"Every academic in the fields of Bible and theology needs to read this book. So many books attempt too little and say even less. This one swings for the fences and hits a home run."

—James M. Hamilton Jr., Southern Baptist Theological Seminary

"This book is both highly relevant and disturbing, as prophetic words often are. Carter gives a critical assessment of the problems besetting hermeneutics in the twenty-first century in biblical studies departments, including the seminary. He argues that such study has left the father's home of rich exegetical tradition (the fathers, the creeds, the Reformers), where it had feasted on the banquet of Scripture, and has wandered off into a barren wasteland of historical criticism, where it dines on the bones, fragments, and husks of the 'assured results' of scholarly study. Carter warns that the recent discipline of theological interpretation will not accomplish a return to the father's house unless it has the right metaphysical equipment. This book is brilliant, incisive, prophetic, witty, extremely well written (I could hardly put it down), and desperately needed. I heartily recommend it!"

—Stephen Dempster, Crandall University

Interpreting Scripture

with the

Great Tradition

Recovering the Genius *of* Premodern Exegesis

Craig A. Carter

B
Baker Academic
a division of Baker Publishing Group
Grand Rapids, Michigan

© 2018 by Craig A. Carter

Published by Baker Academic
a division of Baker Publishing Group
PO Box 6287, Grand Rapids, MI 49516-6287
www.bakeracademic.com

Printed in the United States of America

Library of Congress Cataloging-in-Publication Data
Names: Carter, Craig A., 1956– author.
Title: Interpreting scripture with the great tradition : recovering the genius of premodern exegesis / Craig A. Carter.
Description: Grand Rapids : Baker Publishing Group, 2018. | Includes bibliographical references and index.
Identifiers: LCCN 2017050533 | ISBN 9780801098727 (pbk. : alk. paper)
Subjects: LCSH: Bible—Criticism, interpretation, etc.—History.
Classification: LCC BS511.3 .C3775 2018 | DDC 220.601—dc23
LC record available at https://lccn.loc.gov/2017050533

18 19 20 21 22 23 24   7 6 5 4 3 2 1

To the blessed memory of

John Bainbridge Webster
(1955–2016)

beloved mentor and teacher,
who spoke and wrote so profoundly about our God
and who now beholds him face to face

"I thank my God upon every remembrance of you."
(Phil. 1:3 KJV)

Contents

Preface

The conventional wisdom concerning biblical hermeneutics among the vast majority of evangelical biblical scholars today goes something like this:

> We should interpret the Bible like any other book. The sole purpose of exegesis is to try to understand what the original author meant to communicate to the original audience in the original situation. The text has only one meaning—namely, what the original, human author meant to say. Allegorical interpretation is dangerous because it allows people to read any meaning whatsoever into the text. Maintaining a commitment to the authority of the Bible depends on not departing from the single meaning of the text discovered by historical study. The purpose of a college or seminary education is to train future preachers and teachers in the historical method. It is not the responsibility of the scholar to determine the meaning of the text for today. It is the job of the preacher, teacher, or individual reader to decide how the gap between the ancient meaning and the contemporary situation should be bridged. This is called "application," and it is not the job of the biblical scholar qua biblical scholar to do it, although as a Christian, a biblical scholar must figure out how to apply the text to the present just like everyone else. A scholar's expertise as a scholar, however, is an advantage only insofar as it enables a clear determination of the original, historical meaning of the text.

In this book, I argue that every single component of the conventional wisdom described in the above paragraph is wrong or, at the very least, highly misleading. I argue that we must interpret the Bible in a unique manner because it is uniquely inspired. The purpose of exegesis is to understand what God is saying to us today through the inspired text. The text may have one or several meanings because of the complexity of God the Holy Spirit inspiring the text through a human author. The authority of the Bible is God's self-authenticating Word speaking through it, and in order to hear God's Word, it is crucial that we interpret it as a unified book with Jesus Christ at its center. The interdisciplinary practice of biblical studies as found in academic settings today is an agent of secularization in the church and needs to be reformed so that it becomes a servant of Christian theology and spirituality rather than a confusing amalgam of history, philology, archaeology, literary theory, sociological theory, and philosophy operating with unacknowledged metaphysical assumptions and without any material center. The meaning of the text for today is what we seek to hear as we study the text carefully, intensively, and reverently. Biblical exegesis is a spiritual discipline by which we are gradually made into the kind of readers who can receive with gladness the Word of God. Ancient reading practices, which have never died out completely in the church, can help us hear God's Word in less subjective and more ruled ways than modern hermeneutics makes available to us.

Ironically, many preachers and laypeople who read this book will find in it a more accurate description of what they actually do in day-to-day biblical interpretation than what is found in many hermeneutics textbooks today. That is because the theory taught in those hermeneutics textbooks is not practiced in the church in any kind of consistent manner. This gap between theory and practice occurs because the neopagan philosophical naturalism of the Enlightenment has had a much greater influence on academia and hermeneutical theory than it has had on the actual practice of teaching and preaching in the local church. In many cases, the type of biblical interpretation practiced in evangelical churches today is in substantial continuity with the way the church has read Scripture throughout church history, even though readers in various eras have made use of different reading techniques and employed widely varying terminology to describe what they were doing. The way the church reads Scripture is rooted in a reading culture that nourishes good readers through a tradition handed on from generation to generation through practices and patterns of exegesis that are consistent with one another. Brevard Childs demonstrated a "family resemblance" in exegetical practices that can be seen from the church fathers to the modern period in certain interpreters.[1] The Enlightenment has exercised more influence on scholars who wish to make an impression on the secular academy than it has on faithful pastors who wish to cultivate a love of the Bible in their congregations. Many books seek

---

1. Childs, *Struggle to Understand Isaiah*, 299–300. Childs's conclusions will be discussed more fully at various points in this book.

to bring church practice into line with academic theory; this one seeks to do the opposite. It is my conviction that academic theory needs to be reformed according to church practice when it comes to biblical interpretation.

This book has grown out of a decade of reading, research, and reflection on the Christian doctrine of God. I have become increasingly disillusioned with modern theology in general and with the twentieth century's so-called revival of trinitarian theology in particular. The post-Kantian, Hegelian, trinitarian theology that has dominated the twentieth century is actually not a revival of the trinitarian classical theism of the fourth-century pro-Nicene fathers or of creedal orthodoxy as it has been understood throughout church history.[2] It represents instead a massive revision of the Christian doctrine of God. The Great Tradition of Christian orthodoxy begins with the Old and New Testaments, crystalizes in the fourth-century trinitarian debates, and then continues through Augustine, Thomas Aquinas, the leading Protestant Reformers, post-Reformation scholasticism, and contemporary conservative Roman Catholic, Eastern Orthodox, and Protestant confessional theology.[3] The locus classicus of the Christian doctrine of God is qq. 1–43 of part I of Thomas Aquinas's *Summa Theologica*, which sums up and carefully sets forth in a clear and coherent form the wisdom of Athanasius, the Cappadocian fathers, and Augustine—that is, the trinitarian classical theism that is expressed in the Nicene Creed. The same doctrine of God is also embodied in the seventeenth-century *Westminster Confession of Faith* and in the twentieth-century *Catechism of the Catholic Church*. It has a timeless character that stands in contrast to the shifting winds of doctrinal innovation and cultural fads. I am presently working on attempting to restate this beautiful and rationally compelling doctrine in a companion book to this one, tentatively titled *Trinitarian Classical Theism: An Introduction to the Christian Doctrine of God*.

I originally planned for the material in the present book to be part of the book on the doctrine of God, but it became so complex that I finally recognized the need to make it a separate, though closely related, book. As I studied the history of the doctrine of God, I gradually realized (not without some internal struggle and resistance) that the way the fathers interpreted Scripture, especially the Old Testament, was part and parcel of their trinitarian theology. Modern theologians who reject the fathers' exegetical methods and

---

2. For a penetrating and uncompromising survey of the doctrine of God in twentieth-century theology, see Molnar, *Divine Freedom and the Immanent Trinity*.

3. For more on the contours and importance of the Great Tradition, see Oden, *Rebirth of Orthodoxy*. Especially pertinent to the present book is chap. 7, "Rediscovering the Earliest Biblical Interpreters."

hermeneutical assumptions but still accept the Nicene doctrine of the Trinity often fail to appreciate how this inconsistency threatens to undermine their deepest doctrinal commitments. I have come to see that the modern tendency to move in a unitarian direction is logically (not merely coincidentally) related to the rise of modern historical-critical interpretation of the Bible. Of course, many people do practice historical criticism while maintaining their belief in Nicene doctrine, but I am afraid that this is mostly because their knowledge of the fourth-century debates is shallow and because they lack an appreciation of the implications of basing their belief in the Trinity on the New Testament alone.[4] The intra-Jewish debate of the first few centuries of the church's existence between those Jews who accepted Jesus as Messiah and those Jews who did not was *the* crucial debate in the formation of the church, and it centered on the issue of whether the Old Testament witnesses to Jesus Christ. Only a gentile could imagine that everything does not hang on this point. Either this debate results in conclusions (principally the need to affirm the deity of Christ without denying monotheism) that make the doctrine of the Trinity inevitable, or else we are simply wrong to believe that Jesus fulfills the Old Testament hope and is the one spoken of in the Law, the Prophets, and the Writings.[5] If we are wrong, then the entire Christian faith is one giant mistake and should be abandoned as soon as possible.

As I studied the fourth-century fathers and then Thomas Aquinas, I developed a deep desire to do theology in a classical manner by exegeting the text of Scripture and then reflecting philosophically on the revelation contained in the text in the light of the tradition of the church embedded in creedal orthodoxy. I realized that the study of Scripture is a spiritual discipline by which the Holy Spirit sanctifies us, and I came to understand that true Christian discipleship requires a high view of the divinity of Christ and the triune nature of God. Theology can be a means for building up the church into the image of Jesus Christ, the head of the church, but if this is to happen, theology cannot be a rationalistic enterprise designed to conform Christian doctrine to a system of metaphysics that is at odds with the Christian tradition of orthodoxy, as is the case in so much of contemporary theology. This book is an attempt to recover the approach to biblical exegesis that characterized the Great Tradition.

4. Andrew Louth writes: "The Fathers, and creeds, and Councils claim to be interpreting Scripture. How can one accept their results if one does not accept their methods?" (*Discerning the Mystery*, 100). Jason Byassee is even more provocative: "You cannot have the patristic dogma without patristic exegesis; you cannot have the creed without allegory" (*Praise Seeking Understanding*, 16).

5. The question that the disciples of John the Baptist brought to Jesus is *the* central question: "Are you the one who is to come, or should we look for another?" (Luke 7:20).

It is thus a methodological reflection on the practice I carry out in my book on the doctrine of God.

In reflecting on why the twentieth-century doctrine of God was so detached from the Great Tradition, I came to see in a new way the interconnections between exegesis, metaphysics, and dogma. The Christian Platonism of the Great Tradition was developed in order to express the metaphysical implications of the doctrine of God that emerged from pro-Nicene scriptural exegesis in the fourth century, and as a result the exegesis, the dogma, and the metaphysics are all intertwined together. Creedal orthodoxy is not just verbal formulations on a page; it is, in the words of Lewis Ayres, a "pro-Nicene culture,"[6] and the three essential elements of that culture are a tradition of spiritual exegesis, dogmas emerging from that exegesis, and the metaphysical implications of those dogmas, which in turn provide a hospitable context for the practice of exegesis. To reject any one of the three elements of pro-Nicene culture would be to plunge the whole project into crisis.

Tragically, this is exactly what has happened in modernity. Modern philosophy has systematically rejected the Christian Platonism of the Great Tradition. The nominalist, materialistic, and mechanistic philosophy of the Enlightenment embraced the exact metaphysical views that the pro-Nicene fathers had consciously and decisively rejected. Whereas the fathers found a kinship with the Platonists on a number of points and considered them the best of the Greek philosophers, the Enlightenment thinkers rejected the Platonists and embraced first the Atomists and the Epicureans (in the eighteenth century) and later the Stoics and the Skeptics (in the nineteenth and twentieth centuries). The result was a crisis within Western intellectual thought, and this crisis expressed itself in two ways: (1) in the rise of the historical-critical method of biblical interpretation from Baruch Spinoza onward and (2) in the revisionist or liberal theology that flowed from the impetus provided by Friedrich Schleiermacher. In the historical-critical method of biblical interpretation, methodological naturalism became *the* central presupposition of exegesis.[7] This methodological naturalism led to a concentration on the single meaning of the text—that is, the original meaning the original human author intended to convey to the original readers in the original situation. This is

---

6. Ayres, *Nicaea and Its Legacy*, 274–78.

7. That some scholars today seem not to be aware of how important philosophical naturalism is to their strongly held positions only shows how deeply ingrained in modern thinking it has become. It is the air we breathe as moderns; for pragmatic late modern people it seems like mere "common sense." Such deeply ingrained patterns of thought form a culture and are seldom subjected to critical scrutiny; rather, everything else (especially tradition) is subjected to critical scrutiny on the basis of philosophical naturalism.

what the modern historical critics (consciously departing from the classical tradition) came to mean by "historical meaning."

In this context, the term "critical" meant that older meanings that depended for their coherence on the supernaturalism of the older metaphysics had to be revised or rejected outright. The meaning of the term "historical" was drastically narrowed from its previous meaning of "an interpretation of past events" to its newer meaning of "an interpretation of past events that excludes the supernatural." In the narrowed, modern meaning of the term "historical," many crucially important events of the past are assumed to be impossible, such as the drowning of the Egyptian army in the Red Sea, Isaiah predicting the virgin birth and crucifixion of Jesus centuries in advance of their occurrence, and the bodily resurrection of Christ. When moderns speak of the "literal sense" of Scripture, they often mean the historical sense in the later, narrower sense of historical, whereas in the Great Tradition the meaning of the literal sense was much broader, allowing room for both human and divine (supernatural) authorial intent and also for levels of meaning in the text because of inspiration.

What I term "the liberal project" was launched by Schleiermacher, who intended to save Christianity from becoming utterly irrelevant to modern European intellectual thought and perhaps even from being pushed out of the modern research university altogether. The liberal project was to revise and restate Christian doctrines within the constraints of modern metaphysics— that is, within the limits of philosophical naturalism. This meant, for example, expressing the doctrine of the Trinity within the constraints of the nominalism, materialism, and mechanism of Enlightenment philosophy. These two wings of the liberal project—historical criticism and revisionist theology—have been the foundations on which twentieth-century relational theisms have been built. Theologians after Hegel have embraced various types of relational theism, such as process philosophy (Whitehead, Cobb), modern dynamic panentheism (Moltmann), panentheistic liberation theologies (Cone, Boff, McFague), and open theism (Pinnock, Sanders). In theological systems such as these, God is seen as being interdependent with the world (voluntarily in some cases and involuntarily in others), and creation is viewed as a necessary expression of the divine nature, if not an actual limit on the divine nature. In all of these theological systems, the doctrine of the immanent Trinity is largely eclipsed by an almost exclusive focus on the economic Trinity. But none of them can be considered a legitimate development of the orthodoxy of the Great Tradition. None of them affirm the true, uniquely Christian understanding of divine transcendence. Ironically (in view of their reflexive anti-Platonism), they have more in common with certain aspects of Neoplatonism that were consciously rejected by the Nicene fathers.[8] But this sort of Neoplatonism offers no serious resistance to the philosophical naturalism that animates modernity. Even "Spirit" and "the Absolute"—even "God"—are all part of the one overarching reality that we inhabit; true divine transcendence has been abandoned. God is either *in* history, or God *is* history. Either way, God is not free of history and thus not transcendent in the classical sense.

Twentieth-century trinitarian theology is not even aware of how unorthodox it is because, in the poignant words of Lady Galadriel, "Some things that should not have been forgotten were lost."[9] Modern theology has forgotten that metaphysics cannot be ignored without exegesis and doctrine being negatively affected.[10] And not just any metaphysics will do. Christian Platonism[11] was carefully and painstakingly crafted over centuries to serve as a context for reflection on Scripture that leads to true knowledge of the living God and enables true doctrinal statements about him. The companion book to this one will concentrate on reflecting about philosophical questions that arise from the theological exegesis of Scripture passages concerning God. The present book is an exercise in *ressourcement* that attempts to recover classical theological interpretation of Scripture for the church's benefit today. This book provides the hermeneutical justification for the procedure employed in the other book, lest anyone be tempted to regard it as hermeneutically naive.

This book is an attempt to overcome the negative effects of the historical-critical method by repudiating the methodological naturalism that grows out of its Epicurean metaphysics and cheerfully embracing the supernatural,

8. For an extremely helpful discussion of the massive influence of Neoplatonism on Hegel and all the nineteenth- and twentieth-century theology influenced by him, see Cooper, *Panentheism*.

9. In the prologue to the movie *The Lord of the Rings: The Fellowship of the Ring* (2001), Lady Galadriel speaks these words about the ring of power: "And some things that should not have been forgotten were lost. History became legend. Legend became myth. And for two and a half thousand years, the ring passed out of all knowledge."

10. John Webster reminds us,

A Trinitarian dogmatics of the holiness of God will be an exercise in ontotheology. For its concern is—with fear and trembling—to give a conceptual depiction of the Church's confession of the works and ways of the Holy Trinity. And such a depiction necessarily requires an ontology—an account of the being, nature and properties of God. This ontology must certainly be resolutely dogmatic. . . . But dogmatics ought to be unpersuaded that Christian theology can long survive the abandonment of ontotheology and ought to think long and hard before it hands over the doctrine of God for deconstruction. The undeniably corrosive effects of certain traditions of metaphysics are best retarded, not by repudiating ontology, but by its fully Christian articulation. (*Holiness*, 32–33)

11. "Christian Platonism" is not simply identical with "Neoplatonism" or "the views of Plato" or even "Platonism in general," much less with decadent versions like the various forms of gnosticism. In chap. 3 I will carefully define what I mean by "Christian Platonism" and place it in its historical context. Readers who exhibit symptoms of an allergy to Platonism should read chap. 3 before rejecting the term out of hand.

miracles, providence, inspiration, and other concepts central to the Great Tradition but often brushed aside by modernity. A great deal of the distance between contemporary theology and fourth-century pro-Nicene theology arises because even conservative and evangelical scholars today often view the allegorical methods of biblical interpretation used by the fathers as childishly inept. The fathers, following the explicit example of the writers of the New Testament, interpreted the Old Testament text as having multiple levels of meaning. The biblical text functioned sacramentally for them by manifesting Christ in the present.[12] The christological meaning of an Old Testament text could be discerned on this side of the resurrection because it was always there in the text, even though it was not necessarily discerned (or at least not *clearly* discerned) by those who lived before the incarnation of God in Christ. The lively awareness of divine authorial intent, in addition to human authorial intent, enabled them to see the *sensus plenior* as resident in the text itself and not as something read into the text by readers.[13] Without this way of reading the Old Testament, the New Testament writers could not have interpreted the Old Testament christologically and the apostolic witness to Jesus Christ as the fulfillment of the Scriptures could not have been convincing. So in a very important sense, our faith is dependent on the validity of patristic exegesis. If Christology is not genuinely and objectively *in* the Old Testament text waiting to be discerned by the apostles as they are led into all truth by the Holy Spirit in fulfillment of Jesus's promise given in John 16:32 but rather is *read into* the text by the apostles and church fathers as one possible reading among others, then the question of the relationship of the Triune God of Nicaea to the God of Israel witnessed to in the Old Testament is left hanging.

It is my conviction that recovering a genuinely Nicene doctrine of the Trinity depends completely on first recovering the genius of premodern exegesis. But in order to accomplish that, we must first recover the Christian Platonist metaphysics inherent in the spiritual exegesis that was at the root of Nicene theology and reject both the historical criticism of the Enlightenment and the naturalistic metaphysics on which it rests. In other words, if we wish to draw

12. This is the central thesis of a recently published book that is now the best available introduction to the exegesis of the church fathers: Boersma, *Scripture as Real Presence*. This richly detailed and theologically astute treatment of patristic exegesis should be read alongside my work because it offers many excellent examples of the sort of exegesis I refer to at many points in this book. Boersma's work focuses on how the fathers actually did exegesis, whereas my work focuses on how we can and should appropriate the fruit of their work today. Both of us are seeking to contribute to the work of *ressourcement*.

13. David Steinmetz correctly positions the classic approach as a via media between the extremes of the single-meaning theory, on the one hand, and the postmodern reader-response theories, on the other. See Steinmetz, "Superiority of Pre-critical Exegesis," 13–14.

on the deep, nourishing resources of the Great Tradition, we must come to grips with how exegesis, metaphysics, and dogma hang together in Nicene Christianity. But to do that sort of thing flies in the face of powerful currents of thought in the contemporary culture.

Stanley Jaki reminds us that naming things is an exercise of power and that the misnaming of something, such as an epoch of history, may well be a misuse of power and a form of intellectual domination.[14] The Enlightenment's periodization of Western history into three ages—classical, middle, and modern—helped to demote the peak of Western Christendom in the thirteenth century to the status of an "interlude" between classical antiquity and the revival of paganism in the so-called Enlightenment. What a different picture would be conjured up in the student's mind if the thirteenth century was named "the Enlightenment," and the period from 1650 to 1800 was called something like "the Period of the Decay of Christendom"! The neopagans of early modern Europe drew a contrast between the "age of reason" and the "age of faith" and evaluated the various aspects of the culture of ancient Greece and Rome according to how well or poorly they foreshadowed the "age of reason." This periodization of Western history was itself an act of interpretation and domination as the neopaganism of the Enlightenment sought to overcome Christendom and drive Christianity out of the public square.[15]

The sad contemporary spectacle of the so-called New Atheism is a continuation of the worst manifestations of this "Reason Worship," which led to the attempt to brand Christianity as anti-reason, anti-science, and anti-intellectual during the Enlightenment. Just as current new-atheist writers exhibit an embarrassing lack of self-critical humility by labeling themselves "Brights,"[16] so the neopagans of high modernity flattered themselves by claiming the label "Enlightenment" for their age, which implied of course that the age of faith that preceded them was an age of darkness. It was no accident that the period during which Europe was converted to Christianity ended up being labeled the "Dark Ages."

Using the term "precritical" to describe the way the church has historically read the Bible is meant to be pejorative, even though some writers gamely try to use the term without prejudice. "Precritical" or "premodern" biblical interpretation is often contrasted with "scholarly" or "academic" biblical interpretation, expressing a sentiment like the following: "Well, you may have

14. Jaki, *Genesis 1 through the Ages*, 109.

15. Notice the subtitle of the first volume of Peter Gay's magisterial history of the Enlightenment: *The Enlightenment*, vol. 1, *The Rise of Modern Paganism*.

16. Daniel Dennett actually did this in a piece in the *New York Times* a few years ago. Quoted in Feser, *Last Superstition*, 3.

problems with philosophical naturalism, but surely you don't mean to reject
the scholarly, scientific, and academic study of the Bible during the past two
centuries."[17] Of course not, but the suspicion is inevitable given the way we
have named these periods of history. One of the purposes of this book is to
counter this misuse of the power of naming in which the historic and orthodox way of reading the Bible practiced by Christians from the apostles to the
present is placed under suspicion and ultimately marginalized. My hope is to
overcome the Enlightenment by showing that the Enlightenment movement of
"higher criticism" is a dead end, a sideshow, a deviation from orthodoxy, and
a movement that is now in the late stages of self-destruction. It is my conviction that the church will still be reading the Bible with Irenaeus, Athanasius,
Augustine, Aquinas, and Calvin long after Baruch Spinoza, David Strauss,
Hermann Reimarus, Friedrich Schleiermacher, Rudolf Bultmann, and the Jesus
Seminar are mere footnotes in the history of the decline of post-Christian
Western culture. One of the many reasons for this confidence is that, when
all is said and done, the historic approach to exegesis will be found to be the
truly scientific and rational method of exegesis, and the historical-critical
method will be judged to have been ideologically driven and philosophically
deficient. I am quite aware that many will regard these as bold claims; the
reader is invited to delay judgment about the validity of these claims until
after reading this book. Although this book is a necessary explanation for,
and justification of, the exegetical approach taken in my forthcoming *Trinitarian Classical Theism*, it also stands alone as a contribution to the reform
of biblical hermeneutics through *ressourcement* after the pathologies and
heresies of the Enlightenment have been overcome.

17. The way many scholars reflexively associate "scholarly" and "naturalism" is very telling. "Can a nonnaturalist reading be scholarly?" they sometimes ask. Such a question, asked
sincerely, indicates an alarming state of philosophical confusion.

Acknowledgments

$\mathcal{J}$t is a pleasure to acknowledge that many people have been helpful in the process of writing this book. I would like to thank Ben Reynolds, my colleague at Tyndale, for introducing me to David Nelson, who became my editor for this project. Both David and I studied with John Webster, and we share a mutual appreciation for him as a person and as a theologian. It has been a privilege to work with an editor who is broadly sympathetic to the kind of theology I want to write. I also want to thank Hans Boersma, whose work in patristic exegesis has been an inspiration to me and who was strongly supportive of this project in its early stages.

I also want to thank Tyndale University College for a sabbatical in the winter of 2012, during which time I did research and reading in preparation for this book and the companion volume on the doctrine of God. My students at Tyndale have been a great stimulus in my attempts to explain the things I have been learning as I have moved from a modern to a classical understanding of trinitarian theology. They have responded with enthusiasm to historic orthodoxy and have been thrilled to learn of the spiritual depths, intellectual riches, and biblical truth of the trinitarian classical theism of the Great Tradition. This response, especially in my classes on the doctrine of God and my seminar on theological interpretation of Scripture, has been very encouraging. It makes me think that more students would be orthodox if only their professors had the courage to teach the tradition with conviction.

I also need to thank the pastors and people of Westney Heights Baptist Church, where I have served as theologian-in-residence since 2008. The Reverend Jack Hannah, who brought me on staff a decade ago, and the current senior pastor, the Reverend Don Symons, have been unfailingly supportive and encouraging. My ministry of teaching at Westney has been possible because of the tremendous interest in studying the Bible on the part of the people in this wonderful church. Every Thursday evening this past year I have taught a class on biblical hermeneutics to a group of twenty men; on Sunday morning I teach the book of Isaiah to more than one hundred people. After two years we have just finished chapter 45! Keeping one foot in the academy and one foot in the local church has forced me to think on multiple levels at all times and has kept me grounded in reality while thinking on a philosophical and theological level. This is how theology has been done for most of church history and how it should be done today. The isolated intellectual in the ivory tower is simply out of touch and crippled by the lack of feedback necessary for doing good theology. I thank God for placing me in the midst of people who love God's Word and who are not afraid to study it diligently.

I also want to thank Dale Dawson and Steve Dempster for many good conversations about the topics covered in this book. Dale is a pastor-theologian, who also studied under John Webster and teaches doctrine part-time, so he has been a terrific dialogue partner. Steve is a spiritually discerning student of the Hebrew text of the Old Testament. I have learned much from both of them.

My wife, Bonnie, has been teaching a course on hermeneutics to a group of fifteen women at our church while I have been writing this book. She has put into practice many of the ideas I have written about in this book with amazingly positive results. She is a great source of support and encouragement to me, and without her this book would not have been possible. I would also like to thank my daughter, Rebecca Carter-Chand, for compiling the indexes.

I have dedicated this book to John Webster, my doctoral supervisor and the greatest theologian of his generation. Now that he has been taken from us, it is imperative that those who appreciated his work do whatever we can, according to the measure of grace we have been given, to carry forward the magnificent and inspiring vision of theology he exemplified.

It is customary to add in places like this that the people mentioned above do not necessarily agree with everything in this book and that responsibility for the viewpoints expressed here is mine alone. But surely you knew that already.

All Scripture quotations are from the English Standard Version of the Bible unless otherwise noted. I use, recommend, and thank God for the ESV Study Bible, which is a marvelous tool for anyone wanting to study God's Word today.

Cover note: The picture on the front cover, "Simeon's Song of Praise," was painted by Rembrandt in 1631. It depicts an aged Simeon quoting Isaiah 52:10 as he prophesies that this baby Jesus is "the Lord's Christ" (Luke 2:26). A faithful and skilled reader of Scripture, Simeon sees the messianic thrust of the Old Testament as pointing toward the coming of the Suffering Servant. The text stresses that he understood this by the Holy Spirit. My book is about how to read like Simeon, Anna, and other faithful people of God, who discerned the christological meaning of the Holy Scriptures by the illumination of the Spirit, symbolized in the painting by the bright light shining down on the child and on Simeon's face.

Abbreviations

General and Bibliographic

AT	author's translation	esp.	especially
chap(s).	chapter(s)	etc.	*et cetera*, and so forth
e.g.	*exempli gratia*, for example	KJV	King James Version

Old Testament

Gen.	Genesis	Song	Song of Songs
Exod.	Exodus	Isa.	Isaiah
Lev.	Leviticus	Jer.	Jeremiah
Num.	Numbers	Lam.	Lamentations
Deut.	Deuteronomy	Ezek.	Ezekiel
Josh.	Joshua	Dan.	Daniel
Judg.	Judges	Hosea	Hosea
Ruth	Ruth	Joel	Joel
1–2 Sam.	1–2 Samuel	Amos	Amos
1–2 Kings	1–2 Kings	Obad.	Obadiah
1–2 Chron.	1–2 Chronicles	Jon.	Jonah
Ezra	Ezra	Mic.	Micah
Neh.	Nehemiah	Nah.	Nahum
Esther	Esther	Hab.	Habakkuk
Job	Job	Zeph.	Zephaniah
Ps(s).	Psalm(s)	Hag.	Haggai
Prov.	Proverbs	Zech.	Zechariah
Eccles.	Ecclesiastes	Mal.	Malachi

New Testament

Matt.	Matthew	1–2 Thess.	1–2 Thessalonians
Mark	Mark	1–2 Tim.	1–2 Timothy
Luke	Luke	Titus	Titus
John	John	Philem.	Philemon
Acts	Acts	Heb.	Hebrews
Rom.	Romans	James	James
1–2 Cor.	1–2 Corinthians	1–2 Pet.	1–2 Peter
Gal.	Galatians	1–3 John	1–3 John
Eph.	Ephesians	Jude	Jude
Phil.	Philippians	Rev.	Revelation
Col.	Colossians		

Old Testament Apocrypha / Deuterocanonical Books

Bar.	Baruch	Sir. (Ecclus.)	Sirach (Ecclesiasticus)
1–2 Esd.	1–2 Esdras	Tob.	Tobit
Jdt.	Judith	Wis.	Wisdom (of Solomon)
1–4 Macc.	1–4 Maccabees		

Introduction

1

Who Is the Suffering Servant?

The Crisis in Contemporary Hermeneutics

> Who has believed what he has heard from us?
> And to whom has the arm of the Lord been revealed?
>
> Isaiah 53:1

This chapter is intended to set the stage for the positive proposal I wish to make for the reform of contemporary biblical hermeneutics. I will do this (1) by introducing the problem we face today in interpreting the Bible, (2) by explaining how this problem arose, and (3) by pointing to some positive signs of renewal. The chapter will close with a brief outline of the rest of the book.

The Gulf between Academic Hermeneutics and Church Preaching

The origins of this book go back to an experience I had more than thirty years ago when I had just graduated from seminary and was starting my first full-time pastorate in two small country churches on Prince Edward Island, Canada. It was traditional in these churches to have a Good Friday service, and I was to preach. I wanted to take as my text Isaiah 53, but there was a problem. I knew that the passage was a prophecy of Jesus and that it described his atoning death on the cross, which is why I wanted to preach it. But, alas,

I was too educated to be able to preach this message with a clear conscience! In the seminary studies I had just completed, I had been taught the historical method of interpreting the Bible. I had a liberal-leaning professor who was always going on about "the assured results of higher criticism," and also some more conservative ones who had advocated a grammatical-historical approach. As far as I could see, both liberal and conservative scholars were united in stressing that the text has only a single meaning: what the original author meant to convey to the original readers in the original situation. This is why the seminary had taught me Hebrew, Greek, ancient history, and critical methods like form criticism and source criticism: so that as a pastor I would be equipped to do what laypeople for the most part could not do—namely, recover the historical meaning of the biblical text.

Higher Criticism of Isaiah

I knew that, since Bernhard Duhm's work in the late nineteenth century, Isaiah 53 had been identified as the "Fourth Servant Song" and that the identity of the servant was a matter of wide scholarly disagreement. I also was aware vaguely that the church fathers and the Reformers had interpreted Isaiah 53 as a prophecy of Christ, although I was not as aware then as I am now of how universal that view was in the church prior to the Enlightenment. I knew I was going to preach Christ as the meaning of Isaiah 53, but I could not for the life of me see how to justify doing so on the basis of the hermeneutical theory I had been taught. I knew that the New Testament clearly teaches that Jesus Christ is the Messiah who fulfills the messianic hope in the prophets in general and in Isaiah in particular.[1] But while the fact that the New Testament writers interpret Isaiah 53 in this way gave me confidence in preaching Isaiah 53 as Philip did to the Ethiopian eunuch (Acts 8:30–35), it still did not solve the hermeneutical problem.

After all, maybe the New Testament writers were wrong. Modern historical criticism, I had discovered, was quite ready to declare the New Testament writers wrong about various things, such as the authorship of various canonical books, including the Pentateuch, Isaiah, and the Pastoral Epistles. And there is no way to reconcile the allegorical interpretation of Hagar and Sarah that Paul gives in Galatians 4 or the interpretation he gives of the rock in the wilderness wanderings in 1 Corinthians 10 with the historical-critical method. So the question arises: If the New Testament writers could interpret the Old Testament allegorically, and if the church fathers did so regularly in

---

1. In their widely used textbook, *A Survey of the Old Testament*, Hill and Walton state (745) that there are thirty-eight references to Isaiah 53 in the New Testament.

conscious imitation of the apostles, why could we not do so as well? If the answer to that question is that the historical-critical method is the right way to interpret Scripture, then that means the New Testament writers were wrong in their methods. Yet, if Jesus is the Messiah of Israel, they must have been right in their conclusions. How could that be?[2] How could they have arrived at the right conclusions via a faulty method?[3] Was it a fortuitous mistake? Or does the falsity of their method call their conclusions into question? Should we just appeal to the authority of the New Testament for our messianic interpretation of Isaiah 53 and ignore what Isaiah (or Deutero-Isaiah or whoever it was) meant to affirm?

I was aware of another possibility. Perhaps the apostles were able to interpret the Old Testament allegorically because they were inspired, whereas we should refrain from doing so because we are not inspired and are therefore liable to make errors.[4] Behind this view lay the common perception that the allegorical method is uncontrolled and arbitrary and therefore allows anyone to read anything at all into the text. Many people seem to confuse the allegorical method with postmodern reader-response methods of hermeneutics in which the reader actually reads meaning into the text that was not there initially. The difference between at least some of the allegorical approaches of the fathers and the modern, reader-centered approaches, however, is that the former do not seek to read the reader's ideas into the text, but rather to extract a second layer of meaning from the text itself. As David Steinmetz makes clear in his classic article, "The Superiority of Pre-critical Exegesis,"[5] the allegorical method actually lies between the two extremes of the Enlightenment's single-meaning theory, on the one side, and a postmodern reader-centered approach,

2. Louth rightly presses this question in *Discerning the Mystery*, 100.

3. Holmes wrestles with this dilemma in chapter 2 of *The Quest for the Trinity*. He writes: "We tend to assume today that a text means what the author intended it to mean. If this is right, it will be very difficult to find any treatment of the doctrine of the Trinity in the Old Testament . . . whatever a text like 'You are my son; today I have begotten you' (Ps. 2:7 NRSV) might mean, its use in debates over whether the generation of the Logos from the Father is a volitional and time-bound act, or an essential and eternal one, is completely inappropriate" (34).

4. I was privileged to take courses on Mark and Romans from Richard Longenecker in the 1980s, and he advocated this solution. In the preface to the second edition of his work *Biblical Exegesis in the Apostolic Period*, Longenecker replies (xxxiv–xxxviii) to Richard Hays's criticism of his refusal to follow the apostles in their method as well as in their conclusions. For Longenecker, it is wrong to follow the apostles in doing allegorical exegesis even though they were preserved from erroneous conclusions by the inspiration of the Holy Spirit. He believes that Paul's use of allegory, midrash, and pesher is "culturally conditioned" and needs to be "contextualized" for today. It is difficult to avoid concluding that for Longenecker, modernity gets to decide which methods of biblical interpretation are allowable for theology.

5. Steinmetz, "Superiority of Pre-critical Exegesis," 13–14. This article originally appeared in *Theology Today* 37, no. 1 (April 1980): 27–38.

on the other. The allegorical approach views the text as having more than one meaning, but not an unlimited number of meanings and certainly not mutually contradictory ones. But if one believes (as many evangelical biblical scholars do) that the only thing standing between us and interpretive chaos is the single-meaning theory, one naturally would be loath to give it up lest the whole enterprise of biblical interpretation degenerate into the expression of individual opinions as to the meanings of texts with no way to adjudicate among them.

If the writer of Isaiah 53 believed that the servant was Israel or a righteous remnant within Israel, as major medieval rabbis taught,[6] or some historical figure in Israel like Moses or the prophet himself, as some modern critics say,[7] then clearly there is a problem in getting from the original author's view to the view of the New Testament writers, let alone in constructing an interpretive bridge between the original historical situation (usually construed by historical critics as the Babylonian exile) and the present-day congregation.

How the Church Preaches Isaiah

When one consults the sermons and expositional and devotional commentaries written by pastors throughout the centuries of church history, one finds that the christological meaning of Isaiah 53 is enthusiastically advocated and expounded.

The volume on Isaiah 40–66 in the Ancient Christian Commentary on Scripture series lists examples of the unanimous testimony of the fathers as to the identity of the servant of Isaiah 53. Just to give one example, let us hear Clement of Alexandria: "The Spirit gives witness through Isaiah that even the Lord became an unsightly spectacle: 'And we saw him, and there was no beauty or comeliness in him, but his form was despised and rejected by people.' Yet, who is better than the Lord? He displayed not beauty of the flesh, which is only outward appearance, but the true beauty of body and

6. Brown, "Jewish Interpretations of Isaiah 53," 64.

7. E.g., Whybray, *Isaiah 40–66*, says, "The person referred to throughout this chapter is the same as the 'servant' of the three earlier 'Servant Songs,' 42:1–4; 49:1–6; 50:4–9—that is, the prophet Deutero-Isaiah himself" (171). North, *Suffering Servant in Deutero-Isaiah*, provides a survey of fifteen proposals for the identity of the servant covering Jewish, early Christian, and modern ones, and including both individuals (such as Moses, Hezekiah, and Isaiah) and collectives (such as ideal Israel, the righteous remnant of Israel, and the prophets). There are various forms of messianic identification, both Jewish and Christian. More recently, Blenkinsopp (*Isaiah 40–55*, 355–56) stated that no new options have emerged since North's survey and that none of these fifteen suggestions have been met with unanimous approval. Blenkinsopp himself thinks that the Fourth Servant Song depicts Deutero-Isaiah but was composed by a disciple.

soul—for the soul, the beauty of good deeds; for the body, the beauty of immortality."[8]

Commenting on Isaiah 52:13, John Calvin writes, "After having spoken of the restoration of the Church, Isaiah passes on to Christ, in whom all things are gathered together."[9] It is worth stressing that Calvin here speaks of *Isaiah* (the author of the text) beginning in this verse to speak of Christ. To put it this way is different from saying, as so many have done, that the early church interpreted this passage in christological and messianic terms. The question is whether this meaning inheres in the text or is read into the text by later readers.

The great nineteenth-century evangelical preacher Charles Spurgeon comments: "How clearly you have before you here our blessed Redeemer, and how strong are the expressions used by Isaiah to set forth his substitution. If he did intend to teach us the doctrine that Christ suffered in the place and stead of his people, he could not have used more expressive words; and if he did not intend to teach us that truth, it is marvelous that he should have adopted phraseology so likely to mislead."[10] For Spurgeon, the fact of inspiration makes predictive prophecy easy to imagine, and a text like this one makes it obvious to anyone whose mind is not closed to the possibility that Isaiah could be given a vision of the crucifixion of Christ centuries before it happened.

One of the greatest Bible expositors of the twentieth century was John R. W. Stott, who exercised a worldwide Bible preaching ministry from his home base of All Souls Langham Place, London. In *The Cross of Christ*, published in his sixty-fifth year and summarizing much of the fruit of his expository ministry over the previous forty years, he points out that Paul, John, Peter, Luke, and Matthew—the major contributors to the New Testament—together allude to eight of the twelve verses in Isaiah 53. Stott asks, "What was the origin of their confident, detailed application of Isaiah 53 to Jesus?" He then answers, "They must have derived it from his own lips. It was from this chapter more than from any other that he learnt that the vocation of the Messiah was to suffer and die for human sin, and so be glorified."[11]

8. Elliott, ed., *Isaiah 40–66*, 159.
9. Calvin, *Commentary on the Prophet Isaiah*, 106.
10. http://www.studylight.org/commentaries/spe/view.cgi?bk=isa&ch=53.
11. Stott, *Cross of Christ*, 31. Brevard Childs lists several noted modern scholars as holding to this view, including J. Jeremias, H. W. Wolff, P. Stuhlmacher, and M. Hengel (Childs, *Isaiah*, 420). To this list can be added leading conservative Old Testament scholars such as John Oswalt and J. Alec Motyer. Childs, however, follows the majority in rejecting the view that the authority of the biblical witness is determined by its being anchored in the mind of Jesus. We will revisit Childs's views at several points in this book, so I will not go into my evaluation of them at this point. Suffice it to say that I believe Childs's "third way" has laudable intentions but is insufficiently radical in its critique of modern ideas of "history" and "scholarly neutrality."

Through the centuries the church has believed and taught that the Old
Testament generally, and Isaiah 53 in particular, speaks of Jesus Christ because
it is inspired by the Spirit of God. Enlightenment-inspired higher criticism,
however, operates on the basis of metaphysical assumptions that make this
impossible. What we have is a clash between university and church. Or, to
vary the metaphor, perhaps it is not so much a clash as two solitudes that have
never embraced each other. David Steinmetz ended his famously controversial
article, "The Superiority of Pre-critical Exegesis" with these stirring words:

> The defenders of the single-meaning theory usually concede that the medieval
> approach to the Bible met the religious needs of the Christian community but
> that it did so at the unacceptable price of doing violence to the biblical text.
> The fact that the historical-critical method after two hundred years is still strug-
> gling for more than a precarious foothold in that same religious community is
> generally blamed on the ignorance and conservatism of the Christian laity and
> the sloth or moral cowardice of its pastors.
>
> I should like to suggest an alternative hypothesis. The medieval theory of
> levels of meaning in the text, with all its undoubted defects, flourished because
> it is true, while the modern theory of a single meaning, with all its demonstrable
> virtues, struggles because it is false. Until the historical-critical method becomes
> critical of its own theoretical foundations and develops a hermeneutical theory
> adequate to the nature of the text it is interpreting, it will remain restricted,
> as it deserves to be, to the guild and the academy, where the question of truth
> can endlessly be deferred.[12]

Is there any hope of bringing these two solitudes together? Can historical
criticism be reformed on the basis of orthodox theology? Is it possible to
develop a theory of biblical hermeneutics that can undergird and nourish
ecclesial preaching and teaching? What would such a theory look like? I believe
that it is possible to reform hermeneutical theory and that the prospects for
doing so are better today than they have been for a long time. But the next
step in the argument is to recount how things got to this point, so that we
can see the scope of the reform needed.

How Such a Gulf Developed between Church and Academy

Before we can interpret the Bible, we must decide what it is. If interpretation is to be scientific, it must adapt its method to the nature of the thing
being studied. The methods of astronomy are obviously insufficient to study

---

12. Steinmetz, "Superiority of Pre-critical Exegesis," 14.

biology; one requires a telescope while the other needs a microscope. The methods of logic cannot be used to study history except in a secondary sense in testing the validity of arguments made in the course of evaluating evidence. But using all logic and no evidence at all will not work, for history is not a deductive science. The study of texts requires different approaches, depending on the nature of the text being considered. On the one hand, the historical researcher may scan and discard records until finding the specific piece of information being sought. On the other hand, the literary critic may read the same poem over and over until its rhythm and meter become so familiar they are unforgettable. The philosopher may pore over a few paragraphs and reduce the prose to a series of propositions arranged in logical order, something the literary critic would almost never think of doing. How does one study God?

Methodological Naturalism and Divine Inspiration

According to the confession of the Christian church, the Bible is an inspired book. This is the inescapable fact confronting anyone who wants to interpret the Bible. All agree that this is a religious text used for millennia by religious communities, first Jewish, then Jewish and Christian. But that tells us only that certain people and groups ascribed deep religious significance to these texts and claimed that the Bible is a Word from God in which God reveals himself to us and therefore is different from all other texts. But were they *right* in doing so? Should the interpreter start from the standpoint of faith that God has spoken in these texts, or should a conclusion as to the truth of this claim be part of the results of the interpreter's investigations? In other words, is divine inspiration a necessary premise of good interpretation, or is it preferable to start with agnosticism on the question of the reality of inspiration? Would a presupposition of divine inspiration actually impede good interpretation? Would it be a good compromise to employ methodological naturalism in one's interpretation until one becomes convinced that the texts of the Bible really are the Word of God—perhaps after the work of interpretation proper is finished? But if one begins with methodological naturalism, is it really possible to come to such a conclusion except by repudiating one's starting point? How, exactly, does one change horses midstream? To the extent that it really is a *starting point*, does not repudiating it necessarily mean that one must start all over?

The question, then, is not whether the metaphysical starting point of interpretation potentially conditions the interpretation of the text. It seems clear, to me at least, that it does; I hope that the following chapters will convince any readers who may doubt the validity of this point. But the question I wish to raise is what actual effects metaphysics has had on biblical interpretation throughout history. I invite the reader to consider the possibility that metaphysical beliefs (or denials, which in their own way are just as significant as beliefs) form a context in which interpretation is carried out and that the results of interpretation cannot be separated from the metaphysical assumptions behind the method of interpretation. By "metaphysical," I actually do not mean anything radically different from what theologians traditionally have meant by the doctrines of creation and providence and by ideas such as miracle and inspiration. I find it preferable to use the word "metaphysical" for two reasons. First, some views of theology in the modern world can speak of theological issues as if they did not intersect with history and nature. But I am talking about the way the world actually is, how God relates to the world, and, specifically, how God speaks to creatures. This kind of theology inevitably has metaphysical dimensions. Second, I wish to compare two sets of faith commitments; I choose to call them two sets of metaphysical beliefs, rather than two religions, simply because one does not recognize itself as a religion (even though I must confess that it looks like a religion to me).

The Metaphysics (or Religion) of the Enlightenment

The rationalistic faith of the Enlightenment has a view of God (Deism), revelation (general, not special), truth (known by reason alone), sin (Pelagianism), Christ (teacher of morality and example of love), atonement (via subjective theories only), salvation (through education and technology), the church (the scientific community), and eschatology (utopia on earth through progress). But most modern people who live their lives as though this set of beliefs were true dislike admitting that they follow a *religion*. They would rather it was a choice between religion and reason, which is why the myth of the warfare between science and religion was invented in the nineteenth century.[13] It relieves them of the necessity of confronting the unpleasant fact that they have knelt before the altar of science and bowed to their god, just as surely as the despised Christians bow before the God of the Bible. But they are willing to affirm certain metaphysical doctrines, or at least they are always willing to admit to *denying* certain metaphysical doctrines (which often amounts to the same thing as affirming the opposite of the doctrines

---

13. For an influential example of the propaganda that was instrumental in pushing this myth to the forefront of public consciousness, see White, *Warfare of Science with Theology*. His work is continued a century later by the so-called new atheists. The definition of "new atheist" is one with less philosophical awareness and more bombast than most of the older atheists.

that are denied). For example, they eagerly refute Aristotelian teleology and trumpet mechanism. They oppose design in nature and affirm the power of chance to bring structure and order to the world. They deny universals and the supernatural realm (thus adopting nominalism and materialism), and they especially repudiate what they like to call "Greek metaphysics" or "classical theism."[14] Evidently, however, many of them remain unaware that they have simply traded Christian Platonism for Epicureanism or Stoicism and that they have simply chosen *different* metaphysics, rather than succeeding in freeing themselves from metaphysics altogether.

It is the essence of scientism that one believes that one can be free of all metaphysical influence merely by substituting empirical science and mathematical reasoning for metaphysics.[15] All that is accomplished by this move is to become unconscious of one's actual metaphysical assumptions and therefore uncritical of one's own presuppositions, which increases the odds of ending up holding incoherent views. This is a dangerous self-deception that characterizes many liberal-leaning Christians today, in particular, and it is painfully obvious to an objective observer.

If one denies (as I do) that starting with methodological naturalism can possibly lead to an orthodox, theological interpretation of Scripture as the source and guide to the church's faith, then the starting point becomes crucial. The rise of historical criticism in the Enlightenment took as a basic axiom that the Bible must be "allowed to speak for itself" rather than being "shackled" to a set of dogmas set forth in creeds purporting to represent the true meaning of the Scriptures. Historical critics like Baruch Spinoza, Hermann Reimarus, and David Strauss believed that, historically, church theologians had interpreted Scripture using the ecumenical creeds of the first five centuries as their guide to true interpretation. It seems clear, to me at least, that these Enlightenment thinkers and their heirs today vastly underestimate the degree to which the contents of the creeds had been composed, debated, challenged, and revised on the basis of biblical exegesis. From the seventeenth-century perspective, creedal orthodoxy seemed frozen in time and a barrier to penetrating to the true meaning of the text. Radical thinkers of the Enlightenment,

---

14. The new metaphysics did not arise suddenly in the seventeenth century. It has crucially important antecedents going back to the nominalism of William of Ockham and the concept of the univocity of being in the thought of Duns Scotus in the dark and chaotic fourteenth century. The tragic breakdown of the medieval synthesis of faith and reason, which had been founded on the existence of universals and the doctrine of the analogy of being, after Thomas Aquinas's majestic work in the thirteenth century, created the chaos and ferment in the fifteenth and sixteenth centuries out of which the Enlightenment emerged. More will be said about this history in chapters 3 and 4.

15. For a lucid explanation of "scientism," see Feser, *Last Superstition*, 83–85.

such as Spinoza, rejected the body of dogmas contained in the creeds and tried to interpret the Bible in a way that would be more compatible with their own faith, which was rationalism. They were convinced that ethics and true religion could be derived from "reason" alone and that the Bible should be interpreted like "any other book,"[16] rather than as a uniquely inspired Word from God. They sought religion based on general revelation alone without relying on special revelation. From our jaded, late-modern perspective it may appear to us that they were chasing leprechauns and unicorns, but they were deadly serious about it.

The Political Roots of Enlightenment Religion

The political motivations of the Enlightenment must also be kept in view. The Enlightenment is usually dated from about 1650 to 1800. More precisely, we could say it began with the Peace of Westphalia in 1648, which brought to an end the Thirty Years' War, and ended with the death of Immanuel Kant in 1804. Most Enlightenment thinkers were appalled by the bloodshed of the Wars of Religion, which stretched from the Peasants Revolt of 1524 in Germany through the war against Protestantism in France, the English and Scottish Reformations, to the English civil wars and the invasion of Ireland under Cromwell that did not end until the 1650s. Much of the intelligentsia of Europe, rightly or wrongly, blamed religion of all kinds for the passion and fury of these wars.

The purpose here is not to adjudicate historical blame or decide between competing historical interpretations; the point here is the narrower one of highlighting the motives of those who became convinced that the interpretation of the Bible must be wrested from the hands of bishops, pastors, and theologians and placed under the control of philosophers committed to reason as their highest authority. Those who answered to the church and its tradition naturally saw the Bible as undergirding the dogmas of the faith. Classical interpretation of Scripture involved reading the texts as the inspired Word of God and as teaching orthodox Christianity. But it was not only the orthodox theologians who brought concerns from outside the text itself into the

16. This phrase comes from Leo Strauss, who writes: "In our time scholars study the Bible in the manner in which they study any other book. As is generally admitted, Spinoza more than any other man laid the foundation for this kind of biblical study" (*Spinoza's Critique of Religion*, 35). For Strauss, the significance of Spinoza's approach is that it is a critique of revealed religion. The context of Spinoza's work is, Strauss says, "the critique of Revelation as attempted by the Radical Enlightenment" (35). For further discussion of Spinoza's role in the emergence of historical-critical study of the Bible, see Harrisville and Sundberg, *Bible in Modern Culture*, chap. 2.

interpretive process. Enlightenment philosophers like Spinoza and Thomas Hobbes were convinced that the political power of the church could be broken and peace ensured in civil society *only* if a new method of interpretation could be devised that would make the Bible the symbol of the new religion of reason, although, of course, they would not have put it that way. Their way of putting it was to say that the Bible must be studied like any other book and that the meaning of each text was what the original author had intended to convey to the original readers in their original situation. Since this historical meaning could be uncovered only by a certain methodology, which was regarded by the Enlightenment thinkers as rational and scientific, only those who were committed to this new method and trained in its intricacies could establish the meaning of the Bible. Biblical interpretation would henceforth be a matter for "experts."

This method, however, smuggled naturalistic metaphysics into interpretation under the guise of "historical method" and thus undermined the doctrine of inspiration without launching a frontal assault on the doctrine openly. The result was that political control of the meaning of the Bible gradually shifted from the church to the academy. In the early nineteenth century, the German research university emerged as an instrument of the state and became the model for universities worldwide in the late nineteenth and twentieth centuries. Increasingly, the modern, bureaucratic state tended to justify its authority on a Weberian account of bureaucratic and technological rationality, the very thing that was cultivated in the research university.[17] So, indirectly, the interpretation of the Bible was brought, at least to some extent, under the control of the state, rather than the church.[18]

One of the clearest ways in which modern historical criticism functions as a religion is the way it proselytizes so vigorously for its point of view. Jason Byassee notes how many "deeply skeptical biblical scholars are recovering fundamentalists." He mentions Wheaton College alumnus Bart Ehrman as an example and describes Ehrman as an evangelist for historical criticism.[19] Byassee calls the higher critical guild "a sort of shadow church with saints, canonized texts, hallowed processes of training novices, calls for ascetic renunciation and deferred reward, with its own glosses filling the texts of manuscripts, its own orthodoxy, its own heretics, its own desired political

---

17. See MacIntyre's illuminating discussion of this point in *After Virtue*, 25–27.

18. This control was never total, of course. But the point at which the new Enlightenment method asserted its superiority to classical theological interpretation was when it claimed the title "scientific" for itself. Churches, clergy, and Christians could dissent but only at the price of being "unscientific" or "fundamentalist."

19. Byassee, *Praise Seeking Understanding*, 245.

and spiritual ends."[20] Iain Provan, V. Philips Long, and Tremper Longman III also view the historical-critical guild as a kind of religion. They were disappointed by the reaction to the first edition of their book, A *Biblical History of Israel*, and in an extensive appendix to the second edition, which addresses reactions to the first edition, they reflect on how it feels to be excluded from the community. After expressing frustration with J. J. Collins's failure, as they see it, to engage the arguments of their book and his dismissing of it because it differs from the "standard" approach, they say, "He already knows, as he enters the discussion, which scholars are 'critical' and which are not, and the identification has nothing to do with whether scholars display critical thought via extensive argument in their writings; it has everything to do, rather, with which scholars agree with him in what he considers to be certain assured results of (truly) critical thought."[21]

In language similar to that used by Byassee, they write: "The academy is a community of interpretation with its own presuppositions and traditions, just as are the synagogue and the church."[22] It seems to me that if we take seriously what these (and many other) scholars are saying, it would be very naive to think of the historical-critical guild (as many evangelicals seem to do) as a neutral, objective, scientific group of disinterested scholars united by the sole purpose of seeking truth. That picture is probably less accurate than the other extreme of regarding the historical-critical academy as a heretical sect along the lines of the Jehovah's Witnesses, only with PhDs.

The new method of biblical interpretation that we call "historical criticism" did not appear out of nowhere for no reason, and it was not discovered in a laboratory like insulin. It began with (1) the neopagan metaphysical assumptions of the Enlightenment, which led to (2) the development of a new method of interpretation conducted within (3) a new social location resulting in (4) a whole new set of doctrines. All four elements of this approach to biblical interpretation are very different from traditional ones. Theologians and pastors of the Great Tradition had (1) Christian Platonist metaphysical assumptions (which they believed were exegetically justified), (2) a method of spiritual exegesis (which they believed was the same as the way the New Testament apostles interpreted the Old Testament), (3) a social location within the believing community of faith (to which they saw themselves as accountable), and (4) a set of doctrines (contained in the ecumenical creeds) that were very different from the doctrines of the Enlightenment.

20. Byassee, *Praise Seeking Understanding*, 18.
21. Provan, Long, and Longman, *Biblical History of Israel*, 424.
22. Provan, Long, and Longman, *Biblical History of Israel*, 424.

The doctrines of the quasi-religion of the Enlightenment were described above as follows: The rationalistic faith of the Enlightenment has a view of God (Deism), revelation (general, not special), truth (known by reason alone), sin (Pelagianism), Christ (teacher of morality and example of love), atonement (via subjective theories only), salvation (through education and technology), the church (the scientific community), and eschatology (utopia on earth through progress). In contrast to this description, traditional Christianity of the Great Tradition held to trinitarian classical theism; the necessity of correcting and supplementing general revelation with the special revelation found in Scripture; a view of truth as being found primarily in the incarnation of God in Jesus Christ and in Scripture read as his word; a doctrine of sin as moral rebellion resulting in true moral guilt; the corruption of human nature and the helplessness of humanity to save itself; salvation through faith in the penal, substitutionary sacrifice of Christ on the cross; the church as the fellowship of the redeemed; and eschatology as a living hope centered on the personal return of Jesus Christ to earth at the end of the age.

None of the claims made up to this point are particularly new or controversial in and of themselves. What I am attempting to call attention to here, which may be new for some, is the interconnection between metaphysics, method, social location, and doctrine. To do this, it is necessary to stress the contrast between Christian Platonism, classical interpretation of Scripture, and theology that begins from revelation and that is done in and for the church, on the one hand, and Epicurean metaphysics, historical criticism, theology that takes reason rather than revelation as its highest authority and that is done within the secularized university for a secularized society, on the other hand. Here is the contrast in the form of a chart.

Contrasting Methods of Scripture Interpretation

Classical Theological Interpretation	Modern Historical-Critical Interpretation
1. The metaphysics is Christian Platonism.	1. The metaphysics is Epicurean naturalism.
2. The method of interpretation is faith seeking understanding by means of philosophical meditation on special revelation, which corrects and supplements general revelation.	2. The method of interpretation is the historical-critical approach, which excludes special revelation and relies exclusively on general revelation by employing methodological naturalism.
3. The social location is the church located (ideally) within Christendom.	3. The social location is the secularized research university within a secularizing (post-Christendom) society.
4. The result is the handing on of the core orthodoxy of the ecumenical creeds.	4. The result is the new religion of salvation through technology, education, and social progress (i.e., progressivism).

The thinkers of the Enlightenment wanted to break the power of the church in society, and one key move they made to accomplish this goal was to assert that morality could be based on reason alone without the need for special revelation. The power of the church in European society derived in large measure from the widespread assumption that society would degenerate into lawlessness and chaos without the church's teaching Christian morality on the basis of the Bible. Understanding their motive for the rejection of special revelation and the creedal orthodoxy of traditional Christianity is important for the way that they interpreted Scripture. What I called "methodological naturalism" above was the presupposition of the historical approach they advocated. Naturalism is the key methodological presupposition of the historical-critical method of biblical study; it is what makes the various historical-critical methods different from other methods of biblical interpretation. I will discuss metaphysics in more detail in chapter 3, but here it is necessary to make clear that the two basic starting points for interpretation depend on different metaphysical presuppositions. A fundamental choice confronts the would-be interpreter at the outset: inspiration or naturalism. This basic choice cannot be avoided, only obfuscated.

The choice between inspiration and naturalism is the basis of the gulf between the academy and the church of which Steinmetz spoke. Classical interpretation of Scripture—which was the approach in Western culture from the early centuries up to the Enlightenment and still is the approach followed in the preaching and teaching of much of the worldwide church today—cannot adopt methodological naturalism without rendering inoperative the doctrine of inspiration. This is so because the doctrine of inspiration requires a Christian Platonist metaphysics in which supernatural divine revelation can take place at the moment that the prophets and apostles write the text, in which divine providence can ensure the preservation and transmission of the text, and in which the Holy Spirit can illumine the meaning of the text to readers in every century. There has to be a metaphysical framework in which God is able to speak into history on an ongoing basis in order for special revelation to be possible. This metaphysical framework depends entirely on a uniquely Christian doctrine of divine transcendence that comes from the Bible. A naturalistic metaphysics produces a method that leads to a heretical form of Christianity (or perhaps a whole new religion?) that the church must reject.[23]

23. The judgment of J. Gresham Machen that liberalism is really a whole new religion and not Christian at all, which he offered in 1923, has been ratified rather than refuted by the developments of the past century. He saw liberalism as a "non-redemptive religion" called "modernism," which is rooted in "naturalism." See his *Christianity and Liberalism*, 2.

Can This Gulf Be Overcome? Promising Developments in Recent Scholarship

Are there any signs that biblical scholarship is becoming more self-critical and more open to classical ways of interpreting Scripture? The answer to this question is a qualified yes, although it is not easy to distinguish between fads and actual retrieval of usable resources from the past. Michael Allen and Scott Swain are engaged in a project of retrieving the catholic nature of the Reformed tradition; this is the single most hopeful trend in contemporary theology as far as I am concerned.[24] In chapter 1 of their book, *Reformed Catholicity: The Promise of Retrieval for Theology and Biblical Interpretation*, Allen and Swain enumerate no less than thirteen recent trends in theology and biblical studies that could conceivably come to mind when someone calls for a recovery of classical approaches to biblical interpretation.[25] What these diverse approaches have in common is a sense that modern theology has exhausted itself and needs to go back to classical resources for renewal.[26]

Where would I situate my project with regard to those approaches? It might be helpful to run through them briefly, offering some comments. Some are irrelevant to my proposal, such as the emerging or emergent church movement, which I view as little more than a vehicle for young evangelicals who want to become liberal Protestants. The Evangelical Catholicism of Carl Braaten and Robert Jenson has not really been very influential on me, primarily because Jenson has not viewed classical theism as part of the tradition that needs to be retrieved.[27] The consensual Christianity of Donald Bloesch, the ancient-future approach to worship advocated by Robert Webber, and the modern hymns movement are congenial but not really influential on my thinking. The seminal work of Karl Barth, especially in exegesis, has been hugely influential on the entire twentieth and twenty-first centuries,

---

24. John Webster is the most important and influential figure in this movement. Although he did not live to complete his own projected five-volume *Dogmatics*, his influence through his essays, his supervision of doctoral students, his editorial work, and his interpretation of Barth has been substantial. He published a series of essays in dogmatics that gives a good idea of the overall shape of his theology. See *Word and Church*; *Confessing God*; *Domain of the Word*; *God without Measure* (2 vols.). See also his short monographs *Holiness* and *Holy Scripture*.

25. See also two new series they are editing: New Studies in Dogmatics (Zondervan) and International Theological Commentary (T&T Clark).

26. Allen and Swain, *Reformed Catholicity*, 4.

27. See Swain, *God of the Gospel*, for an explication of the concerns about Jenson's theology. I am in agreement with Swain's basic criticisms of Jenson's "evangelical historicism" (233) and with his call for *ressourcement* (234). And I can only echo Swain's appreciative reference to John Webster as "the supreme contemporary example of dogmatic theology in a (shall we call it?) Reformed and Thomistic key" (7). This description of Webster points to the central reasons why I see Webster, not Jenson, as the way forward.

but Barth's influence on me is mostly mediated through the work of John Webster. This means that I value Barth most where he is in line with the Great Tradition, which is just the opposite of how many influential readers of Barth receive his work. Certainly it must be recognized that exegesis of Scripture is one area in which Barth has deep roots in the Great Tradition; his exegesis is very fruitful and helpful to those who are trying to do theology in the tradition of classical orthodoxy, even when his specific conclusions may be challenged.[28] The growth in interest in reception history of the Bible, in part fostered by Barth's influential example as an exegete, is a very encouraging sign, because it shows an interest in taking seriously the way the Spirit has led the church in interpreting Scripture through divine providence in history that preserves the gospel from generation to generation, just as Jesus promised (John 16:13). The church is not infallible, but the Spirit is and, to the extent that the Spirit's preserving work is visible, we can get help in understanding Scripture.

One of the most encouraging trends in the past few decades has been the degree of interest evangelicals and other conservative Protestants have shown in the exegesis of the church fathers. One of the most important religious publishing events of the twentieth century was the appearance of the Ancient Christian Commentary on Scripture series from InterVarsity Press.[29] Studying the history of how the Bible has been interpreted is a trend I wish to extend and reflect on theologically in this book. The work of John Milbank and Radical Orthodoxy has been very helpful in understanding the role of the breakdown of medieval realism and the growth of nominalism in the development of modernity.[30] It has helped me to see that modernity needs to be rejected at a much deeper level than most conservative Protestants have imagined up to now. Thomas Oden's "paleo-orthodoxy" also has been very influential in my

28. One of the most helpful books on Barth's exegesis is Gignilliat, *Karl Barth and the Fifth Gospel*. The weakness of Barth's exegesis is related to his reluctance to challenge the modern Enlightenment understanding of history. But sometimes he is happily inconsistent on this score when it comes to the actual practice of exegesis.

29. This landmark work was done under the general editorship of Thomas C. Oden and made a selection of the best of patristic commentary on all sixty-six books of the Bible available in modern English for the first time. In the wake of this earthquake in the world of religious publishing, many publishers are now publishing translations of classic commentaries from the fathers, the medieval schoolmen, and the Reformers. Most notable in this regard is InterVarsity Press's own follow-up series, the Reformation Commentary on Scripture, under the general editorship of Timothy George. See also The Church's Bible being published by Eerdmans under the general editorship of Robert Louis Wilken, which is a project similar to the Ancient Christian Commentary on Scripture series.

30. See Milbank, *Theology and Social Theory*. Also helpful are Gillespie, *Theological Origins of Modernity*; and Tyson, *Returning to Reality: Christian Platonism for Our Times*.

thinking,[31] along with the emphasis on *ressourcement* in the Roman Catholic nouvelle théologie movement spearheaded by Henri de Lubac[32] and in the evangelical *ressourcement* movement as seen in the work of D. H. Williams and Hans Boersma.[33] The welcome rise of *ressourcement* Thomism in the work of scholars such as Gilles Emery, Thomas Joseph White, and Matthew Levering has facilitated a new reading of Thomas Aquinas that situates him within the living tradition of patristic exegesis and theology.[34]

Another trend that I welcome is the theological interpretation of Scripture movement,[35] although it has become something of a victim of its own success. Because everybody wants on the bandwagon, the movement has become so diverse as to be in danger of petering out without making the impact some of us originally envisioned. The emphasis on the spiritual exegesis of the fathers is welcome, as is the recognition of the importance of the rule of faith for disciplining exegesis. But there are problems.

Three of the most significant problems in contemporary discussions of theological interpretation of Scripture are (1) the unresolved relationship of theological interpretation to modern, historical-critical approaches;[36] (2) the

31. See *Agenda for Theology*; *Requiem*; and *Rebirth of Orthodoxy*. In these books Oden complains about modernity. In editing the Ancient Christian Commentary on Scripture series, he did something highly significant to counter the hold that modernity has on the Christian mind.

32. Three volumes have now appeared in English translation of Henri de Lubac's seminal work, *Medieval Exegesis*. These works are part of the valuable Ressourcement series published by Eerdmans. See the bibliography for publishing information on these works.

33. Boersma's emphasis on "sacramental ontology" has been valuable as one of the few contributions, other than Radical Orthodoxy, to bring philosophical considerations into the exegetical conversation. See his *Nouvelle Théologie and Sacramental Ontology* and *Heavenly Participation*. An important recent publication by Boersma is *Scripture as Real Presence*. See also his *Sacramental Preaching*, which demonstrates how exegesis and preaching come together within a sacramental worldview. Louth's *Discerning the Mystery* is also helpful in this regard.

34. I would mention Levering, *Scripture and Metaphysics* as being of great importance for my understanding of Thomas Aquinas's conception of theology as contemplative wisdom. This, more than anything else, enabled me to see the kinship between Thomas and the fourth-century Cappadocian fathers. This book also makes clear that Aquinas's trinitarian theology is both rooted in fourth-century Nicene thought and a clear alternative to twentieth-century relational theisms.

35. An excellent introduction to the movement is *Manifesto for Theological Interpretation*, ed. Bartholomew and Thomas. Also see Billings, *Word of God for the People of God*; and Treier, *Introducing Theological Interpretation of Scripture*. The *Dictionary for Theological Interpretation of the Bible*, ed. Vanhoozer, is useful as well.

36. This is seen most clearly in the work of Brevard S. Childs. His final commentary, *Isaiah*, was a typical historical-critical work that barely touched the rich mine of theologically significant issues in Isaiah. However, his final book, *Struggle to Understand Isaiah as Christian Scripture*, is immensely fruitful and stimulating, not to say encouraging. But why could he not do the kind of theological interpretation that he so lucidly described having been done by the fathers, medieval schoolmen, and Reformers? It seems that his exegetical work proceeds

failure to distinguish between spiritual exegesis that honors the literal sense, and thus is compatible with *sola Scriptura*, and that which does not do so; and (3) the inability of some contemporary practitioners of the approach to rule out revisionist readings of Scripture, which leads to the suspicion that the approach is a wax nose liable to be made subservient to the contemporary communities of readers in such a way that the authority of Scripture over the church is rendered inoperative in practice. My sense is that two other issues lie behind these problems. First, it is a typically modern tendency to overvalue method and to undervalue culture and tradition. Method by itself cannot save us. Theological (or spiritual or figurative or allegorical) exegesis must be deeply embedded within a pro-Nicene culture that involves the fruitful interaction of spiritual exegesis, Nicene dogma, and the theological metaphysics generated by that dogma. This means that we have to pay attention to the metaphysical context in which exegetical work is done as well as the metaphysical implications of the exegesis. In chapters 3 and 4 of this book, I will address this issue by seeking to overcome the influence of the Enlightenment's philosophical naturalism on biblical interpretation. Second, with regard to the second and third problems, any concept of "theological interpretation" that undermines the Reformation's emphasis on the unique authority of Scripture over individual and communal human experience and ecclesiastical structures must be

---

on two rails that never meet: (1) historical-critical insights into what John Webster calls "the natural history of the text" (Webster, *Domain of the Word*, 43), which are largely unhelpful for preaching or theology, and (2) canonical exegesis, which is often very theologically fruitful. It is a tragedy that he found himself unable to extend the great tradition of historic Christian exegesis himself. The reason why may be his unwillingness to challenge the metaphysical presuppositions on which higher criticism is based. Francis Watson contends that Childs's *Biblical Theology of the Old and New Testaments* never lives up to its promise: "Childs in practice so concerned to preserve the integrity of the Old Testament that its dialectical relationship to the New virtually disappears" (*Text and Truth*, 14). The shortcoming about which Watson is speaking results from viewing the Old Testament as having only a historical meaning and not a christological layer of meaning that requires acceptance of the existence of divine authorial intent in the text. The refusal to integrate the human author's intent with the divine author's intent in defining the meaning of the text results in the spiritual, christological sense never quite being rooted in the historical meaning of the text. Childs certainly saw that the main tradition of Christian exegesis did take divine authorial intent into account. Why he exhibited ambivalence about doing so himself is difficult to understand. Matthew Levering has a penetrating analysis of Childs's thought on this topic in his *Participatory Biblical Exegesis*, 8–13. Levering points to the unresolved problem of the nature of history in Childs's thought and contends that Childs could not bring himself to accept the idea that a theological concept of history is compatible with the integrity of historical-critical research. According to Levering, Childs always viewed human authorial intent as inviolable if one is pursuing historical-critical study. Here is where we need to move beyond Childs to recover a properly orthodox theological metaphysics if we are to be able to interpret the Bible with the Great Tradition. Much more must be said about these issues as this book progresses.

rejected as incompatible with orthodox Christian faith. In the second half of this book, I will endeavor to describe an approach to biblical interpretation that does not fall prey to this danger.

Perhaps an example will help to clarify the issue. When Stephen Fowl argues that the inclusion of unrepentant, practicing homosexuals in the church may be analogous to the inclusion of uncircumcised gentiles in the church in Acts 10–15,[37] we have a perfect example of why so many people fear allegorical readings of the Bible and why theological interpretation of Scripture in general seems to be dangerous. It seems that he is making the text say something it does not say by imposing a contemporary agenda onto the text and inserting a meaning into the text that is foreign to the plain sense of the Bible. It does nothing to ameliorate this fear when, in response to Christopher Seitz's concern that such a reading undermines the plain sense of Scripture, Fowl says, "It does . . . raise again the sharp issue of how compatible a static notion of the 'plain sense' of scripture, a plain sense located in the text rather than the believing community, is with Christian theological approaches to the Old Testament."[38] Fowl gives every indication of being willing to allow the experience of the contemporary community to override the plain sense of Scripture, thus fatally undermining biblical authority. This tendency has been the Achilles' heel of modern, revisionist theology and liberal Protestantism in general ever since Schleiermacher. It is, therefore, not a way forward and has virtually nothing in common with the way the historic mainstream of Christianity has read the Bible. It is a dead end.

Notice that Fowl's proposed interpretation of Acts 15 drives a wedge between the literal sense of the text and the purported "spiritual sense." In Acts 15:20, the gentiles are required by the Jerusalem Council to abstain from sexual immorality. That is what the literal sense conveys, whether we view it as simply the historical sense or as the plain sense.[39] In this text, sexual immorality would clearly include homosexual acts. Fowl is talking about extending the meaning of that text in such a way that the spiritual sense would permit a positive moral evaluation of homosexual acts. This sets the spiritual sense in direct contradiction to the literal sense, so it *clearly* is a wrong exegetical move. We will discuss this issue more extensively in chapter 6. The point here is to note that merely proposing a spiritual or theological sense or extending the meaning

37. Fowl, *Engaging Scripture*, 119–26.
38. Fowl, *Engaging Scripture*, 126.
39. In this case, as is often the case in the New Testament, there is no gap between the literal sense and the historical sense of what the original human author meant to convey in the original situation to the original audience. It is not necessary to assert that the historical sense is always the single meaning of the text in order to see that in many cases it is exactly that.

of a text in a certain direction is not automatically to be accepted. So let no one labor under the illusion that just calling it "theological interpretation of Scripture" automatically guarantees good interpretation. Theological interpretation can be done on the basis of good or bad theology; bad theological interpretation, of course, leads to unhelpful and wrong exegetical results.

The Decline of Historical Criticism

Speaking of dead ends, another major trend in contemporary theology that is promising is the continuing disintegration of the historical-critical approach to biblical interpretation. This is encouraging in the sense that it demonstrates the need for a radical reform of biblical studies as an academic discipline. If we think of historical-critical scholarship as a tradition stemming from Spinoza and coming down to the Society of Biblical Literature today, we can point to four characteristics of the tradition in its current form.

First, it is characterized by chronic instability. The "assured results of higher criticism" may be assured while they last, but they do not last long. Modern higher criticism is typically modern insofar as it is firmly in the grip of what Alexander Solzhenitsyn, in another context, termed "the relentless cult of novelty."[40] New theories and new twists on old theories seem to be the lifeblood of the discipline; as a result, the clear impression given those outside the guild is that the Bible has no stable meaning.

Second, we see methodological fragmentation. New methods proliferate and are used to get contradictory results. Scholars working in feminist or liberation modes can work without much communication with those practicing literary criticism or rhetorical criticism. The practitioners of the various methods do not seem to need one another. Under such circumstances, is it even meaningful to speak of a "discipline" (singular) at all? Or is there a hidden, underlying set of methodological presuppositions that needs to be exposed and evaluated?

Third, there is increasing relativism as to the results of the investigation of the biblical text. The historical-critical method was supposed to be objective

40. See Solzhenitsyn, "Relentless Cult of Novelty," an address to the National Arts Club in New York City in 1993 on the occasion of his being awarded the Medal of Honor for literature. In this paper Solzhenitsyn writes: "This relentless cult of novelty, with its assertion that art need not be good or pure, just so long as it is new, newer, and newer still, conceals an unyielding and long-sustained attempt to undermine, ridicule and uproot all moral precepts." While he is speaking of art in particular, what he says applies to many areas of academic life in the twentieth century, including biblical studies. Nothing is stable and nothing lasts. The contrast with consensual trinitarian and christological orthodoxy, which has existed in a stable form for over 1,500 years, could not be more stark.

and scientific; it was supposed to be the antidote to the subjectivism of the allegorical approach. Yet anyone who studies the Old Testament knows that hardly any two scholars agree on the dating, composition, and authorship of most of the books and sections of books, let alone their meaning. Entire volumes are written that never even get around to discussing the meaning of the biblical book as a whole, let alone how its meaning contributes to the meaning of the Bible as a whole. Only "fundamentalists" seem to do that.

Fourth, higher criticism causes the Bible to go silent in the churches. In denominations in which higher criticism dominates the seminaries, there has been a steep decline in preaching and teaching the Bible in the churches. Laypeople are told that they cannot interpret the Bible correctly without advanced degrees, and so they do not read it very much. Who can blame them? There is a famine of the Word of God in liberal Protestantism. With numerical decline since the 1960s continuing to accelerate, the prognosis is that the continued existence of these denominations for more than another generation or two is very much in doubt. In summary, historical criticism, like liberal theology in general, has done much to weaken the conviction of the church that the Bible is a unified book, uniquely inspired and authoritative, with a crucially important message for all of humanity that one can understand by reading it and listening to sermons that explain it. In short, historical criticism makes it hard to hear the message of God to us in the Bible.

The churches and denominations that are growing or stable tend to have preaching and teaching ministries that draw on the accumulated wisdom of the Great Tradition of Christian orthodoxy by standing in a linear tradition passed on from pastor to pastor and not relying exclusively on seminary education to do the job. It would be safe to say that more pastors derive more of their preaching and teaching material and methods today from the Tim Kellers and the John Pipers of the world than from academic hermeneutics textbooks. When I as a young pastor decided to preach Isaiah 53 as a prophecy of Christ's atoning death, it meant more to me that I was following the example of John R. W. Stott and D. Martyn Lloyd-Jones than that I was violating the rules laid down by the historical-critical method. The more liberal Protestantism disintegrates, the less relevant the historical-critical method of biblical interpretation will appear to be; this fact should serve to encourage more people to take a second look at what the Great Tradition of Christian orthodoxy has to offer.

Biblical Theology and a Theology of the Bible

Before I conclude this all-too-brief survey of promising trends in contemporary theology, I want to mention two other trends that I think hold great potential for nourishing the christological interpretation of the Old Testament and traditional exegesis of the Bible.

First, there has been a flowering of whole-Bible biblical theology in the late twentieth and early twenty-first centuries. There are two main sources from which these writers drew inspiration: the work of Geerhardus Vos and Brevard S. Childs, respectively. Childs published his *Biblical Theology of the Old and New Testaments* in 1992 as the culmination of a decades-long publishing program highlighted by his major work *Introduction to the Old Testament as Scripture* in 1979. A decade later Charles Scobie's massive, one- thousand-page work, *The Ways of Our God: An Approach to Biblical Theology*, appeared. In the preface to this work he spoke of inhabiting two worlds: the world of the academy, in which the historical-critical approach dominated, and the world of the church, where he often preached and led Bible studies for laypeople. He says, "The tension between these two worlds was often acute."[41] He mentions Childs as one of his inspirations for undertaking this project, as Childs was one of the few who deliberately tried to inhabit both of the solitudes.

The influence of Geerhardus Vos (1862–1949) has been disseminated through the faculty of Westminster Theological Seminary for the past half-century and has recently stimulated evangelical efforts in biblical theology more widely. G. K. Beale's *A New Testament Biblical Theology: The Unfolding of the Old Testament in the New* is an outstanding example.[42] Vos viewed biblical revelation as redemptive historical (rather than as historical critical) and as christocentric. His high view of revelation and inspiration provided a basis for a presentation of a unified biblical theology.[43] This approach is exemplified in his classic *Biblical Theology: Old and New Testaments*, published in 1948.

Recently, there has been an outburst of biblical theology at the Southern Baptist Theological Seminary, with three whole-Bible biblical theologies appearing within a span of only four years. First came the excellent *God's Glory in Salvation through Judgment: A Biblical Theology* by James M. Hamilton Jr. in 2010, a book that every pastor should own and use regularly. It was followed by *Kingdom through Covenant: A Biblical-Theological Understanding of the Covenants* by Peter J. Gentry and Stephen J. Wellum in 2012 and then by *The King in His Beauty: A Biblical Theology of the Old and New Testaments* by

---

41. Scobie, *Ways of Our God*, ix.

42. See also Beale's important monograph, *Temple and the Church's Mission*. Another book that exemplifies a kind of biblical interpretation that is not supported by the historical-critical method but stands in the historic tradition of the church is Letham, *Message of the Person of Christ*.

43. Gaffin, "Introduction," in *Redemptive History and Biblical Interpretation*, xv.

Thomas R. Schreiner in 2013. By attempting to present the meaning of the Bible as a single unified witness to Jesus Christ, all of these works make a significant contribution to undoing the considerable damage done over the past two centuries by the atomizing effects of historical criticism.

Second, John Webster has articulated an ontology of Scripture that is based in trinitarian classical theism and offers tremendous potential as a theological framework for biblical interpretation. We have to piece together his perspective from the many articles and papers he published, which offer a glimpse of what he was planning for his dogmatics.[44] Here I want to point to three aspects of Webster's project that hold promise for biblical interpretation in the Great Tradition of Christian orthodoxy, although we will discuss them more extensively in chapter 2. First, he understands the need for theology to delineate an ontology of Scripture that gets beyond an ontology of "pure nature" in which the Bible and its readers inhabit a reality in which God does not act, which is what Spinoza meant by interpreting the Bible out of its own history. Webster stresses that the doctrine of creation is the basis of such an ontology, and he argues that we can have an adequate doctrine of creation only by means of an appeal to the Christian doctrine of God.[45] Second, he stresses that the most important factor in good biblical interpretation is a proper appreciation of what the Bible actually is: "divinely instituted signs in the domain of the Word."[46] The nature of interpretation depends on the inspired nature of the Bible. Third, he stresses the mystery of Scripture—namely, that "the Word accomplishes his act of *self-utterance* through these human auxiliaries."[47] Interpretation of Scripture cannot proceed with a focus on the human authors and their intentions alone; it must pay attention to what the divine author is saying through the human authors as well, which necessarily involves the interpreter in mystery, because no human interpreter can grasp all that God is or all the knowledge that God has of himself.

The strength of the recent revival of whole-Bible biblical theology is that it seeks to present the message of the Bible as a unified, coherent, meaningful, relevant Word from God given through the human words of the authors. The weakness of this movement, like the weakness of modern evangelical theology generally, is that it does not address in an adequate manner the philosophical, dogmatic, and theoretical issues that render biblical theology problematic. This is not to say that there are no answers to these problems; it is merely to observe that contemporary evangelical theology and biblical interpretation

---

44. See the bibliography for a listing.
45. Webster, *Domain of the Word*, 5–6.
46. Webster, *Domain of the Word*, 9.
47. Webster, *Domain of the Word*, 8, emphasis added.

need to be more historically grounded in the Great Tradition, more critical
of modernity's philosophical deviations from the Great Tradition, and more
aware of the way that exegesis, dogma, and metaphysics interrelate in the
Great Tradition. It is my conviction that John Webster's theology of the Bible
can serve as an adequate basis for the biblical theology that evangelicals have
always written and are continuing to write today. It is my hope that this book
contributes in some small way to making this happen.

The Argument of This Book

This book seeks to address the problem outlined in this chapter of the gulf
between the theories of academic hermeneutics and the practice of ecclesial
preaching and teaching. In part 1 (chaps. 2–4), I critique modern hermeneutical theory by beginning with a discussion in chapter 2 of how the doctrine
of Scripture is grounded in the classical doctrine of God. Next, I turn to
metaphysics in chapter 3 and summarize the Christian Platonist metaphysics
of the Great Tradition and how it embodies the metaphysical implications
of the biblical doctrine of God. I also show that the Enlightenment was a
point-by-point rejection of Christian Platonism and an embrace of ancient
Atomist, Epicurean, and Stoic ideas instead. Chapter 4 proposes a revised
template for the history of hermeneutics in which the modern hermeneutics of
the Enlightenment is demoted from being the goal toward which all previous
history led to being considered instead a dead-end road leading to nihilism.
Part 1 ends with a call for *ressourcement*.

Part 2 (chaps. 5–7) answers this call by describing resources in the Great
Tradition of Christian exegesis that can help us understand what it would mean
to interpret the Bible as the Word of God. The goal is to introduce the reader
to some of the riches of the Great Tradition's theological reflection on, and
practice of, biblical interpretation. Limits of time and space here necessitate
selectivity; we just sample the riches that lie for the most part barely tapped.
The question of arbitrariness and subjectivism, which is such a big concern for
modern interpreters, is addressed head-on, and the view is put forward that
the historic manner in which the church has interpreted Scripture is actually
more scientific and *more* objective than modern historical-critical methods.

This book tries to restore the delicate balance between biblical exegesis,
trinitarian dogma, and theological metaphysics that was upset by the heretical, one-sided, narrow-minded movement that is misnamed "the Enlightenment." It is an attempt to recover the pro-Nicene culture of the fourth
century—to inhabit the tradition of Nicene orthodoxy in a substantial way

and not just by mimicking certain vocabulary in superficial ways while actually operating as if the neopagan metaphysics of the Enlightenment were true. In some ways, the original Enlightenment is over, but in other ways its legacy continues to exert a malign influence on Western culture. We could summarize it this way: the naive faith in reason as an adequate source of morality and truth has run its course and is dissipating into the acids of postmodernism, but the cult of the autonomous individual unfortunately continues without diminishment in the romanticism and postmodernism that followed the Enlightenment. With the rise of nineteenth-century romanticism, the individual remained central, but the romantic thinker looked to feeling instead of reason as the source of meaning. By the beginning of the twentieth century, romantic concepts of feeling were seen to be devoid of objective moral content and the Nietzschean will-to-power triumphed.[48] In the postmodern context, the reader-centered approaches to hermeneutics are essentially romantic in essence insofar as they see the individual as the source of meaning, which is then read into the text. But this kind of interpretation must inevitably degenerate into a form of the will-to-power.

In attempting to recover classical interpretation of Scripture, we must be aware of the history of Western thought since the Enlightenment; we must avoid the temptation to replace the single-meaning theory with as many meanings as we have readers (and we must be *seen* to avoid doing so). In a nutshell, my argument shall be that the classical approach to interpretation has always allowed for a fuller meaning (*sensus plenior*) under the guidance of the Holy Spirit without opening the door to interpretive anarchy. Reading the text of Scripture under the guidance of the tradition of creedal orthodoxy allows for new light to break forth without that new light shattering the vessel that contains it. The Enlightenment can be overcome by recovering some of the things that should not have been forgotten.

---

48. MacIntyre provides a clear explanation of what he calls "the failure of the Enlightenment project" in *After Virtue*, chaps. 5–6.

Part 1

Theological
Hermeneutics

2

Toward a Theology of Scripture

God is not summoned into the presence of reason;
reason is summoned into the presence of God.

John Webster[1]

*T*his chapter is foundational to my entire proposal. If academic hermeneutics is to be reformed so as to become an adequate basis for the
preaching and teaching ministry of healthy, growing churches, it must be
reformed on a *theological* basis. But what does this mean? One thing it must
mean is that the role of philosophy in hermeneutics must be secondary to
theological description rooted in special revelation. Theology must shape the
philosophy that shapes hermeneutics.

Theology is the study of "God in himself" and of "all other things relative
to him."[2] In this chapter, we are focusing on the work of God in which he
communicates with his fallen, estranged creatures in such a way as to save
them. So we are looking at the nature of God and the nature of creatures in
relation to the One who created them and who is now engaged in redeem-
ing them. We begin from revelation and therefore from a knowledge of the
mighty acts of salvation done by God in history culminating in the death,
resurrection, ascension, and heavenly session of our Lord Jesus Christ. Our
task here is not to argue for the reality of God or his acts of salvation, but
rather to understand who God is on the basis of what he has done.

1. Webster, *Holiness*, 17.
2. Webster, *God and the Works of God*, 3.

The possibility of the reception of revelation by the creature is not primarily a matter of human capacity but is rather a possibility created by the powerful ability of the Triune God to make himself known to his creatures through his Word in the power of his Spirit. It is a matter of the capacity of God's energetic, saving grace to overcome slothful creatures, penetrate the resistance of the rebels, and transform erstwhile enemies into friends. It is activity pictured vividly in the miracles by which Jesus Christ healed the deaf: "And they were astonished beyond measure, saying, 'He has done all things well. He even makes the deaf hear and the mute speak'" (Mark 7:37).[3] The resurrected Jesus Christ is the Word of God and because he is alive and all-powerful, he is able to overcome the obstacles to the receipt of revelation, which are chiefly a matter of sin, rather than being merely epistemological in nature. Or, rather, we could say more precisely that the obstacles, which are epistemological in nature, have their deepest roots in the effects of Adam's fall and our willing complicity in his sin.

The act of reading a biblical text is not a secular act. It actually is a divine-human encounter. John Webster writes: "The act of reading Scripture— because it is the act of reading *Scripture*, the herald of the *viva vox Dei*—is not an instance of something else, but an act which, though it is analogous to other acts, is in its deepest reaches *sui generis*."[4] Nothing is more fundamental to the Christian life than reading the text of Scripture and submitting one's life to the One who speaks His Word through the human words of the inspired text. And nothing is more damaging to the Christian life than the attempt to secularize this act of reading; to do so is to act like an atheist. If reading in faith is how we become Christians, reading without faith is how we become atheists. So the stakes are high.

We need not a general hermeneutics but a special hermeneutics. This does *not* mean, however, that we cannot use reading techniques that are used to interpret other kinds of writings. It just means that in the borrowing process, these methods must be transformed in light of the theological truth found in the Bible. For people trained in the spiritual practice of biblical interpretation, the reading of *all* texts (and writing itself) is transformed as a result of this spiritual training.[5] The simple act of working out the grammar of a Greek

3. Here Mark pictures Jesus as fulfilling the prediction of a new exodus by Isaiah: "Then shall the eyes of the blind be opened, and the ears of the deaf unstopped" (Isa. 35:5). The fact that this miracle happens in the Decapolis (outside Israel) should not be missed; God's people are being led home from the nations, and the healing of both the desert and the people is occurring in the ministry of Jesus.

4. Webster, *Holy Scripture*, 72.

5. It seems highly improbable, for example, that the modern, realistic novel could have emerged in a culture that had not been shaped by the Bible.

sentence is something non-Christians do all the time, but in the case of the Christian interpreter, it is taken up into a larger matrix of reading practices and is thus sanctified for use by the Holy Spirit. Accurate translation is *Christian* translation when it is done by a believer who seeks to hear the living God speak and stands ready to obey. Reverence for God engenders reverence for the text, which leads to careful attention to the details of the text and its transmission. As Webster puts it, "Like other acts of Christian existence it is a human activity whose substance lies in its reference to and self-renunciation before the presence and action of God."[6] Texts that are memorized are regarded in a different light from texts that are not; all biblical interpreters should spend time memorizing Scripture. Careful, attentive, slow, meditative reading expresses reverence for the text of Scripture. The transformation of the various methods of reading texts derived from the surrounding culture and the process of adapting them in the service of biblical interpretation are testimonies to the fact that, in biblical interpretation, method is less important than what one believes about the nature of the biblical text and the divine reality to which it points: its *res*.

We need a theological description of the entire event of biblical interpretation in its context, and this means that we need a special hermeneutics that arises out of a true understanding of the inspired status of the text we are reading. As Webster pithily expresses it, "bibliology is prior to hermeneutics."[7] But, as he also pointed out, bibliology itself cannot be the starting point; the nature of the text is inseparable from the *res* of the text, its subject matter and substance. Bibliology is the account of *God* speaking through the text, so bibliology itself must be grounded within the doctrine of God. We do not really know *what* the Bible is until we know *who* it is who commandeers these human words and reveals himself through them. According to Webster, "Countering the hegemony of pure nature in bibliology and hermeneutics requires appeal to the Christian doctrine of God."[8] The doctrine of God generates a theological understanding of who we are as readers and the nature of the situation in which we read. But note well, it is the *Christian* doctrine of God to which we must appeal. We are talking about appealing to the specific understanding of God that is derived from the prophets and apostles of Holy Scripture by means of exegesis. It is an appeal to the Holy Trinity. This means that a certain kind of circularity is inevitable in talking about a "Christian doctrine" of anything—not a vicious circle, but rather an expanding circle of understanding.

6. Webster, *Holy Scripture*, 72.
7. Webster, *Domain of the Word*, viii.
8. Webster, *Domain of the Word*, 6.

We must take seriously the back-and-forth nature of dogmatic theology; we as theologians are not Moses coming down from the mountain but are more like Paul reasoning in the synagogue, trying to convince his fellow Jews that Jesus is the Messiah of the Scriptures. Theology involves reading the text, meditating on it, drawing conclusions from it, arguing over it, reflecting on the dogmatic and philosophical implications of those (perhaps revised) conclusions, and then coming back to the text and reading it again from our new perspective. Later readings are shaped by prior readings, yet result in further insight. Is this not everyone's experience? Who reads the text once and understands it, and all the implications that flow from it, instantaneously? Who has never changed an interpretation based on further reflection and discussion? And yet, who does not have settled convictions about the meaning of the text that one could not imagine changing?

This process of reading, meditating, formulating dogmatic propositions, rereading the text, gaining further insight, and so on is the context in which a theological metaphysics develops that allows us gradually to realize who we are, where we are, what our situation is, who is speaking to us, and how we should respond. This is the setting in which theology is done. Part of becoming a theologian is learning our true identity, the truth about our world, the true nature of our problem, and the true nature of the text we are reading and who is speaking to us. Hans Boersma calls this a "sacramental ontology,"[9] which is a good way to describe the biblical understanding of reality that is depicted imaginatively in the fiction of J. R. R. Tolkien and C. S. Lewis.[10] Matthew Levering calls for "participatory exegesis," which is done on the basis of a metaphysics in which history is seen as participating in God.[11] Webster speaks of "a textual and hermeneutical ontology."[12] I prefer the language of "theological metaphysics," by which I mean the metaphysical implications of the Nicene doctrine of God. This variation in terminology should not obscure fundamental agreement on the main point. What we are all talking about is the nature of God, the inspiration of Scripture, our fallen human nature, and the process by which communication between God and us takes place. What is crucial is that we recognize that *we* do not define the situation into which God is allowed to speak, and *we* do not set limits on what God is allowed to say. Instead, we come to realize our true situation only as we actually read the Scriptures and believe the Word of God. We

9. See Boersma, *Nouvelle Théologie and Sacramental Ontology* and *Heavenly Participation*.
10. See *The Silmarillion, The Hobbit,* and *The Lord of the Rings,* by Tolkien, and *The Space Trilogy* and *The Chronicles of Narnia,* by Lewis. They are widely available in many editions.
11. Levering, *Participatory Biblical Exegesis,* 33–34.
12. Webster, *Domain of the Word,* viii.

are *hearers*, which places us in a subordinate position ready to receive what is given as gift.

The double meaning of "Word" as referring to the Second Person of the Trinity, who became incarnate in Jesus of Nazareth, and also as the spoken Word of the Triune God, which is inscripturated in the words of the prophets and apostles of Holy Scripture, is a very significant double meaning. We will need to reflect on how to think about the relation between these two meanings of the word "Word" by meditating on the relationship of the eternal Son who became incarnate to the words in the text of Holy Scripture that refer to him. We need to see an analogy but not an identity; not everything that can be said of the incarnation can rightly be said of Scripture.[13] Commenting on Telford Work's proposal in *Loving and Active: Scripture in the Economy of Salvation*, Webster says that while it is one of the few contemporary works to take seriously the need for a theological ontology of the Bible, it "goes awry" in failing to maintain the Creator-creature distinction with sufficient rigor. As Webster says, "Scripture does not have a divine nature." But this does not mean that we must secularize Scripture as purely natural, and it does not mean that we "uncouple scriptural signs and divine Word" in "nominalist fashion."[14] What Webster is after here is the distinction between incarnation and sacrament. For him, Scripture functions sacramentally; the doctrine of inspiration (which he unpacks as providence, sanctification, and inspiration) is the theological explanation for how that happens. Scripture functions sacramentally for him, just as it does for Hans Boersma, who shows what deep roots in the Christian tradition such a concept actually has.

Boersma's recent book, *Scripture as Real Presence: Sacramental Exegesis in the Early Church*, describes in great detail and with penetrating insight the sacramental exegesis of the early church fathers. Far from being a dispassionate historical description, his book actually is an argument for the contemporary relevance of patristic exegesis. His point is not that we must slavishly copy and repeat the exact exegetical choices of the fathers in every respect but rather that their conviction that "Christ is the hidden treasure present in the *visibilia* of the Old Testament Scriptures" is as true today as it ever was.[15] He notes that the weakness of modern historical exegesis is that "it doesn't treat the Old Testament as a sacrament (*sacramentus*) that *already contains* the New Testament reality (*res*) of Christ."[16] Boersma points out that Augustine

13. Webster, *Domain of the Word*, 13.
14. Webster, *Domain of the Word*, 13.
15. Boersma, *Scripture as Real Presence*, 17.
16. Boersma, *Scripture as Real Presence*, xv, emphasis original.

"regularly refers to scriptural texts as *sacramenta*,"[17] which indicates the deep roots of this view of Scripture in the Great Tradition. Webster's work on Scripture is firmly rooted in the classical Christian understanding of what Scripture is. On the issue of the sacramental nature of Scripture, there is no disagreement between the early church fathers and the Protestant Reformers. As Timothy George points out: "The preaching of the Gospel as a sacramental event is at the heart of Reformation theology. Preaching is also at the heart of Reformation faith—preaching as an indispensable means of grace and a sure sign of the true church."[18]

At one point, Webster poses the question, "What is theological interpretation of Scripture?" and answers, "interpretation informed by a theological description of the nature of the biblical writings and their reception, setting them in the scope of the progress of the saving divine Word through time."[19] This is what I mean when I say in chapter 1, "Before we can interpret the Bible, we must decide what it is." Of course, in the order of discovery, we have to read the Bible first, and the Holy Spirit teaches us through the words of the prophets and apostles the saving truths of the faith. It is not as if the inspiration of the Bible were somehow known from some external source. But in the order of exposition, the nature of the Bible precedes the interpretation of the Bible. What the Holy Spirit teaches us as we read Scripture is that Scripture is *inspired Holy* Scripture and that, because of that ontological reality, it is possible to regard what we learn from the Bible as the Word of almighty God.

Here we will probe a mystery that stretches our limited human minds as far as they can go before we reach the limits of human comprehension. Even so, a full account of the metaphysics of interpretation will require the discussion in the next chapter; here we describe the situation theologically, and in the next chapter we will reflect on the metaphysical implications of this theological description. But, with God as our enabler, by the end of the next chapter we should have a rough sketch of the metaphysics of revelation based on a theological description of the act of biblical interpretation, which can serve as a touchstone to guide us through the history of the complex issues surrounding the process of interpreting the Bible in chapter 4.

There are thus two parts of the theology of Scripture that we seek to explicate in this chapter: (1) a description of what Scripture is—namely, inspired writing that comes from God and leads us to God—and (2) a description of

17. Boersma, *Scripture as Real Presence*, 2.
18. George, "Reformational Preaching" (accessed on Feb. 24, 2017). For more on the continuity of the Reformation with the Great Tradition of Christian exegesis, see George, *Reading Scripture with the Reformers*, 26–36.
19. Webster, *Domain of the Word*, 30.

the kind of God that God is. In other words, theology explicates the characteristics of the God who is capable of inspiring Scripture and who does, in fact, inspire Scripture for the benefit of his wayward human creatures.

The Inspiration of Scripture

We begin by noting for the record that the divine inspiration of the Bible is not a particularly controversial point of theology in the Great Tradition. There are two possible reasons why some point of theology is not found in the Apostles' Creed: one is that it is not central to the faith, and the other is that it is so central and so taken for granted that no one would have thought to put it in. The inspiration and authority of Holy Scripture is in the latter category. The framers of the Apostles' Creed would never have thought of using the creed as some sort of substitute for, or alternative to, the Bible. Scripture and creed have always functioned together as the basis of the Christian faith.

The ecumenical creeds are not meant to be summaries of all the important points made in the Bible in the sense that whatever the creeds omit is thereby signaled to be unessential or unimportant. The creeds, it is well to remember, were meant to be guides to reading Scripture. Every Sunday, going back to the days of the apostles, the Scriptures were read in Christian worship in every congregation, just as they were in my church last Sunday morning. At first Scripture was only what we now call the Old Testament. Then letters from apostles like Paul were read along with the Old Testament writings as helps in interpreting the meaning of the (Old Testament) Scriptures. Eventually, Gospels were written and read for the same purpose.[20] As the apostles began to pass away, the church realized that because of the uniquely historical fact of the incarnation of our Lord, there could never be another generation of "eyewitnesses of his majesty" (2 Pet. 1:16). Therefore, steps were taken to preserve for all time the apostolic interpretation of the Old Testament in the form of letters, narrative accounts, and Gospels. Thus the New Testament came to be accepted as apostolic and therefore as the authoritative interpretation of the Scriptures.

Inspiration, Providence, and Miracle

The doctrine of divine inspiration consists of two complementary parts: miracle and providence. The canonization of the New Testament writings

---

20. The degree to which the New Testament is consumed with interpreting the Old Testament is revealed by the fact that approximately 32 percent of the New Testament consists of quotations or allusions to material in the Old Testament (Hill and Walton, *Survey of the Old Testament*, 744).

is an example of divine providence at work. But there would have been no writings to canonize if the miraculous aspect of inspiration had not already occurred. All attempts to reduce inspiration to merely providence or merely miracle must inevitably fail. An inductive study of the Bible itself reveals that both aspects of inspiration are seen as equally important. On the one hand, some texts came into existence by clearly miraculous means. We can cite as the paradigmatic example the giving of the law to Moses at Sinai. The Ten Commandments are described as having been written by "the finger of God." We are told in Exodus, "And he gave to Moses, when he had finished speaking with him on Mount Sinai, the two tablets of the testimony, tablets of stone, written with the finger of God" (Exod. 31:18).

Now it is somewhat amusing that conservative theologians have been accused by liberal theologians repeatedly over the past two centuries of believing in the "outdated" and "intellectually bankrupt" doctrine of verbal plenary inspiration, which they say is a mere "dictation theory" of inspiration. It is by now a well-established tradition that one positively melts in fear whenever that foreboding imprecation "dictation theory" is hurled over the rampart like some sort of bomb. Well, the undeniable fact is that some of the text of Scripture *was* given by dictation, and this is not a theory but a simple fact reported by the text of Scripture itself. John says so plainly in the opening chapter of the book of Revelation: "I was in the Spirit on the Lord's day, and I heard behind me a loud voice like a trumpet saying, 'Write what you see in a book and send it to the seven churches, to Ephesus and to Smyrna and to Pergamum and to Thyatira and to Sardis and to Philadelphia and to Laodicea'" (Rev. 1:10–11).

What is this but dictation? John does as he is told and records both what he sees in the vision and what the angel says. This is what the text claims for itself; it is not a theory invented by the conservative theologian to buttress certain conservative dogmas. It is not theory, but a fact about which we need to theorize. Somehow we have to fit at least *some* dictation into our doctrine of inspiration. Inspiration is, at least in part, a miracle.

On the other hand, not all of Scripture has such a spectacularly miraculous provenance; some of it seems to have come into existence by means that we understand as more "normal." For example, in Luke 1 we read: "Inasmuch as many have undertaken to compile a narrative of the things that have been accomplished among us, just as those who from the beginning were eyewitnesses and ministers of the word have delivered them to us, it seemed good to me also, having followed all things closely for some time past, to write an orderly account for you, most excellent Theophilus, that you may have certainty concerning the things you have been taught" (Luke 1:1–4). Here we have a picture of a process that looks very familiar to us. It looks like a biographer writing a book about the life of a highly significant figure (Jesus) by conducting interviews with eyewitnesses, doing research, and then engaging in a writing process similar to the one in which I am engaged as I write this book.

This kind of very human writing and editorial work can be discerned all over the canon. For example, 2 Kings 18–20 appears to have used the book of Isaiah as a source, because it repeats some of the material found in Isaiah 36–39. We know that the author of Kings used Isaiah, rather than the other way around, because the material in Isaiah is not in chronological order.[21] Hezekiah's illness and recovery actually preceded Sennacherib's siege of Jerusalem, even though in both Isaiah and Kings, Sennacherib's siege of Jerusalem is presented first (Isa. 36 = 2 Kings 18:13–37) and Hezekiah's illness and recovery afterward (Isa. 38 = 2 Kings 20). It is clear that the rest of 2 Kings records historical events in the order in which they occurred; that is a feature of Kings. But Isaiah has a clear and specific literary purpose in placing chapters 36–37 where they are as the end of the "Assyrian section" and chapters 38–39 where they are as the beginning of the "Babylonian section,"[22] even though that puts them out of chronological order. This means that the author of Kings probably borrowed this material from Isaiah; if it had been the other way around, the material in Kings would likely be in chronological order. This sort of literary borrowing is quite different from Moses receiving supernatural revelation on Sinai or John having a vision on Patmos.

The Bible also bears unmistakable marks of having been worked on by editors, and some material has clearly been added later. For example, the passage describing the death of Moses in Deuteronomy 34 reads as though it was written by whoever wrote (or edited) Joshua. It refers to Moses in the third person, calling him "Moses, the servant of the LORD" (Deut. 34:5). Then it refers to Joshua as Moses's successor upon whom Moses had laid hands (Deut. 34:9). Joshua 1 opens with "After the death of Moses, the servant of the LORD . . ." (Josh. 1:1), thus linking back into Deuteronomy by using the same title for Moses: "the servant of the LORD." Throughout the book of Joshua, Moses is referred to repeatedly as "the servant of the LORD"; finally at the very end of the book, Joshua is referred to as "Joshua the son of Nun, the servant of the LORD" (Josh. 24:29) in the context of the record of his death at the age of 110. An editorial intention to link Moses and Joshua is apparent in these references. Later writers of Scripture often engaged in such editorial

21. For a clear discussion of the issues involved in coming to this conclusion, see Walton, "Date of Isaiah," 129–32.

22. For a good discussion of this ordering of material, see Beyer, *Encountering the Book of Isaiah*, 143–45.

shaping and completing of previous writings; we do not know the names of many of those who did so. Here is where a high doctrine of providence allows us to have confidence that "all Scripture is breathed out by God" (2 Tim. 3:16), even if we are not sure of the identity of the human author or editor in a particular instance.

This is one of the major problems with making "human authorial intent" the "be-all and end-all" for biblical interpretation, as we shall explore further in later chapters. Some of the material we are interpreting does not have a single author/editor, so whose intention are we talking about? Historical criticism gets all tangled up at this point. If you are operating in a framework of methodological naturalism, then it seems almost inevitable that there is going to be a tension between the conscious intention of the original author and the conscious intention of some or all later editors. The meanings of the various layers of the text and the various sources potentially become contradictory; the ability to determine what *the text* means is therefore undermined. Whose intentions determine the meaning? It would truly be ironic if the defenders of the single-meaning theory were forced to reply that in some cases the text must have multiple meanings. At least traditional theories of multiple meanings in the text did not view the various meanings as mutually contradictory. I prefer the terminology of "layers of meaning" rather than "meanings" for this reason. Again, full discussion of this point must be postponed until later.

The crucial thing to note for our present purposes, however, is that when the Bible claims inspiration for itself no distinction is made between the texts that originated in obviously supernatural ways and the texts that originated in normal human ways. Paul explicitly says that *all* Scripture is God-breathed (θεόπνευστος): "All Scripture is breathed out by God and profitable for teaching, for reproof, for correction, and for training in righteousness, that the man of God may be complete, equipped for every good work" (2 Tim. 3:16–17). "All Scripture" here undoubtedly refers to the entire Old Testament and at least some of the New Testament writings already in circulation.[23] Peter also offers no qualifiers to the scope of inspiration of the Scriptures when he writes: "For no prophecy was ever produced by the will of man, but men spoke from God as they were carried along by the Holy Spirit" (2 Pet. 1:21).

23. This can easily be demonstrated by paying close attention to Paul's quotations of Scripture in 1 Timothy. In 1 Tim. 5:18, Paul quotes Deut. 25:4 and Luke 10:7 (= Matt. 10:10), introducing both quotations with the formula "For the Scripture says." This would be as jarring as my quoting the apostle Paul and John Webster and introducing both quotations by saying, "For the Scripture says," unless, of course, Paul and his readers shared a belief that Luke's Gospel was actually Scripture.

Whatever "carried along" may be taken to mean, the presence in the text of the words, thoughts, and personalities of the human authors must not be taken to imply that the text is any less than exactly what God intended it to be or that the text says anything other than exactly what God intended it to say. "Providence" should not be taken to mean "partly divine and partly human" or "somewhat inspired" as opposed to the Scripture that comes into existence by a miraculous action of God (as at Sinai or on Patmos), which might by contrast be viewed as "wholly divine" or "completely inspired." Sometimes one gets the impression that when people talk about the Bible being both God's words and human words, they mean that by virtue of being human words they must be less than fully divine words or even that some of the words of Scripture are likely untrue for that reason. For example, the Bible says that God ordered the extermination of the Canaanites, but surely that cannot be right, they say. That must be a human erroneous word in the midst of a lot of other divine, true words. Maybe God's providence just slipped up there for a moment! But this is not how the Bible presents itself. God can work equally effectively through providence and inspiration; that is a sign of how complete and perfect his sovereignty is. So "All Scripture is breathed out by God" (2 Tim. 3:16).[24]

The New Testament and the church fathers make no significant distinction between the authority of the Old Testament and the authoritative christological interpretation of the Old Testament provided by the apostolic eyewitnesses to Jesus Christ. Since the christological interpretation is viewed as the correct interpretation of the Old Testament, no wedge can be driven between them as far as the early church is concerned. One of Brevard S. Childs's conclusions in *The Struggle to Understand Isaiah as Christian Scripture* is "A basic characteristic of Christian exegesis has been its acknowledgement of the authority of Scripture" and that only after the rise of philosophical rationalism in the Enlightenment was this called into serious question.[25] He notes that we see this conviction of the authority of Scripture most clearly, not in the occasional formal doctrinal statements of the inspiration and authority of Scripture (such as the ones we have just discussed), but rather in the use made of Scripture by both the New Testament apostles and the church fathers—namely, the way it is assumed to be "a single vision of both testaments as a unified and authoritative telling of one story of salvation through Jesus Christ."[26] This is how Scripture has been understood throughout the Great Tradition.

24. For a good discussion of biblical inspiration, see Swain, *Trinity, Revelation, and Reading*.
25. Childs, *Struggle to Understand Isaiah*, 300–301.
26. Childs, *Struggle to Understand Isaiah*, 301.

So, to sum up, God's providential work is responsible for the preparation of the historical situation in which the human authors wrote, for the preparation of the human authors themselves, for the writing of the text, for the preservation of the inspired text once it was written, and for the process of canonization. In the midst of the process, however, certain events occurred that cannot be explained by the usual laws of nature. If God's providence is his *usual* way of acting in the world, God's miraculous acts are his *unusual* ways of acting in the world. Inspiration is made up of both miracle and providence. In his miraculous acts, God introduces novelty into history in the form of special revelation.

The Indispensable Role of Miracle in Inspiration

We think of providence as arranging events in such a way that the biblical author states this particular view, rather than some other one. But how does God convey to us through human writers what "no eye has seen" (1 Cor. 2:9)? In this verse, Paul is quoting Isaiah 64:4, which says,

> From of old no one has heard
> or perceived by the ear,
> no eye has seen a God besides you,
> who acts for those who wait for him.

The Isaianic context is the longing for God to act decisively and powerfully in history. As verse 1 puts it: "Oh that you would rend the heavens and come down" (Isa. 64:1). Isaiah is praying for the power of God to manifest itself in history in an unmistakable manner. The point is that Israel does not believe in a version of the Epicurean/Deist God who cannot or will not intervene. Also, God is not merely the personification of the irrational forces of nature, which cannot be addressed personally with any expectation of a response. Instead, God is personal and alive and active in history, yet transcendent in power and might. Miracles are his calling card. He is not like the lifeless idols; he can even foretell the future. How can he do that? He can do that because he is in control of history. He is transcendent.

If God is determined to reveal himself in a truly new way, miracle is necessary. When the sacred text has the LORD say, "Behold, I am doing a new thing" (Isa. 43:19), we should not be surprised that the imagery of miraculous deliverance at the Red Sea is used in the immediately preceding verses. Basically, this chapter declares: "If you thought the first exodus was something, wait until you see what I am going to do to deliver Israel this time. If you thought deliverance from Egypt was a display of power, wait until you see the deliverance from Babylon!" The second exodus of which Isaiah speaks was not complete until the redemption of the world accomplished by Jesus on the cross as the divine Messiah acting in his capacity as Suffering Servant. And it was not fully revealed until the resurrection of Christ from the dead. In fact, the implications and effects of that exodus are still rippling across history in the form of the deliverance of the elect from the pagan nations, which will culminate in the second coming of Christ and the establishment of God's heavenly kingdom on earth, the consummation of the new exodus. The point I am trying to make here is that, just as we can know the existence of God as first cause of creation by means of general revelation and yet we still need special revelation to inform us of the triune nature of God, so inspiration by providential means can go only so far in revealing what God wishes us to understand; the revelation of what is truly new requires miraculous acts and prophetic interpretation of those acts.

In his wonderfully concise and incisive book, *The Bible among the Myths*, John Oswalt argues that there is a world of difference between the content of the Bible and the myths of the ancient Near East to which the Bible is often compared. He contends that the similarities of the Bible to the religious literatures of the ancient Near East are often overemphasized. Actually, the similarities are merely "the result of cultural adaptation, using readily available forms and terms to say something quite new."[27] There is a link between God's miraculous revelation and what is totally new in the Bible. I do not think it is an accident that it was Oswalt who wrote the standard conservative commentary on Isaiah, which upholds the unity of the book and the authorship of Isaiah of Jerusalem.[28] If one thinks that inspiration can be only a matter of providence (which can often be explained away as "coincidence" within a naturalistic worldview), then it is always tempting to view the teaching of the Bible as saying *no more than* what is said in other ancient Near Eastern texts. For example, if one thinks this way, one may well say that Genesis 1:1 does not teach creation *ex nihilo*, but rather that God exercised his shaping power on eternally existing matter, because that is what the *Enuma Elish* teaches. How could we expect the author of Genesis to rise above his culture and say something unthinkable and unprecedented for people of his time and cultural background?

The traditional Christian answer to that question has always been "inspiration"; implicit in the concept of inspiration is the possibility that God could

---

27. Oswalt, *Bible among the Myths*, 85.
28. Oswalt, *Book of Isaiah 1–39* and *Book of Isaiah 40–66*.

actually convey new information to the human author (or inspire the human author to write "better than he knew"). First Peter 1:10–12 seems to take this sort of inspiration for granted:

> Concerning this salvation, the prophets who prophesied about the grace that was to be yours searched and inquired carefully, inquiring what person or time the Spirit of Christ in them was indicating when he predicted the sufferings of Christ and the subsequent glories. It was revealed to them that they were serving not themselves but you, in the things that have now been announced to you through those who preached the good news to you by the Holy Spirit sent from heaven, things into which angels long to look.

Peter pictures the prophets preaching and writing their prophetic oracles without fully comprehending what it was they had said or written. This is astonishing; it speaks of mystery in the text of Scripture. It also reminds us that what was inspired (that is, God-breathed) was not the prophet but the words we have in Scripture. It is the text that is inspired, which makes the single-meaning theory of hermeneutics highly problematic. Once you reduce the meaning of the text to human authorial intention, you relocate inspiration from the text to the author of the text, which is extremely problematic, since we do not have access to Peter, Paul, and Moses (let alone the author of Hebrews) but have access only to the texts they wrote. This move also makes the meaning of the Bible forever uncertain and indeterminate because proving the intention of a long-dead author is never an easy thing and sometimes impossible. Determining the intention of an anonymous author/editor is even more difficult; arbitrating among the obscure intentions of an unknown number of authors and editors is hopeless.

I suggest that there is a direct link between Oswalt's ability, on the one hand, to believe that God revealed the name of Cyrus to Isaiah a century and a half before the rise of Cyrus and Persia and his ability, on the other hand, to believe that God could inspire the author of Genesis to proclaim a doctrine of creation totally unlike anything found anywhere else in his cultural milieu. A God who could do one could do the other. A God incapable of one would be incapable of the other. There is an important connection between novelty of revelation and miracles such as predictive prophecy. To approach the Bible with a conviction that it contains new revelation, which is not merely the product of the human imagination or of human insight, is central to what it means to believe in the inspiration of Scripture.

The miracle of revelation through the writers of Scripture is balanced and complemented by the parallel miracle of the illumination of the readers of

Scripture. Both are works of the Holy Spirit, and neither could occur in a world in which philosophical naturalism was the truth about reality. Neither could be described adequately on the basis of methodological naturalism.[29] The problem with a naturalistic approach to the book of Isaiah is not merely that it leads to the rejection of the unity of the book and the traditional authorship by Isaiah of Jerusalem. A naturalistic approach leads one inevitably to see it as a mishmash of fragments from different centuries written by different authors and jammed together without regard for contradictions and incompatibilities. Competing theologies jostle for position cheek by jowl. Various authors and editors put forward competing perspectives. Believers who ask, "What does it all mean?" receive very little help from historical-critical scholars. In such circumstances, who can blame ordinary Christians for giving up on reading the Bible? Given the nature and provenance of the Bible (written in three languages by forty different authors over fifteen hundred years), the only way it could have a coherent and consistent message is by virtue of divine inspiration. For such a book to have a unified message would be a miracle. In fact it *is* a miracle!

Those who have ears to hear let them hear. Through prayer, docility, and receptivity, and with an open heart, we read the Scriptures expecting God to speak to us through them. We hear in the inspired text the voice of the living God and, in hearing, we are transformed into both hearers and doers of the Word. We know so little about God, but God knows himself perfectly and graciously shares a tiny fragment of that knowledge with us creatures. For that we can thank God, not our own weak intellectual powers or our modern scientific methods. God bears us up with wings as eagles and lifts us up to heavenly places by his power. That is what it means to read Scripture under the illumination of the Holy Spirit.

The God Who Speaks

We must now say more about the God who does these things. It is God who by miracle and providence inspires the sacred text. It is God who is the *res*, the subject matter about which the Bible speaks. It is God who illumines the meaning of the text to us as we read it in humble faith. So our question is, What must the God be like who can do, and has done, such things? In

---

29. One could very well argue that the interpreter working on the basis of methodological naturalism would be blind to the existence of novelty in the text of Scripture even if it were present. To be working on the basis of methodological naturalism would lead one to concoct alternate explanations for the presence of what appears to be sheer novelty in the text.

moving from the works of God to the nature of God, we are following the path taken by fourth-century pro-Nicene theology.[30] What we see revealed in the economy does not exhaust the infinite being of the Triune God, but we can be sure that God is at least capable of doing what revelation shows us he has, in fact, done. His works require that he has certain powers in order for him to be able to do those works; we can reason from the works to the powers to the nature that has those powers and thus make true, though of course not exhaustive, statements about what God is. Since the cause must be greater than the effect, we can know that God is greater than what he has caused, although we can never know the totality of his inexhaustible being. God, in the unfathomable depths of his perfect and beautiful being, is much more than what he reveals himself to be—but never less. And, we must add, his immanent being is never contradictory to his revealed nature. Therefore, knowledge of God gained by revelation is true, though not comprehensive, knowledge. Based on what God has done, according to Scripture, what can we say about him? There are many things we could say, but because of limited time and space, let me suggest that the two essential things we must say here are that such a God must be transcendent and such a God must be personal.

God Is Transcendent

The God who revealed himself to Israel is constantly contrasted to the gods of the nations, the idols, and the dark spiritual forces that utilize the human weakness for idols to exploit our fallen nature and lead us away from the true and living God who created us for fellowship with himself. The contest between Yahweh and the gods of Egypt was formative in the consciousness of Israel. The ten plagues humiliated the magicians of Pharaoh's court and the gods worshiped by the Egyptians. The power of Yahweh was supreme; even the great military prowess of an ancient and powerful civilization was unable to stand against Israel's God. After this triumph, Moses sang:

> I will sing to the Lord, for he has triumphed gloriously;
>   the horse and rider he has thrown into the sea.
> The Lord is my strength and my song,
>   and he has become my salvation;

30. For a helpful discussion of this pattern, see the discussion of Basil of Caesarea's *Hexameron* in Ayres, *Nicaea and Its Legacy*, 314–17. As he so often does, Thomas Aquinas concisely sums up pro-Nicene theology when he writes, "Because therefore God is not known to us in His nature, but is made known to us from His operations or effects, we can name Him from these" (*Summa Theologica*, pt. I, q. 13, art. 8, p. 67).

> this is my God, and I will praise him,
>> my father's God, and I will exalt him.
> The LORD is a man of war;
>> the LORD is his name. (Exod. 15:1–3)

The prophet Isaiah, whose poetry is full of exodus themes, goes Moses one better. He mocks Babylon, the great imperial power that destroyed Jerusalem, in a taunt song *before* the LORD has acted in judgment on Babylon (Isa. 14:3–21).[31] Isaiah also mocked the idols of Babylon by pointing out that the Babylonians had to carry their heavy idols from place to place on beasts, whereas the God of Israel has borne his people from their birth (Isa. 46:1–4). The idols are made by the peoples, but the LORD creates his people from nothing. In chapter 44, Isaiah makes fun of those who cut down a tree and use half of it for firewood to cook dinner and the other half to make an idol before which they pray and say "Deliver me for you are my god!" (Isa. 44:9–17). In Isaiah 41:23, he contrasts the false gods of the nations with the LORD by challenging the gods to predict the future, which is something only the LORD can do.

So how do we describe the difference between the LORD and the gods of the nations? First, the gods of the nations are material,[32] while the LORD is spiritual in the sense of not material; that is, he is invisible.[33] The LORD's works are visible, but he is not. For this reason, the second commandment prohibits the fashioning of images (Exod. 20:4). Second, the LORD is able to hear and answer prayer, while the false gods of the nations are deaf and dumb. The God of Israel entered into covenant with Abraham, renewed that covenant with Isaac and Jacob, and then heard the cries of his suffering people in Egypt

---

31. I consider all of Isaiah to stem in substance from Isaiah of Jerusalem, who lived approximately 760–680 BC. So the book was in its final form, or nearly final form, by the early seventh century, which means that the references (Isa. 44:28; 45:1) to Cyrus's decree (issued in the 530s BC) are a prediction made by Isaiah on the basis of revelation. Such detailed revelation about the future is unusual (though not unprecedented) in biblical prophecy, but clearly necessary in this instance because of the high degree of importance associated with the prediction of the exile before it happened so that everyone would know that it was part of the Lord's plan. For a defense of predictive prophecy and the unity of Isaiah, see Allis, *Unity of Isaiah*. Also see Oswalt's two-volume commentary on Isaiah listed in the bibliography.

32. The idols are material. This does not mean, however, that dark, demonic forces do not lurk behind the idols and use the idols to deceive the nations. No biblical writer would deny that possibility in any given situation. But even if people are understood to be worshiping spiritual beings and not merely the wood or metal idols that represent those beings, they still deserve the mockery expressed in Isaiah 44 because they are still worshiping mere creatures of the one true God.

33. A recent and interesting discussion of divine invisibility can be found in Sonderegger, *Systematic Theology*, 1:49–144.

(Exod. 3:7). Third, having heard the cries of the enslaved, he is able to deliver them because of his great power. The LORD has a mighty arm and is powerful to save. So does all this add up to what we mean by "transcendent"? Not quite.

We have not penetrated to the full meaning of what the Old Testament texts are saying about the God of Abraham, Isaac, and Jacob by saying that he is invisible, able to hear and speak, and all-powerful. Why not? The Bible does not present God as merely *more powerful* than the pagan gods, for example, but as *all-powerful*. In saying this, we must recognize first of all that the gods of the nations are not all completely powerless. We are told that after Moses and Aaron turned the Nile into blood, "the magicians of Egypt did the same by their secret arts. So Pharaoh's heart remained hardened" (Exod. 7:22). What was happening there? The gods of Egypt (that is, the demons behind the idols) were real and could perform some miracles. The biblical worldview includes room for spiritual beings that are not God and yet are not merely mythological projections.[34] Jesus casts out demons; Paul warns us to put on the whole armor of God in order to stand against the schemes of the devil (Eph. 5:11). Why do we need to do this? It is because of the battle we are caught up in as the people of God. Paul writes, "For we do not wrestle against flesh and blood, but against the rulers, against the authorities, against the cosmic powers over this present darkness, against the spiritual forces of evil in the heavenly places" (Eph. 6:12). Yet this same Paul could write to the Corinthians, "Therefore, as to the eating of food offered to idols, we know that 'an idol has no real existence,' and that 'there is no God but one.' For although there may be so-called gods in heaven or on earth—as indeed there are many 'gods' and many 'lords'—yet for us there is one God, the Father, from whom are all things and for whom we exist, and one Lord, Jesus Christ, through whom are all things and through whom we exist" (1 Cor. 8:4–6).

There is no contradiction here. Paul is saying clearly that there is only one true God, the God of Israel, the Father revealed in Jesus Christ his Son and through the Holy Spirit. Of course no human ruler, no material idol, and no created spiritual entity could ever be considered to be in the same category as the one true God. In fact, that is a basic truth about God that Thomas Aquinas stresses: God is *sui generis*. He is not a member of a genus. He is utterly unique. Isaiah writes:

> "You are my witnesses," declares the LORD,
> "and my servant whom I have chosen,

34. See Heiser, *Unseen Realm.*

that you may know and believe me
    and understand that I am he.
Before me no god was formed,
    nor shall there be any after me." (Isa. 43:10)

The God of the Bible is not merely the biggest, strongest spiritual being of all. He is not merely a being among other beings. He is the Creator of all that exists. There are only two categories of existing things: God in one category by himself and, in the other category, all that is not God, including angels, demons, human beings, and the entire spiritual and material realms of creation (as Gen. 1:1 puts it: "the heavens and the earth"). Everything in that second category has its existence as a gift from the One who created all that exists and is himself uncreated.

God is, in the terms used by scholastic theology to express this feature of biblical revelation, the One whose being includes existence. All other beings have existence in addition to their essence, but God's being is his existence. Part of what it means for God to be the kind of being he is, is that he necessarily exists. For Thomas Aquinas, this gets at an essential aspect of what God's mysterious words to Moses at the burning bush mean: "I am that I am" (Exod. 3:14). For God to name himself "I am" is tantamount to his saying, "I am my own existence. Nothing gave me my existence and I did not bring myself into existence. I could never fail to exist or cease to exist, because I am." The deepest meaning of the tetragrammaton is "I am myself."[35]

In meditating on what it means for God to name himself "I am," one realizes that God is utterly, totally unique. Divine being is not the same as created being; the difference is qualitative, not merely quantitative. That is a big problem for anyone who wishes to speak about God. How does one speak meaningfully of something or someone who is utterly different? Christian theology gives two answers to this question, both of which are conscious of the danger of idolatry and try to avoid it. The first is that God is ultimately unknowable and mysterious. We can apprehend God but never comprehend God. Our knowledge of God is always a drop in the ocean compared to God's knowledge of himself. God is beyond comprehension for us limited creatures. The second answer, however, is more hopeful. It is that we can use analogical language chastened and corrected by special revelation to speak truly of God—even if we can never speak comprehensively of God.

The Great Tradition uses analogical language to speak of God. The classical exposition of the meaning of analogy is that of Thomas Aquinas,

35. Thomas Aquinas, *Summa Theologica*, pt. I, q. 13, art. 12, p. 70. Also see pt. I, q. 3, art. 4, p. 17.

although it would be false to say that he invented it. As is often the case,
Thomas is simply summing up more clearly and systematically the implications of what the fourth-century fathers said.[36] Analogical language allows us to say things about God without falling prey to the false idea that
any comparison we utilize captures God totally. All language falls short,
yet some language can be adequate for our purposes. It can be adequate
without comprehensively describing God's essence in a total way. Here is
how analogical language works. It is the middle way between univocal and
equivocal language.

Univocal language would be that which speaks of God using a word drawn
from creaturely reality that is taken to mean exactly the same when applied
to God and when applied to a creature. Equivocal language is the opposite. It
thinks of a word as having no overlapping meaning whatsoever when applied
to God and to a creature. So, for example, take the word "father." I am a
father, and God is a father. If language is equivocal, then the word "father"
applied to God has no overlapping meaning whatsoever with the word applied to me. But if language is univocal, then the word "father" applied to
God and to me means exactly the same thing. God has a son, and I have a
son. But I needed a wife in order to have a son; God, however, has no wife
and needs none. So when we say that language is analogical, we mean that
the word "father" means the same when applied to God and to the creature
in *some* respects, but that in *many more* respects it does not have the same
meaning. Analogical language for God always falls short of capturing the
exact nature of God's essence, but it does manage to say some true things
about God nonetheless. Analogical language preserves the mystery of God's
being, which is beyond our human comprehension, but allows us to say some
true things about God.

So when we say that God is transcendent, we mean that God is higher,
better, greater, more powerful than anything else that is. But we mean more
than that. We also mean that God is utterly and totally unique. We mean
that God is a mystery beyond our comprehension who has, nevertheless,
revealed himself to us. We have no theory to explain how this is possible; all
we have to go on is that God has spoken in his Word, and so we try our best
to repeat, like a child learning to talk, what he has said to us in the Scriptures.
All our theorizing about the fact of revelation is done after the fact of revelation. Our theory does not make revelation possible; revelation makes our
theorizing necessary.

36. Thomas Aquinas, *Summa Theologica*, pt. I, q. 13, art. 10, p. 69. The discussion in this
paragraph and the next follows Thomas's explanation closely.

God Is Personal

The second thing we need to say about the God who has revealed himself in the history of Israel and in Jesus Christ is that this God is personal. We have said that God is transcendent, which means that when we say that God speaks through the inspired text of his appointed prophets and apostles, we are not merely hearing an echo of our own human thoughts. We are hearing a voice that is truly transcendent and therefore not merely the kind of thing we normally hear when we read the writings of great philosophers, poets, or theologians. We are addressed by *God*. But now we must emphasize the other key term of that statement: We are *addressed* by God. The voice we hear is the personal address of one who is revealed to be our heavenly Father speaking through his only Son in the power of the Holy Spirit. In short, God is personal.

Fine distinctions are very important in every complicated field of thought, and here we must make a fine distinction that makes all the difference in the world: God is personal, but God is not a person. What is meant by this distinction? The Bible clearly teaches monotheism, but theologians and philosophers debate exactly what monotheism entails. By monotheism here I mean the doctrine that there is only one God, that God is totally unique, and that there is no class of which God is a member.

I take this understanding of monotheism to be not a philosophical opinion but the clear meaning of many biblical texts. For example:

> Thus says the LORD, the King of Israel
> and his Redeemer, the LORD of hosts:
> "I am the first and I am the last;
> besides me there is no god." (Isa. 44:6)

This is not an isolated text pulled out of context; it is representative of a large number of biblical texts throughout the book of Isaiah and, indeed, throughout both Testaments that declare the uniqueness of God. Many false gods pretend to be in the category of "gods" alongside the true and living God of Israel, but they are just pretenders. The true God has many imitators but no peers. Notice that God himself declares that "besides me there is no god," that is, no real god. In the context, Isaiah is well aware of and discusses thoroughly the gods of the nations and declares that the LORD will judge them and triumph over them. It would be hard to judge nonexistent entities, but it is easy to judge pale imitations of the real thing, that is, demons posing as gods and the idols of stone and gold that people make to visualize them. The fact that they can be visualized proves that they are fakes, which is one reason for the giving of the second commandment. As soon as you start thinking of God as a member of a class of gods (even if you think he is the biggest, smartest, strongest of them all), you are committing idolatry.

What we are talking about here is the difference between what Brian Davies calls "classical theism" and "theistic personalism."[37] These are two contrasting forms of theism. Classical theism has been the mainstream view of the Great Tradition from the fourth century, when many of its distinctive points were decisively clarified, through Augustine to the scholastic tradition culminating in Thomas Aquinas. The *locus classicus* of the classical theist view of God is found in the first forty-three questions of the first part of the *Summa Theologica*. This understanding of God (which I usually refer to as trinitarian classical theism) was never challenged by the Reformers and passed into Protestant scholasticism, becoming the basis of Protestant reform movements such as Pietism, Puritanism, and, from the 1730s onward, evangelicalism. This view of God is taught by all the major Protestant confessions of faith, including the Augsburg Confession, the Thirty-Nine Articles of the Church of England, and the Westminster Confession. The lightly edited Baptist version of the Westminster Confession, known as the Second London Confession of 1689, is the confession under which I work as a theologian; it is the basis of various reformed Baptist confessions that form the doctrinal basis of my denomination. Trinitarian classical theism is also embedded solidly in the twentieth-century catechism of the Roman Catholic Church. As a confessional Protestant, I stand within the Great Tradition of the church, at the heart of which stands the conception of God known as trinitarian classical theism; that makes me catholic, though not in communion with Rome for doctrinal reasons other than the doctrine of God itself. I say this to make the point that the teachings of classical theism described below are not mere philosophical opinions about which individual Christians are free to disagree. Many people do disagree with classical theistic teachings, but to the extent that they do so they place themselves outside the Great Tradition; the root of such disagreement is, in my view, exegetical. I have had people say to me that the reason I believe in divine immutability and impassibility is that I am a Thomist, as though it would be no surprise if non-Thomists thought differently. But the fact is that Augustine, Calvin, and Thomas Oden (a Methodist) all affirmed God's immutability and impassibility, so clearly such teachings are not somehow unique to either Thomists or Roman Catholics.

What do classical theists teach about God? As Davies explains, the doctrine of creation *ex nihilo* is at the root of classical theism. The doctrine of creation out of nothing means that the true God is unique. As we saw above, all existing

37. Davies, *Philosophy of Religion*, 1–16.

things fall into one of two categories: (1) God, who has existence as part of his essence and cannot not exist; and (2) all things that are not part of God, which have existence not in themselves, but only as God upholds them in existence. Only God exists necessarily; all created things, including material ones (such as animals), spiritual ones (angels and demons), and material-spiritual ones (human beings), have a beginning and are created by God. They are, therefore, contingent beings. The doctrine of creation *ex nihilo* is not based on a philosophical argument about what must be the case; rather, it is a revealed truth found in Scripture.[38] It ensures that the Creator-creation distinction is preserved and is the foundation of God's sovereignty, omnipotence, uniqueness, and transcendence. It makes both providence and miracle possible.

As the divine cause of all that exists, God is different from creatures, which is why the category of "mystery" has always played such a large part in classical theism. As the first cause of all that is, God is not merely one of the beings operating within the causal order. God is the one who causes all things to be, causes their natures to be what they are, and preserves these natures in being so long as they exist. This does not mean that God cannot do miracles, but it does mean that he does not do miracles by interfering in an otherwise self-sustaining and self-existent system. That conception of what constitutes a miracle is based on a modern Enlightenment concept of a self-sufficient universe, which is foreign to the Great Tradition. All God's acts are basically the same; the providence versus miracles distinction is valid only from *our* point of view. God does not "suspend natural law" in doing a miracle; he simply causes something to happen that is not comprehensible to our scientific classification of natural laws, because all we can study are the regularities of nature, not the exceptions. Miracles have to be recognized as infrequent and unusual acts of God, as opposed to the repeated and usual acts of God that we describe as natural or scientific laws. The fallacy is to suppose that these scientific laws are somehow autonomous and independent of God in the first place, so that a miracle then must be understood to be a contravention of those laws—God *acting* (for once!) instead of letting the machine hum along on its own. The mechanical picture of the universe has a strong grip on the modern mind, but it is an idolatrous invention of the human mind and incompatible with the Christian understanding of creation and providence. It is a kind of mythological thinking.

38. Thomas Aquinas believed that it is not possible to demonstrate that the world had a beginning by reason alone. He accepted it as a revealed truth found in Scripture: "By faith alone do we hold, and by no demonstrations can it be proved, that the world did not always exist, as was said before of the mystery of the Holy Trinity" (*Summa Theologica*, pt. I, q. 45, art. 2, pp. 242–43).

As the divine Creator, God does not change. God is not a being impris-
oned in time like us. He is transcendent over time as the Creator of time and
space. God cannot be affected by creatures in the way that one creature can
be affected by another. Nothing we do can force or elicit a certain change,
emotion, or action from him. But he does answer prayer, judge sin, and forgive
the repentant sinner. He does these things, however, not because he is forced
to do so by our actions, but because he acts graciously toward us by his own
free decision. To think that we can force God to do something is to fall into
mythological thinking and to be skirting dangerously close to the occult—
which, as Scripture shows, is a perennial temptation for human beings.

To sum up: according to classical theism, which is simply the position of
mainstream orthodoxy throughout history, God is the first cause of all that exists other than God. God is utterly unique and therefore mysterious. The human
mind cannot fathom the depth of his being. God is perfect, simple, immutable,
impassible, and sovereign. All things that exist, including both material and spiritual beings, depend entirely on God for their existence in the first place and for
their continuation in existence. God's entire relationship to his creation is one
of grace; God is the one who acts in freedom. In sum, God is personal in such a
way that his transcendence is not in any way mitigated, jeopardized, or limited.

What then is theistic personalism? This is an understanding of God that has
arisen in modernity. It can reject many of the basic tenets of classical theism,
including divine simplicity, immutability, impassibility, and the utter uniqueness
of God. Not all theistic personalists reject all these attributes of God; some
reject just one or two, while others are more radical. Theistic personalists such
as Alvin Plantinga adopt a Cartesian view of the nature of persons by claiming
that a person is the incorporeal aspect of a human being, as Descartes put it,
"a thinking thing."[39] Philosophers in the Aristotelian tradition tend to view
persons as embodied, that is, as essentially corporeal. The Bible sees people
in this way also; even when the continuing existence of the soul is envisioned
as happening apart from the body during the intermediate state, this form of
existence is viewed as temporary, anomalous, and destined to end in a future
resurrection of the body. This is one reason why the Great Tradition has never
been willing to see God as a person; God qua God has no material body, which is
one reason why the incarnation is such an overwhelmingly astonishing mystery.

Theistic personalists, however, are willing to say that God is "a person"
despite not having a body.[40] Richard Swinburne says that God is something

39. René Descartes, as quoted by Davies, *Philosophy of Religion*, 11.
40. But some open theists actually go so far as to speculate that God has a body or that the
world might be God's body. E.g., see Pinnock, *Most Moved Mover*, 34–35.

like a "person without a body."[41] They conceive of God as a mind without a body, and they understand the difference between God's mind and our minds as basically one of degree. While the Great Tradition uses analogical language for God, theistic personalism tends to speak of the divine attributes and nature using univocal language. Thus, for theistic personalists, we have a mind and God has a mind, and the word "mind" means the same thing in both cases. But God is a mind with infinite understanding, knowledge, power, and so forth. The difference is one of degree, not kind. According to classical theism, God is not a part of the universe or a being in the universe, but rather the source and cause of the universe and therefore transcendent of it. God is not a mixture of act and potency, but pure actuality. God is not a complex being made up of parts, but entirely simple. All creatures are mixtures of act and potency and are made up of parts (body and soul, for example), and so all creatures are coming into being or passing out of being. But God is not a creature.

Theistic personalism does not necessarily and in every case lead to a view of the God-world relationship in which the world is in some way a necessary emanation of the divine being or in which God is in some way interdependent with the world. But, quite often, theistic personalists do adopt some sort of relational theism. Since Georg Hegel, most academic theology in the West has tended toward some sort of relational theism (process theology, dynamic panentheism, open theism, etc.). All such theology constitutes a serious departure from the Great Tradition. Classical theism has now become a minority position in the modern Western university, just as orthodox Christianity has been forced to the margins of late modern Western culture.

Theistic Personalism and Inspiration

The impact of the general theological situation of modernity on biblical interpretation is widespread and highly detrimental. The notions of providence and miracle suffer immensely in such a theological environment, and so the doctrine of inspiration becomes highly problematic. One way in which this can be seen is in the tendency to view human and divine acts in a competitive manner. If one takes a theistic personalist position, then one is automatically

41. Swinburne, *Coherence of Theism*, 1. In a later book, Swinburne says that he wishes to clarify that in his earlier statement he did not mean to rule out the possibility that God might temporarily acquire a body, so he would now wish to affirm God's being "essentially bodiless." He speaks of God as a "divine individual" and says that while a person normally requires a body to exist, God exists insofar as he is a divine individual with certain properties, which include being "omnipresent, creator and sustainer of any universe there may be, perfectly free, omnipotent, omniscient, perfectly good, and a source of moral obligation" (*Christian God*, 127).

driven in an Arminian direction in which God's acts and our acts are on the same plane and therefore in direct competition. The more God acts, the less we do; the more we act, the less God does. It is a zero-sum game: both actors are beings within the universe in competition with each other. In the Great Tradition (not just in Calvinism), God operates on an entirely different plane than creatures do. God is the first cause of creatures and upholds them in being, which means that he is the context in which creatures live. But it remains true that creatures have creaturely freedom to act according to their own natures without outside interference. This is what creaturely freedom is—the ability to act according to one's own nature without having some external, coercive force usurp the role of one's own nature and force one to go against one's own free will.

Creaturely freedom is not absolute freedom to do anything the mind can imagine. Creaturely free will is thus not libertarian free will; only God could have libertarian free will, but even God cannot act against his own nature. This way of phrasing it suggests a lacking in God or a limitation on God, but this is not so; the inability to act against his perfect nature is one of God's chief perfections. So, in actual fact, libertarian free will does not exist and could not exist. The concept is not even coherent. To be absolutely free to do whatever one willed to do would mean that nothing, not even one's own nature, could constrain the totally uncaused will. But a totally uncaused will, that is, one not even constrained by one's own nature, would be random and irrational. Acts of such a will would be more like spasms. No reason could be given for any action. All one could say would be "I willed it," but the meaning of "will" in this sentence would be indeterminate. In such a case, nothing would cause one to will anything as opposed to anything else. One might just as well be evil as good; indeed, it is unclear what meaning those terms would even have for one possessing absolute freedom. We could possibly understand the serpent's words to Eve (Gen. 3:5) as a promise of libertarian free will, but if we do, then we need to remember that Jesus said the devil was a liar from the beginning (John 8:44).

In a modern, theistic personalist, Arminian system of thought, inspiration of Scripture becomes a highly suspect doctrine because the possibility of God working through the creaturely natures of human writers to achieve the exact, foreordained result that God desired cannot be conceived except as an infringement of human, libertarian free will. And that, I strongly suspect, is really what lies behind the shock and outrage of those who cannot believe that one might dare to suggest a theory of inspiration that conjures up the specter of "dictation." How could real human freedom result in the text containing only and exactly what God wanted in the text? The force of this problem is

felt by those who have been influenced by theistic personalism, while classical theists do not see it as a problem, because they understand freedom in a
compatibilist manner.

What results from the discomfort with the idea of inspiration in a theistic
personalist context are usually various forms of "fudging." Perhaps the basic
ideas are inspired but not the exact words. Maybe teaching on faith and
practice is reliable, but matters of science and history are not. The problem
becomes especially acute at points where something entirely new, humanly
unknowable, or inaccessible to normal human intelligence is revealed. This
is why Enlightenment higher criticism has such an animus toward predictive
prophecy. This is also why historical critics resist interpreting Genesis 1:1 as
teaching creation *ex nihilo*. For Moses to be given a revelation of something
foreign and contradictory to his cultural context of beliefs regarding the
origin of the universe seems to inhibit his freedom. It seems like God imposing a meaning arbitrarily and to that extent preventing Moses from really
being the author of the text. It seems to make Moses a mere passive object
instead of a person. If possession of libertarian free will is the basis of human
personhood, then we obviously have a problem in that the classical idea of
inspiration seems to constitute a threat to human dignity.

In the worldview of classical theism, however, God and humans are *not* in
competition. God's sovereignty does not consist of forcing human beings to
go against their natures by twisting their arms until they submit their wills
to God, so to speak. Rather, God is the underlying cause of all that exists
and has created the universe in such a way that it participates in him. This is
what is meant by a "sacramental ontology." God is not a "thing" or "person"
alongside other persons within a self-existent universe. Instead God is the
cause and source of the universe as a whole, and the universe has its being in
him. Speaking of God as Creator, Paul affirms, "And he is before all things,
and in him all things hold together" (Col. 1:17). In the universe God actually has created, the prophets and apostles of Holy Scripture are the properly prepared, sovereignly appointed, and completely effective instruments
of God's will in the writing of Scripture with the result that the words of
Scripture are exactly what God wants them to be. In such a context, God is
able to endue these words with as much meaning as he chooses, and he does,
in fact, endue them with more meaning than is apparent at first glance. This
is why the single-meaning theory is inadequate. As Peter explains in 1 Peter
1:10–12, Isaiah may not have fully understood his own vision of the Suffering
Servant, but the Triune God who spoke through the prophet and sanctified his
words for divine use had a greater understanding than the prophet had. The
task of exegesis is that of probing into the well of divine meaning with the

awareness that the multiple layers of meaning all come from a single divine mind and therefore will never contradict one another. Spiritual exegesis is not an exercise in finding ways to interpret the text against itself or against the literal sense or against the conscious intention of the human author. These are all misunderstandings of spiritual exegesis. Spiritual exegesis is a way of thinking God's thoughts after him and deepening our understanding of the meaning inherent in the inspired text.

The Word in the Words

The Bible is the Word of God insofar as it participates in the divine Word of God, the Second Person of the Trinity.[42] God has sanctified the human words of Scripture for his use in revelation. As John Webster puts it, "Sanctification is the act of God the Holy Spirit in hallowing creaturely processes, employing them in the service of the taking form of revelation within the history of the creation."[43] He goes on to discuss why this concept seems to us to be so problematic in late modernity and points to the modern separation of the sensible and intelligible realms of reality: "Part of what lies behind this denial is the complex legacy of dualism and nominalism in Western Christian theology, through which the sensible and intelligible realms, history and eternity, were thrust away from each other, and creaturely forms (language, action, institutions) denied any capacity to indicate the presence and activity of the transcendent God."[44]

For Webster, only "a Christian doctrine of the Trinitarian works of God," that is, "the free, active self-presence of the triune God in creation . . . inspiring the biblical writings"[45] can adequately account for the relationship of revelation and Scripture. The trinitarian works of God include his immanence (presence) and his transcendence (uniqueness). God is the first cause of creation, so all created things have their being in him (Col. 1:16–17); recognition of this truth is necessary to see how Scripture is related to God, that is, how the biblical Word is related to the incarnate Word.

Scripture, like all things, participates in the being of God by virtue of its creaturely status and so there is no gap to overcome in speaking of the

---

42. After writing this chapter, I discovered that this section heading is actually an almost direct quotation from Karl Barth, which just shows that Stanley Hauerwas was right when he wryly observed that half of what we think is originality is just forgetting where we first read something. See Barth, *Epistle to the Romans*, 8.

43. Webster, *Holy Scripture*, 17.

44. Webster, *Holy Scripture*, 19–20.

45. Webster, *Holy Scripture*, 18.

relationship. This is what it means for creaturely realities to participate in God in a sacramental ontology. It is significant that when Jesus spoke to the two disciples on the road to Emmaus about how the Scriptures testified to him, they listened without recognizing him, but when he broke bread, they recognized his true identity (Luke 24:28–32). Biblical interpretation is sacramental, not in the Roman Catholic sense of being one of the seven sacraments of the church, but rather in the sense that participation in the risen Lord Jesus Christ is the means by which we understand the words of Scripture as what they truly are: the Word of God. By participating in the risen Lord Jesus Christ by faith, we learn from him what the meaning is of the words of Scripture, which testify to him. As the Word of God speaks through the human words of Scripture, so the words of Scripture participate in the Word of God and thus mediate him to us creatures sacramentally. The scriptural words mediate the reality of the Second Person of the Trinity to us as creaturely realities taken up into God and sanctified for this purpose. Such a sacramental understanding of Holy Scripture requires what Boersma calls a "sacramental ontology" and what Webster calls "the domain of the Word." I shall describe Nicene theological metaphysics as "Christian Platonism" in the next chapter; this is how I identify what all three of us are referring to when we speak of the context in which the saving self-revelation of God occurs to our benefit.

Webster's comments noted here, as well as my comments on Colossians 1 and Luke 24, help to explain the nature of biblical interpretation theologically. But they also raise many metaphysical questions: What does "participate" mean exactly? Why are "dualism and nominalism" so bad? How do the sensible and intelligible realms relate? How does history participate in the eternal? Are we not getting close to talking about Platonism? Indeed we are, and this is what we must discuss in the next chapter: the nature of Christian Platonism, why it is so central in the Great Tradition, and why the Enlightenment attack on it was such a disaster. It is time to talk metaphysics.

3

The Theological Metaphysics
of the Great Tradition

So we do not lose heart. Though our outer self is wasting away, our
inner self is being renewed day by day. For this light momentary
affliction is preparing for us an eternal weight of glory beyond all
comparison, as we look not to the things that are seen but to the
things that are unseen. For the things that are seen are transient,
but the things that are unseen are eternal.

2 Corinthians 4:16–18

At the beginning of the previous chapter, I said that, in order to interpret Scripture well, we need a special hermeneutics rooted in a
bibliology that itself is rooted in the Christian doctrine of God. I also said
that we needed to describe the act of reading by answering the following
questions: Who is God? What does it mean to say that the Bible is inspired?
Who are we? How does God communicate with us? In that chapter, we saw
that God is transcendent and personal and that the Bible is the set of human
writings that has come into existence by means of divine providence and
divine miraculous actions and has been sanctified by the Holy Spirit for use
in divine-human communication. We saw that we are hearers who need to
understand ourselves as ready to receive what is given to us as a gift by the
God of grace. Because we are fallen sinners in rebellion against our Creator,
we are in need of God's persistent, powerful, overcoming grace—grace that
overcomes our resistance by the attraction of its sheer goodness. Now that we

have at least an outline of answers to these questions, we are well on the way to a theological description of the act of reading and interpreting Scripture. But now we have to fill in the background. Where does this action take place? What account of the nature of the world is necessary for all this talk of grace, participation, communication, hearing, and so forth to be possible? We now turn to the question of theological metaphysics.

Everyone who has theological opinions has metaphysical doctrines that guide the way that one interprets reality and the way that one understands Christian teaching. Our metaphysical beliefs inevitably shape our conception of the meaning of Scripture. They form a kind of grid on which we super-impose our theology; they are a kind of filter for how we understand what the Bible is saying. Upon first hearing this kind of talk, one common reaction is to be scandalized and to vow never to let it happen to us. We might think that the solution is to free our biblical interpretation from all metaphysical influences—as if that were somehow possible. In reality that is not possible; it is part of the human condition to read from within a set of presuppositions. It is not possible to advance deeply into the study of any subject without first adopting certain basic assumptions that form the basis of that subject and not rethinking them in every moment. There is nothing evil or wrong with this; it is simply a matter of the natural limitations of human creatures, and it is vanity to object to it. It is not a matter of being naive about what John Webster rightly called "the undeniably corrosive effects of certain traditions of metaphysics,"[1] but, rather, it is a matter of recognizing the need to articulate a fully Christian description of ontology that results from the contemplation of special revelation in full awareness of philosophical questions.

The goal is not to rid ourselves of all metaphysical presuppositions, but rather to allow our metaphysical presuppositions to be reformed by Scripture. As Matthew Levering shows, Thomas Aquinas is exemplary in the tradition for doing this. Levering writes, "Aquinas deploys metaphysical (theocentric) analysis to raise or *convert* the mind to the self-revealing God who is triune spiritual substance and uncaused cause of all things."[2] He speaks of Aquinas's method as "theocentric contemplative ascent, which deepens the participation in God's knowledge that the believer already has in faith, and which is per-fected in the beatific vision."[3] This is what theology ought to be, but seldom does theology measure up to this ideal in the contemporary academy. We need to unpack the metaphysical assumptions underlying the classic concept

1. Webster, *Holiness*, 33.
2. Levering, *Scripture and Metaphysics*, 36, emphasis original.
3. Levering, *Scripture and Metaphysics*, 37.

of theology and try to shake ourselves free from assumptions that are all around us in our contemporary culture in order to work ourselves back to the contemplation of the true and living God.

As we begin, we must bear in mind that the concept of the nature of theology as contemplation in the Great Tradition is very different from the pragmatic concept that dominates both conservative and liberal modern theology, which is oriented toward supporting immediate action in the world to improve society and/or the self. Ironically, it is precisely the impatience of modern theology with metaphysical questions that often causes it to adopt unwittingly the materialism, mechanism, and nominalism of modern culture without pausing to ask if doing so might deform, or even emasculate, Christian doctrine. We need to be not less, but *more*, suspicious of metaphysics than we often are, especially the metaphysical doctrines of Epicurus, Zeno, and Democritus.[4] If you do not know who they were and what their ideas were, you are in mortal danger of absorbing their errors without even realizing that you have done so, for these ideas are in the air we breathe today in the late modern West. We need to understand why the church fathers consciously and deliberately chose to reject their metaphysical views, while finding at least a few usable ideas in Plato and Aristotle. We need to realize that the Augustinian-Thomist tradition has already spent centuries wrestling with metaphysical questions on which most modern theologians, and almost all modern biblical scholars, are mere novices. Since the late medieval period and increasingly so in the Enlightenment, mainstream Western philosophy has diverged from Christian revelation in such a way as to undermine the theological metaphysics of the Great Tradition. Anyone who desires to understand Great Tradition exegesis and dogmatics as contemplation of the beauty of God needs to understand these philosophical trends.

What Is Theological Metaphysics?

Let me begin by defining terms. By "theological metaphysics" I mean *the account of the ontological nature of reality that emerges from the theological descriptions of God and the world found in the Bible.* In metaphysics, we are concerned to penetrate beyond the surface descriptions of things to comprehend their true natures. Ontology deals with the nature of being; metaphysics is the science that seeks to describe the ontological reality of the world and

---

4. These are the founders of ancient Epicureanism, Stoicism, and atomism. They are always lurking around the neighborhood, ready to climb in the windows of the house that is our worldview as Plato and Aristotle are being ushered out the front door.

things in the world. In other words, it seeks to describe the being of the world
and the things in it. Theology is the study of God and all things in relation to
God. Metaphysics is theological when it allows biblical revelation to determine
the true ontological nature of reality as it contemplates the biblical teaching
on God and all things in relation to God. The doctrine of the creation of all
things by the Triune God is obviously central to shaping a theological metaphysics, but the doctrines of sin and redemption, as well as the Trinity and
Christology, are also crucial. In summary, metaphysical doctrines are arrived
at by contemplation of the special revelation contained in Holy Scripture,
that is, by exegesis and dogmatic reflection on the exegetical results in the
light of philosophical questions and analysis.

Serious philosophical and/or theological thought, including hermeneutics,
cannot be coherent without explicitly considering metaphysical questions.
When certain writers make a big show of rejecting metaphysics, what they
are really doing is rejecting certain widely held metaphysical doctrines, usually without specifying what doctrines they themselves propose to replace
them. This is highly irresponsible, since we cannot engage in any scientific
thought whatsoever without making metaphysical assumptions. For example, when a person says that all metaphysics should be rejected and then
discusses human reproductive technology or assisted suicide as if humans
did not have a soul, that person has, in effect, smuggled an unexamined,
materialist assumption into the discussion, one that makes a great deal of
difference at every step in the debate. Fallen human beings are rather good
at hiding their own unpalatable metaphysical presuppositions even from
themselves. Metaphysics can be avoided only by dishonest and sloppy thinking; such thinking results in disobedience to this scriptural command: "Do
not be conformed to this world, but be transformed by the renewal of your
mind, that by testing you may discern what is the will of God, what is good
and acceptable and perfect" (Rom. 12:2). The reason why sloppy thinking
is disobedience to the command to be transformed by the renewal of our
minds is that, in practice, such thinking almost always involves accepting
some of the anti-Christian metaphysical assumptions that surround us in
a post-Christian, neopagan culture. The Bible specifically and repeatedly
calls us away from doing so.

The Bible also makes statements about God's actions that presuppose
certain doctrines about the nature of reality. Although the Bible sometimes
explicitly teaches metaphysical doctrines, such as creation *ex nihilo*, for
example,[5] other times the metaphysical doctrine is arrived at by a process of

5. E.g., see Gen. 1:1; Pss. 33:6, 9; 90:2; John 1:1–3; Acts 14:15; Rom. 4:17; Col. 1:16; Heb. 11:3.

contemplating revealed truth, such as the doctrine of the participation of material things in the ideas in the mind of God.[6] It needs to be stressed that what we are talking about here, however, is not merely a matter of "speculation" and "opinion," as opposed to the settled truth revealed directly in Scripture. That is too simplistic a distinction. We are talking about what God teaches us in his Word as we listen to his Spirit illumining our minds as to the deeper truth of scriptural passages. We are talking about what the early church called "dogma," which is not a matter of personal opinion in which one person's views are as good as anyone else's. We are talking about a serious quest for truth based on the conviction that Jesus meant what he said when he said to his disciples:

> I still have many things to say to you, but you cannot bear them now. When the Spirit of truth comes, he will guide you into all the truth, for he will not speak on his own authority, but whatever he hears he will speak, and he will declare to you the things that are to come. He will glorify me, for he will take what is mine and declare it to you. All that the Father has is mine; therefore I said that he will take what is mine and declare it to you. (John 16:12–15)

This last statement is stunning in its scope. All that the Father has belongs to the Son, and the Spirit will take what belongs to the Son and declare it to the disciples and, through them, to the church as a whole. God actually allows us—his human creatures—to share in some of his own majestic and inexhaustible self-knowledge. There is no limit to what is revealed except the limited human capacity to assimilate truth.

It seems clear that the Spirit carries out the mission described by Jesus both by inspiring Holy Scripture, part of which would later be written by some of the disciples in that room that night, and also by illumining the meaning of the Scriptures to generation after generation of believers as they ponder the deepest meaning of the sacred texts. No wonder John remarks at the end of his Gospel, "Now there are also many other things that Jesus did. Were every one of them to be written, I suppose that the world itself could not contain the books that would be written" (John 21:25). And that would cover just the things Jesus did. How many more worlds would be necessary to contain the books written to ponder and describe all the meaning and implications of those deeds! The depth of the meaning of the Scriptures should be evident from what Jesus says here: all that the Father has belongs to the Son; from this inexhaustible storehouse of truth and reality, the Spirit draws when he

6. See Doolan, *Aquinas on the Divine Ideas*, for an excellent discussion of Thomas Aquinas's Christian Platonism as it relates to this point.

speaks through the written words of Scripture. Thus Paul prays that Christ, by his Spirit, will fulfill this promise in the lives of believers:

> For I want you to know how great a struggle I have for you and for those at Laodicea and for all who have not seen me face to face, that their hearts may be encouraged, being knit together in love, to reach all the riches of full assurance of understanding and the knowledge of God's mystery, which is Christ, in whom are hidden all the treasures of wisdom and knowledge. I say this in order that no one may delude you with plausible arguments. . . . See to it that no one takes you captive by philosophy and empty deceit, according to human tradition, according to the elemental spirits of the world, and not according to Christ. (Col. 2:1–4, 8)

Part of what the Spirit has said to the church, according to the Great Tradition of Christianity, is the theological metaphysics I am attempting to sketch here.

Why Christian Platonism?

The theological metaphysics of the Great Tradition can be described as Christian Platonism. Andrew Louth quotes Endre von Ivánka: "The phenomenon which characterizes the whole of the first millennium of Christian theological thought . . . is the use of Platonism as the form for [its] philosophical expression and the framework of the world-picture in terms of which the proclamation of revealed truths was made—in other words, Christian Platonism."[7] As Louth goes on to explain, both Platonism and Christianity teach that we have a spiritual nature that can participate in the "realm of eternal truth, the realm of the divine."[8] But whereas Platonism sees human nature as continuous with divine being and as capable of ascending to the realm of the divine, Christianity views man as a creature created out of nothing. Therefore, in Christianity there exists an ontological gulf that can be overcome only by God descending in Christ to save us. Yet, as Louth points out, we have been made in God's image and have the possibility of communion with God, even though this possibility is realized only in Jesus Christ. What is open to us in Platonism by nature is only open to us in Christianity by grace.

Given that there is such a fundamental disagreement between Christianity and Platonism, the question naturally arises: Why is the theological metaphysics of the Great Tradition best described as "Christian Platonism"? The best source for answering this question is one of the greatest minds among the early

---

7. Louth, *Origins of the Christian Mystical Tradition*, xii.
8. Louth, *Origins of the Christian Mystical Tradition*, xii.

fathers of the church, Augustine of Hippo. First, we will review how Platonism aided Augustine in his conversion to Christianity by examining book 7 of his *Confessions*. Then we will turn to book 8 of his *City of God*, in which he discusses the history of Greek philosophy, points out what is superior about the Platonists, and then levels some serious critiques against the Platonists. Then we will discuss how Christian Platonism differed from other kinds of Platonism by examining briefly the history of Platonism from Plato to late antiquity, the era of Augustine. It is not the point of this discussion to write a history of Platonism, a project that would extend well beyond the scope of this book; rather, it is to make clear how Christian Platonism is different from what Plato himself believed, from Neoplatonism and from gnosticism, and also why it is legitimate to refer to the theological metaphysics of the Great Tradition as "Christian Platonism."

How Platonism Helped Augustine Become a Christian

Augustine was a Manichaean for about nine years before his conversion and baptism in 387 at the age of thirty-three. It is important to understand something of what Manichaeism was in order to understand the intellectual and spiritual problem with which Augustine was struggling in *Confessions*, book 7, and, specifically, how Platonism helped him escape from the grip of Manichaeism.

Manichaeism was a gnostic offshoot of Christianity mixed, as all gnostic religions are, with elements of other religions and philosophies. It began in Babylonia, which was under Persian rule when Mani received "revelations" and claimed to be bringing to the world the fullness of revelation: what he called the "Religion of Light."[9] He often called himself an "apostle of Jesus Christ," but this obscures the fact that he saw himself as bringing much greater religious insight than Christ ever did.

Manichaeism starts from the problem of evil and offers a solution by proposing a cosmogony in three phases. In phase one (which is past), there were two opposing eternal principles completely separated from each other: the good or God (characterized by light) and evil or Satan (characterized by darkness). There is thus an eternal, ontological dualism, according to Manichaean teaching.

In the second phase (our present situation), a series of conflicts occurs between the evil principle and the good principle, which involves the evil principle capturing and imprisoning light. The creation of the material universe was part

9. The information in this paragraph and the next few paragraphs is taken from the excellent article by Coyle, "Mani, Manichaeism," 520–25.

of the strategy of the good principle in warring against the evil principle, but the creation of humans was the work of the evil principle, which wanted to create a rival to the good principle's "primal human." The creation of Adam and Eve by the evil principle was designed to keep as much light trapped in the visible world as possible; this goal was to be achieved through procreation. Jesus, as the good principle's response, was sent to reveal knowledge (*gnosis*) to Adam and Eve. Mani's "Jesus" is not a sin-bearing savior, but a bearer of saving knowledge, another common feature of gnostic heresies. The Jesus of Christian orthodoxy was considered evil because he had a physical body; in fact, Mani regarded him as the devil in disguise.

Manichaeism had a clergy (the elect) and a laity (the hearers). The purpose of the elect was to be saviors by releasing light from this world so it could go back to the good principle. They did this by a strict asceticism that included celibacy, vegetarianism, intensive times of prayer, and refraining from killing animals even for food. The purpose of the hearers was to serve the basic needs of the elect, to be catechized into the Manichaean religion, and to practice a less severe ritualistic asceticism than the elect. Marriage was allowed for hearers, but procreation was highly discouraged. Their hope was to be reincarnated as members of the elect. Hearers were eligible for salvation after death by permanent separation from the material realm. All physical bodies were destined for hell.

In the third phase (the future), there will be a return to the original separation of good and evil, which will happen when as much of the light as possible has been reclaimed by the good principle. The material universe will then disappear, and all substance will withdraw into the realm of darkness. But the restored order will not be as good as the original one, because not all the light will be set free. The principle of good will therefore be "eternally wounded or diminished."

A central paradox (or perhaps contradiction) in this religious system is that matter is evil, and yet there is no real ontological distinction between God and matter. Augustine writes of his changing views during the latter part of his Manichaean period at the beginning of book 7 of his *Confessions*: "I was no longer representing you to myself in the shape of a human body, O God, for since beginning to acquire some inkling of philosophy I always shunned this illusion, and now I was rejoicing to find a different view in the belief of our spiritual mother, your Catholic Church. Yet no alternative way of thinking about you had occurred to me; and here was I, a mere human, and a sinful one at that, striving to comprehend you, the supreme, sole, true God."[10]

10. Augustine, *Confessions*, 7.1.1, p. 158. References will include the book, chapter, and section numbers as well as the page numbers to the English translation.

At the outset of book 7, Augustine is having difficulty with the issue of how to understand God. Although he was not tempted by crudely anthropomorphic thinking, the only way he could conceive of God was as "a vast reality spread throughout space in every direction." He writes, "I thought that you penetrated the whole mass of the earth and the immense, unbounded spaces beyond it on all sides, that earth, sky and all things were full of you."[11] As a Manichaean, Augustine had a basically materialistic conception of God. As we just saw, there is no real transcendence in Manichaean cosmogony even though there are beings that are not physical in the sense of being visible. But we know that many things that are not visible are still part of the material universe, such as gravity or radio waves. The point is that Augustine had no real concept of a transcendent God who is ontologically unique and not part of the universe in some sense; he had no such idea because Manichaeism had no such idea. Even though Manichaeism could easily distinguish between the material and the spiritual, it still saw both as aspects of one more-fundamental reality.

But Augustine had been listening to Ambrose's preaching for a while by this point, and he knew Christianity taught that God is immutable and thus incorruptible, unlike the good principle in Manichaeism. The problem was how to conceive of God as both *real* and also as *not* in any way part of the material universe or the unified reality of which the universe is an expression. Augustine found himself on the horns of a dilemma: either God is immutable but unreal, or God is part of the universe and thus mutable. Christianity seemed to want it both ways: God is immutable because he is not part of the universe, yet somehow God is real. No matter how hard he tried, this was what Augustine could not understand to be possible until he read some of the books of the Platonists.

At the end of book 5, when he was struggling with the issue of how to prove the falseness of the Manichaean view of God, Augustine says, "If only I had been capable of envisaging a spiritual substance, all their elaborate constructions would have fallen to pieces. . . . But this I could not do."[12] It turns out that this concept of a "spiritual substance" was exactly the concept that the books of the Platonists helped him come to understand. The way Augustine discusses the books of the Platonists is very interesting; he never names the titles and does not quote directly from them. Here is the way he explains what he learned from them in his own words:

In them I read (not that the same words were used, but precisely the same doctrine was taught, buttressed by many and various arguments) that *in the*

11. Augustine, *Confessions*, 7.2, p. 159.
12. Augustine, *Confessions* 5.25, p. 132.

beginning was the Word, and the Word was with God; he was God. He was with God in the beginning. Everything was made through him; nothing came to be without him. What was made is alive with his life, and that life was the light of humankind. The Light shines in the darkness, and the darkness has never been able to master it; and that the human soul, even though it bears *testimony about the Light* is not itself the Light, that God, the Word, is *the true Light*, which illumines *every human person who comes into this world*; and that he was in this world, *a world made by him, but the world did not know him.* But that he came to his own home, *a world made by him, and his own people did not receive him; but to those who did receive him he gave power to become children of God; to those, that is, who believe in his name*—none of this did I read there.[13]

This is a complicated passage that merits careful consideration. Note carefully the word "But" at the beginning of the final sentence. Augustine is saying that he read in the books of the Platonists the same doctrine as he found in the prologue to John's Gospel, but he says that not all that is found in John 1 is in the books of the Platonists. What he found in both was the concept of God's Word as God, and this proved to be key to Augustine's search. In effect, he read the prologue to John's Gospel through the grid of the concept of "spiritual substance" that he learned from the Platonists, and suddenly everything made more sense. Augustine could see that the Bible is saying that God is both a substance (i.e., a real thing) and also spiritual (i.e., not material) at the same time in the same way as the Word of God is fully God when it goes out from God in creative action. There is a sense in which both God and things in this world have being. But there is a great difference between divine and created being. Augustine writes: "I turned my gaze to other things and saw that they owe their being to you"[14]; he notes that while these other things come into being and pass away, God is eternal. The contrast between beings that come into existence and pass out of existence, on the one hand, and God, who is eternal, immutable, and perfect, on the other hand, is the basis of the theological metaphysics of the Great Tradition; it provides Augustine with a way to say that God is real, but not a part of this created reality. This distinction is the fundamental basis of divine transcendence taught in Scripture.[15] But

13. Augustine, *Confessions* 7.9.13, pp. 169–70, italics in original.
14. Augustine, *Confessions* 7.15.21, p. 176.
15. We need to understand that the distinction between divine and creaturely being is not quantitative, but qualitative. It is not that God is older than created things; it is rather that, by virtue of being eternal, God is an entirely different kind of thing. He is *sui generis*. His being is eternal being, while our being is created being. His superb and perfect reality means that he has actual existence, but even his existence is different from our existence, being necessary and not contingent.

while the Platonists could articulate a metaphysical concept that helps make the Christian understanding of creation comprehensible, they had no idea of the doctrines of incarnation or redemption (the topics of the final sentence in the quotation above).

Augustine tells us that he followed the advice of the books of the Platonists (likely Plotinus's *Enneads*) by preparing himself by purification for the ascent of the soul to the vision of God. Here is how he describes what happened:

> O eternal Truth, true Love, and beloved Eternity, you are my God, and for you I sigh day and night. As I first began to know you you lifted me up and showed me that while that which I might see exists indeed, I was not yet capable of seeing it. Your rays beamed intensely upon me, beating back my feeble gaze, and I trembled with love and dread. I knew myself to be far away from you in a region of unlikeness, and I seemed to hear your voice from on high: "I am the food of the mature; grow then, and you will eat me. You will not change me into yourself like bodily food: you will be changed into me." And I recognized that you have chastened man for his sin and caused my soul to dwindle away like a spider's web, and I said, "Is truth then a nothing, simply because it is not spread out through space either finite or infinite?" Then from afar you cried to me, "By no means, for *I am who I am*."[16]

The crucial part of this quotation is the question: "Is truth then a nothing, simply because it is not spread out through space either finite or infinite?" In other words, Augustine is asking if something like truth (a name for God) can be real without being a finely diffused material substance spread out through space (the Manichaean concept of God). Augustine realizes that God is not nothing simply because he is not "spread out through space either finite or infinite." He finds that God is "I am who I am"—a clear allusion to Exodus 3:14. God has his own unique mode of existence as part of his essence. Augustine finds himself unable to doubt that God exists and "is seen and understood through the things that are made," that is, through contrast with created things. The latter phrase is obviously an allusion to Romans 1:20. The Platonic concept of "spiritual substance" allows Augustine to understand what Scripture means—namely, that God transcends creation precisely in the sense that he is immutable in contrast to the things in the world and that the things in the world depend on him for existence.

But we need to note that in this attempt at Platonic ecstasy, Augustine is "beaten back."[17] He does not achieve union with God; he only perceives God

---

16. Augustine, *Confessions* 7.10.16, p. 172.
17. This phrase is from the editor's headings in the New City Press edition of *Confessions*, 172.

"from afar." He thus comes to realize the need for Christ as mediator: "Accordingly I looked for a way to gain the strength I needed to enjoy you, but I did not find it until I embraced the mediator between God and humankind, the man Christ Jesus, who is also God."[18] Neoplatonism took him only so far. Just as Thomas Aquinas will later teach that we can prove the existence of a first cause of the universe by reason alone, but cannot know the triune nature of God or the incarnation except by special revelation, Augustine here says that he was able to perceive the reality of God as creator, but not the doctrines of incarnation, sin, or redemption, through the teachings of the Platonists. He never sees Platonism as sufficient in itself, nor does he view it as right about everything. At best it is incomplete and at worst it is idolatrous, as we shall see. Nevertheless, it provided Augustine with the intellectual tools that enabled him to reject the Manichaean doctrine of God and accept the Christian doctrine of God. And that, surely, is no small thing. In his own personal quest, Augustine sees it as providential that God brought the books of the Platonists to his attention at a crucial moment. In terms of the history of Christian theology, as a whole, the role Platonism played in the formation of the creedal orthodoxy of the first five centuries can also be seen as providential. The incarnation and birth of the church took place at just the right time in history for the truth to be unfolded in the way it needed to be.

Augustine's Mature and Balanced Evaluation of Platonism

In book 8 of the *City of God*, Augustine engages the Platonists in a critical manner. He begins by stating that philosophy is "the love of wisdom" and, since God is wisdom, true philosophy must be the love of God. But just calling oneself a philosopher does not make one a real philosopher, that is, "a lover of God."[19] Augustine's purpose in this book is to refute the idea that the worship of the pagan gods is either necessary or right. In the second section of this book, he goes through the history of Greek philosophy from Thales down to his own day covering both the Italian and the Ionian schools. It was Plato who brought the two schools together and thus unified the mathematically oriented Pythagorean thought with the empirical science of the Ionian school to bring philosophy into existence as a wisdom tradition. Socrates was the first to link natural philosophy with morality; he saw that the true nature of the universe could be grasped only by a purified intelligence. He taught

18. Augustine, *Confessions* 7.18.24, p. 178.
19. Augustine, *City of God* 8.1, p. 242. References will include book and chapter numbers as well as the page numbers to the English translation.

that the weight of lust weighs down the soul and prevents it from ascending to the contemplation of the truth. It was Plato who systematized this insight by bringing together the practical bent of Socrates with the contemplative approach of Pythagoras and the empirical bent of the Ionian tradition.

Plato divided philosophy into three parts: (1) natural philosophy or metaphysics, which focuses on the nature of what is (reality); (2) moral philosophy or ethics, which discerns how to conform human action to the nature of reality; and (3) rational philosophy or logic, which distinguishes truth from falsehood and thus prevents the other two branches from making errors. The path of wisdom is thus to understand reality as it actually is, to adapt one's behavior to reality, and to avoid errors in reasoning while doing so. This is wisdom or philosophy. Many Platonists also hold that God is the cause of existence, the source of reason, and the source of the rule of life.[20] Thus to love God is to love wisdom and become a true philosopher.

In the light of this understanding of philosophy, it is little wonder that Augustine selects the Platonists as his primary dialogue partner in the discussion of idolatry and true worship. He concludes that theological questions are to be discussed with the Platonists rather than with any other philosophers, whose opinions must be counted inferior. He writes:

> Thus, if Plato has stated that the wise man is one who imitates, knows and loves this God, and who is blessed by participation in him, what need is there to investigate other philosophers? No one has come closer to us than the Platonists. Let the mythological theology, then, which delights the minds of the ungodly with the crimes of the gods give way to the Platonists; so too, the civic theology in which impure demons, under the name of gods, have seduced people devoted to earthly delights and have wanted to take human errors as divine honors.[21]

Augustine thinks that if Plato came back to life today, he would become a Christian. Note, however, Plato would not automatically *be* a Christian; he would have to *become* one, which would involve rejecting erroneous views and adopting new doctrines based on biblical teaching as part of what repentance and faith would mean for him. Above all it would mean accepting Christ as his divine Lord and Savior. But Augustine's main point is that Plato was near the truth on some very important points.

In chapter 6 of book 8, Augustine discusses what he finds attractive and helpful in Platonism. The first point he stresses is that the Platonists rightly realize that no material object can be God: "They saw that no material body

20. Augustine, *City of God* 8.4, p. 246.
21. Augustine, *City of God* 8.5, p. 247.

is God and therefore they went beyond all bodies in their search for God."[22] So the first way in which they are helpful is their rejection of the materialism of Democritus and other materialists. Platonism, like the Bible, views reality as consisting of both a material dimension (the earth) and a spiritual dimension (the heavens). Trying to fit the Bible into a materialistic metaphysics is impossible. Second, Augustine makes the point that the Platonists also realize that nothing changeable can be the supreme God. He writes, "They saw that nothing mutable is the supreme God, and therefore they went beyond every soul and all mutable spirits in their search for the supreme God."[23] This is what makes true transcendence possible; God is not part of the totality of the cosmos including both its visible and invisible, its material and spiritual, dimensions. God is not the "chief angel." He is not a being among other beings, but rather being itself. Third, Augustine points out that the Platonists grasped that God is the uncaused cause of all that is not God:

> They also saw that in every mutable thing, the form that makes it what it is, in whatever measure and of whatever nature it is, can only have its existence from him who truly *is* because he exists immutably. It follows then that the whole material world, with its shapes, its qualities, its ordered motion, with the elements arrayed from heaven down to earth, and with whatever bodies exist in them, and that all life, whether life which only nourishes and sustains existence, like the life in trees, or life which also has feeling and sensation, like the life in animals, or life which has all this and has intelligence as well, like the life in human beings, or life which has no need to take nourishment but still sustains existence and has sensation and intelligence, like the life in angels—it follows, then, that all these can have existence only from him who simply *is*. For, to him, it is not one thing to exist and another to live, as if he could exist without being alive; nor is it one thing to live and another to have intelligence and another to be happy, as if he could have intelligence without being happy. To him, rather, to exist simply is to live, to have intelligence, and to be happy.[24]

Here we have an articulation of the core doctrines of classical theism: immutability and simplicity in the service of proving that God is the first cause of all existing reality other than himself. Augustine says that the Platonists were correct to discern from the nature of the changing flux that constitutes the universe that "the primary form" that makes things what they are could not come from the things themselves, because if it did it would be subject to change and unable to perform the function of maintaining things in existence

22. Augustine, *City of God* 8.6, p. 249.
23. Augustine, *City of God* 8.6, p. 249.
24. Augustine, *City of God* 8.6, pp. 249–50.

throughout the life cycle of birth, growth, maturity, old age, and death. If things did not receive their form from something unchanging, nothing would be stable. Therefore, Augustine concludes, "God, as well as his eternal power and divinity, were understood and seen by them through the things that he made" (Rom. 1:19–20). Augustine is not in the least surprised that the best of human philosophers are saying exactly what Paul claims is true in Romans 1, nor is he surprised that these same philosophers have given themselves over to irrational idolatry as well, as Paul also said.

A major school of modern philosophy is empiricism, and from this school of philosophy, best represented by David Hume, has flowed a great deal of the skepticism and relativism of the modern era.[25] Augustine considers the Epicureans of his day and compares them to the Platonists. He describes the Epicureans as those who "though much enamored of the skill in debating which they call dialectic, still imagine that this is to be derived from the bodily senses. It is from the senses, they assert, that the mind conceives of the ideas . . . of those things which they explain by means of definition and it is from the senses, they claim, that their whole account of learning and teaching is derived and deduced."[26] Augustine pointedly wonders, however, what fleshly eyes such philosophers (if they can properly be called "philosophers") use to "catch sight of the form and the splendor of wisdom."[27] The same question can be addressed to moderns like David Hume or Karl Marx, who deny the existence of universals like wisdom or beauty. At least the Platonists have a philosophical explanation for universals, even if they disagree among themselves as to the details. Modernity, however, is in the process of dissolving into Nietzschean nihilism and postmodern relativism, because Epicureanism and atomism cannot build or sustain an advanced culture, which can be based only on a belief in goodness, truth, and beauty.[28]

Augustine's main purpose in book 8, however, was not merely to praise the Platonists. That was just the first part of his argument; the second part was to argue the folly and evil of worshiping pagan gods. The fact that the Platonists have such a high and profound concept of God makes their participation in pagan idolatry all the more egregious. In chapter 10, Augustine warns the reader that we must be wary of those whose philosophy is "based on the elements of this world" and not on God, the world's Creator. We should heed

25. See Feser, *Last Superstition*, 138–41, and chap. 5 in general.
26. Augustine, *City of God* 8.7, p. 251.
27. Augustine, *City of God* 8.7, p. 251.
28. For a concise, clear, and convincing account of this descent of modernity into barbarism, see Feser, *Last Superstition*, chap. 5. See also Weaver, *Ideas Have Consequences*; and MacIntyre, *After Virtue*.

Paul's warning: "See to it that no one takes you captive by philosophy and empty deceit, according to human tradition, according to the elemental spirits of the world, and not according to Christ" (Col. 2:8). Paul, who quoted the Greek poets but avoided their theological errors, is our example.[29] Augustine thinks that the Platonists' participation in polytheistic worship is inconsistent on their part, as well as inexcusable. On this point, there is no possibility of compromise or rationalization; the Platonists are wrong, utterly wrong, destructively wrong. Plato thought that all the gods are good, but Augustine finds this incredible. How can Plato describe as good the gods whose shows and poets he banished from his ideal republic as despicable? How can Plato not have seen that gods who delight in scandals, immorality, and so on can never be considered good?[30] Although Augustine spends pages examining the problem from every possible angle, he can find no way to justify or mitigate the guilt of the Platonists in this matter.

Augustine's attitude to Platonism is hardly naive or uncritical. He finds things to criticize as well as things to admire in Platonic thought. But overall he finds the Platonists worth debating, unlike most of the other schools of philosophy. Their errors can be refuted using their own first principles. One could hardly call Augustine's overall attitude to pagan philosophy positive. The Platonists are the best of a bad lot, and even they have serious faults and errors mixed in with the truth. Why then would we want to call the theological metaphysics of the Great Tradition, to which Augustine contributed so much, Christian Platonism?

How Is Christian Platonism Related to Platonism in General?

The first thing we need to keep in mind is that Augustine believed that certain philosophers had demonstrated as true certain doctrines concerning God and his relation to the world. He believed this in much the same way as many modern Christians believe that science has demonstrated as true certain truths concerning the nature of the physical universe.[31] Most Christian theologians today are concerned to reconcile the truths of natural science with biblical doctrine, because the doctrine of creation is at stake. If the Bible teaches errors concerning nature, how can we believe in the doctrine of creation? If it

29. Augustine, *City of God* 8.10, p. 253.
30. Augustine, *City of God* 8.13, p. 257.
31. I do not mean to imply here that everything said by modern scientists has to be accepted as true, especially when scientists stray out of their narrow areas of specialization into the territory of metaphysics and history. The point is merely that Christianity is not a form of antirealism and so is committed to dealing with reality, as it actually exists.

is true that God created the world, then nature is his work just as the inspired Scriptures are his work and, properly interpreted, the book of nature should not contradict the book of Scripture. Augustine held that some philosophers had discovered the truth that God exists and is simple, immutable, and the cause of all that exists apart from God. This inevitably raises the question of the relationship of the God of the Bible to the god of the philosophers. Perhaps the God of the Bible is merely the tribal god of the Christians and Jews, just as Horus is a god for the Egyptians, Zeus for the Greeks, and so on.

The crucial question is how we can do justice to the pervasive biblical contrast between the gods of the nations and the one true God who created heaven and earth, rules the nations, and guides history to its fulfillment by his providence. Think of what Isaiah says about the God of Israel:

> Who has measured the waters in the hollow of his hand
>   and marked off the heavens with a span,
> enclosed the dust of the earth in a measure
>   and weighed the mountains in scales
>   and the hills in a balance?
>
> Who has measured the Spirit of the LORD,
>   or what man shows him his counsel?
> Whom did he consult,
>   and who made him understand?
> Who taught him the path of justice,
>   and taught him knowledge,
>   and showed him the way of understanding?
> Behold, the nations are like a drop from a bucket,
>   and are accounted as the dust on the scales;
>   behold, he takes up the coastlands like fine dust. (Isa. 40:12–15)

Does this sound like the tribal god of Jews and Christians? Or does it sound more like the first cause of all things? Augustine had no doubt that the God of the Bible is much *more* than the god of the philosophers, but he could never be *less*.

When we look at Greek philosophy as a whole during the patristic era, we can see a range of views about the gods/God. First, we have those who either denied the existence of the gods (like Lucretius) or denied that the gods involved themselves in the affairs of human beings (like Epicurus). Then there are those who saw God as the "soul of the universe" (like the Stoics) or as the universe itself at the most general level of description (Eastern pantheism). Most ancient people were polytheistic, although many intellectuals doubted the crudely anthropomorphic accounts of the gods given in the myths, and a few held to a philosophic concept of God above and behind the polytheism of the masses (like the Platonists). Then there were those who acknowledged that there is one, simple, immutable, perfect, transcendent God who created all things and upholds all things in existence. Some of these Platonist philosophers compromised their beliefs by engaging in polytheistic rituals. But those who had the courage of their convictions and resisted polytheistic worship tended to convert to Christianity as soon as they heard the gospel.[32] They adopted the teaching of the church and submitted their minds to Scripture, but they saw no reason to give up their previous philosophical beliefs where those beliefs were not contradicted by Christian dogma. They were Christian Platonists. They became major dialogue partners in the development of patristic dogma.

What is Platonism? The answer to this deceptively simple question is very complicated. Scholars of ancient Greek philosophy have to contend with the fact that there is a striking diversity of views held by philosophers who claim to be Platonists between the death of Plato and the end of Roman antiquity (roughly Augustine's era). The neologism "Neoplatonism" was invented by nineteenth-century German historians of philosophy to describe what they saw as a "new" type of Platonism in the third to fifth centuries AD that deviated significantly from the thought of Plato himself. "Middle Platonism" is another historical construct that signifies philosophers of an earlier period who inhabited Plato's Academy and called themselves Platonists yet who seem to have disagreed with Plato on important issues. Then there are the "Academic Skeptics," who doubted almost everything and yet claimed to be Platonists in doing so. Scholars have to contend also with the fact that there is an oral tradition discussed by Platonist philosophers; some think that the most important doctrines Plato taught were never written down. Then again, there is the strange case of Aristotle—Plato's greatest student, who seems to many moderns to be the antithesis of Plato in crucial respects. Yet, in antiquity, nobody thought Aristotle was anything but a Platonist. Platonism is a highly complex phenomenon.

Friedrich Schleiermacher, who was a scholar of Plato before becoming the father of modern, liberal theology, was among the first to propose the thesis that holds that the development of Plato's thought can be discerned by arranging the dialogues into early, middle, and late categories.[33] The same

32. Augustine recounts the story of one such convert, Gaius Marius Victorinus Afer, in *Confessions* 8.2.3–4.9, pp. 186–92.

33. For a discussion of the development of scholarship on Plato and Platonism in the nineteenth century and of Schleiermacher's influence in particular, see Gerson, *From Plato to Platonism*, 34–35.

evolutionary paradigm that Georg Hegel and Charles Darwin used was employed by nineteenth-century writers (who were practically obsessed with evolution as the engine of progress) to describe the development of Plato's own thought in much the same way as the Old Testament was reinterpreted as the development of Hebrew thought from primitive mythology to something approximating what an educated, upper-class, scientifically minded, nineteenth-century German gentleman took to be true. In yet another parallel to the Bible, the history of Platonism was so chopped up and segmented that by the dawn of the twentieth century it was hard to see that anything vaguely resembling "Platonism" still existed. It was as difficult to talk about what "Platonism" teaches as it was to talk about what "the Bible" teaches. Should we then conclude that the question "What is Platonism?" cannot be answered?

In a series of scholarly books and articles, Lloyd P. Gerson has proposed a model for understanding Platonism in such a way that both unity and diversity can be accounted for, and both ancient and modern interpretations can be seen as partially right.[34] The ancients saw Platonism as a unity, and philosophical scholarship up to the eighteenth century perhaps overestimated the unity in the tradition. But the nineteenth and twentieth centuries went to the opposite extreme, reflecting first the Enlightenment myth of progress of nineteenth-century culture, and then the postmodern relativism of twentieth-century culture, in emphasizing first orderly development and then interpretive chaos. Gerson poses the question "Was Plato a Platonist?" as a way to suggest a distinction between Platonism as a general paradigm that sets it apart from other schools of ancient philosophy and individual Platonist philosophers, including Plato himself, Aristotle, the various members of the Academy, the Skeptics, the Neoplatonists, and so on, all of whom can be seen as part of a tradition, which can be defined as a research program.

In order to make this coherent, Gerson argues convincingly for a construct he calls "Ur-Platonism," which defines the unity binding together all Platonist philosophers. In a brilliant move, he expresses the five points of this construct in negatives, which permits a wide variety of possibilities for constructive solutions to the various problems the Platonic tradition seeks to address. The five points of Ur-Platonism are antimaterialism, antimechanism, antinominalism, antirelativism, and antiskepticism. We need to understand what he means by each of these terms before we go any further.

First, antimaterialism is "the view that it is false that the only things that exist are bodies and their properties."[35] The antimaterialist maintains that

---

34. See, in addition, Gerson, *Aristotle and Other Platonists.*
35. Gerson, *From Plato to Platonism*, 11.

entities exist that are neither bodies nor properties of bodies yet exist independently of bodies. There are many ways this could be true, but that is for Platonists to debate. Ur-Platonism merely asserts that the material world is not all that exists.

Second, antimechanism is "the view that the only sort of explanations available in principle to a materialist are inadequate for explaining the natural order."[36] Although antimechanism is closely related to antimaterialism, it really is aimed at any position that suggests that an adequate explanation for the behavior of physical things is inherent in the things themselves. Behind this is the idea, widespread in antiquity, that an adequate explanation for a thing must be a different sort of thing from the one being explained. This is a corollary of the idea that things need an explanation for their existence, which is a rejection of the divinity and aseity of the cosmos.

Third, antinominalism is "the view that it is false that the only things that exist are individuals, each uniquely situated in space and time."[37] The antinominalist insists on this view primarily to explain how two things can be the same in some way without being identical, and a causal explanation is sought. The usual approach is to affirm some sort of view of universals.

Fourth, antirelativism is the "denial of the claim that Plato attributes to Protagoras that 'man is the measure of all things, of what is that it is and of what is not that it is not.'"[38] In his dialogues, Plato discusses both epistemological and ethical relativism. Epistemological relativism is not yet skepticism, because rather than denying the possibility of truth, it merely defines truth as "true for me" or "what appears to be true to me." Ethical relativism is really hedonism; it says that the good is what is "good for me" or "good for my group." Antirelativism, however, says that goodness and truth are properties of being.

Fifth, antiskepticism is "the view that knowledge is possible."[39] Gerson writes, "Knowledge (*episteme*) refers to a mode of cognition wherein the real is in some way 'present' to the cognizer."[40] Skeptics do not deny cognition, only knowledge. If either materialism or nominalism were true, skepticism would necessarily follow because it would not be possible for the real to be present to the cognizer; there could be only representations of the real. This, of course, describes what David Hume takes to be the only possibility when it comes to the act of knowing—or, I should say, cognizing. No wonder his

36. Gerson, *From Plato to Platonism*, 11.
37. Gerson, *From Plato to Platonism*, 12.
38. Gerson, *From Plato to Platonism*, 13.
39. Gerson, *From Plato to Platonism*, 13.
40. Gerson, *From Plato to Platonism*, 13.

skepticism was so drastic that he even came to doubt causation.[41] Plato's attacks on the Sophists apply in spades to Hume; Plato knew the type all too well.[42] So much for Hume's empiricism and skepticism being the result of a modern, scientific worldview; he is merely reviving ancient sophistry, which is the enemy of all science.

This brief sketch of Ur-Platonism is a description of what all Platonists held in common from Plato to Plotinus and the last of the major Neoplatonic philosophers such as Porphyry and Proclus.[43] Obviously, there is room for what Gerson calls "a host of 'dogmatisms,' among which are many contradictory positions"[44] within the parameters of this construct. Gerson is not claiming that every single Platonist philosopher began every work with a creed-like summary of the "Five Holy Antis" or any such thing. The five points of Ur-Platonism constitute a modern heuristic construct that helps us understand from our vantage point what was much more intuitively grasped and passionately believed by Platonist philosophers in antiquity.

Is there any way to state what unified Ur-Platonism is in less than five points? Gerson thinks so. He suggests that the main thrust of the five points is explanatory; all forms of Platonism believe that true explanation is always a top-down, never a bottom-up, process and that the true explanatory framework will converge on the smallest possible number of principles. The one explains the many; the many do not explain themselves. This means that all forms of Platonism tend to be hierarchical in one way or another.[45] An additional way to get at the essence of Platonism, according to Gerson, is to see that Platonism is fundamentally antinaturalism; one could say that all five points of Ur-Platonism, taken together, constitute a comprehensive antinaturalist

41. Feser, *Last Superstition*, 265.

42. Feser (*Last Superstition*, 274) quotes Elizabeth Anscombe's characterization of Hume as a "mere—brilliant—sophist."

43. Lewis Ayres has a very similar definition of Platonism:

> The "Platonic" school is presented as the underlying movement of all Classical philosophy except Epicureans and some Skeptics. Thus, Augustine can confess membership in this 'school' while holding in the same work to a theory of cognition and of the unity of the soul that owes most to anicient Stoicism. . . . Belonging to this school involves acceptance of the immateriality and reality of Truth and the soul, of the participation of beings in Being, and of the possibility of reliable knowledge. . . . Note also that Augustine sees himself as belonging to this school even as he sees Christ as the ultimate authority. (*Nicaea and Its Legacy*, 368n14)

44. Gerson, *From Plato to Platonism*, 15.

45. This is one of the main ways Christians find Platonism to be biblical. Thomas Howard describes the sacramental worldview of medieval Christendom: "Nature and politics and animals and sex—these were all exhibitions in their own way of the way things are. This mind fancied that everything meant everything, and that it all rushed up finally to heaven" (*Chance or the Dance*, 13).

position. Platonism is the most important and coherent alternative to philosophical naturalism in the history of Western thought. Yet another way of
getting at the essence of Platonism is to say that it is the view that the world
is meaningful, as opposed to random, purposeless, or chaotic. In other words,
for all Platonists, teleology is inherent in reality; the task of philosophy is to
discover it. For Christian Platonists, teleology is known by natural reason as
corrected and supplemented by the biblical doctrine of creation.

By now it should be clear why Christians like Augustine felt an affinity
with Platonism that they did not feel with atheism, atomism, materialism,
skepticism, and other forms of ancient thought. David is convinced that the
heavens declare the glory of their Creator (Ps. 19), Genesis 1:3–25 portrays
the heavens and the earth as spoken into being by the divine Word, and the
Psalms see creation as set in order by the rationality of the divine wisdom (e.g.,
Ps. 104). The doctrine of creation certainly creates a reasonable expectation
of teleology and order in nature that can be investigated by human reason.
Natural theology, natural law, and natural science thus all have a basis in
reality. Platonism and Christianity together form a unified foundation for
the development of empirical science on a foundation of mathematics. To
oppose Christian Platonism, therefore, is to oppose philosophy itself and, in
so doing, to set oneself in opposition to reason, the moral law, and natural
science.

The Bible emerged out of the ancient Near Eastern mythological worldview and was influenced by an encounter with Greek rationalism during the
Second Temple period. The Old Testament prophets and the New Testament
apostles, as well as the early church fathers, had the task of encountering the
metaphysical assumptions of their culture and correcting those assumptions
in the light of divine revelation. One consistent feature of the biblical worldview is its understanding of created reality as consisting of what is called
throughout the canon "the heavens and the earth." As Karl Barth points out,
following Augustine and the Great Tradition in general, this phrase is used
from Genesis 1:1 onward to designate the revealed truth that all of reality that
is not God is the creation of God.[46] Both what we call the material cosmos,
and also the spiritual realm of heaven, are neither eternal nor part of God
but created *ex nihilo*. Platonism has room for this basic metaphysical truth,
unlike the materialism of the Atomists or the pantheism of certain Stoics

46. Barth writes, "The object to which the statement about creation refers is 'heaven and
earth.' . . . There can be no doubt that in the sense of the biblical witness from Genesis to
the Revelation of John, they denote the sum of the reality that is distinct from God" (*Church
Dogmatics*, III/1, 17). Barth is notable as one of the few twentieth-century theologians to have
written on angelology, which he treats in paragraph 51 in *Church Dogmatics*, III/3, 369–531.

or the agnosticism of the Skeptics. Unlike Epicureanism, Platonism refused to regard the spiritual realm as irrelevant or unconnected in any way to this world that we inhabit. Hans Boersma observes that "the church fathers were convinced of a close (participatory) link between this-worldly sacrament (*sacramentum*) and otherworldly reality (*res*)."[47]

The only thing left to explain in this section is how Christian Platonism is related to Ur-Platonism; by this point, that should require very little discussion. If one thinks about orthodox dogma and patristic interpretation of Scripture and then imagines Ur-Platonism as the metaphysical context in which the fathers did their exegesis and dogmatics, it is easy to see how both those who articulated the Nicene faith and the Platonists, insofar as both worked within the framework of Ur-Platonism, had common enemies: materialism, mechanism, nominalism, relativism, and skepticism. Christianity, as the true philosophy, joins together a philosophical account of the truth about reality with a theological account of the revelation of God's saving work in Israel's history culminating in Jesus Christ.

Christianity could thus be described as "sacramental-historical" in nature. It is sacramental because it holds to the reality of universals, which Thomas Aquinas understood to be ideas in the mind of God. Since individual created things providentially participate in universals and thus are upheld in being by Christ (Col. 1:15–17), we know God sacramentally. Our being is upheld in existence by divine being, and we can know God as the source of our being. There is a vertical dimension of existence because this world that is accessible to our empirical senses is not the sum total of reality. Rather, this world participates in a reality greater than itself and is only a shadow of this greater reality. As far as this goes, the "Platonism" side of the label "Christian Platonism" is being stressed. But what makes Christian Platonism uniquely "Christian" is a cluster of doctrines centered on creation and the incarnation. God is the transcendent, self-existent Lord who brought the cosmos into existence *ex nihilo* as an act of his will. And God has entered into history in the person of Jesus Christ in order to redeem the fallen creation and redeem it to his glory. The church is the community of the saved, who form the nucleus of the new humanity that God is fashioning to populate the new heavens and new earth that he intends to bring into being at the end of history through the return of Christ, the resurrection of the dead, the last judgment, and the transformation of all things according to the pattern known to God from

---

47. Boersma, *Scripture as Real Presence*, 12. Boersma says on the same page that what he terms "sacramental ontology" is identical to the widely acknowledged Christian Platonism of the fathers.

eternity and revealed in Christ. Christianity is thus also a matter of horizontal relationships as well as vertical ones.

It is crucial to see that Christianity cannot be reduced either to sacramental participation in God alone (the temptation faced by Roman Catholicism) or to historical redemption alone (the temptation to which theological liberalism yields). Christianity is thus sacramental-historical in its fundamental nature; it is a *narrative of redemption*, but it is a narrative of the redemption *of the cosmos*, that is, of all created reality and nothing less. Without the sacramental, vertical dimension of Christianity, the faith is reduced to a form of gnosticism. Without the historical, redemptive dimension, the faith is reduced to the modern ideology of progress—the "immanentization of the eschaton" in the justly famous phrase of Eric Voegelin.[48] Crucially, it must be noted that Voegelin saw this form of modernity as a form of gnosticism. So Christian Platonism is the sacramental-historical alternative to gnosticism and the theological metaphysics of the true, biblical, orthodox faith—the Great Tradition—that comes out of the patristic age with the Nicene Creed as its leading symbol. Christian Platonism is a synthesis of the best of rational Greek philosophy and biblical revelation and is responsible for the flowering of Western Christendom.

Although there were many disagreements between the orthodox, pro-Nicene fathers and the Platonists, it is easy to see how the fathers could have perceived themselves as working within the metaphysical paradigm of Ur-Platonism. It would have seemed as natural to them as a contemporary theologian seeking to interpret Genesis in a way that does not totally contradict natural science. It would have been a great deal stranger if the fathers had categorically rejected Platonism. Such a move would likely have caused nascent Christianity either to sink below the waves of the various combinations and varieties of ancient gnostic religions or to dissolve into skepticism and agnosticism. The idea of the fathers advancing an Atomist interpretation of the doctrine of the human person or a nominalist explanation of creation by the Logos is too bizarre even to contemplate. Such weirdness would not occur until humankind had "progressed" to the level it attained only in the modern era.

The Modern Rejection of Christian Platonism

Speaking of the modern era, it should be obvious to anyone familiar with trends in modern thought and culture that Christian Platonism is not exactly

48. Voegelin, *New Science of Politics*, 163.

the dominant metaphysical account of reality in Western culture today. The amazing thing about the so-called Enlightenment is that its adherents droned on endlessly about "reason" and yet ended up eventually undermining it. When we look around us, we see a society that views rational proofs for the existence of God as silly and is in rebellion against the natural moral law.[49] Christian Platonism is not even upheld by most modern theologians and, incredibly, not even by all evangelical ones. All too often evangelicals try to pretend that they are uninterested in and unaffected by metaphysics, which simply means, more often than not, that they are unconscious disciples of some anti-Christian sophist.

How did this happen? The rise of modern science took place on the foundations of Christianity and Platonism, as Pope Benedict XVI explained clearly in his masterful Regensburg Lecture.[50] But just as experimental science was taking off in Western culture, the Enlightenment philosophers kicked the foundations out from under it; the long-term implications were destructive of religion, morality, and science, in that order. If we want to understand modernity, we need to see it as an astonishing *reversion* to the pre-Christian naturalism of the ancient world that Christian Platonism had, by great effort, managed to overcome in the process of shaping and developing Western culture. Modernity is the irrational rejection of Christianity as the true religion and also the point-by-point rejection of Christian Platonism as the metaphysical framework for Western culture; the two rejections are intricately bound up with each other. As we bring this chapter to a close, we need to pause to reflect on how these claims explain so much of what our culture is currently experiencing. Doing so will provide a foundation for comprehending the history of biblical interpretation that we will consider in the next chapter. It will also highlight what is at stake in the struggle to interpret Scripture rightly, not just for the church, but also for Western culture.

What is modernity? *Modernity is a cultural pathology caused by the breakdown of the Great Tradition and the rise of neopaganism in Western civilization.* It is partially a reversion to ancient paganism, but it properly should be called "neopaganism" because the new paganism incorporates certain ideas derived from Christianity (preeminently the idea of history as linear and progressive). Thus, from one angle the current cultural malaise is a form of neopaganism, but from another it could equally well be defined as a Christian heresy. We will consider this ambiguity further in what follows. There

---

49. These two characteristics of modernity are not unrelated; they are mutually reinforcing, as Paul explains in Romans 1.

50. For a perceptive introduction to the lecture and a text of the lecture itself, see Schall, *Regensburg Lecture*.

are three phases in modernity: early modernity (1300–1650), high modernity (1650–1800), and late modernity (1800–present). We will consider each of these three phases in turn.

Early modernity has two stages, which together constitute the first phase of modernity: the breakdown of the medieval synthesis and the creation of the modern, mechanistic worldview in the context of the rise of modern, technological science. The late Middle Ages saw the tragic breakdown of the Christian Platonism of the High Middle Ages, symbolized above all by Thomas Aquinas's great work of genius, the *Summa Theologica*. The metaphysical realism of the medieval synthesis was replaced by the rise of voluntarism and nominalism, and the doctrine of God underwent a fundamental change. Many books deal with this period, but one of the most helpful is Michael Allen Gillespie's *The Theological Origins of Modernity*.

Gillespie rightly points to the origins of the medieval world (and thus of Western culture) in the synthesis of Christianity and pagan philosophy in late antiquity. This is the formation of Christian Platonism that I have been describing. He notes that in the medieval synthesis, nature and reason reflected each other.[51] I would add that the basis of this fact was the Nicene doctrine of the Trinity insofar as it was the rationality of the Logos, imprinted on the natural world because God created according to his Word (see Genesis and John's Gospel), that made this coherence of nature and reason possible. Gillespie discusses the work of Duns Scotus and William of Ockham in the formation of nominalism as an alternative to realism. William of Ockham worked from a base of divine omnipotence and saw universals as incompatible with divine sovereignty.[52] He saw creation as contingent, not only in the sense that it might not have existed if God had not willed it but also in the more radical sense that it cannot be stable if God is to retain sovereignty. This idea is dramatically at odds with the biblical notion of covenant; the Bible sees God as binding himself to his covenant freely and understands this not as a limitation on God but rather as an expression of the perfection of his nature described by the term "faithfulness." But Ockham's radical notion of God's freedom veered alarmingly close to denying the intricate relationship between covenant and creation so ably expounded recently by Karl Barth.[53] For Ockham, God is not the predictable God of Aquinas, who could be counted on to maintain his relationship to creation on the basis of a knowable moral law. Instead, God is liable to do anything whatsoever tomorrow, because the

51. Gillespie, *Theological Origins of Modernity*, 19.
52. Gillespie, *Theological Origins of Modernity*, 22.
53. Barth: "If creation was the external basis of the covenant, the latter was the internal basis of the former" (*Church Dogmatics*, III/1:231–32).

only basis of his action is his total sovereignty and his utterly unpredictable will. Gillespie raises a very good question when he asks: "How could anyone love or venerate such an unsettling God?"[54] So a further question arises: Why on earth would a view like this be able to overcome and replace the view of the Great Tradition? Yet somehow it did. Although the church censured Ockham's thought in 1326, his influence grew over the next 150 years until it had become one of the most powerful intellectual movements in Europe. By the time of Luther, all the universities in Germany, except one, were dominated by the nominalists.[55]

Nominalism eventually led to a new concept of God, which in turn led to a new view of the human person in the image of God. The new concept of God was one in which the will played a more prominent role than reason or love. This led to a new emphasis on the human will as central to the definition of the human person. Gillespie writes:

Nominalism sought to tear the rationalistic veil from the face of God in order to found a true Christianity, but in doing so it revealed a capricious God, fearsome in power, unknowable, unpredictable, unconstrained by nature and reason, and indifferent to good and evil. This vision of God turned the order of nature into a chaos of individual beings and the order of logic into a mere concatenation of names. Man himself was dethroned from his exalted place in the natural order of things and cast adrift in an infinite universe with no natural law to guide him and no certain path to salvation. It is thus not surprising that for all but the most extreme ascetics and mystics, this dark God of nominalism proved to be a profound source of anxiety and insecurity.[56]

This is not the God of the Bible, not the God of Nicaea, not the God of Augustine. It is a heretical concept of God—at best an idol and, at worst, the devil in disguise. So why did it seem so plausible that many people accepted it? The answer surely has something to do with the terrifying and cataclysmic events of the fourteenth century.

The fourteenth century was the worst century in European history until the horrors of the twentieth. Like the twentieth century, it was characterized by horrible and long-lasting wars. It was the era of the Hundred Years' War between England and France and also the era of the Black Death, which claimed the lives of a third of the population all by itself. It was the period of the Great Schism, when there were two popes (and for a time three popes).

54. Gillespie, *Theological Origins of Modernity*, 25.
55. Gillespie, *Theological Origins of Modernity*, 27.
56. Gillespie, *Theological Origins of Modernity*, 29.

It was also the time of the Little Ice Age, when the amount of arable land shrank—a disaster in a feudal society in which most of the population farmed the land. Town life declined, trade and travel declined, and the failures of the Crusades robbed Europe of much of its best leadership, not to mention much of its wealth. In such an age, the dark god of sheer will proposed by nominalism somehow began to seem plausible.

As Europe recovered during the next two centuries, the time was ripe for new ideas, especially ones that might allow human beings to enhance their security in a fragile world by gaining control of the forces of nature. The rise of technological science during this period took place on the foundations of rationality created by the medieval synthesis, but within the context of a new mechanistic view of nature and a new pragmatic view of science as technology, rather than as wisdom. Departing from Christian Platonism, European thinkers at the beginning of the Enlightenment sought not to accommodate themselves to reality but rather to take control of nature and bend it to purposes invented by human will. If the nominalist God can never be our source of security, then technology would replace God. In such a climate, the motto of the Enlightenment was operative already, as later articulated by Immanuel Kant in the only pithy thing he ever wrote: "Dare to think for yourself."[57]

The second phase of modernity, high modernity, was the Enlightenment (1650–1800); it was characterized above all by materialism. Reason was viewed as an alternative to a supernatural worldview. The individual will, which was central in early modernity, was not dislodged from its place, for it was specifically *human* reason that was practically worshiped. Nature was seen as raw material on which the human will could and should imprint its own image. We should *use* nature, *manipulate* nature, and even *alter* nature to further human projects. This attitude was strongly reinforced by the stunning technological successes throughout the modern era, which began to accelerate during the eighteenth and nineteenth centuries.

The Enlightenment ended in a sense in 1804 with the death of Kant, but in another sense it is ongoing. It ended in the sense that the romantic movement supplanted it because of its successful critique of the Enlightenment's inability to account for higher human values like art, beauty, love, mystery, and above all, freedom. But it did not end in the sense that Enlightenment nominalism, materialism, and mechanism continue to exercise a stranglehold on the Western concept of nature. Insofar as human persons are bodies, they are subject to the natural laws of science and wholly determined. But insofar

57. Kant, "What Is Enlightenment?," 58.

as one is a soul, one is free in the modern sense of freedom from constraint or freedom as uncaused action. The concept of the human person as simultaneously determined and free is one of the unresolved contradictions of modernity. Cartesian dualism organizes the problem but does not solve it. The human person, considered as a body-soul unity, cannot be free within the worldview of modernity; yet neither can the essence of the human person be truly human without being free. Thus we see the development of a view of the human person in which the body is incidental to the essence of the person. This is why the concept of "transgender" makes some sort of twisted sense to the late modern mind.[58]

Throughout the nineteenth century, romanticism continued to coexist with Enlightenment rationalism, but around the beginning of the twentieth century it began to break down. After Friedrich Nietzsche, World Wars I and II, coupled with the rise of communism and fascism and the horrors of the Holocaust, crippled European cultural confidence and decimated much of the best of its leadership, thus causing a gaping wound in the European soul. The skepticism that had been a powerful force since Hume and Kant morphed into epistemological and ethical relativism as postmodernism undertook to question not just Enlightenment metanarratives but also the ability of reason to discover a natural moral law and even natural scientific laws. Science itself became politicized. Human technology began to view not only nature, but also human nature itself, as raw material at the disposal of human will.[59] New reproductive technologies, the separation of procreation from love and marriage, the breakdown of the family, the rise of drug addiction, the increase in loneliness and suicide, and the rise of crudeness, lewdness, and cruelty make a sad mockery of the supposedly ongoing and inevitable cultural "progress" that is widely supposed to be the fruit of modernity.[60] Modernity has become so antiscience and irrational that it is widely considered unacceptable today not

58. This dualism is diagnosed, critiqued, and superseded in John Paul II's magisterial work, *Man and Woman He Created Them*. See the introduction for a lucid discussion of the modern anthropology and John Paul II's critique of it (34–63).

59. C. S. Lewis, one of the twentieth century's most prominent Christian Platonists, issued a prophetic warning about this in his 1944 book, *The Abolition of Man*. He saw quite clearly that this necessarily meant the rule of some over others, not freedom for all. He also foresaw the end of humanity itself as the final outcome.

60. Aldous Huxley's 1932 dystopian novel *Brave New World* outlines a world in which all aspects of life are ruthlessly controlled by social engineers who have gained total control of the all-powerful state. The family has been utterly destroyed, and human reproduction occurs in the laboratory under the supervision of state officials. The goal of totalitarian socialism has been attained. The technology that makes such top-down control possible is advancing at a rapid rate today, and Western societies seem incapable of placing any limits on it. See Greely, *End of Sex*; and Smith, *Consumer's Guide to a Brave New World*.

to believe that a man can turn himself into a woman just by an act of the will any time he chooses to do so. The biological reality of sexual differentiation is viewed as subject to human will; even nature itself must not be allowed to stand in the way of the autonomous individual will.

The rise, growth, and fall of modernity can be summarized as the systematic, point-by-point rejection of Christian Platonism. The coming into existence of Christian Platonism laid the foundation for Christendom; its dissolution threatens to cause the fall of Christendom. The fourteenth and fifteenth centuries saw the rise of nominalism. The sixteenth to eighteenth centuries witnessed the growth of materialism and the mechanistic view of nature enshrined in the Newtonian worldview. Atheism during the Enlightenment can be seen as a reaction against the dark God of sheer will; Deism can be viewed as a compromise between conservative forces who wanted to maintain belief in God and modern ones who wanted full-out atheism to triumph everywhere. Deism provided a context in which philosophical naturalism could gradually take hold of the Western mind. In the nineteenth century, skepticism was practically institutionalized in the dominance of the philosophy of Kant, which was a restatement of the sophistry of Hume in fancy philosophical terminology. Finally, the twentieth century embraced relativism and rejected natural theology and natural law and is now in the process of rejecting natural scientific law.

Christian Platonism is today the philosophy of a culturally despised minority. But antimaterialism, antimechanism, antinominalism, antirelativism, and antiskepticism still constitute the core ideas of the nonnaturalistic theological metaphysics of the Great Tradition of Christianity. As we shall see in the next chapter, the massive changes in the way the Bible has been interpreted during the past two centuries make perfect sense when viewed in the context of the narrative I have just sketched. The rise of historical criticism since Baruch Spinoza and the rise of revisionist theology since Friedrich Schleiermacher are the two main components of what I term the "liberal project." The liberal project is, quite simply, the attempt to do Christian exegesis and restate Christian doctrines on the basis of modern metaphysics, which is to say, on the basis of a metaphysics consisting of the rejection of each of the main points of Ur-Platonism. If we recall Gerson's view that Platonism can be defined as antinaturalism, we see that the liberal project is thus the attempt to fit Christianity into a naturalistic worldview. It is the attempt to retain Christianity while acquiescing to modernity's rejection of Ur-Platonism. But in this process "Christianity" is transformed into the neopagan culture religion of the post-Christian West. We need to understand that Christian Platonism and *ressourcement* constitute a rival tradition to modern metaphysics and the liberal project. Christianity and modernity cannot be reconciled and cannot coexist permanently; they must inevitably clash in the struggle for cultural supremacy. The interpretation of the Bible is the key battleground on which this struggle has played itself out for the past three centuries. In the next chapter, therefore, we turn to the history of hermeneutics in the modern period.

4

The History of Biblical
Interpretation Reconsidered

The historical-critical method is a way of explaining away what does
not fit within a fairly narrowly defined, rationalistic enterprise. As
we have seen, it was first used to explain away miracles.... Nothing
like traditional Christianity can survive in such an environment, for
such traditional Christianity claims that through certain specific
events in the past God has revealed himself to men.

Andrew Louth[1]

*T*he purpose of this chapter is to show that the currently dominant narrative about the history of biblical interpretation needs to be replaced
with a new and better version that interprets historical facts more accurately.
Where the modern narrative sees ineptitude and confusion, a more accurate
interpretation would see skill and spiritual insight; where the modern narrative sees progress, a more sober estimation would see decline. The currently
fashionable story of biblical interpretation is a subset of the general modern
myth of progress, which sees history as a gradual rise from superstition to
science, from religion to atheism, and from supernaturalism to naturalism.
This narrative is a product of the Enlightenment; it is the story that modernity
tells about itself to prove that it needs no story. It is the particular story that
claims to be universal. Everything is subject to the acids of historicism except

1. Louth, *Discerning the Mystery*, 16.

the narrative about the rise of reason and science in seventeenth-century Europe itself. But now even this core narrative of modernity is breaking down. I remember a professor of Old Testament in seminary who constantly proclaimed this or that view as "the assured results of higher criticism." But that was over three decades ago; who talks like that today? In an age when all grand rationalistic metanarratives have come under postmodern suspicion, it is amusing to think that biblical scholars may turn out to be the last "true believers" in the Enlightenment myth of progress.[2]

On the contrary, the Great Tradition of Christian orthodoxy has an almost two-millennia tradition of consensus on Christian dogma—the doctrines of the Trinity and Christology—built on the foundation of a tradition of objective exegesis. Theologians keep coming to the same consensus about what the Bible means, and preachers keep proclaiming that message of salvation through Jesus Christ to the world; the result is growing, thriving churches that witness to Christ in various centuries and diverse cultures all over the world. In contrast, the historical-critical movement spawns atheists and heretics, is consistently rejected by the faithful when it tries to preach its message openly, and results in the numerical, doctrinal, moral, and spiritual decline of any denominations that make the mistake of allowing it unfettered control of its seminaries and pulpits. Faithfulness to Jesus Christ, not some vaguely defined myth of progress, is the true goal of Christian mission; the Great Tradition is the tradition in which faithfulness to that goal is nurtured.

With regard to biblical interpretation, the myth of progress divides history into two phases: the precritical period and the critical period. It is less common today to encounter a section of a commentary on the history of the interpretation of a biblical book that starts in the 1700s, as if nothing of significance to our consideration of the meaning of that book occurred during the patristic, medieval, and Reformation periods. But most treatments of the premodern era still emphasize how untenable premodern exegesis was. Even conservative evangelical hermeneutics textbooks can speak of patristic exegesis as being amateurish, almost childish, notable only as an example of how not to do exegesis.[3] Bernard Ramm wrote, "Calvin's Commentaries are considered the first real scientific, philological exegesis of Scripture in the

---

2. For one of the early critiques of grand metanarratives, see Lyotard, *Postmodern Condition*.

3. E.g., see the widely used college-level introduction to hermeneutics by Duvall and Hays, *Grasping God's Word*. Duvall and Hays are dismissive to the point of caricature of allegory, and they totally ignore premodern exegesis except to ridicule it. For example, they write, "Once the author loses control of the meaning, many readers will naturally drift into overspiritualizing the text through fanciful allegorical interpretation" (208).

history of the Church."[4] He explains that the reason the fathers did not fall into heresy was that they used the literal method sometimes "unconsciously" and only allegorized the Old Testament.[5] Their motive was good in wanting to affirm the Old Testament as a Christian book, he says, but they had a very infantile understanding of the progress of revelation. He views their methods of interpretation as tending to obscure the truth of the Word.

Ramm is a typical example of the general trend of scholarship until very recently. Insofar as any of the fathers are praised, it is only for isolated instances in which a few of them might have anticipated modern methods in some way. For example, the Antiochene fathers are often said to pay more attention to history and the literal sense than the Alexandrians, who are written off as hopelessly subjective allegorizers.[6] The point of this distinction is to make the Antiochenes appear to be forerunners of the modern historical critics. But scholars point out real problems with this superficial interpretation in that most of the Alexandrians and Antiochenes have much more in common with each other than either group has with the Enlightenment.[7] Frances Young points out that in Platonism, not only words but also the world itself is an imperfect copy of the reality to which both pointed. She argues persuasively that to classify the Alexandrians as employing allegorical interpretation and the Antiochenes as employing literal interpretation is too clumsy a distinction. Young holds, "The difference between 'literal' and 'allegorical' references was not absolute, but lay on a spectrum."[8] We also need to be aware that "history" and the "literal sense" turn out to mean very different things for the fathers and the moderns, so comparisons are anything but straightforward.[9]

The irrational bias of the myth of progress can be seen in the tendency to criticize orthodox church fathers for reading Greek metaphysics into the

4. Ramm, *Protestant Biblical Interpretation*, 117.

5. Ramm, *Protestant Biblical Interpretation*, 29.

6. Brevard S. Childs calls the contrast between the spiritual concerns of the Alexandrians and the historical concerns of the Antiochenes "particularly misleading" (*Struggle to Understand Isaiah*, 130). For a good discussion of the spiritual exegesis of the Antiochenes, see Nassif, "Spiritual Exegesis of Scripture," 437–70.

7. E.g., see Boersma, *Scripture as Real Presence*, chap. 3, where he compares Origen and John Chrysostom on the theophany in Genesis 22. While recognizing that they "emphasize different aspects of the paradox of divine descent" (60), Boersma also stresses that their approaches are not mutually exclusive. Boersma draws attention to the fact that Origen's approach stressed the vertical aspect and the condescension of the transcendent God, while Chrysostom's approach stresses the horizontal aspect and the ability of God to enter into interpersonal relationships. The concerns of both approaches, Boersma says, are recognized as valid by sacramental exegesis.

8. Young, *Biblical Exegesis and the Formation of Christian Culture*, 120.

9. Childs, *Struggle to Understand Isaiah*, 67. Childs has a good discussion of Origen's method in general (62–72).

text, while overlooking the influence of Baruch Spinoza's rationalism and Bruno Bauer's Hegelianism on their own biblical interpretation. Is this because "Greek" metaphysics is bad, but "German" metaphysics is good? According to the history of hermeneutics as told from an Enlightenment perspective, if it were not for the pagan Enlightenment, Christians would still be reading Greek metaphysics into the Bible like Augustine and making it say whatever they pleased like Origen. Is it not rather bizarre that this narrative asks us to believe that it took the pagan Epicureanism of the Enlightenment to rescue us from the "subjectivism" of the Nicene fathers, medieval schoolmen, and Protestant Reformers?

In reality, crucial aspects of the dominant narrative do not withstand serious, scholarly scrutiny by experts in patristics, medieval theology, and Reformation history. Predictive prophecy was central to the interpretation of the Old Testament by the fathers and cannot be excised without drastically revising the meaning of the Bible.[10] The Antiochenes and John Calvin were not forerunners of historical criticism; they consciously rejected the naturalistic metaphysics at the root of historical criticism.[11] Typology is no more compatible with historical criticism than is allegory.[12] Allegorical methods used by the fathers were not entirely subjective, and (contra Adolf von Harnack) Greek metaphysical doctrines were not used naively to warp a pristine "Hebraic" worldview. And so on it goes. But challenging specific points of the overall narrative is not enough; we must also specify how the overall narrative needs to be revised. That is the goal of this chapter: to synthesize recent developments in patristic, medieval, Reformation, and modern hermeneutics and set down some markers for a revised narrative of the history of biblical interpretation.[13] Of course this is an ambitious project, but it is less irresponsible to make at least a beginning in the right direction than to continue driving in the wrong

10. For an excellent discussion of this issue, see Allis, *Unity of Isaiah*.

11. See Childs, *Struggle to Understand Isaiah*, chaps. 10 and 14.

12. The attempt by Jean Daniélou and others to distinguish between allegory, which they regard as subjective, and typology, which they see as embedded in the text and thus not subjective, is a complex issue that has a point but is an oversimplification. See Daniélou, *From Shadows to Reality*. Childs states that although Daniélou's thesis was greeted with favor in the 1950s, it later was widely recognized that "the sharp distinction between allegory and typology could not be sustained" (*Struggle to Understand Isaiah*, 65).

13. I am not trying to write a history of biblical interpretation here, although that is a great need that I hope someone inspired by the perspective offered here will address. This chapter is an exercise in historiographical revisionism drawing on the work of such scholars as Henri de Lubac, John Milbank, Brevard Childs, Lewis Ayres, Robert Wilken, Matthew Levering, David Steinmetz, Richard Muller, and Thomas Oden. None of these writers, however, provides a synthesis of the whole story in the way I am attempting to do here, and it is not likely that any of them would agree with every detail of what I have written.

direction by doing biblical interpretation on the basis of the highly question-able foundations of the currently fashionable narrative.

First we will examine the consensus of the Great Tradition on biblical interpretation, and then we will look at the great disruption caused by the Enlightenment-inspired rise of higher criticism and how the liberal Christian response to the Enlightenment, the liberal project, falls short in its goal of reconciling Christianity and the Enlightenment. The last section will suggest how the modern narrative needs to be revised.

The Orthodox Consensus: Exegesis of Scripture in the Great Tradition

The early church unified around the Nicene doctrine of the Trinity and the Chalcedonian doctrine of the two natures of Christ and enshrined this unity in the ecumenical creeds of the undivided church of the first five centuries. The degree to which this consensus has endured as the common ground of the church, despite all the divisions and disagreements over other doctrines, is truly astonishing. It should cause us to exclaim: "Great and amazing are your deeds, O Lord God the Almighty!" (Rev. 15:3). The schism between East and West in the eleventh century did not disturb this consensus; neither did the Protestant Reformation of the sixteenth century. In the modern era, some of the most fervent trinitarians are low church, Bible-believing evangelicals in cultures far removed from both the Greco-Roman society of late antiquity and Western Christendom—in places like sub-Saharan Africa, India, and mainland China. What is often overlooked is that this dogmatic consensus rests firmly on patterns of exegesis preserved in the church throughout its history, which produced the dogmas so firmly confessed. These churches have no bureaucratic authority enforcing creedal orthodoxy on them; they have the Scriptures and the guidance of the Holy Spirit, as well as a common exegetical heritage handed down generation by generation. It is this common exegesis of the church that I am interested in bringing to the fore in this book.

Brevard S. Childs performed a great service to the church when, in his last book, *The Struggle to Understand Isaiah as Christian Scripture*, he presented the results of his research on the history of the interpretation of Isaiah from the beginning of the patristic era to the twentieth century. In his research, he sought to discover the answer to this question: "Is there a 'family resemblance' that emerges from this analysis of many generations of Christian biblical study? Are there any parameters that identify exegesis as Christian? How do successive generations of expositors exert critical judgment in rejecting, correcting, and enriching exegetical moves made by their predecessors in order to address different audiences and changing historical conditions?"[14] His conclusion was that there are seven "discernible characteristic features that constitute a family resemblance within the Christian exegesis of the Old Testament."[15] Childs's primary-source research is far too detailed to summarize here, but we need to examine his conclusions to identify the common characteristics of Great Tradition exegesis.[16]

1. The Authority of Scripture

First, Childs notes that there has been widespread agreement that God is the author of "the Bible's Word."[17] The early church inherited a high view of biblical inspiration from Judaism and then simply assimilated the New Testament to the Hebrew Bible as the apostolic key to interpreting Scripture. According to Childs, biblical authority was manifested in the struggle against gnosticism most clearly in the way that Scripture was seen as a unified telling of one story of salvation through Christ. Irenaeus spoke for all the fathers in viewing the Bible in this way. Childs notes that the inspiration and authority of the Bible did not come under serious attack until the Enlightenment. I would just add that we should note carefully that the form that attack took was the undermining of the unity of the Bible as a single narrative, which was done by ignoring divine authorship and concentrating on human authorship alone.[18] The ancient gnostics would not be the last group in church history to attack Scripture as a coherent revelation from God.

2. The Literal and Spiritual Senses of Scripture

Second, Childs notes that Christian exegesis has always recognized both a literal and a spiritual sense of Scripture. The warrant for this move is far from being a "late Hellenistic intrusion." In fact, Childs notes, the warrant for spiritual interpretation is found within the New Testament itself, so to employ such a method is to interpret Scripture the way that Scripture interprets itself. He expresses agreement with Andrew Louth, who says that

14. Childs, *Struggle to Understand Isaiah*, xi.

15. Childs, *Struggle to Understand Isaiah*, 300.

16. In the following section, I critically evaluate pp. 300–321 of Childs's *Struggle to Understand Isaiah*. I recommend that everyone interested in biblical interpretation read his entire book carefully.

17. Childs, *Struggle to Understand Isaiah*, 300.

18. The post-Enlightenment debate over the inerrancy of Scripture, which occurred primarily in the Anglo-Saxon world, is a serious debate, but behind it stands the bigger issues of divine authorship of Scripture, the unity of the Bible, and the coherence of its message of salvation centered on Jesus Christ.

allegory is "constitutive of Christian interpretation as a means of discerning the mystery of Christ."[19]

Childs notes that older attempts to paint Origen as a quasi-gnostic who irresponsibly read foreign meanings into the text of Scripture have been greatly revised in recent decades.[20] He notes that earlier treatments of the Alexandrians as "fanciful allegorists" and the Antiochenes as forerunners of the modern historical method have also been reconsidered. Both schools of interpreters agreed in recognizing the presence of a literal and a spiritual meaning in the text; much of the confusion that has arisen is caused by various terms—such as *theoria*, *allegoria*, *skopos*, and *nous*—being used in different ways. The main concern of the Alexandrians was that the literal sense apart from the spiritual killed the meaning; while the main concern of the Antiochenes was that "the biblical historical sequence could be lost in timeless symbolism."[21] Childs points out that Christian exegetes recognized the validity of both concerns and eventually incorporated aspects of both schools into the mainstream Christian tradition.

A major contribution that helped to keep the exegetical tradition within consistent parameters was made by Irenaeus, who emphasized the rule of faith as the theological content of Scripture. The rule of faith arises organically out of Scripture and provides a guide to further interpretation of Scripture. The rule of faith is summarized in the Apostles' Creed, but it arises out of Scripture itself.[22]

Childs notes that Thomas Aquinas, while accepting the by-then traditional fourfold sense of Scripture in theory, actually stressed literal interpretation in his exegetical practice. Yet, as Henri de Lubac shows, Thomas's concept of the literal sense includes within itself much of the exegetical and homiletical wealth of meaning that previously had been seen as the spiritual or allegorical sense. Something similar happened with the Reformers, Luther and Calvin. Calvin could be highly critical of certain allegorical interpretations; yet in his own interpretation of the literal sense, much of what previously had been regarded as the allegorical meaning was included within the literal sense. Calvin stressed the "plain sense" of the text. The point to note is that for him the plain sense included the christological meaning that the tradition

19. Childs, *Struggle to Understand Isaiah*, 302. See Louth, *Discerning the Mystery*, for a strong defense of allegory and an incisive critique of the influence of the Enlightenment on Christian theology and exegesis.

20. Recent scholarship is much less harsh toward Origen. See Boersma, *Scripture as Real Presence*, chaps. 3, 4, 8, and 9. For a recent treatment of Origen stressing the role of exegesis in the spiritual development of the interpreter, see Martens, *Origen and Scripture*.

21. Childs, *Struggle to Understand Isaiah*, 303.

22. See chap. 5 below for further discussion of Irenaeus and the rule of faith.

100   Theological Hermeneutics

had always seen in the Old Testament and called the spiritual sense. If one examines Calvin's exposition of Isaiah 53, for example, it is obvious that he interprets the meaning of this chapter as plainly speaking of Jesus Christ, the suffering Messiah.[23]

3. Scripture's Two Testaments

The entire Christian exegetical tradition has worked on the basis of the conviction that the Bible consists of an Old Testament and a New Testament. The sequence is not only chronological; it is also grounded in a trinitarian theology that sees the one Triune God at work in both Testaments in complementary ways. From Marcion in the second century to Enlightenment higher critics to the German Christians in the 1930s, there have been repeated attempts to subordinate the Old Testament to the New or even discard the Old altogether. Various schemes of progressive revelation and evolutionary development have also been proposed, although they often tend to end up relegating the Old Testament to an inferior status.

The church fathers and Calvin made a kind of different move. They distinguished between the modes of God's revelation in the two Testaments but at the same time "insisted that the substance of the revelation—that is, its content (*res*)—was the same."[24] Childs makes a very helpful and insightful comment when he says that Calvin's approach "did not need an additional level of allegory by which to render the text's spiritual meaning."[25] But if Calvin is representative of the tradition and if Childs was right when he said that the recognition of the literal and spiritual senses is common to the entire tradition, then how can he say that Calvin did not need allegory in order to render the text's spiritual meaning? Does that mean that allegory is not necessary for the spiritual meaning? The answer to this question is yes. Not all those who discerned a spiritual or christological meaning in the Old Testament called what they were doing "allegorical interpretation." Yet those who used the term "allegory" and those who did not use it *did* see a christological layer of meaning in a text like Isaiah 53, in addition to the literal sense or as part of the literal sense.

This is one of the points where the terminology is confusing, and the virtue of Childs's study is that he penetrates the terminological jungle all the way to the clearing in which the truth can be discerned. It is just as true to say that allegory, as a reading technique, is not indispensable to Christian exegesis as

23. Calvin, *Commentary on the Prophet Isaiah*, 106–32.
24. Childs, *Struggle to Understand Isaiah*, 305.
25. Childs, *Struggle to Understand Isaiah*, 306.

it is to say that the rejection of allegory is often the rejection of the essence of the Christian exegetical tradition. The latter occurs when allegory is conflated with all the possible ways that a christological meaning or spiritual sense can be seen in the text. As Childs shows, in Nicholas of Lyra, Thomas Aquinas, and Calvin we see the spiritual sense drawn back into the literal sense by means of what could be termed the "double-literal sense" or the "extended literal sense." One could also call it the christological dimension of the plain sense. I prefer to talk of it in terms of layers of meaning in the text, but further discussion of this point must be deferred to later chapters, where my constructive proposal for interpreting Scripture with the Great Tradition will be set forth. The main thing to see here is that the connection between the literal sense and the expanded literal or spiritual sense must be preserved and that the literal sense must always control and limit any additional senses. This is a common theme throughout Great Tradition exegesis.

One other point in Childs's summary of this issue of the relationship of the Testaments must be mentioned. Childs rightly notes that patterns of prophecy and fulfillment and typology were the most common ways of relating the Testaments. But he does not seem to appreciate that these ways of relating the Testaments are part and parcel of the approach he favors, as discussed above—namely, the focus on the ontological substance of the text, the Triune God revealing himself through the text. This is one of the few weaknesses of Childs's analysis. He does not give the prophecy-fulfillment motif its due as being absolutely fundamental to the relationship between the Testaments. He seems not to appreciate that for the New Testament apostles, the flip side of the christological meaning in the Old Testament is the fulfillment of Old Testament prophecy by Jesus Christ. From an Enlightenment viewpoint, of course, predictive prophecy is simply impossible on metaphysical grounds. But for the vast majority of human beings in the vast majority of cultures, who have not been corrupted in their thinking by the bad philosophy of the Enlightenment, there is widespread agreement with the apostles on this point.[26]

Some of those in the modern era, who have been influenced by Enlightenment naturalism, attempt to deal with the question of the christological interpretation of the Old Testament by viewing the apostles as setting the example for us by reading Christ into the Old Testament. They would argue that this is a plausible or valid reading of the Old Testament, but not necessarily the one correct reading for everyone. Such individuals sometimes find

26. For a scintillating discussion that explains what is so bad about Enlightenment philosophy, see Feser, *Last Superstition*, esp. chap. 5.

support for their approach in various types of postmodern hermeneutics in which the reader's contribution to the interpretation is seen as inevitable and even desirable. Others, however, claim that we should hear the Old Testament's voice for what it is without reading the Christian interpretation into the Old Testament. In such a debate, the unfortunate choice seems to be between respect for the true meaning of the Old Testament and the loss of the Old Testament's relevance for the church. Must we choose, or is this a false dilemma? Important for this debate is Childs's criticism of the suggestion of Rolf Rendtorff and Walter Brueggemann that the church should not attempt to understand the Old Testament as preparation for the New, but rather should see it as intrinsically not Christian. They seem to think that viewing the Hebrew Bible as Christian is an insult to the Jewish community—a kind of theft of their sacred Scripture. Childs notes, however, that to take the advice of Rendtorff and Brueggemann is to judge the New Testament's interpretation of the Old as "in no sense normative" but only as "a creative imaginative construal."[27] He calls this a "fundamental theological error." In Childs's view, such proposals fall outside the scope of the common Christian exegetical tradition: "Christians see in the Old Testament a genuine continuity with the New, integral to its textual meaning, whether expressed in a pattern of sacred history or of an ontological unity undergirding the two testaments."[28]

This is a highly significant point, because it reminds us that the crucial issue is not what the apostles read into the Hebrew Scriptures, nor is it the christological interpretation they gave those Scriptures. Rather, the crucial question is what those Scriptures mean. When Paul went into the synagogue in a new city on his missionary journeys and debated about whether Jesus was the Messiah prophesied by the Scriptures, the only issue that mattered was whether Paul was reading Christ *out* of the text or reading Christ *into* the text. This was all that mattered, both to him and to his debating partners. On that point hung the question of the appropriateness of conversion to Christianity. Paul's whole life (and those of the other apostles) was staked (both figuratively and literally) on the belief that Jesus was correct when he said that the Scriptures testified to him. This conviction must be seen as absolutely central in the exegetical approach of the Great Tradition and must be a cornerstone of any hermeneutic that could be considered adequate for the church today or tomorrow.

27. Childs, *Struggle to Understand Isaiah*, 307. The phrase is used by Childs to describe Brueggemann's proposal.
28. Childs, *Struggle to Understand Isaiah*, 308. I find Childs to be crystal clear on this issue here, but in his earlier writings this same clarity is often missing.

4. The Divine and Human Authorship of Scripture

Childs notes that the church has always confessed that Scripture is both human and divine speech. For Thomas Aquinas, God is the author of Scripture, and the human authors are the "instrumental cause." Childs continues, "Thus for Thomas there was no great tension between the two. The literal sense is what the human authors intended in their writings, but because God, the ultimate author of scripture, comprehends everything all at once in his understanding, a multiplicity of senses can also be derived from the one divine intention."[29] There is much here that is right, but there is a slight overemphasis on the link between the human intention and the literal sense, which implies that the spiritual sense must derive from divine authorship. The problem is that this separates the two senses too sharply, which was the problem with which the tradition wrestled during the patristic and early medieval era, when the literal sense and the allegorical sense threatened to pull the text apart. How can Augustine's "christological literalism" or Thomas Aquinas's "double-literal sense" work if the literal sense is restricted to human authorial intention and the spiritual sense is restricted to divine authorial intention? We will return to this problem in chapters 6 and 7, but just to anticipate a little, I suggest that we should consider moving the exclusive focus away from human authorial intention to the meaning of the text itself. We are not *simply* listening to the human prophets and apostles themselves; rather, we are seeking to understand texts that they wrote under the influence of inspiration. Ultimately, it is the divine author who speaks through these texts; the human writers are mere servants of the Word, as are contemporary preachers and teachers. I believe that some such account is the logical outcome of the trajectory of the tradition described by Childs, which is why I raise it here.

Childs notes that for Calvin there was little tension between the divine and human authorship of Scripture. As in the case of Aquinas, for Calvin the undeniable fact that the Scriptures were written by human beings and reflect the unique literary style of the different authors did not in any way lessen the truth that the Scriptures are also the words of God addressing us with authority. However, Childs also observes that, under pressure from the English Deists, this coherence began to fall apart and orthodox apologists sought new strategies to defend divine authorship by means of emphasizing its inerrancy. The nineteenth-century emphasis on human authorship "overwhelmed" such efforts, in Childs's opinion. I think it would be possible to view the history a bit differently. The decline of liberal Protestantism and the continuing health and growth of worldwide evangelicalism renders the word

---

29. Childs, *Struggle to Understand Isaiah*, 309.

"overwhelmed" a bit of an overstatement. Maybe it describes the current situation in left-wing-dominated Ivy League universities. It is also true, however, that the nineteenth century saw the translation of Calvin's commentaries into English and the phenomenal growth of Calvinism throughout the world during the next century. Liberals in every generation are surprised all over again to discover that Calvinism is not just something found in dusty history books. The Christian church has exhibited a surprisingly strong resistance to the theological liberalism that renders the Bible a merely human work.

5. The Christological Content of the Christian Bible

The next common feature of the exegesis of the Great Tradition is the christological focus of the Bible as a whole, which is a question that cannot be separated from the related one of whether the Bible has a determinate meaning of any kind. Childs puts the question squarely:

> Is there a determinate meaning within the biblical texts of the Christian Bible? Traditional Christian exegesis took it for granted that the biblical witness was directed toward a specific reference. Its testimony provided access to the mysteries of divine reality. At times the reality perceived was earthly, bound in time and space. At other times it was a transcendent reality related directly or indirectly to sense perception, but requiring divine inspiration for its full comprehension. Accordingly, Scripture contains multiple meanings, but all joined in some manner to a referent. The derogatory dismissal of myths and fables in the New Testament (1 Tim. 1:4; 4:7; 2 Tim. 4:4; 2 Pet. 1:16) was set in contrast to a proclamation based on what "we have heard, . . . seen with our eyes, . . . looked upon and touched with our hands" (1 John 1:1).[30]

I have reproduced this long quotation because it is such a good summary of how the various aspects of the exegetical tradition intersect and support one another. Here Childs says that the Bible has a "determinate meaning." This is called in theology the clarity of Scripture; it has a message that can be understood by those open to hearing what God has to say, even if the reader does not have a PhD in ancient history. The "specific reference" is the "divine reality," which is to say that the *res* (or subject matter or content) of the Bible is God. This message is not always clear in the sense of being easily perceived by earthly means, yet the multiple meanings or layers of meaning all refer back to the one referent, God. The fact that God is the referent means that the witness of the Bible is something entirely different from the mythological

---

30. Childs, *Struggle to Understand Isaiah*, 313.

talk of "the gods" in ancient Near Eastern and Greco-Roman cultures. Those gods are merely personifications of the forces of nature or nature considered as a whole or else created spiritual beings posing as the true God. In myth, humans talk about the cosmos of which we are a part. But in Scripture, it is not just that the prophets and apostles are talking about the transcendent Creator and Lord (which in itself would make the Bible unique), but it is also that God actually speaks through them to us today.

Childs notes that the historical-critical approach, which he says arose from the Enlightenment, assumed that the referent of the Bible could be understood according to its literal/historical sense. What Childs does not note at this point is the way in which the Enlightenment redefined the meaning of "history." No longer was history what John meant by "what we have heard . . . seen . . . looked upon and touched" (1 John 1:1), meaning both the earthly Jesus and the divine Christ; for the historical critics, history could be only the earthly Jesus and nothing more. Thus the referent was changed from God to earthly realities contained within the naturalistic concept of the cosmos. By defining the "literal/historical" sense in naturalistic terms, historical criticism cut itself off irrevocably from the referent of the Bible and thus could never hope to understand the Bible's true meaning. By making this move, modern historical criticism became unscientific. It substituted mythology for theology.

Childs then notes that a powerful assault has recently been launched against the historical-critical method by postmodernists, who "challenge the self-confidence of the historical modernists as ignoring their own time-conditionality."[31] For postmodernists, meaning arises as a result of an interaction of reader, text, and context; no meaning is ever fixed or absolute. Postmodernists therefore make meaning more about the struggle for power than the search for truth. Childs says that the church thus finds itself being challenged on two fronts and needing to reaffirm its faith in a definite divine referent to which the text witnesses. He understands the canon to play a role here insofar as the concept of a canon is a witness to the christological meaning of the Bible. Childs singles out Walter Brueggemann as a postmodern interlocutor and, very surprisingly, seems to agree with him that the appeal to the rule of faith and canon is, in a sense, "a creative imaginative construal."[32] But Childs's position is seriously weakened by this apparent concession. At most, Childs can say that traditional exegesis rests on the faith of those making up the tradition: "a stance of faith."[33]

31. Childs, *Struggle to Understand Isaiah*, 314.
32. Childs, *Struggle to Understand Isaiah*, 315.
33. Childs, *Struggle to Understand Isaiah*, 316.

There are two problems with Childs's response. First, is it really true that the church today is being challenged on two fronts? Rather than seeing postmodernism as an alternative to modernism, we could better understand it as modernity in its decadent period. When the historical critics, under pressure from Enlightenment naturalism, backed off from acknowledging the divine voice speaking through the human authors of the Bible, they destroyed any hope of objective exegesis. There can never be objective truth in a cosmos characterized by the endless, purposeless flux of philosophical naturalism. Such a reality cannot even be called a "cosmos," because a cosmos means a unified reality. If history is simply narratives about events within the endless, purposeless flux, then historical texts merely present myths (descriptions of eternal, immanent, cyclical processes) or power struggles—or both. That conclusion was baked into modernity once Christian Platonism was rejected and nominalism, materialism, and mechanism were accepted. This conclusion preceded (and caused) the rationalism of the Enlightenment. Then, once rationalism failed, skepticism followed as surely as night follows day. Predictably, the historical critics attempted to respond to skepticism using only the historicist and rationalist weapons allowed them by modernity.[34] But they failed to stem the tide, and twentieth-century relativism inevitably followed.

The exegesis and dogmatics of the Great Tradition are objective in that they are a response called forth by the reality who speaks in the words of the prophets and apostles, the One who created the cosmos and guides it to its eschatological destiny in Christ. Skepticism is rooted in a lack of faith and cannot be defeated with rationality alone. Pure reason is as usable by those who are insane as by those who are sane. Only faith seeking understanding can overcome skepticism; yet it is crucial that Christians understand what it is that we confess. We confess that we believe in objective truth, not our "creative imaginative construal." We do not confess to have an eccentric faith stance that we can understand if others do not share, since there are many faith stances (and so also many gods). No, we confess faith in the one and only Creator of the universe and Lord of history, the one true God; we bear witness that this One has spoken in the Bible and has acted to save his people in the life, death, resurrection, ascension, heavenly session, and promised future return of the Lord Jesus Christ.

Second, and this is to anticipate the next section, Childs seems reluctant to challenge the concept of history presupposed by both the Enlightenment and postmodernists. The concept of history in the Great Tradition is not one

---

34. The greatest contemporary exponent of this strategy is N. T. Wright. For a critique of Wright's theology based on this insight, see Adams, *Reality of God and Historical Method*.

of "creative imaginative construals" about an eternal and purposeless flux. Jason Byassee astutely points out that Augustine is no less interested in history than any historical critic; he just has a different understanding of what history is. For Augustine, history is "creation called forth out of nothing in Christ to participate in the fullness of God, on its way to that goodness through its restoration in Christ."[35] What a marvelous definition! Teleology is central to this understanding of history. It is the distinctive feature of the uniquely Christian understanding of time and is what makes history *history* instead of myth. This notion of history is what modernity attempted, but ultimately failed, to secularize. Modern Western culture has attempted to jettison the theological metaphysics of the Great Tradition while maintaining a secular version of teleological history, but the dissolution of the Enlightenment into so-called postmodernism has revealed the utter failure of this project. We need to recover the Great Tradition's concept of history, which will necessitate a recovery of Christian Platonism as well. When we do this, we will find ourselves doing something that neither Enlightenment rationalism nor postmodern relativism can accept. This, however, should be no cause for panic on the part of the church; we just need to wait for modernity to finish collapsing and then carry on throughout the process of rebuilding culture on the ruins of Western modernity.[36] The church has done this before and can do it again.

6. The Dialectical Nature of History

Unfortunately, when Childs comes to the last two points of his seven-point description of the common exegetical approach of the Great Tradition, he stumbles. The central problem, already exposed in the discussion of history above, is that the "dialectical nature of history" that he puts forward in this sixth section is not a description of the understanding of history that has been held in the Great Tradition since the patristic age. Instead, it is a version of history that attempts to straddle the fence between the Great Tradition and the Enlightenment. In essence, a view derived from liberal theology instead of from the Great Tradition, it tries to paper over the great chasm between two irreconcilable worldviews.

Childs correctly observes that the fathers, such as Irenaeus, understood history in terms of "a special and unique purpose at work in the events of the world." He is also correct in saying that, up until the Enlightenment, Christian theologians attempted to describe the special quality of biblical history

---

35. Byassee, *Praise Seeking Understanding*, 252. Byassee is actually quoting Michael McCarthy's argument here. See McCarthy, *Revelatory Psalm*.

36. For a similar perspective, see the concluding paragraph of MacIntyre, *After Virtue*, 243.

in terms of the supernatural. But then he claims, without any explanation or supporting argumentation, that the concept of the supernatural was "not biblical." He also claims that when the Bible speaks of the miraculous, it is actually describing "surprising and unexpected activity of God, and often part of the natural world."[37] It is not entirely clear to me what this means, but it sounds like a repristination of early twentieth-century neoorthodoxy. God is somehow behind it all as a whole, but he does not speak or act personally into the flow of history in a supernatural way. So history, for Childs, turns out to be only naturalistic history, just as the Enlightenment said, although with an "interior" meaning that can be attributed to God *without impinging on the outer, naturalistic history*. There is lots of providence but a severe shortage of miracles. On this understanding of history, what would you have seen if you had been standing in front of Christ's tomb on Easter morning? Would the stone be rolled away or in place? Would the body be there or not? It is difficult to answer such questions on the basis of Childs's theory of "dialectical" history. Maybe it is unfair to imply that Childs left open the possibility of the resurrection not being an event of time and space and thus "historical" in the sense that the New Testament proclaims it to be, but he certainly left himself open to that interpretation. This theory of "dialectical" history fits with his response to Brueggemann, discussed above, and would explain in what sense he meant the statement that the canonical interpretation of the Bible could rightly be termed a "creative imaginative construal." Childs writes, "God's unique action in history cannot be fused with empirical history, nor can it be separated."[38] In this quotation, it must be observed, Childs is unable simply to say that God's action occurs *in* history or that history *is* God's action. God's action and empirical history remain two discrete entities, which somehow must be related dialectically to each other by scholars.[39]

37. Childs, *Struggle to Understand Isaiah*, 318. This sort of statement is typical of early twentieth-century neoorthodoxy and the biblical theology movement. As is well known, both neoorthodoxy and the biblical theology movement collapsed in the early 1960s because of trying to have it both ways on the issue of history. In chap. 2 I described the biblical doctrine of inspiration as composed of both providence and miracle; the biblical theology movement wanted revelation without miracle. Childs's earlier book, *Biblical Theology in Crisis*, 62–66, outlined the issues clearly. When one reads these two books by Childs, written thirty years apart, one is struck by the lack of progress made in resolving the problem of history, despite the clarity of vision he displayed in identifying the problem.

38. Childs, *Struggle to Understand Isaiah*, 320.

39. One can observe this same struggle to bring together an Enlightenment naturalistic view of history and the witness of the biblical text to God's supernatural activity in history in Childs's discussion of the resurrection of Christ in his *New Testament as Canon*. Childs points out that Barth opposes Bultmann's interpretation that the faith of the early church created the resurrection (the subjective interpretation) with his own view that the resurrection created

I contend that the problem of bringing God's action and empirical history together cannot be resolved except by means of a metaphysics that provides a context in which they are not foreign to each other in the first place. This is the problem when one does not reject philosophical naturalism root and branch. It was the Enlightenment (building on ancient Greek philosophical skepticism) that first demanded that "history" be understood in a naturalistic sense. Without that biased and unwarranted assumption, the so-called problem of faith and history would not exist in the first place. Secularists accuse Christians of not being able to put empirical history and God's action together, but it was the secularists who separated them in the first place. If a guest takes an expensive piece of china from your table and smashes it on the floor, it is irrational to blame the owner for not being able to reassemble it adequately. The fault lies with the one who did the smashing. The most the owner can do is to bar the guest from having access to the dining room in the future. It is time to expel the Enlightenment culture-wreckers from positions of cultural, or at least ecclesial, influence. Failing that, we should at least lock up the china.

What is required in place of the philosophical naturalism of the Enlightenment is a "participatory metaphysics," such as Matthew Levering proposes in a helpful act of *ressourcement*. Levering is responding specifically to the problem Childs bequeaths to us; his advice is that the road to the future runs through the past. The virtue of Levering's book *Participatory Biblical Exegesis* is its detailed tracing of participatory exegesis through the Christian tradition in the way that one can only wish Childs had been able to do in *The Struggle to Understand Isaiah as Christian Scripture*. What we learn from Levering is that the problem of history is really a clash of metaphysical systems and that the biblical and traditional Christian understanding of history cannot be sustained within a naturalistic worldview such as that of the Enlightenment

---

the faith of the early church (the objective interpretation). Childs speaks of these two views as being at a "stalemate" and seeks to find a way that does not simply accept one and reject the other. The tension between his dialectical approach and the biblical text itself is palpable, however, and comes out into the open when he writes: "The problem with the usual application of the historical-critical method—the so-called subjective option—is not in its recognizing the sociological setting of the tradents of the tradition. Rather, it rests in allowing these factors to determine the text's meaning even when such an interpretation runs against the explicit testimony of those who shaped the texts. As a result of claiming to know better than the text itself, they only succeed in rendering its theological witness mute" (209). This judgment is clearly correct; the mystery is why Childs feels the need to move back and forth in hopes of somehow reconciling a true and responsible interpretation of the text (Barth's) with a clearly false and unbelieving one (Bultmann's). This seems to be a case of knowing the truth but hoping there is some way to reconcile truth and error in one system of hermeneutics, which would seem to be a hopeless and unproductive endeavor.

and postmodernism. This is why my sketch of Christian Platonism in chapter 3 was necessary prior to this chapter. In Christian Platonism we have a metaphysical basis for a participatory exegesis. In Christian Platonism, history exists as an aspect of creation, and creation continues in existence only by virtue of its participation in ideas in the mind of God. Creation, including the history of creation, is not separate from God or autonomous or self-existent. History occurs within the realm of divine providence and is directed by God to its appointed end. So there is no need to "bring together" God's action and empirical history, because they were never separated in the first place. Let us waste no more time on pseudoproblems created by skepticism and unbelief; instead, let us attend to the task of explicating how history participates in God's providence, a task greatly in need of attention by theologians.

7. History and the Final Form of the Text

In his final section, Childs tries to defend his (and the Great Tradition's) decision to focus on the final form of the text (the canonical form) against critics who charge him with neglecting the importance of the prior compositional stages. The lurking implication of the accusation is the postmodern concept that one stage of the text is as authoritative as another, since all are human efforts. Why should the final form be singled out as authoritative? Childs does not appeal to the miraculous preservation of the text as a work of the Holy Spirit, since he does not view the divine activity as something that can be perceived from the historical standpoint. He argues that both historical criticism of the Bible, using a history-of-religions approach, and theological interpretation of the canonical form are legitimate enterprises, and thus he basically appeals for a nonaggression pact between philosophical naturalism and theological interpretation. The terms are something like the following: I will not ask you to believe in miracles, if you allow me to use the Bible as sacred Scripture for my Christian community. Tensions arise, however, from fractious elements on both sides. The hotheads called the "new atheists" cannot keep themselves from attacking what they perceive Childs to have admitted to be merely a "creative imaginative construal"—a soft target if there ever was one. And the preachers, evangelists, and apologists of the church cannot agree to stop proclaiming that the LORD is the one true God of creation and history, who calls all people everywhere to bow before him in worship. He is not merely our "creative imaginative construal" but the objectively existent first cause of the universe, who has revealed himself supremely in Jesus Christ as the only Savior of the world. For atheists and philosophical naturalists, the unpleasant truth is that the world we inhabit is a purposeless flux that we have to try to manage as best we can by the human will exerted through technology. For the Christian Great Tradition, the world is "creation called out of nothing by Christ, on its way to its fulfillment in the New Heavens and New Earth."[40] Both versions of the nature of history cannot be correct, and no "dialectical" concept of history will suffice to reconcile them.

The Great Disruption: Exegesis of Scripture in Modernity

The Great Tradition was a three-legged stool made up of spiritual exegesis, Nicene dogma, and Christian Platonist metaphysics. By pressing deep into the meaning of the text contemplatively, spiritual exegesis yielded the trinitarian and christological dogmas, which in turn generated certain metaphysical doctrines such as creation *ex nihilo* and the reality of the spiritual realm. The metaphysics then created a hospitable context for further spiritual exegesis in which the interpreter penetrated through the literal sense to that to which the text referred, the spiritual or heavenly realities that led upward eventually to participation in the divine radiance. It was all based on a sacramental ontology in which creaturely things—words—were taken up into the divine and made into signs, which conveyed the reality to which they pointed. Great Tradition exegesis was and is a profoundly spiritual and moral act in which the interpreter who succeeds in grasping the true *res* or subject matter of the text is irrevocably transformed in the process—sanctified and turned into one who possesses eternal life.

To some Protestants, all this talk of sacramental ontology and trinitarian dogma may sound vaguely Roman Catholic and therefore suspect. But nothing could be more quintessentially Protestant than the sacramental nature of the Word of God. Nothing could be more quintessentially evangelical than the transformation of sinners into saints through the preaching of the Word. The Word of God is the link between God and sinners; through the Word of God, we experience union with Christ through calling, regeneration, justification, adoption, sanctification, and preserving grace. So when we talk about biblical interpretation, we are not just talking about some sort of academic exercise in which people argue about the best intellectual construct to use in describing their faith. We are talking about the heart of the gospel itself—the essence of our faith.

This is why the great disruption of modernity is so serious. It is a dagger in the heart of our faith. In the previous chapter I proposed a reading of

40. Michael McCarthy as quoted by Byassee, *Praise Seeking Understanding*, 252.

Western intellectual history in which modernity is defined as the systematic, point-by-point rejection of Christian Platonism as the key to understanding the rise and fall of modern Western culture. In this section, my goal is to try to use this reading of Western intellectual history to understand the nature and reasons for the changes in biblical interpretation since the eighteenth century. In the previous chapter, we saw that modernity can be divided into three basic stages: early modernity (1300–1650), high modernity or the Enlightenment (1650–1800), and late modernity (1800–present). The first period saw the breakdown of the medieval synthesis of faith and reason and the rise of nominalism, mechanism, and materialism. The second period saw the rise of atheism and rationalism, along with the beginning of skepticism. The third period saw the romantic rebellion against Enlightenment rationalism followed by the slow decay of Western modernity into relativism, nihilism, and despair. But here our main focus must be on the interpretation of the Bible during this period. It is arguable that the changes in how the Bible was interpreted during this period constitute the key to understanding contemporary Western culture. This should not be surprising, since the Bible was foundational to the creation of Western culture in the first place.

Early Modernity: From Christian Platonism to Nominalism, Mechanism, and Materialism

In his illuminating book *The Theological Origins of Modernity*, Michael Allen Gillespie explains that the breakdown of the medieval synthesis in the fourteenth century led to the emergence of a new conception of God in Western Europe. Ironically, this "new" view of God is amazingly similar to at least some interpretations of the Islamic view of God, which is a central point in Pope Benedict XVI's Regensburg Address. The view of God in Western modernity is growing closer to the view of God in Islam as it moves away from trinitarian classical theism. It could be described as a concept of God stripped of his Logos (or Reason or Word).[41]

One sixteenth-century European intellectual who resisted the gravitational pull of the new concept of God as sheer will, unconstrained by universals, was John Calvin.[42] Calvin thought from within the theological metaphysics of the

41. Speaking of late-medieval voluntarism, Benedict points out that developments in this line of thinking "clearly approach those of Ibn Hazm and might even lead to the image of a capricious God, who is not even bound to truth and goodness" (in Schall, *Regensburg Lecture*, 137, pars. 25–26).

42. For a discussion of Calvin's attacks on late-medieval nominalism, see Muller, *Unaccommodated Calvin*, chap. 3, esp. 46–52. Muller writes that Calvin's comments on scholasticism were "a rather pointed and precise attack *not* on the older scholastic tradition but on a strain

Great Tradition; he was a Christian Platonist in the sense in which I am using the term. [43] He famously remarked at the beginning of his *Institutes of the Christian Religion* that our concepts of God and man are bound together so closely that our concept of one is always affected by changes in our concept of the other. [44] This insight contains a crucial clue to understanding the relationship between the rise of technological science in the Enlightenment and the Enlightenment concept of God. As early modern European culture moved away from special revelation, there was a tendency to see both God and humans in God's image as primarily "willing beings." Early modernity witnessed a new concept of God as characterized primarily by will. The seventeenth century saw the rise of Arminianism and the concept of libertarian or uncaused free will as a defining feature of human beings. The essence of humanity in the image of this new God of sheer will is—what else?—absolute, uncaused will.

The God of nominalism—the God of sheer will—is a terrifying being to us limited, fragile human beings. This kind of God is eerily similar to the ancient mythological gods, who were personifications of the blind, irrational forces of nature. The essence of pagan religion is fear; it is the response of terrified human beings in the face of forces they could not control, which threatened their livelihoods and even their lives. But in the Enlightenment, the new physics led to technological applications that promised to give human beings the possibility of at least some measure of control over the blind, irrational forces of nature that seemed to their ancestors to be beyond human control. God, in the early modern mind, was a symbol of a nature that threatened human life

---

of contemporary scholastic theology viewed by Calvin as especially problematic in view of its extreme nominalism" (52).

43. Some historians of ideas tend to lump the Reformation in with the breakdown of the medieval synthesis, the Renaissance, and the Enlightenment as all part of one movement called "modernity." See, e.g., Gregory, *Unintended Reformation*. However, I would follow Richard Muller in pointing out that the Reformation led to Protestant scholasticism and that much of the work of Thomas Aquinas was received enthusiastically in both Lutheran and Reformed scholastic theology. The whole picture is complex and does not lend itself to easy summary. John Owen is one of many examples of Protestant theologians who engage Aquinas appreciatively and reject nominalism. See Muller, *After Calvin*. I would argue that although both Roman Catholic and Protestant theology include figures who stood against the cultural tide as modernity swelled, both traditions were greatly influenced by modernity in negative ways as well. The negative influence of the Enlightenment affected all Christian theology in the West, which is why the *ressourcement* movement led by thinkers like Henri de Lubac in the mid-twentieth century was necessary. One could argue that evangelical Protestants are just awakening to the need for *ressourcement*.

44. The opening words of Calvin's magisterial *Institutes* are "Nearly all the knowledge we possess, that is to say, true and sound wisdom, consists of two parts: the knowledge of God and of ourselves. But, while joined by many bonds, which one precedes and brings forth the other is not easy to discern" (Calvin, *Institutes*, 35).

with chaos and death and was thus a symbol of that which must be overcome, tamed, and brought under rational, scientific, human control.

High Modernity: Enlightenment Rationalism

Something new emerged in the Enlightenment in terms of biblical interpretation; the question is how to define it. Many authors make the perfectly valid point that the historical-critical method is not actually one method but a family of methods.[45] But we should notice that most modern biblical scholars are quite clear on which methods are in the family and which are not. There is no doubt that source criticism, form criticism, and redaction criticism are all historical-critical methods and that allegory, typology, and discerning the *sensus plenior* are not. What is not always made clear is the criterion or criteria by which this distinction is made. Some evangelical biblical scholars today seem naively to think the difference is that modern methods are careful, scholarly, and based on original language study, while premodern methods are a hodgepodge of baseless opinion, carelessly proffered and accepted credulously. In other words, modern methods are scientific, but premodern ones are crudely amateurish. Anyone who has ever actually read a premodern commentator like Origen, Augustine, or Thomas Aquinas knows that this is a wildly irresponsible exaggeration at best. And such a fantasy can be sustained only by ignoring the Kantian and Hegelian elephants in the room of nineteenth-century historical criticism.

It was the heretical Jew, Baruch Spinoza, who blazed the trail for the development of rationalistic biblical criticism, and his motives were political in nature. In his *Theological-Political Treatise*, he laid down the basis for a new kind of biblical interpretation. The goal is "to free society from the destructive force of religious passion."[46] As a cosmopolitan, antimonarchist, capitalist, and internationalist, Spinoza regarded all religions as based in superstition and as breeding grounds for cruelty, fear, hatred, and violence. Basically, he mistook human nature in its fallen condition for religious faith.[47] Eradicating religion from seventeenth-century Europe was not a feasible possibility, so the next best thing was to place it under the control of "reason," which basically is code for Epicurean metaphysics. This is why Spinoza thought that historical-critical

45. E.g., see Watson, "Does Historical Criticism Exist?," 307–18.
46. Harrisville and Sundberg, *Bible in Modern Culture*, 42.
47. Spinoza would have been shocked to find that the irreligious and even antireligious regimes in twentieth-century Russia and China engaged in antihuman brutality and murder to an extent that made the seventeenth-century Wars of Religion look like a mere dress rehearsal. How could this be if the true solution to the problem of violence is to get rid of religion?

study must be free of ecclesiastical control. He reduces the truth of Scripture to "what agrees with the understanding of the autonomous biblical critic free of dogmatic commitments."[48] Spinoza insists that the Bible be treated like any other book, and he "rejects the dogmatic tradition of exegesis."[49] For him, the truth of Scripture is "that which is recognizable to unaided human reason."[50] Basically, this is a dismissal of special revelation; Spinoza rejects all forms of miracle and revives ancient Epicureanism. Epicurus (341–270 BC) had viewed the fear of the gods as the basic source of human unhappiness; he taught that the gods are indifferent to humans. Happiness consists of ridding oneself of the fear of God.[51] When Richard Dawkins's atheist group put an advertisement on the London transit system in 2009 that read "There's probably no God. Now stop worrying and enjoy your life," he was promoting ancient Epicureanism all over again.[52] Whether he had any idea that he was parroting the ideas of an ancient Greek philosopher and some seventeenth-century Enlightenment thinkers is not known. It is not as if these ideas were discovered by modern scientists in a lab somewhere; they are quite old-fashioned.

Spinoza's ideas led to much controversy, eliciting both followers and opponents; gradually, however, those who supported his ideas found that they were gaining the ascendency in European cultural life. Richard Simon (1638–1712) published his *Critical History of the Old Testament* in 1678, which disputed Mosaic authorship of the Pentateuch.[53] John Toland (1670–1722) and Matthew Tindal (1657–1733) were examples of radical Deist writers who asserted, "For a religion to be true it must correspond to universal human experience."[54] As for the sophist Protagoras in Plato's dialogue *Protagoras*, man is, for these rationalists, "the measure of all things."[55] The Bible must be treated like any other book. Insofar as it conforms to "rational religion," it is to be respected; when it does not, it must be subjected to critique. This was the complete rejection of biblical authority.

48. Harrisville and Sundberg, *Bible in Modern Culture*, 39. Spinoza assumed that anyone free of ecclesiastical control would think as he did and embrace Epicurean metaphysical views. For a discussion of ancient pagan philosophical ideas that were important to the early modern philosophers, see Wilson, *Epicureanism at the Origins of Modernity*. Her discussion of Spinoza can be found on pp. 125–35.

49. Harrisville and Sundberg, *Bible in Modern Culture*, 41.

50. Harrisville and Sundberg, *Bible in Modern Culture*, 42. "Unaided human reason" means for Spinoza something suspiciously like "thinking like Baruch Spinoza."

51. See Festugière, *Epicurus and His Gods*.

52. See https://humanism.org.uk/campaigns/successful-campaigns/atheist-bus-campaign. See also Wilson, *Epicureanism at the Origins of Modernity*.

53. Harrisville and Sundberg, *Bible in Modern Culture*, 47.

54. Harrisville and Sundberg, *Bible in Modern Culture*, 48.

55. As quoted by Feser, *Last Superstition*, 31.

Hermann Samuel Reimarus (1694–1768) embodied in his person the clash between orthodoxy and Enlightenment rationalism. He was born to devout parents who taught him scholastic Protestant orthodoxy, and he studied classical languages and philosophy. Exposed to the radical ideas of Enlightenment rationalism, he nevertheless took a post teaching Oriental languages at the Hamburg gymnasium, which included lecturing on the preaching texts from the Gospels assigned to the various Sundays of the church year. He attacked the faith in private while defending it in public and found comfort in reading Spinoza.[56] After his death, his work, *Apology or Defense for the Rational Worshippers of God*, finally came to light and revealed his private views. He clearly rejects special revelation, miracles, prophecies, and the resurrection of Christ. Roy Harrisville and Walter Sundberg sum up his position: "It is clear that in the view of Reimarus, Augustinian Christianity, with its electing God, atoning Lord, and salvation by imputed grace is alien to natural religion—the latter conceived to be a process of humanization and a struggle for political freedom."[57] The Enlightenment founders of the historical-critical study of the Bible had a faith, but it was a different faith from Christianity; it was progressivism based on philosophical naturalism.

While many people were content to follow the logical implications of naturalism into atheism and to reject Christianity altogether, others sensed the shallowness of naturalism and its inadequacy as a foundation for a healthy and thriving civilization. Biblical interpretation in the nineteenth century would be influenced by such people who desired to overcome the deleterious effects of naturalism by working from within naturalism. Such people followed Hegel in elevating History (with a capital *H*) to the status of the cause of all things and the moving force by which all things are directed to their final destiny. It was an attempt to overcome the Enlightenment from within the myth of progress advocated by the Enlightenment and from within the Epicurean metaphysics presupposed by the Enlightenment. What is important to see is that the Hegelian metaphysics did not really challenge naturalism; it merely reinterpreted it in such a way that what seemed to its proponents to be crucially important—ethics, art, humanistic ideals in general—could be preserved amid the acids of modernity. Such a reinterpretation of naturalism applied to biblical interpretation involved the application to the Bible of an evolutionary scheme in which biblical religion was interpreted as mythical and seen as the first stage of Christianity, which must progress from myth to history and finally to philosophy.

56. Harrisville and Sundberg, *Bible in Modern Culture*, 52.
57. Harrisville and Sundberg, *Bible in Modern Culture*, 58.

One of the prime movers in this application of myth to the New Testament was David Strauss.

Late Modernity: Romanticism, Skepticism, and Relativism

In the life and thought of David Friedrich Strauss (1808–74), we see the contours of this alternative religion sketched out quite clearly in *The Old Faith and the New*, written two years before his death. Strauss rejected theism altogether and the doctrine that God created the world, the possibility of miracles, the divinity of Christ, and Christianity in general. He proposed a new religion based on Hegelian philosophy and Darwinian evolution in which man creates the future by means of technological science. How did Strauss get to this point?

As a student, Strauss was opposed to rationalism and even won an essay competition put on by the Catholic faculty of Tübingen on the topic of the resurrection. Afterward he wrote, "I proved the resurrection of the dead with full conviction and when I made my last point, it was clear to me there was nothing to the entire story."[58] He began to study Hegel's philosophy, since those who are throwing off Augustine and Plato need some sort of metaphysics to take the place of what they are abandoning. He wrote his *Life of Jesus Critically Examined* because he thought that Schleiermacher's *Life of Jesus* was not radical enough. Of special interest to us is the fifty-page introduction that sets forth his method of biblical interpretation. Basically, Strauss argues here for the application of the category of myth to the New Testament.

In the introduction, Strauss sketches the history of modern higher criticism. He begins with the Greek philosophical critique of Greek religion in which two different courses were pursued: one was to reject the miraculous parts and treat the stories as myths expressing an idea; the other was to reject the miraculous and accept a historical kernel as true, with miraculous details added later to embellish the narrative. These two approaches could be termed historical and mythological, and Strauss explains that it was mainly the historical approach that was applied to Christianity during the Enlightenment. The only church father he mentions is Origen, whom he basically equates with Philo, and he interprets Origen's allegorical method as an example of the mythological approach.[59] This, however, does not begin to do justice to Origen, as more recent scholarship makes clear.

Strauss contrasts the Deists and naturalistic thinkers of the Enlightenment with those who sought a mythological meaning. He contrasts the naturalists,

---

58. As quoted in Harrisville and Sundberg, *Bible in Modern Culture*, 88.
59. D. F. Strauss, *Life of Jesus*, 41.

who simply opposed Christianity and all forms of revealed religion, with the rationalists, who wanted to remain within the church. The rationalists viewed the biblical writers as having no choice but to write in mythological terms. Strauss writes, "Eichhorn observes that before the human race had gained a knowledge of the true causes of all things, all occurrences were referred to supernatural agencies, or to the interpositions of superhuman beings."[60] However, as Strauss points out, previous writers have been hesitant to apply the mythological understanding to the New Testament narratives. He considered Kant to be doing something similar to the allegorical interpretation of the church fathers when he distilled the meaning of the Scriptures into a moral sense that he believed was latent in the human mind and came to expression in the biblical narratives. According to Kant, the Bible must be interpreted "in a sense which agrees with the universal practical laws of a religion of pure reason."[61] Essentially, Strauss regarded the allegorical method as extracting a rational idea from the text that the interpreter represents as the "kernel," while the "husk" of historical truth is discarded. For Strauss, both Origen and Kant read meaning into the text from outside the text (not that Strauss thought that there was necessarily anything wrong with doing that).

Strauss also distinguishes between historical myth and philosophical myth. Historical myth understands a text as containing narratives that mix the natural and the supernatural, which means that the interpreter's job must be to separate these elements from each other. Philosophical myth, however, sees the meaning of a text as a simple idea, thought, or precept that the narrative conveys in the form of a story.[62] Essentially, a philosophical myth is like a parable in that the basis in historical fact, or lack thereof, is quite irrelevant. In a passage important enough to quote at length, Strauss writes:

> In adopting the mythical point of view as hitherto applied to biblical history, our theologians had again approximated to the ancient allegorical interpretation. For as both the natural explanations of the rationalists, and the jesting expositions of the Deists, belong to that form of opinion which, while it sacrifices all divine meaning in the sacred record, still upholds its historical character; the mythical mode of interpretation agrees with the allegorical, in relinquishing the historical reality of the sacred narratives in order to preserve to them an absolute inherent truth. The mythical and the allegorical view (as also the moral) equally allow that the historian apparently relates that which is historical, but they suppose him, under the influence of a higher inspiration known or unknown

60. D. F. Strauss, *Life of Jesus*, 49.
61. D. F. Strauss, *Life of Jesus*, 51.
62. D. F. Strauss, *Life of Jesus*, 53.

to himself, to have made use of this historical semblance merely as the shell of an *idea*—of a religious conception. The only essential difference between these two modes of explanation is, that according to the allegorical this higher intelligence is the immediate divine agency; according to the mythical, it is the spirit of a people or a community. . . . Thus the allegorical view attributes the narrative to a supernatural source, whilst the mythical view ascribes it to that natural process by which legends are originated and developed.[63]

In this passage, Strauss tries to justify his mythological approach to the Bible by showing how close it is to the ancient practice of allegorical interpretation and how different it is from Enlightenment naturalism and its view of the text as historical myth. He says that both the allegorical view and his view of philosophical myth see the meaning of the text in an idea pictured in the narrative.[64] Naturalism, in contrast, sacrifices the religious meaning of the text by saving its historical kernel, which it sees as the true meaning. The only difference between allegory and philosophical myth is that the former sees the meaning as coming directly from God, while the latter sees the meaning as arising out of the "spirit of a people or community." That means that the latter works on the basis of philosophical naturalism.

Two questions need to be asked of Strauss's position. First, is he fair to the church fathers, by which I mean, does he describe the allegorical method correctly? If the research discussed earlier in this chapter has any validity whatsoever, it is clear that the answer to this question must be an emphatic "No." Strauss spectacularly misunderstands the relationship between the literal and spiritual senses in the Great Tradition. He presents it as a crude reading of "higher" ideas into the biblical text, which is a fair description of the Enlightenment, but not even close to being a fair description of the fathers, who wrestled conscientiously and continuously with the problem of the relation of the literal and spiritual senses. Second, we must ask if there is any significant difference between the "philosophical myth" position and the naturalist position that Strauss contrasts to it. Is it not a distinction without a real difference? It would seem that to regard the Bible as containing philosophical myth is, in substance, not all that different from regarding it as superfluous, primitive, and irrelevant to the modern world. We can see this clearly in Strauss's discussion of miracles and creation.

Since Strauss has already accepted a mechanistic metaphysics of nature, the idea of providence no longer makes any sense to him. He writes, "Our

63. D. F. Strauss, *Life of Jesus*, 65.
64. The background of this concept of the relationship between religion and philosophy is, of course, Hegelian.

modern world . . . has attained a conviction, that all things are linked by a
chain of causes and effects, which suffers no interruption . . . the totality of
finite things forms a vast circle which, except that it owes its existence and
laws to a superior power, suffers no intrusion from without."[65] He defines
his opponents' view, that is, "supernaturalism," as the belief that the world
is a self-sufficient entity operating by its own immanent laws on which God
acts from the outside.[66] He believes that this idea that God can intervene to
do miracles is inconsistent with the doctrine of God: "The proposition that
God sometimes works mediately, sometimes immediately, upon the world,
introduces changeableness, and therefore a temporal element, into the nature
of his action."[67] The problem here is clear: Strauss finds the Christian doctrine
of miracles problematic because of his attempts to fit it into a mechanistic,
materialist metaphysics.

Since Strauss is working from a mechanistic view of the universe, rather than
a Christian Platonist view, he does not see God's involvement with the world
as a constant upholding of the universe in being, as Scripture teaches and the
theological metaphysics of the Great Tradition elaborates. He understands
the world to be self-sustaining, even if it required a Creator to get it started.
(Eventually Strauss denied even that.) But Christian orthodoxy understands
God alone to be self-sustaining; the being of the world participates in the
Logos and thus has existence. Since God is not at work all the time in the
world, according to the mechanistic metaphysics, a miracle is an "interference" with the creation from the outside. It is easy to see why people might
think that such interference is illogical. Why make it able to operate on its
own by cause and effect, only to meddle with it occasionally? The answer, of
course, is that God did not make the world to operate on its own, according

---

65. D. F. Strauss, *Life of Jesus*, 78.

66. This definition, of course, is quite different from the definition of supernaturalism in
the Great Tradition, in which the world is not self-sufficient and does not operate according
to its own laws with God on the "outside." In the Great Tradition, God is immanent as well
as transcendent and upholds the being of the world in existence at every moment of every
day, which makes God the ultimate cause of all that happens. The Great Tradition, therefore,
understands a miracle as God acting in a way that seems unusual to us, but such action is not
in principle different from the ongoing providential action of God that occurs all the time. God
is not foreign to the world in the Great Tradition, as he is in modern philosophy. In modern
metaphysics, the attribute of self-existence (aseity) is transferred from God to the world, which
makes the world equal in divinity to God and thus reduces God to a being among beings (theistic
personalism). God and the world confront each other as two self-existent and self-sufficient
entities in modernity, which sets up all sorts of pseudophilosophical problems including free
will versus determinism, the mind-body problem, the problem of causation, the problem of
miracles, and so on.

67. D. F. Strauss, *Life of Jesus*, 79.

to the classical Christian understanding of creation and providence.[68] Once again, the Enlightenment has created a pseudoproblem that is not a problem in the Great Tradition and exists only when the Christian Platonism of the Great Tradition is arbitrarily rejected.

Miracles are the *unusual*, as opposed to the *usual*, manner of God's action, but they are not in essence different from the action of God that is going on at every moment of history. God's action is God's action, whether it is providential or miraculous is a secondary point. It is only from our human perspective that an unusual action is surprising. Strauss cannot understand how God could act in history without changing, but, of course, no Great Tradition thinker has ever been presumptuous enough to think it possible for a human being to comprehend that from our finite perspective. What the Great Tradition says is that we confess it to be true that God *does* work in history even though God is simple, perfect, immutable, and transcendent. That he does so is a central point of the Christian confession; *how* he does so is beyond our comprehension. We believe it only because it happened. We do not believe in the incarnation because we can comprehend it rationally or derive its necessity from pure reason alone. We believe it because it is a fact that confronts us and calls us to believe; Jesus rose from the dead and ascended to the right hand of the Father. The apostolic testimony of the New Testament is astonishment at what has happened. The resurrected Christ creates faith in the disciples by appearing to them and convincing them that he is alive from the dead. That is the origin of Christian faith, not theorizing about what may or may not be possible. We believe because the apostolic witness is preached to us, and the Holy Spirit enables us to respond in faith to the good news. The rejection of Christian Platonism makes the mystery seem suspiciously like a contradiction instead of a paradox. But, we might wonder, why reject Christian Platonism in the first place? In fact, a Christian has no reason to do so, and the felt need of atheists to distance God from the world because they misunderstand the nature of God and mistakenly consider him a threat to their freedom does not constitute a valid reason.

Strauss, however, does have one valid point, and it is an important one. He makes clear that conservative modernists who oppose naturalism by searching for the historical core truths in the narrative are fighting a losing battle. He writes, "So true it is that supernaturalism clings with childlike fondness to the empty husk of historical semblance, though void of divine significance, and estimates it higher than the most valuable kernel divested of its variegated

68. See chap. 9, "On the Theology of Providence," in Webster, *God and the Works of God*, 127–42.

covering."[69] The temptation to abandon divine authorial intent and spiritual meaning and to accept the challenge to defend the historicity of the text as alone the source of meaning was very strong for those conservatives *who conceded the mechanistic view of the universe that drives modernity*. It would have been better for theological conservatives to be much *more* conservative than they were by never embracing modern, mechanistic metaphysics in the first place. The lesson we learn from this is that the mechanistic metaphysics must be resisted lest pseudoproblems be created and require solutions that dissolve the orthodox doctrine of God into heresy. Unfortunately, however, there is a conservative wing of the liberal project that strives to adapt Christianity to modern metaphysics at the lowest cost possible by arguing for as large a kernel of historical fact at the heart of the myth and legend surrounding it as possible. Strauss is right to discern this as a losing proposition, and so should we.

Strauss never renounced philosophical naturalism. His distinction between historical myth and philosophical myth was, in the end, a distinction without a difference. In the final analysis, all forms of myth deny the literal sense of Scripture. We must understand that the Bible, including the Old Testament no less than the New Testament, is not myth.[70] It is not comprehensible in terms of ancient Near Eastern mythological writings, nor is it comprehensible on the analogy of Greek and Roman myths. There is a vast chasm between myth and biblical history. It is Strauss's fable of the world as a self-existent, self-moving machine that is a myth. The Bible witnesses to a transcendent God who created all that is, upholds it all in being, and is Lord of history. By a combination of providence and miracle, God guides creation toward its appointed destiny to be redeemed through Christ as the kingdom of God. The difference is stark. In the Bible, God cannot be reduced to one being among beings within the overall cosmos; however, in all forms of mythology, the cosmos is all there is, so God must be conceived in one of three basic ways: (1) as a being within the cosmos (theistic personalism), (2) as a name for the cosmos as a whole (pantheism), or (3) as interdependent with the universe (panentheism). The first and third options are forms of relational theism, while the second is the oldest alternative to classical theism. The one thing God cannot ever be in any form of myth (historical or philosophical) is truly *transcendent* in the sense in which the Bible says God is.

Similarities between the Bible and the religious writings of the surrounding cultures do exist, but should not be overemphasized. As John Oswalt puts it:

---

69. D. F. Strauss, *Life of Jesus*, 66.

70. For a handy summary that spells out the difference between ancient Near Eastern myth and the Bible in a clear and concise manner, see Oswalt, *Bible among the Myths*.

To this point I have argued that the Bible is essentially different from the religious literatures of the ancient Near East, and indeed, of the rest of the world. I have maintained that the thought world of the Bible is so radically different from that of the others that the similarities that undoubtedly do exist between the Bible and the others are superficial and not essential. . . . The similarities do not indicate unity with the thought world around Israel but are the result of cultural adaptation, using readily available forms and terms to say something quite new.[71]

The basic problem with the position of Strauss and all the Enlightenment thinkers who adopted the nominalist, mechanistic, and materialistic metaphysics of modernity is that this metaphysics does not and *cannot* acknowledge what the Bible really is. That is a fatal error from which there is no recovery except repentance. There is no room in modern metaphysics for a special revelation from a transcendent God, so of course those committed to philosophical naturalism must fit the Bible onto the procrustean bed of myth. What else *could* they do if they are determined not to repent and believe the Christian gospel?

How the Narrative Needs to Be Revised

As the influence of the radical Enlightenment slowly seeped into every nook and cranny of European intellectual life through the eighteenth century, Western academic theology sank into a state of crisis. When Immanuel Kant died in 1804, the crisis consisted of three related problems. First, the influence of Hume and Kant seemed to many to close off any return to the theological metaphysics of the Great Tradition. Christian Platonism, which was now referred to in a condescending tone as "Greek metaphysics," was viewed as a burden to be shed as soon as possible. Adolf von Harnack worked diligently to craft a narrative of the rise of Christianity that made metaphysics an imposition on the simple faith of early Christians, but he was merely clearing the ground for the reconceptualizing of Christianity in terms of modern metaphysics. Second, special revelation was seen as a giant mistake resting on the old metaphysics and thus it had to be abandoned. This meant that Christianity had to be reinvented as the culture religion of modern progressivism, so it had to symbolize ideals that could be known by human reason apart from special revelation. Albrecht Ritschl was one who worked hard to make Christianity into an ethical religion compatible with modern progressivism. Third, with the demise of metaphysics, it was necessary to inflate "history" to "History"

71. Oswalt, *Bible among the Myths*, 85.

in such a way as to move the ideal of perfection from "up there," as in Christian Platonism, to "up ahead," as in the idea of history as progress. In other words, the cosmos was now viewed as a natural system in which there exists no other layer of reality or realm of universals or heaven or any such thing. We see this sort of thing all over twentieth-century academic theology; it can be traced back to Hegel. Philosophical naturalism had triumphed.

A great deal of Christian theology and biblical language now seemed to be in desperate need of reinterpretation. Sin, for example, was rethought in evolutionary terms as human nature that still retained elements of its animal ancestry. Heaven could be moved from "up there" to the end of history as the utopian goal of history. Whatever the specific details, and there were extensive debates about the right way to proceed, some such expedients were seen as absolutely necessary if Christianity was going to retain its respected place in European culture and in the burgeoning new research universities that grew up in the later nineteenth and early twentieth centuries, first in Germany, then in the rest of Europe, Britain, and North America, and finally around the world. Should there even be a faculty of theology in these new cultural institutions? If theology were locked into the metaphysics of the fourth or thirteenth centuries, why should it have any more claim on a place in the universities than astrology or alchemy? But if it were transformed into the religious expression of the spirit of modernity, then it obviously would have an honored place both in the university and in the culture. The purpose of the liberal project was to ensure the latter, rather than the former, outcome.

There are two aspects of the liberal project: historical criticism of the Bible and revisionist (or liberal) theology. Spinoza launched the historical-critical aspect of the project; Schleiermacher launched the revisionist-theology aspect. Both were basically pantheists[72] who accepted the philosophical naturalism that animated the French Enlightenment and became dominant in Western modernity after Hume and Kant. In this book, I am interested primarily in historical criticism and hermeneutics, but it is important to bear in mind that the changes in the interpretation of the Bible in Western culture during the past two centuries are not isolated phenomena and did not take place in response to scientific discoveries. They are part of an attempt to remake Christianity into the culture religion of the modern, progressive left and are of central importance to the triumph of naturalism in Western culture. The liberal project seeks to convince the members of Christian churches that they

72. Cooper, *Panentheism*, 67–72 (Spinoza), 80–88 (Schleiermacher). Cooper concludes that Spinoza is a pantheist who has influenced panentheism (72), while Schleiermacher could be categorized as a panentheist who is very close to pantheism (88). These are very fine distinctions.

can accept the metaphysical beliefs of modernity while remaining Christians in some meaningful sense by reinterpreting the doctrines of the Bible in the context of modern metaphysics. The basic reason why the liberal project must be rejected is that it is trying to square the circle. It is simply impossible to domesticate the Christian faith to the extent that would be necessary for Christianity to be made compatible with modernity. Let me explain why I say that.

Recent hermeneutics has become more and more distant from preaching and theology as it has attempted to reinterpret Christian doctrine within the constraints of modern metaphysics. Some scholars simply continue in the Enlightenment tradition assuming that meaning can be found through historical reconstruction of the circumstances that gave rise to the text. Many of those who have despaired of finding religiously meaningful results in historical reconstruction, however, have moved into various forms of literary criticism. Literary analysis of the text, while bracketing questions of reference, can shed light on the meaning of the text and can allow biblical books to be read as coherent entities, instead of as mere "sources." But the question "To what do the texts refer?" never goes away. Many of those who embraced the fad of poststructuralism over the past fifty years have now simply given up on truth and are left with the logical end point of modernity: the will to power. The reading of texts is nothing more or less than the exercise of the will to power. Ironically, the poststructuralists often think they are critiquing the will to power of others, but actually they embody it themselves; their critique can be based on nothing more than their personal dislike of certain manifestations of power (colonialism, racism, sexism, etc.). They are emotivists with a persecution complex who tend to become caricatures of what they critique.

In a world in which all texts are merely tools to be used in power struggles, the sole remaining source of legitimacy for these critics is the claim that "we" are good and "they" are bad because "they" have more power than "us." But this is less than credible coming from highly pampered, well-paid, sometimes famous, tenured university professors before whose wrath administrators and government bureaucrats tremble. The problem of these "tenured radicals" is the problem that the Marxists always have after they win power. Stripped of their only remaining claim to superior virtue—their powerlessness—they are exposed as mirror images of the previous regime and thus lose all moral credibility just as happened in the Soviet Union and Communist China. This is where Enlightenment hermeneutics ends. The metaphysics of modernity leads to no truth, no reality, and no moral virtue; nothing remains except the raw will to power. The worship of a God of sheer will (or, what amounts to the same thing, the furious rejection of such a "God") ends with human beings viewed as wills in eternal conflict in the meaningless flux of directionless change.

The liberal project needs to be abandoned because it is a dead end. Modern historical-critical study of the Bible is based on a false conception of created reality, a false conception of history, and a false conception of the Bible. The study of the Bible is not enhanced by historical criticism; it is only eroded and demeaned. Of course there is much that is good in the modern, scholarly study of the Bible, because much of it is just a continuation of the kind of scholarship that existed prior to modernity. But, as a general rule, *what was good in the Enlightenment was not new, and what was new was not good.* The Enlightenment did not invent textual criticism; Origen did that. The Enlightenment did not invent history; Augustine wrote a great philosophy of history. The Enlightenment did not invent reason; Thomas Aquinas wrote possibly the most rationally beautiful work in history.

The narrative of the history of biblical interpretation needs to be revised in such a way as to regard modernity in general, and the Enlightenment in particular, as a wrong turn in biblical interpretation. What is needed is to go back to where the wrong turn was made and pick up the trail from that point; only by doing so can we make progress. Fortunately for academic theologians, the Great Tradition continues to flourish today outside the modern university. We need to understand the history of biblical interpretation as a continuous and successful one, while we view the Enlightenment and historical criticism as a dead-end side path. We need to get academic hermeneutics back on track by grounding it in the preaching of the evangelical churches and by linking contemporary evangelical best practices to the best strands of patristic, medieval, and Reformation exegesis. In short, we need *ressourcement* as the way forward. The second part of this book will try to make a contribution to this task by mining the riches of the Great Tradition for help in interpreting the Bible faithfully in our day.

Part 2

Recovering Premodern Exegesis

5

Reading the Bible as a Unity
Centered on Jesus Christ

The Historical Point of View, put briefly, means that when a learned
man is presented with any statement in an ancient author, the one
question he never asks is whether it is true. He asks who influenced
the ancient author, and how far the statement is consistent with
what he said in other books, and what phase in the writer's development, or in the general history of thought, it illustrates, and how
it affected later writers, and how often it has been misunderstood
(specially by the learned man's own colleagues) and what the general
course of criticism on it has been for the last ten years, and what
is the "present state of the question." To regard the ancient writer
as a possible source of knowledge—to anticipate that what he said
could possibly modify your thought or your behavior—this would
be rejected as unutterably simple-minded.

C. S. Lewis[1]

*B*revard Childs recounts a story told by James Smart in his book, *The
Interpretation of Scripture*, about an unnamed scholar who, in a
speech at a meeting of biblical scholars, referred to himself as a historian
and not a theologian.[2] This remark brought forth thunderous applause from
the gathered assembly. No doubt the papers given at that meeting matched

1. Lewis, *Screwtape Letters*, 172, letter 27.
2. Childs, *Biblical Theology in Crisis*, 77.

up well with the description C. S. Lewis gives in the quotation above of "The Historical Point of View." In this chapter, I wish to recommend what many no doubt would call an "unutterably simple-minded" approach to learning how to interpret the Bible—namely, that we learn how to do so from the Bible itself. This entire chapter is an exposition of the truth of two texts: 1 Corinthians 2:14 and Luke 24:25–27.

As I said in the preface, the overall goal of this book is to contribute to reforming hermeneutical theory by bringing it into harmony with the best preaching and teaching of the church; faithful pastors are much better at interpreting the Bible than the learned professors of the modern academy. In my introduction I suggested that before we can interpret the Bible well, we first need to decide what exactly it is. So in the first part of the book (chaps. 2–4), the focus was on theology and metaphysics, that is, on theological hermeneutics. In the second part of this book, we get down ("Finally!" some might say) to the practice of exegesis and, in particular, what we can learn from the church fathers about how to do it well. The present chapter will focus on reading the Bible as a unity centered on Jesus Christ as a spiritual practice. Chapter 6 will discuss what it might mean to let the literal sense control all meaning without constricting the literal sense by a naturalistic definition of history. Chapter 7 will examine how the fathers interpreted the Old Testament christologically and how those who came before us saw Jesus Christ in the Old Testament so clearly. The emphases of these chapters have one thing in common: they were all undermined by the modern rejection of pro-Nicene culture, which included the rejection of spiritual exegesis in the name of historical criticism, the rejection of Christian Platonism in favor of a revived Epicureanism, and the rejection of Nicene dogmas as the proper guide to accurate interpretation of Scripture. Our goal here is to locate, dust off, and restore to a place of honor the precious jewels of past generations of faithful teachers of the faith, who have left for us a rich legacy of interpretive methods and exegetical results.

In this chapter, I argue that we should read the Bible as a unity centered on Jesus Christ. As John Webster puts it: "Holy Scripture is a unified attestation of Jesus Christ, and so in an important sense a single, coherent text."[3] This general proposition will be developed by means of three subtheses: (1) biblical interpretation is a spiritual discipline, (2) the apostles are our models, and (3) the rule of faith is our guide. The bottom line, the nonnegotiable foundation of the Great Tradition, is the firm conviction that the Bible is a unified book. Therefore, it is to be interpreted more along the lines of a sprawling historical novel than as an anthology of short stories by various authors.

3. Webster, *Domain of the Word*, 17.

It is one book with one Author, and its many subthemes all relate in some way to its one overall theme. To understand the Bible this way, we need the illumination of the Spirit, and we need to pay attention to the example of the apostles and keep closely to the rule of faith as our guide. What follows is an explanation of how these things can happen.

Biblical Interpretation Is a Spiritual Discipline: Ambrose of Milan

In this first section, we will consider the theme of biblical interpretation as a spiritual discipline. We will take as our example a bishop who is best known for his spiritual interpretation of Scripture and his role in Augustine's conversion: Ambrose of Milan. My organization of the material will expound the following thesis.

Thesis: Biblical interpretation is a spiritual discipline because perceiving the unity of the Bible requires the illumination of the Holy Spirit (1 Cor. 2:14).

Many years ago, in a private conversation about hermeneutics, John Webster made a comment to me to this effect: "Hermeneutics—it is really all a matter of the Holy Spirit, isn't it?" He was quite right, of course, and for this reason we begin this chapter with a consideration of the role of the Holy Spirit in interpretation and will conclude chapter 7 with a description of interpretation as a sacramental activity. God leads his people to true interpretation of his Word, so there is no substitute for prayer and obedience in the task of interpreting Scripture.

When modern interpreters approach the Bible in the expectation that any neutral and objective scholar should be able to understand its meaning, they risk distorting both the nature of the Bible and the nature of its message.[4] John Webster defines exegesis as "the attempt to hear what the Spirit says to the Churches,"[5] which locates biblical interpretation within the church and requires faith of the interpreter for true interpretation. To do anything else would have been unthinkable for, and incomprehensible to, the church fathers. Like Webster, the fathers took Paul's words seriously when he wrote "The

4. E.g., most of the leading historical-critical commentary series do not make confessional Christianity a prerequisite for contributors. An atheist with a PhD is apparently qualified to interpret the Bible. This is a radical, modern notion with no support in the Great Tradition. Of course, no one is denying that an atheist may give us a "thundering good book" (as C. S. Lewis would put it) on Hellenistic Greek grammar or Egyptian archaeology, but these academic disciplines do not necessarily purport to tell us what the Bible means. When they try to do so, they overstep their bounds.

5. Webster, *Holiness*, 3.

natural person does not accept the things of the Spirit of God, for they are folly to him, and he is not able to understand them because they are spiritually discerned" (1 Cor. 2:14). By looking at patristic exegesis, we can gain some comprehension of why the church fathers would have been appalled by the unspiritual language that even conservative interpreters use in approaching Scripture today.

In his indispensable book on Nicene theology between the outbreak of the Arian controversy just before the Council of Nicaea in 325 and the work of Augustine in the next century, Lewis Ayres develops a thick description of pro-Nicene culture. Too often, fourth-century theology is treated in textbooks as a list of isolated propositions about doctrinal matters that are debated in the same rational, "scientific" way as we do today. Does the literal sense of Proverbs 8 really assert the preexistence of the Son? Can the doctrine of God as three persons yet one being really be derived from the Gospel of John? These questions are not illegitimate and do need to be engaged, but there is a danger that in doing so, we will read our own metaphysical and theological presuppositions into the writings of the fathers and thus misinterpret what they say. It is important to understand what *they* thought they were doing when they interpreted Scripture, and it is here that Ayres is a sure-footed guide.

Ayres begins by asserting, "All pro-Nicene authors believe that at the heart of the purification necessary for Christians lies a reordering of human knowing and desiring."[6] We are not ready to desire the right things in our natural state; nor are we prepared to know truth in such a way that we can sort out what is good for us and what is not just by virtue of being educated human beings. Rather, what is necessary, above all, for human beings who really want to know and desire the good is what Ayres terms "dual-focus purification." He elaborates, "An anthropology is 'dual-focus' where problems with unsanctified human thinking and action—and the cure for those problems—are described by exploring how human beings should possess a trained soul that animates the body and attends to their joint *telos* in the divine presence through contemplation of God."[7] Ayres is pointing out that the fourth-century Greek and Latin fathers worked with an anthropology in which humans (1) are made up of souls and bodies and (2) are fallen because of sin. Due to our fallenness, our desires are disordered and need to be sanctified. We need to learn how to know and desire what is *truly* good rather than whatever is superficially attractive or temporarily desirable in the moment of lust or temptation. We need purification of both body and soul in

6. Ayres, *Nicaea and Its Legacy*, 326.
7. Ayres, *Nicaea and Its Legacy*, 326.

order to realize the *telos* of our nature, so our understanding of theological anthropology must be "dual-focus." This dual-focus purification will lead to growth in our ability to know the good and to desire the good. Of course, God is our ultimate good, but we have many subordinate goods—food, beauty, friendship, sensual pleasure of various sorts, and so forth—that can be used moderately and lawfully to direct our thankful hearts upward toward our ultimate good or can become idolatrous substitutes for our ultimate good when we turn them into ends in themselves. Thus the problem we face in Christian sanctification cannot be reduced solely to one of knowing or one of desiring. We have both to know the good *and* to desire it above all else in order to be sanctified and grow in faith.

Ayres gives several examples, but I want to mention just one and urge the reader to become familiar with Ayres's incredibly helpful and perspective-enlarging book. Ambrose of Milan, in his *On the Holy Spirit*, speaks of the Spirit as "the fount of water shaping the Church."[8] Quoting Proverbs 5:15–16 and Matthew 6:19, he urges us not to lay up treasures on earth where rust and moth destroy but to avoid the filth of vices, which dim the vision of the mind. He sees vice as "distorting the focus of the soul on God."[9] Ayres comments: "From here he argues that if someone loses their grasp of the truly divine power welling forth into the Christian, they will develop doctrines that do not recognize the unity of the Spirit with the Father. Arius and Photinus are both named as examples. Amid the polemic in this text we see a distinctively pro-Nicene linking of appropriate spiritual progress and growth in correct doctrinal belief."[10] He is making a radical statement here; Ambrose is saying that correct doctrine is necessary for spiritual growth. And, just as shockingly, he claims that spiritual growth is necessary for correct doctrine. (Imagine how *that* would have gone over at the meeting of biblical scholars mentioned above!) What we believe or fail to believe is crucial for growth in the Christian life, and growth in the Christian life is necessary for sound doctrine and correct biblical interpretation. Ambrose is typical of the Nicene fathers in understanding sanctification and correct doctrinal understanding as arising from true biblical exegesis and as viewing these two things as intricately intertwined. He sees the disciplining of the body as necessary to the clear perception of spiritual truth by the soul because it is only as we prevent rust and moths (Matt. 6:19) from corrupting the well from which flows the Spirit (Prov. 5:15–16) that we experience the full flow

8. Ambrose of Milan, "On the Holy Spirit," chap. 16, p. 114.
9. Ambrose, "On the Holy Spirit," chap. 16, p. 114. See also Ayres, *Nicaea and Its Legacy*, 328.
10. Ayres, *Nicaea and Its Legacy*, 328.

of the pure water of the Spirit. Ambrose shows that Scripture speaks of both Christ and the Holy Spirit as "the fount of eternal life."[11] To be full of the Spirit is to have eternal life. Yet to be filled with the Spirit, we must have the pure water of the Spirit flowing into our lives.

Ayres goes on to elaborate on the kind of spiritual discipline necessary for sound doctrinal understanding: "Whether one conceives of the training of the soul and body as controlling or eliminating the passions, only by this training can the soul appropriately 'govern' the body while attending to the Good 'in' which it exists."[12] I would argue that sanctification involves the control, rather than the elimination, of the passions (self-control is a fruit of the Spirit—Gal. 5:22–23), but that is not the main point here. The main point is that our disordered desires need to be rightly ordered. Note that for the Christian Platonist Ambrose, the soul is "in" the Good (that is, God). Pauline theology is presupposed here as the *ground*, as well as the *goal*, of sanctification, which is understood to happen as we are "in Christ," not just positionally or experientially, but ontologically (the doctrine of union with Christ). We are sanctified once for all by the blood of Christ (Heb. 13:12), but we gradually grow into a full realization of sanctification by a process that goes on all through the Christian life (Rom. 6:19) and does not culminate until we are glorified in our resurrection bodies (1 Cor. 15:34–44).

Ayres continues: "Achieving clarity in the soul's vision is directly associated with learning to speak of (or 'see') the presence of the unmediated and con-substantial Word and Spirit in the soul. Pro-Nicene insistence on shaping patterns of speech about God governed by the formal conditions of divine simplicity and infinity is here incorporated into a conception of the Christian life as spiritual discipline."[13] So for Ambrose, and the fathers in general, Ayres argues, reading the Bible is not merely an intellectual exercise. It is an exercise in gaining a true knowledge of God and of being sanctified by coming to desire God above all. Whether the right knowledge is more fundamental than the right desire or vice versa is impossible to tell.

Another Christian Platonist, John Calvin, makes a very similar point in the opening lines of his *Institutes of the Christian Religion*:

> Nearly all the wisdom we possess, that is to say, true and sound wisdom, consists of two parts: the knowledge of God and of ourselves. But, while joined by many bonds, which one precedes and brings forth the other is not easy to discern. In the first place, no one can look upon himself without immediately

11. Ambrose, "On the Holy Spirit," chap. 16, p. 114.
12. Ayres, *Nicaea and Its Legacy*, 328.
13. Ayres, *Nicaea and Its Legacy*, 328.

turning his thoughts to the contemplation of God, in whom he "lives and moves" (Acts 17:28). For, quite clearly, the mighty gifts with which we are endowed are hardly from ourselves; indeed, our very being is nothing but subsistence in the one God.[14]

Here we see the linking of the true knowledge of ourselves with the true knowledge of God; advance in one brings advance in the other, while mistakes in one cause mistakes in the other. Calvin sees our being as subsisting in God, and contemplation of ourselves occasions thoughts of God; for the entire Great Tradition, this explains why no human being can ever be neutral with regard to God, oceans of Enlightenment sophistry notwithstanding.

This basic theology is rooted in Paul's discussion of why humans are without excuse; "what can be known about God is plain to them, because God has shown it to them" in the created order. Here is the actual passage:

> For the wrath of God is revealed from heaven against all ungodliness and unrighteousness of men, who by their unrighteousness suppress the truth. For what can be known about God is plain to them, because God has shown it to them. For his invisible attributes, namely, his eternal power and divine nature, have been clearly perceived, ever since the creation of the world, in the things that have been made. So they are without excuse. For although they knew God, they did not honor him as God or give thanks to him, but they became futile in their thinking, and their foolish hearts were darkened. Claiming to be wise, they became fools, and exchanged the glory of the immortal God for images resembling mortal man and birds and animals and creeping things.
>
> Therefore God gave them up in the lusts of their hearts to impurity, to the dishonoring of their bodies among themselves, because they exchanged the truth about God for a lie and worshiped and served the creature rather than the Creator, who is blessed forever! Amen. (Rom. 1:18–25)

Here is why the fathers thought we needed sanctification; here is where they got the idea that purification of the body from uncontrolled lust went hand in hand with grasping the true Good with the mind. The rational control of the body by the soul is intricately bound up with knowledge of God. But knowledge never stands alone. True knowledge comes only through purification because of the dynamics of fallen human existence.

J. Alec Motyer has been one of the very best evangelical interpreters of Scripture over the past half century or so. He has written, "There is an old jingle which is certainly simple and verges on the simplistic, but our forebears

---

14. Calvin, *Institutes*, 35.

were fundamentally right when they taught that: the Old Testament is Jesus predicted; the Gospels are Jesus revealed; Acts is Jesus preached; the Epistles, Jesus explained; and the Revelation, Jesus expected. He is the climax as well as the substance and centre of the whole. In him all God's promises are yea and amen (2 Cor. 1:20)."[15] This is a typical evangelical claim that Jesus Christ is the true center and meaning of the Bible as a whole and that the Bible is a unity. But is this affirmation a purely doctrinal or intellectual statement, or is it a restatement of the dual-focus purification advocated by the fathers as necessary for true understanding of Scripture? We need to consider this question carefully.

Charles E. Shepherd has written a very interesting doctoral dissertation comparing the hermeneutics of Bernhard Duhm, Brevard Childs, and Alec Motyer, with a focus on Isaiah 53. Unfortunately, however, he fails to see the similarity between what Motyer is doing and patristic exegesis. He does recognize the affinity that Childs felt for patristic exegesis (evident especially in *The Struggle to Understand Isaiah as Christian Scripture*); he also recognizes that Childs failed to provide a very profound spiritual reading of Isaiah 53 in his 2001 Isaiah commentary, especially in comparison to the rich theological reading provided by Motyer.[16] But he fails to make the connection between what Childs and Ayres have described the fathers as doing and what Motyer is doing, even though Shepherd discusses the abundant evidence for such a link in a fully competent manner.

Shepherd draws attention to a surprising move that Motyer makes in interpreting Isaiah 53:10–12, the last stanza of the fourth Servant Song. He points out that Motyer goes back to Isaiah 51:1, which characterizes the remnant as those who pursue righteousness and *seek Yahweh*, in order to point out that the Servant is the end (in the sense of the goal or *telos*) of their quest. Shepherd writes:

> In addition to the propositional knowledge possessed and disbursed by the servant, Motyer finds a twofold function in the specific reference to the "righteousness" of the servant. First, the designation of the servant as "righteous" (צַדִּיק) underscores his "moral fitness" for the task. More importantly for Motyer, however, is the second function of this righteousness: the servant will "justify" the "many" (לָרַבִּים). Here we pick up the second divine speech, signaled with the use of עַבְדִּי. The language slowly gains momentum for Motyer: not only does the servant "make" the many righteous, but given that the verb is followed by a לְ, indicating an indirect object, he translates

15. Motyer, *Look to the Rock*, 22.
16. See Childs, *Isaiah*, 407–23; and Motyer, *Prophecy of Isaiah*, 422–43.

the phrase as "bringing righteousness to the many"—righteousness, then, is a gift bestowed.[17]

In a footnote, Shepherd rightly compares Motyer's understanding of righteousness to Lutheran and Reformed notions of "justification," but then he concludes the discussion in a disappointingly anticlimactic way by saying that "for Motyer, a certain notion of revelation is central to understanding the chapter's message."[18] Throughout the dissertation, Shepherd refers frequently to the uniqueness of Motyer's position, over against the positions of Childs and Duhm, as consisting of his evangelical doctrine of inspiration and revelation that requires him to interpret Isaiah 53 within the context of the canon as a whole and thus as teaching the meaning of the death and resurrection of Jesus Christ. Shepherd writes that for Motyer, "inspiration is best defined as God's preparatory work to enable 'human minds' to receive his self-revelation" and that therefore revelation, for Motyer, is primarily a matter of doctrine.[19] Shepherd sees Motyer's emphasis on inspiration as the guarantee of propositional revelation as a response to Enlightenment rationalism. The implication is that the evangelical emphasis on propositional revelation and doctrine is, at least in part, shaped by its opposition to Enlightenment rationalism. This is all true as far as it goes, but is it the whole story?

I would contend that it is also true that Motyer's position is similar to that of Ambrose, who believed that "achieving clarity in the soul's vision is directly associated with learning to speak of (or 'see') the presence of the unmediated and consubstantial Word and Spirit in the soul."[20] This requires some explanation. When Motyer interprets the Servant's work as including the justification of the remnant—as actually making them righteous—he is describing the same thing as the fathers meant by "dual-focus purification." The Servant, Motyer grasps, makes the believing remnant able to see him for who he really is. As Shepherd noted, Motyer can affirm that "the Servant is the end of their quest." Isaiah 51:1 refers to a remnant, which is described as "you who pursue righteousness," and verse 5 says, "My righteousness draws near." The paradox is that only those who recognize the Servant as their sin-bearer are justified, yet only those who are justified are able to see the Servant as their sin-bearer. Hence, it is highly significant that Isaiah 51:5 reveals the

17. Shepherd, *Theological Interpretation and Isaiah 53*, 195. See Motyer, *Prophecy of Isaiah*, 423–44, esp. 441–42.
18. Shepherd, *Theological Interpretation and Isaiah 53*, 196.
19. Shepherd, *Theological Interpretation and Isaiah 53*, 154.
20. Ayres, *Nicaea and Its Legacy*, 328.

LORD as taking the initiative by inviting the remnant at the beginning of the fourth Servant Song to "Behold my servant . . ." (Isa. 52:13). The act of being made righteous by the shed blood of Christ is what makes a person able to read Isaiah 53 and discern who the Servant actually is, and it is in this recognition of the true identity of the Servant that a person is made righteous. This may seem very odd, but not incomprehensible if one reflects on it in light of the Reformed doctrines of effectual call and regenerating grace.

In his discussion of Exodus, Motyer makes the point that "what the Lord does precedes what the Lord demands," that in Exodus covenant theology, *grace* comes before *law*: "his holy law is . . . his appointed and required pattern of life for those who, by redemption, have been brought to him already, who already belong to him."[21] This kind of Reformed theology recognizes that both justification and sanctification are the work of God; both occur as a result of the divine initiative. Yet sanctification calls forth (elicits) human action, which is intricately bound up with God's saving action. Just as the fathers understood to be the case with their emphasis on dual-focus purification, salvation involves both a reordering of knowing and of desiring, and which comes first is mysterious.

My contention, therefore, is that for both Ambrose and Motyer a doctrinal point (the consubstantiality of the Spirit and the Word for Ambrose, the doctrine of inspiration for Motyer) is intricately intertwined with a spiritual activity (sanctification for Ambrose, justification for Motyer). For both writers, true doctrine cannot be separated from spiritual insight into the real nature of God and his saving action. In neither Ambrose's nor Motyer's case can the relationship of the believer to the Word of God be reduced to doctrine alone, whether it be the doctrine of the inspiration of Scripture in Motyer's case or the doctrine of the Trinity in Ambrose's. In both cases, the exegetical results that become doctrine are attained only through prayer and the purifying work of the Holy Spirit drawing us to Jesus Christ. This links the two across the ages as sharing a similar basic approach to Scripture that is different from that of most modern academic hermeneutics.

I also would argue that Motyer is far from being an isolated case so far as evangelical exegetes and preachers are concerned; therefore, the standard critical evaluation of evangelical exegesis, which is reflected in Shepherd's evaluation of it, needs correcting. It is not modern and rationalistic exegesis, despite what the official textbook theory might lead one to think. The motor that drives the discernment of Jesus Christ in the Old Testament in evangelical exegesis and preaching is not merely rationalistic belief derived from the

21. Motyer, *Look to the Rock*, 41.

doctrine of verbal inspiration but that doctrine *plus* a spiritual discernment that comes through piety and prayer and, ultimately, by means of the grace of the Holy Spirit. Insofar as this is the case, the practice (if not always the theory) of evangelical exegesis and preaching stands in the center of the Great Tradition, in stark contrast to Enlightenment higher criticism, which has eliminated piety in favor of rationalism in search of an elusive and, in the end, unattainable goal of "objectivity."

To see that, as Augustine put it, "the New is in the Old concealed, the Old is in the New revealed"[22] requires that one read under the guidance of the Holy Spirit. It is only as one grows in the grace of sanctification by the Spirit that it is possible to understand the Bible as a unity centered on Jesus Christ and thus to see the Bible for what it really is. Jesus promised his disciples that when the Holy Spirit came, he would guide them into all truth by glorifying the Son and taking what belongs to Jesus and declaring it to them (John 16:12–15). The role of the Spirit is to guide us toward the one who said, "I am the truth" (John 14:6). The Spirit originally did this by inspiring the writings of the apostles that became the New Testament; now the Spirit continues this work by illuminating the minds of those who read the Bible with a genuine desire to know the truth. Knowing the nature of the Good and desiring the Good with all our hearts are inseparable. We cannot desire what we do not know, and we cannot know what we do not desire. The more we desire God, the more clearly we can see him. No wonder we need the grace of sanctification through the ministry of the Holy Spirit if we are going to interpret Scripture rightly. And so, it is little wonder that John Webster said of hermeneutics: "It's all about the Holy Spirit, isn't it?"

The Apostles Are Our Models: Justin Martyr

In this second section, we will consider that the apostles are our models in biblical interpretation, taking as our example the philosopher, convert to Christianity, and eventual martyr Justin Martyr. I will organize my thoughts using the following thesis.

Thesis: The prophecy-and-fulfillment approach linking Jesus to the Hebrew Scriptures goes back to Jesus himself and is modeled by the apostles (Luke 24:25–27).

---

22. Augustine, "Questions on the Heptateuch 2.73," as quoted in Cameron, *Christ Meets Me Everywhere*, 248.

In Luke 24:13–35, we see the risen Lord Jesus Christ opening up the Scriptures to enable the two disciples on the road to Emmaus to see how the Scriptures speak of him. The key verses are as follows:

> And he said to them, "O foolish ones, and slow of heart to believe all that the prophets have spoken! Was it not necessary that the Christ should suffer these things and enter into his glory?" And beginning with Moses and all the Prophets, he interpreted to them in all the Scriptures the things concerning himself. (Luke 24:25–27)

Certain words jump off the page as we read this passage in view of the discussion so far in this book. First, we note the word "foolish." Jesus calls his own followers "foolish." In Psalm 14:1 we read, "The fool says in his heart, 'There is no God.'" Knowing God, as we saw above, is a spiritual issue. These disciples "knew" about the crucifixion and resurrection of Jesus, yet apparently they were unable to see how these events were not just hints or possibilities within the parameters of scriptural teaching but were the clear and central teaching of the Scriptures. These events *were* predicted plainly in the Scriptures; that these disciples could not see that the prophets spoke of Christ's passion and glory meant that they were "foolish," in Jesus's opinion. Does this not suggest a spiritual problem such as a lack of faith in Christ?

The second word that jumps out at us is "necessary." What Jesus thought they should have seen in the Scriptures was the "necessity" of the death and resurrection of the Messiah. They were struggling to see how the true Messiah *could* die, and they were struggling to believe that he was alive. But even if Jesus was alive, a dying and rising Messiah still did not make sense to them; even an appearance of Jesus to them would not, in and of itself, have given them the insight they needed. So the risen Christ had to "interpret" the Scriptures to them, which is the third word that jumps out at us. Two implications of this word as used in the context are obvious. First, Christ *had to interpret* the Scriptures in order for the disciples to understand. Jesus told his disciples in the upper room the night before the crucifixion that it was good that he went away (referring to the ascension—John 16:7) because the Holy Spirit would then come and "guide [them] into all the truth" (John 16:13). Since the ascension had not yet occurred, the risen Lord Jesus himself here guides them into all truth. Second, Christ *could rightly interpret* the Scriptures as "concerning himself" (Luke 24:27). Surely, it is obvious to any Christian that Jesus would not give the wrong interpretation of the Scriptures. The entire Hebrew Bible (Moses and all the prophets) really does speak of him and refers to him. So we understand from this passage that the Scriptures needed interpretation but could properly and rightly be interpreted as referring to the necessity of the Messiah dying and rising from the dead and that one would have to be foolish not to see that this is the case.

How far back in Moses did Jesus begin his interpretation for these disciples? We are not told explicitly, but a good guess would be with the story of creation and the fall with a focus on the *protoevangelium* of Genesis 3:15. The entire Hebrew Bible is about Jesus Christ; the purpose of the New Testament is to interpret it that way so as to bring out its true meaning. As we consider the meaning of this text, we also need to observe the function of this story in Luke's Gospel and the New Testament generally. It links the apostolic interpretation of the Old Testament as christological at its core with the teaching of the risen Lord Jesus Christ himself. The reason why the apostles taught that Christ fulfills the Old Testament is because they received this teaching directly from the Lord himself.

One of the main characteristics of patristic exegesis was a confidence in the authority of Scripture that led the fathers to believe that the apostles themselves model biblical interpretation for us in the way they interpret the Old Testament. Scripture itself therefore not only teaches us what Scripture is; it also teaches us how to interpret Scripture. About a third of the New Testament consists of quotations, allusions, or echoes of the Old Testament; it is no exaggeration to say that the primary purpose of the New Testament is to proclaim that Jesus Christ fulfills the Old Testament and therefore is the key to understanding it correctly. In interpreting the Old Testament christologically, the fathers considered themselves to be faithful followers of the apostles, who were teaching what the risen Lord had taught them. Ultimately, the christological interpretation of the Old Testament is a matter of Christ's personal authority. It is something very close to what Paul calls "the gospel" in Galatians and therefore not something made up by human beings. It is the gospel of God. That Jesus has in his death and resurrection fulfilled the Old Testament messianic hope is definitely good news. Believing the gospel is integral to becoming a Christian, and only a Christian believer can interpret Scripture properly. Sound biblical interpretation depends on personal faith in Christ. Thus the thesis we are currently discussing supports and extends the one we discussed in the first part of this chapter.

We can see this approach of viewing the Old Testament as prophesying Christ in all the church fathers. It was ubiquitous and done, as mentioned already, in conscious dependence on the apostles, who consciously imitated Christ. As an example, let us examine one of the earliest of the fathers, a philosopher who converted to Christianity in the middle of the second century and who, therefore, represents the generation that immediately followed the apostles. Justin Martyr was born in Samaria to a Roman father and spent his early life apprenticing himself to various philosophers in a search for truth. In his *Dialogue with Trypho*, he describes his early philosophical studies. Both before and after his conversion he considered philosophy to be the search for truth and wisdom and the highest form of life. He considered Christianity to be the true philosophy, much as Augustine would two centuries later. He describes his studies with a Stoic teacher, a Peripatetic teacher, and a Pythagorean teacher before he encounters the Platonists, under whom he finally seemed to be advancing. He says that he made great progress, "and the perception of immaterial things quite overpowered me, and the contemplation of ideas furnished my mind with wings, so that in a little while I supposed that I had become wise; and such was my stupidity, I expected forthwith to look upon God, for this is the end of Plato's philosophy."[23]

Like the other church fathers, all of whom were one sort of Christian Platonist or another,[24] Justin does not hesitate to specify the incompleteness of Platonist philosophy. It did aspire to lead people to God, which is the true purpose of philosophy. The problem was that it was unable to achieve this noble purpose. At this point, Justin narrates his conversion experience as a result of meeting an old man on the seashore who engages him in dialogue. As a result of this dialogue, Justin realizes that the soul is not naturally immortal and cannot, on its own, see God. The soul can perceive that God exists, but it cannot rise up and be joined to God by its own power. Philosophy reaches its limit in Platonism and cannot go further.

The old man tells Justin that what is needed is to listen to the prophets, rather than the philosophers. Here is the key passage:

> There existed long before this time, certain men more ancient than all those who are esteemed philosophers, both righteous and beloved by God, who spoke by the Divine Spirit, and foretold events which would take place, and which are now taking place. They are called prophets. These alone saw and announced the truth to men, neither reverencing nor fearing any man, not influenced by a desire for glory, but speaking those things alone which they saw and which they heard, being filled with the Holy Spirit. Their writings are still extant, and he who has read them is very much helped in his knowledge of those matters which the philosopher ought to know, provided he has believed them. For they did not use demonstration in their treatises, seeing that they were witnesses to the truth above all demonstration, and worthy of belief; and those events which have happened and those which are happening, compel you to assent to

23. Justin Martyr, *Dialogue with Trypho*, 195.
24. See chap. 3 above for a discussion of Christian Platonism.

the utterances made by them, although indeed, they were entitled to credit on account of the miracles which they performed, since they both glorified the Creator, the God and Father of all things, and proclaimed his Son, the Christ [sent] by Him.[25]

The theme of prophecy and fulfillment is at the core of the faith to which Justin was converted, and note especially the superiority of prophecy to philosophy. The prophets "spoke by the Divine Spirit, and foretold events which would take place, and which are now taking place." Justin's testimony is that these words spoken to him by this mysterious old man kindled a flame within him that led him into the church and to become a Christian.

In his *First Apology*, addressed to the emperor, Justin seeks religious toleration for Christians, "who are unjustly hated and wantonly abused, myself being one of them."[26] In this work, he discusses why he believes Christianity to be true. Central to his understanding of the faith is the way that Christ fulfilled the prophecies of the ancient Israelite prophets. In this work, he explains Christianity to a pagan audience and strives to show that Christians are not lawless, atheistic, or immoral. He says that Christ taught obedience to the civil authorities and that the kingdom Christians look for is not a human kingdom like that of Rome, but a spiritual kingdom that involves life after death through the resurrection of the body.

Justin discusses the Hebrew prophets as critical to our knowledge of the significance of Christ,[27] teaching that Christ was predicted by Moses, the first of the prophets, and mentioning the messianic text Genesis 49:10, "the scepter shall not depart from Judah." Justin says that messianic prophecy foretells that all nations shall be glad of the advent of the Messiah and points to the current spread of the gospel to all nations in his day as fulfillment of that expectation. In other key examples of fulfilled prophecy, he writes that the manner of Christ's birth was predicted in Isaiah 7:14 and the place of his birth in Micah 5:2. Isaiah's words "Unto us a child is given and unto us a young man is given, and the government shall be upon His shoulders" (Isa. 9:6 AT) are interpreted as being fulfilled in the crucifixion. Justin also finds Isaiah 65:2, "I have spread out my hands to a disobedient and gainsaying people, to those who walk in a way that is not good" (AT), to be applicable to the many present-day Jews who reject their Messiah. Details from Psalm 22 were fulfilled in the crucifixion, and Zechariah 9:9 in the triumphal entry by Jesus into Jerusalem on Palm Sunday. In Justin's reading, certain Old

25. Justin Martyr, *Dialogue with Trypho*, 195–98.
26. Justin Martyr, *First Apology*, 173.
27. Justin Martyr, *First Apology*, 173–80.

Testament texts contain the words of the Father and others utterances of
the Son. The coming of Christ was foretold, as was the crucifixion itself. He
discusses the finer points of the prophetic literature by explaining how the
prophets used the past tense to describe future events as certain. He also asserts that the responsibility of those who crucified Christ is not nullified by
the existence of prophecy concerning those events. In common with many
of the church fathers, Justin believed that Plato learned certain truths from
Moses; he stressed the antiquity of the Hebrew prophets, which in the ancient
world (unlike today) was evidence of credibility. Christ's heavenly session and
preexistence are both discussed and also his rejection by so many of his own
people. The conclusion of Justin's section on prophecy includes these words,
which we need to note carefully:

> For with what reason should we believe of a crucified man that He is the first-
> born of the unbegotten God, and Himself will pass judgment on the whole
> human race, unless we had found testimonies concerning Him published before
> He came and was born as man, and unless we saw that things had happened
> accordingly—the devastation of the land of the Jews, and men of every race
> persuaded by His teaching through the apostles, and rejecting their old habits,
> in which, being deceived, they had had their conversation; yea, seeing ourselves
> too, and knowing that the Christians from among the Gentiles are both more
> numerous and more true than those from among the Jews and Samaritans?[28]

For Justin, Christ as the fulfillment of Old Testament prophecy was absolutely
central to his understanding of the nature of the Christian faith and to its
proclamation in the world.

   Brevard Childs agrees that the prophecy and fulfillment motif is central to
Justin's exegesis and quotes the study of Justin by Oscar Skarsaune in support
of the idea that "Justin's exegesis was shaped by his conviction of his trans-
mitting a received apostolic tradition from his predecessors."[29] Many modern
evaluations of Justin's exegesis have viewed it as "primitive," an assessment
that underlines the Enlightenment rejection of predictive prophecy in favor of
philosophical naturalism. Childs notes also that in the *First Dialogue*, Justin's
use of the phrase "the grace to understand" is technical language pointing to
the idea that "no one can understand the scriptures before Christ reveals the
meaning of the prophecies."[30] Justin stands with the apostles and the other

28. Justin Martyr, *First Apology*, 180.
29. Childs, *Struggle to Understand Isaiah*, 33.
30. Childs, *Struggle to Understand Isaiah*, 35. Note how this idea aligns perfectly with the
discussion in the first part of this chapter.

church fathers in seeing the grace to understand the true meaning of the Scriptures as coming to readers from the Holy Spirit as part of the spiritual discipline of biblical interpretation. Justin extends this idea specifically to the proof-from-prophecy approach to understanding Christ as the center of the Bible. Childs notes Justin's extensive use of large sections of Isaiah, not merely adducing a few scattered proof texts but appealing to the meaning of the book as a whole. In his conclusion, Childs asserts, "Justin thus stands in close continuity with what became the New Testament and the received apostolic tradition he inherited."[31]

Childs's main criticism of Justin's exegesis is that it seems to be supersessionist in its insistence that the Jews ought to have seen the fulfillment of their own Scriptures in the life, death, and resurrection of Jesus Christ. To the extent that Justin teaches this position, however, he is one with the Jewish apostles. Childs is also not pleased with what he sees as Justin's "widespread Christianizing of the Old Testament."[32] But, once again, Childs's quarrel on this point is not with Justin alone but with all the writers of the New Testament, as well as with the church fathers. Childs also criticizes Justin's understanding of the relation of prophecy and fulfillment as "rationalistic," but once again we remember that most of the tradition would be liable to the same charge. Childs clearly tries to be fair to Justin, but in the end it is Childs, not Justin, who stands outside the mainstream of the history of Christian exegetical thought on how Jesus Christ functions as the center of a unified Bible by fulfilling the prophecies of the Old Testament in his virgin birth, sinless life, atoning death, bodily resurrection, glorious ascension, and imminent second coming.

The philosophers of the Enlightenment, such as Baruch Spinoza, rejected the fulfillment of prophecy as incompatible with their understanding of sound reason. They often called the traditional orthodox position "naive," and it is important to understand why they did so. The first and the main reason why Enlightenment higher criticism finds patristic exegesis so foreign and unacceptable is that the metaphysical doctrines of the early modern period made predictive prophecy impossible to understand apart from a problematic divine incursion into the "foreign territory" of the self-contained, self-existent material cosmos. Within the context of modern metaphysics, such divine action is a threat to human autonomy and freedom in a way it never was within the theological metaphysics of the Great Tradition. In the metaphysics of historic Christian orthodoxy, divine action was already pervasive throughout the

---

31. Childs, *Struggle to Understand Isaiah*, 39.
32. Childs, *Struggle to Understand Isaiah*, 41.

cosmos (that is, creation), and miracles would just be more of the same kind of action. Just because God acts in an unusual way does not mean that it is strange that God would act, since divine action is continuous and pervasive in creation even apart from miracles.[33] But there was still another problem besides the fact that predictive prophecy was a species of miracle, and miracles, as we have seen, go against the grain of materialism and mechanism.

This second problem was that predictive prophecy implies the sovereignty of God over history, and this belief raises the same set of questions for moderns that the doctrine of inspiration does (see chap. 2). To summarize, the basic problem is that, within modernity, human freedom and divine freedom are viewed as competing with each other. It is a zero-sum game: the more you have of one, the less you necessarily have of the other. This is because in a theistic personalist theological perspective, God is a being among beings, one actor on the historical stage alongside other autonomous angelic and human actors. In this scenario, whatever God does impinges on the freedom of the other actors, as if a playwright wrote himself into a play and began murdering the other characters. As the cause of the play as a whole, his freedom operates on an entirely different level from the freedom of the characters within the drama. But once the playwright inserts himself into the play as one of the characters, his relation to the characters changes. One of the characters now has "absolute" freedom in contrast to the limited, creaturely freedom of the others and is now perceived as a threat. In the theological metaphysics of the Great Tradition, divine action and human actions operate on different planes.[34] Divine action is what brought created being into existence and is what holds the nature of each created thing in place so that creatures (including human beings) are able to fulfill their natures. But we are free as creatures to act according to our natures without outside interference.

Of course, given the conditions of the fall, we experience a significant loss of freedom due to the weakness and perversity of our sinful natures. This lack of freedom is precisely what the Holy Spirit repairs, which is why, for Paul, walking in the Spirit *is* freedom (Gal. 5:1, 16) and why rejecting the gospel entails falling back into slavery (Gal. 4:8–9). As Jesus says, "So if the Son sets you free, you will be free indeed" (John 8:36). The gospel is all about receiving back the freedom we squandered in our rebellion in the person of

33. This discussion builds on the account of providence and miracle given in chap. 2 above.

34. Of course, the incarnation presents a thorny nest of conceptual problems that took centuries to think through. But the point we need to bear in mind here is that the incarnation is a unique event in history, not a general symbol of the way things eternally are. It is not a symbol of the way God usually works in history; it is miracle rather than providence, and no "ordinary" miracle at that.

the first Adam. But our freedom is always creaturely, limited freedom; it is never the kind of sovereignty that God has.

Our creaturely freedom is the freedom to act so as to express our own human natures; divine freedom is that of the creator of all things and thus of all the natures of things. Divine freedom (or sovereignty) is on a completely different plane from that of creatures. God is free to create this kind of cosmos rather than that kind, and in this kind of cosmos his providence ensures that certain things will inevitably happen without any need to override or nullify any creature's freedom to realize its nature. We see this sort of paradoxical truth taught by the apostle Peter in his Pentecost sermon in Acts 2 when he says, "Men of Israel, hear these words: Jesus of Nazareth, a man attested to you by God with mighty works and wonders and signs that God did through him in your midst, as you yourselves know—this Jesus, delivered up according to the definite plan and foreknowledge of God, you crucified and killed by the hands of lawless men" (Acts 2:22–23). The response of the hearers, after Peter declares that God has raised up this Jesus, whom they crucified, and made him both Lord and Christ (v. 36), is to cry out in repentance and ask Peter what they must do. They recognize their personal guilt even though the cross was ordained by the "definite plan and foreknowledge of God" (v. 23). This is the picture of reality that we find everywhere in Scripture: God is in overall control of history and so actually sovereign that his will is worked out even in the disobedience of his creatures.

This biblical worldview (that is, the theological metaphysics of the Great Tradition, which is to say Christian Platonism) is the context in which the question of predictive prophecy must be considered. Modern historical critics are convinced—sometimes by a chain of reasoning of which they are not conscious but that they accept by authority from other moderns—that long-term predictive prophecy is (a) impossible and (b) not found in Scripture. However, theologians, biblical interpreters, and preachers of the church have found predictive prophecy in Scripture in every century of church history from Justin Martyr to J. Alec Motyer. And they do so in conscious imitation of the apostles.

The fathers (as well as the medieval scholastics and the Reformers) sought to follow the method of interpreting the Old Testament that they discovered in the works of the apostles who wrote the New Testament. Since the apostles declare that the Christ event is the hermeneutical key to understanding the true meaning of the Old Testament, the hermeneutical methods employed by the apostles in interpreting the Old Testament became models for the fathers in their own interpretation of the Old Testament. The Enlightenment animus against the fathers is thus actually a rejection of the Bible's own teaching on how it should be interpreted. It is a rejection of the authority of Christ. It is thus quintessentially a spiritual issue.

The Christian church is not, and has never been, interested merely in affirming that viewing Jesus as the Messiah of Israel and the Savior of the world is merely *one possible way* to read the Hebrew Scriptures, as if the view that Jesus is a usurper of these titles was another equally possible way of reading them.[35] We, as Christian theologians, are not interested in saying that the apostles read Jesus *into* the Old Testament. We insist that they read Jesus *out* of it; actually we go further and assert that the apostles were imitating Jesus in doing so because *Jesus* read Jesus out of the Old Testament (Luke 24:25–27)! Whether the Old Testament texts themselves speak of Jesus or not is the crux of the issue.[36] Any theory of biblical interpretation that cannot assert with Luke 24:27 that the entire Old Testament is full of the things concerning Christ is inadequate for any church that claims the title apostolic.

The Rule of Faith Is Our Guide: Irenaeus

In the final section of this chapter we will consider the rule of faith as our guide to interpreting Scripture using the great second-century bishop, Irenaeus of Lyons, as our example. Again, we will organize the exposition around a thesis.

35. Many contemporary theologians are reluctant to assert what Paul, Peter, and the rest of the Jewish apostles had no difficulty asserting—namely, that all people (Jew and gentile alike) need to believe in Jesus Christ as the Messiah (Acts 4:12). To assert that those Jews who reject Christ as the Messiah are nevertheless saved and do not need to convert to Christ is to take one's stand against the Scriptures. The apostle Paul would find such a view incomprehensible; he was filled with anguish over those who rejected Christ (Rom. 9:1–3). His hope for Israel (Rom. 10:1; 11:1–2) is that they have been "hardened" only temporarily so that the gentiles could be grafted into the covenant like a wild olive shoot (11:25). But eventually, he writes, the hope is that "all Israel" will be saved through Christ (Rom. 11:26). In the case of Jewish believers being tempted to turn away from Christ, the writer of Hebrews avers that the stakes could not be higher because salvation comes only through Christ.

36. In this regard, I depart from the forms of contemporary biblical theology that work in the tradition of Childs by trying to hold together modern, historical criticism and a Christian reading of the Old Testament. The idea that the text has a single meaning located in the intention of the original human author is finally incompatible with the idea that the text has a multilayered meaning that exists because of divine inspiration and is only gradually unveiled through the action of God in shaping the canon and shaping his people that culminates in the incarnation of the Son in the person of Jesus the Messiah and the sending of the Holy Spirit to lead the church into the fuller truth of the Triune God. Childs strives mightily to hold these two things together with his dialectical approach, but my assessment is that he is trying to square the circle and would be better off simply admitting that we must choose between two metaphysical systems, two ultimate authorities, and two incompatible ways of reading Holy Scripture. We must choose between the Enlightenment and the Great Tradition—between naturalism and inspiration.

Thesis: The rule of faith is a summary of the *skopos* of the Bible, which helps to ensure that the interpretation of a given text does not contradict the Bible as a whole.

So far in this chapter we have unpacked two basic assertions. First, we have said that biblical interpretation is a spiritual discipline because perceiving the unity of the Bible requires the gracious illumination of the Holy Spirit (1 Cor. 2:14). Second, we have said that the prophecy-and-fulfillment approach linking Jesus to the Hebrew Scriptures goes back to Jesus himself and is modeled by the apostles (Luke 24:25–27). These two statements are foundational for the third thesis to be expounded in this final section of the chapter, which is an expansion of the exposition of these two texts. We need to address two questions in this section: first, what does this third thesis mean and, second, why does it require the foundation of the first two theses? The example of the church father, Irenaeus of Lyons, will serve to help us answer these questions.

In his work *Demonstration of the Apostolic Preaching*, the second-century bishop of Lyons, Irenaeus, describes "the rule of truth received in baptism" of which the three key articles are the Father, the Son, and the Holy Spirit.[37] He mentions the baptismal creed near the beginning of the work (chaps. 6–7) and again at the end (chap. 100).[38] John Behr comments in his introduction:

> However, rather than being a detached system of doctrinal beliefs, these three articles, the kernel of the rule of truth, are inextricably connected, for Irenaeus, with "the order (τάξις) and the connection (εἱρμός) of the Scriptures" ([*Against Heresies*] 1.8.1). And it is, of course, this order and connection that Irenaeus describes, in a summary fashion, in the *Demonstration*, so that "by means of this small [work you may] understand all the members of the body of the truth" (chap. 1), that is Scripture itself (25–26).

The rule of faith (or rule of truth) is the baptismal creed (Apostles' Creed) that accompanies baptism in the threefold name. The expansion of this creed

---

37. Irenaeus of Lyons, *Apostolic Preaching*, 25. This accessible English translation has an excellent introduction by John Behr, which I highly recommend. The work is usually known by the title *Demonstration of the Apostolic Preaching*.

38. In accordance with the custom followed in many ancient works, the book is divided into short sections, called chapters, which are included in all editions and translations regardless of pagination. This allows the reader to find citations in any edition, including the original language edition. I will put most references to chapter numbers in brackets in my text. Direct quotations, however, will be footnoted. I will give page numbers from the Popular Patristics edition.

is described as the *skopos* or main theme of the Bible. Thus we have three concentric circles: the baptismal formula of the threefold name itself, the Apostles' Creed or rule of faith with its three articles based on the threefold name, and then the *skopos* of Scripture as spelled out here in the *Demonstration*. A complete biblical theology would comprise yet another circle. The *Demonstration* is as much like a whole-Bible biblical theology as anything stemming from the patristic age.

For Irenaeus, the apostolic preaching is the proclamation that Jesus Christ has, in his birth, life, death, resurrection, and ascension, fulfilled the Old Testament. As Behr puts it, "The whole content of the apostolic preaching is derived, for Irenaeus, from the Old Testament."[39] Behr sees Irenaeus as the first patristic writer to maintain "the unity of God's dealings with the human race throughout history."[40] For Behr, as for Augustine in his *City of God*, the Bible tells the story of the totality of created reality from creation to consummation. Jesus Christ is not just the center of the New Testament; he is the center of the Bible as a whole, and not just the center of the Bible but of all history.

Behr very helpfully explicates the second-century background in which Irenaeus wrote. As a young man in Smyrna, Irenaeus heard Bishop Polycarp preach. Polycarp had himself been a student of the apostle John. Irenaeus writes less than a century after the death of the last apostle and was taught by someone who himself was a disciple of an apostle. So he considered himself, with some justification, to be knowledgeable about what the apostles had taught and faithful to their proclamation.

In view of Irenaeus's proximity to the apostles, it is significant that he understands their relationship to the Old Testament as proclaiming the fulfillment of those Scriptures by Christ. Behr notes that this is a theme common to other important second-century writers, including Justin Martyr and Ignatius. He comments, "For Ignatius, it is Christ who is both the content and the ultimate source of our faith, as it has been laid down for us by the apostles."[41] Scripture for these second-century writers is still very much the Old Testament, while the gospel is still very much a proclamation. Irenaeus is the first figure for whom the complete Bible consisting of the Old and New Testaments is assumed as the norm.[42]

The reason the New Testament came into existence is that it embodied the conviction of the apostles that Jesus Christ is the fulfillment of the Old Testament. Behr summarizes Ignatius's attitude toward the Old Testament:

39. Behr, "Introduction," in Irenaeus, *Apostolic Preaching*, 8.
40. Behr, "Introduction," in Irenaeus, *Apostolic Preaching*, 8.
41. Behr, "Introduction," in Irenaeus, *Apostolic Preaching*, 9.
42. Behr, "Introduction," in Irenaeus, *Apostolic Preaching*, 15.

Jesus Christ, His passion and resurrection is, for Ignatius, the only complete revelation of God; this alone is salvific. . . . When Ignatius states that "To me the archives [i.e., the books of the Old Testament] are Jesus Christ," he is not implying that Jesus Christ is a different, higher authority than Scripture; rather, for Ignatius, the Old Testament simply is Jesus Christ—the Word made flesh. All Scripture pertaining to the revelation of God is identical with the revelation of God given in Christ as preached by the apostles; and, in reverse, all that the Gospel proclaims has already been written down as Scripture.[43]

We should not pass lightly over the statement that "the Old Testament simply is Jesus Christ." In a Christian Platonist context, what is being said is that the Old Testament writings do actually participate in the reality that is Jesus Christ. Although these writings predate the incarnation, they do not predate the preexistent Christ, who pervades them with his power and presence as the Word and Wisdom of the Father.

Another significant point for reading Irenaeus correctly is that the christo-centric reading of the Old Testament is much more (though never less) than predictive prophecy. As Behr explains, "For Ignatius and the other apostolic fathers, the Christian Gospel, the revelation of Jesus Christ, was essentially a Christocentric reading of Scripture, as it had been delivered by the apostles, though their writings were never cited to substantiate this teaching nor were they ever cited as Scripture."[44] In the second-century context, the Old Testament reveals Christ; this is true for all the church fathers. Commenting on Justin Martyr, Behr writes, "Although Justin has certainly begun to utilize some apostolic writings, he follows the apostolic fathers in seeing the Christian revelation as having been foreshadowed in the Old Testament Scripture . . . as Justin claims that the prophecies have been fulfilled in Christ, so also the Christian revelation, given by the apostles, is the key to understanding the message proclaimed by the prophets."[45] This is the context in which Irenaeus wrote, and these are the convictions that formed his framework of interpretation.

Another crucial point is that because the Old Testament is fulfilled in the New, not only is the apostolic preaching crucial to the full understanding of the Old Testament, but the Old Testament is crucial to understanding Christian revelation. As Behr puts it, "That the apostolic preaching is nothing other than the various predictions made by the prophets, proclaimed as having been realized in Jesus Christ, means that, on the one hand, the apostolic preaching is both the key to understanding the Old Testament and the confirmation

43. Behr, "Introduction," in Irenaeus, *Apostolic Preaching*, 11.
44. Behr, "Introduction," in Irenaeus, *Apostolic Preaching*, 11.
45. Behr, "Introduction," in Irenaeus, *Apostolic Preaching*, 12.

of its fulfillment, while, on the other hand, it is the Old Testament which shapes the whole of the Christian revelation itself."[46] In this context, one can appreciate that the challenge of Marcion was a life-and-death threat to the very essence of the faith of the church. If his views had prevailed and the Church had jettisoned the Old Testament, the very essence of the gospel would have gone with it.

What is Irenaeus's purpose in *Demonstration of the Apostolic Preaching*? According to Behr, he had two main purposes, each of which could be described as a "demonstration." First, he wanted to demonstrate or unfold the contents of the Old Testament as it pertains to the revelation of Christ preached by the apostles. Second, he wanted to urge the recognition of the scriptural authority of that preaching by demonstrating that the apostles' proclamation of what had been fulfilled in Jesus Christ was indeed prophesied by the prophets beforehand. Irenaeus begins with the necessity of prayer and obedience to God for understanding the Scriptures (chap. 3). He refers to Isaiah 7:9 as expressing the critical principle that if one does not believe, one will not understand. Interestingly, for Irenaeus to "keep the rule of faith" is closely associated with performing the commandments of God, believing in him, and fearing him. There is no gap here between piety and sound biblical interpretation. In fact, each requires the other. In this regard, Irenaeus is typical of the church fathers as a group.

In part 1 of the work (chaps. 3b–42), Irenaeus gives what we can term a biblical theology of the Old Testament in which he covers the history of redemption according to the Scriptures. In part 2 of the work (chaps. 43–97), he describes how everything proclaimed about Christ by the apostles was prophesied beforehand. He discusses the preexistence of Christ as the central meaning of the Old Testament, including how Christ appeared to Abraham and Jacob and spoke to Moses from the burning bush. He discusses how David and Isaiah spoke of the Father and the Son, and he goes on to discuss the life of Christ as an extension of his preincarnate work.

The fundamental idea of Irenaeus's hermeneutics is that "it is on the basis of Scripture that Scripture should be understood."[47] This should be regarded as a bedrock principle of all patristic exegesis and should also be understood as the foundation of all biblical exegesis worthy of the name "Christian." Of course, this principle was replaced in the Enlightenment with the principle that texts should be understood in their historical sense (where "historical" means "history as understood on the basis of philosophical naturalism").

---

46. Behr, "Introduction," in Irenaeus, *Apostolic Preaching*, 13.
47. Behr, "Introduction," in Irenaeus, *Apostolic Preaching*, 24.

Modern historical criticism views "history" as hypothetical reconstructions of the extrabiblical reality in which the author of the text functioned. The Enlightenment theory of exegesis is contradictory to the patristic one, not only because to interpret Scripture in the light of Scripture is to deny the necessity of these changing, unstable historical reconstructions for knowing the meaning of the text but also because it is to interpret the text in a context (the canon of Scripture) in which philosophical naturalism is not accepted. Whatever else they are, the writers of Scripture are not Epicurean naturalists. Our question is which is the primary and most important context for Scripture: history as reconstructed by scholars operating on the basis of philosophical naturalism or the canon of Scripture as a whole as interpreted according to its own intrinsic *skopos*? This issue gets to the heart of the conflict between the Great Tradition and the Enlightenment.

Irenaeus's famous illustration given in his work *Against Heresies* regarding the shortcomings of the gnostic approach to the interpretation of Scripture is as follows:

> Their manner of acting is just as if one, when a beautiful image of a king has been constructed by some skillful artist out of precious jewels, should then take this likeness of the man all to pieces, should re-arrange the gems, and so fit them together as to make them into the form of a dog or of a fox, and even that but poorly executed; and should then maintain and declare that *this* was the beautiful image of the king which the skillful artist constructed, pointing to the jewels which had been admirably fitted together by the first artist to form the image of the king, but have been with bad effect transferred by the latter one to the shape of a dog, and by thus exhibiting the jewels, should deceive the ignorant who had no conception what a king's form was like, and persuade them that that miserable likeness of the fox was, in fact, the beautiful image of the king.[48]

For Irenaeus, the apostles arrange the jewels of the Old Testament in such a way that the image that appears is the face of Jesus Christ.

John Webster argues that we today are "weighed down by spiritual and intellectual custom" and therefore "stiff and clumsy" in making the kind of doctrinal moves the fathers made naturally. He says "we need the training which comes from watching and trying to keep pace with earlier generations who did not share all our compulsions."[49] In his summary of the unity of Scripture, Webster expresses much the same thought as Irenaeus in a contemporary context:

48. Irenaeus of Lyons, *Against Heresies*, 326 (1.8.1).
49. Webster, *Domain of the Word*, 17.

Unity is given by the fact that these texts, in all their incontrovertible diversity of origin and composition and matter, are gathered and formed into a unity by Christ. All things cohere in him, for he recapitulates all things. There is, again, a certain obscurity to this unity, which does not reside on the surface of the texts but in the one of whom the texts are servants, the eternal Son. He—not their discrete occasions—is their primary context and referent; by him they are held together. . . . Jesus Christ guarantees the unity of Scripture, and the propriety of reading it as such, because he is its *auctor primarius* and its *res*.[50]

Webster shares with the fathers, such as Irenaeus, the Christian Platonist conviction that Christ is present in the text and that the text becomes the sacramental means by which we are united with Christ. It is not going too far to assert that the unity of the Bible *is* Christ.

It should come as no great shock to discover that the Enlightenment higher critics denied not only the unity of the Bible but also the unity and coherence of the thought of Irenaeus. In his excellent study of Irenaeus, Eric Osborn states, "No one has presented a more unified account of God, the world and history than has Irenaeus."[51] Yet Osborn also notes that the nineteenth century found the opposite in him. Adolf von Harnack, for example, saw Irenaeus's writings as a compilation of separate traditions. Building on Harnack, F. Loofs applied source criticism to Irenaeus's writings; the not unexpected result was that Irenaeus came out looking like a bad theologian and a "much slighter figure than was previously supposed."[52] One is reminded of Jesus calling Peter to follow him in his death (John 21:18–19). If the disciple is not greater than his Lord, it is hardly surprising that the writings of the fathers should have the same indignity inflicted on them as the apostolic writings themselves. But Osborn's work is a reasoned defense of the unity, coherence, and profundity of the theology of Irenaeus, just as Irenaeus's work is a reasoned defense of the same characteristics of the Bible.

Osborn discusses how the prophets take precedence over the philosophers in Irenaeus, just as we saw in Justin Martyr. He describes Irenaeus's thought as a kind of "horizontal Platonism" in which "the prophets, saints and apostles, and above all the words of Jesus, take the place of the Platonic forms. . . . The prolixity of Irenaeus is not a problem when we see it as an attempt to convey the richness of the mind of God as found in scripture."[53] The use of the metaphor of the picture of the beautiful king is no accident in Irenaeus,

50. Webster, *Domain of the Word*, 18.
51. Osborn, *Irenaeus of Lyons*, 9.
52. Loofs as quoted by Osborn, *Irenaeus of Lyons*, 11.
53. Osborn, *Irenaeus of Lyons*, 15–16.

for he is a writer who understands that what Scripture contains is much too deep, mysterious, and profound to be conveyed in mere theological statements alone.

Osborn develops the unity and beauty of Irenaeus's thought by proposing that in reading Irenaeus we should be guided by four crucial theological concepts and two standards of truth. The four concepts are intellect, economy, recapitulation, and participation. By "intellect" he means that, for Irenaeus, "God is universal Intellect, embracing all things in knowledge and vision, indivisible and simultaneous, entire and identical, the source of all good things."[54] By "economy" he means the overall plan of God that can be discerned from his action in history. History makes sense as the unfolding of the unchanging forms of the divine mind. It is God's action in history that reveals truth. By "recapitulation" he means that all change finds meaning in the person and work of Jesus Christ, who is the "first principle of truth, goodness and being." By "participation" he means that "as God has ever been a presence from which man could not escape, now that presence is an intricate immediacy apart from which neither God nor man can be understood." Osborn continues: "The purpose of the divine exchange is that man might become what God is . . . the end of all things is the participation of God in man and of man in God." Osborn structures his exposition of the theology of Irenaeus around these four concepts.

Osborn also discusses Irenaeus's two criteria of truth. Irenaeus uses logic, but because of what he was trying to talk about, he was "driven" to use aesthetics as well.[55] According to Osborn, in interpreting Irenaeus, we must ask how he combines logic and aesthetic, argument and image. Irenaeus argues against the gnostics using arguments held together by imagery. Gnosticism thought in pictures only and was not really capable of assimilating paradox, but in the thought of Irenaeus, "transcendent love implied nearness and the exclusiveness of Christ brought all things together."[56]

The closest thing we have in contemporary theology to the kind of thinking that Irenaeus is doing in *Demonstration of the Apostolic Preaching* is what I would term "Vosian biblical theology," meaning the tradition of whole-Bible biblical theology in which the Bible is interpreted as a unity centered on Jesus Christ by means of a hermeneutic that sees the most important context of

---

54. The four definitions in the paragraph all come from Osborn, *Irenaeus of Lyons*, 21–22.
55. Osborn, *Irenaeus of Lyons*, 22.
56. Osborn, *Irenaeus of Lyons*, 24. I think that Irenaeus would appreciate the argument in chap. 2 of this book that it is precisely the transcendence of God that is the basis for God's ability to act in history. Theistic personalism misses the paradoxical truth that God as pure being itself is thus able to be *more* personal than a being among beings could ever be.

every biblical text to be the canon of Scripture as a whole. Vosian biblical theology can be contrasted to other kinds of biblical theology: "Gablerian biblical theology" and "Childsian biblical theology." Briefly, they can be differentiated as follows.

Gablerian biblical theology goes back to J. P. Gabler, who is a representative of the Enlightenment; it is opposed to the creeds and dogmas of the Great Tradition. It seeks to drive a wedge between what the text "meant" and what it "means."[57] This is a historical approach that tries to isolate the "theology of Paul" from the "theology of John" and the "Deuteronomistic theology" from the "priestly theology," and so on. For this reason, it is confusing and perhaps inappropriate to call this enterprise "biblical theology" at all. According to Otto Betz, J. P. Gabler in his famous inaugural address at the University of Altdorf in 1787 forthrightly declared biblical theology to be a historical science.[58] It is really more a matter of doing ancient history on the basis of naturalistic presuppositions than it is a form of theology. It is the study, not of God, but rather of human thoughts about God. The unity, clarity, sufficiency, necessity, and authority of Scripture are all denied in principle and ignored in practice. To call this sort of thing "theology" is quite a stretch; to call it "Christian theology" makes no sense whatsoever.

Vosian biblical theology begins with the work of Geerhardus Vos in the early twentieth century[59] and is an attempt to reform the Gablerian approach so as to remove its considerable deficiencies, which are seen as deriving from the Enlightenment. Instead of a historical-critical approach, the Vosian approach advocates a redemptive-historical approach. In many ways, it has been very successful, despite two significant, though not fatal, flaws. One problem is that it fails to perceive clearly enough the nature of its own kinship to the Great Tradition and to writers like Irenaeus and Augustine. The second flaw is the source of the first. Because Vosian biblical theology often lacks the philosophical sophistication to perceive its own affinity to the Christian Platonism of the Great Tradition, it is not able to critique Enlightenment philosophy in the light of that Christian Platonism. If practitioners of Vosian biblical theology could grasp the importance of recovering Christian Platonism and

---

57. See the famous article by Stendahl, "Biblical Theology, Contemporary," 418–32. The entire thrust of this article revolves around the purported need to distinguish between what the text "meant" and what it "means." What it meant is discerned by investigating what the original human author meant in the original historical context, assuming that philosophical naturalism is true. The validity of the rejection of Christian Platonism and the embrace of atomism, nominalism, and materialism in the Enlightenment is the unstated premise on which the whole article rests.

58. Betz, "Biblical Theology," 433.

59. See Vos, *Biblical Theology* and *Redemptive History and Biblical Interpretation*.

using it to critique modern philosophical errors, they could reestablish a link with the Great Tradition that would allow them to draw on the riches of the Christian intellectual past in the work of reconstructing Western civilization after the coming collapse of modernity.

Christian Platonist metaphysics provides a conceptual way of expressing what many evangelicals working in Vosian biblical theology seem to grasp intuitively—namely, that in some mysterious but real way Jesus Christ meets them and transforms them through the texts of the Old Testament that traditionally have been interpreted christologically in the preaching of the church. This kind of preaching is common in the contemporary, conservative, evangelical Reformed tradition. Nevertheless, even without being able to mount a philosophical critique of modernity, those working in this tradition today are doing wonderful work in reviving the practice of whole-Bible biblical theology that was launched by Irenaeus and that has been a constant theme throughout the history of the Great Tradition. In my opinion, the single best example of Vosian biblical theology available today is the deeply insightful work of James M. Hamilton Jr., *God's Glory in Salvation through Judgment*.[60]

Childsian biblical theology is an attempt to offer a mediating approach that appropriates many of the benefits of the Vosian approach without challenging the narrow philosophical naturalism-inspired redefinition of history promoted by the Enlightenment. To the extent that it tries to be a dialectical approach that moves back and forth between the naturalistic view of history and the biblical understanding of history, it achieves some notable successes in interpretation, but in the end it is just not radical enough to reconnect church preaching with the Great Tradition in the way that is needed. Childs has done extremely helpful work in pointing us back to the Great Tradition, but like Moses he has not entered the promised land himself; he has only made it possible for others to do so if they wish.

Both Childs and Vos provide part of what we need in order to move biblical interpretation forward. Childs, on the one hand, has identified the rich resources available to us in the Great Tradition, as we saw in our discussion of his *Struggle to Understand Isaiah as Christian Scripture* in chapter 4. Vos, on the other hand, has demonstrated the theological unity of the Bible as a whole; what Childs writes about, Vos actually puts into practice. But both need to be brought into conversation with the voices of the Great Tradition discussed in this chapter and the two to follow. This book is only a modest

---

60. For more examples of Vosian biblical theology, see the footnotes in chap. 1 above in the section titled "Biblical Theology and a Theology of the Bible."

beginning of such a conversation. But we have to begin somewhere, and listening to the voice of the fathers seems like a good place to start.

Summary and Conclusions

We have examined three church fathers who embody foundational aspects of the Great Tradition of Christian biblical interpretation: Ambrose of Milan, Justin Martyr, and Irenaeus of Lyons. We could have discussed far more than these three. We could have multiplied examples of how the fathers connected piety, prayer, right interpretation, and true doctrine. We could have discussed the role of the *skopos* of Scripture in Athanasius's arguments against the Arians. We could have talked about Augustine's theology of history as similar in important ways to that of Irenaeus. But I hope that enough has been said to show that this is a line of investigation worth pursuing further.

The church fathers believed that the christological reading of the Old Testament is the *true* reading of the Bible. For them, the Bible is not a jumble of often contradictory human thoughts about divine matters but the unified product of a divine Author who worked through providence and miracle to put meaning into the text that was partly, but not totally, comprehended by the human authors. The fathers further believed that seeing this for oneself required being sanctified by the Holy Spirit in the sense that sanctification was both the result of initial understanding and the precondition for deeper understanding. They saw the Christian life as a process and always thought of biblical interpretation as a process of spiritual growth and increasing insight into truth. They also believed that the Scriptures should be interpreted according to the rule of faith (the Apostles' Creed), which is simply a summary of the *skopos* of the Bible. Its role is to remind the exegete of the overall shape of the biblical message as a guide to exegesis so that our interpretations of particular verses do not contradict the rest of Scripture. Because of its divine authorship, Scripture cannot contradict Scripture.

The use of the creed to interpret Scripture is not a device used to import extrinsic meaning from outside the canon into the Bible, but precisely the opposite. Augustine, in his comments on Psalm 73, explains that the unity of Scripture means that Christ really is present in the Old Testament and not just in the New. When Hans Boersma speaks of "Scripture as real presence," he means that Christ is present in the Old Testament ontologically and not just read into the Old Testament text by overzealous Christian interpreters.[61] In

---

61. Boersma, *Scripture as Real Presence*, is the best resource now available for examples of patristic biblical interpretation.

a sermon delivered in 411, Augustine explains how Christ can be simultaneously present and hidden in the Psalms:

> At that time the New Testament was hidden within the Old, as fruit is in the root. If you look for fruit in a root you will not find it; yet you will not find any fruit on the branches either, unless it has sprung from the root. . . . Christ himself, inasmuch as he was to be born according to the flesh, was hidden in the root, that is to say, in the bloodline of the patriarchs. At the appointed time he was to be revealed, like fruit forming from the flower, and so scripture says, *A shoot has sprung from Jesse's stock, and a flower has opened* (Isa. 11:1).[62]

Augustine uses this image of root and fruit to stress that Christ really is present in the Old Testament, which functions sacramentally to bring us to him.

When the higher critics of the modern period claim that the creedal orthodoxy of the Great Tradition is a foreign set of concepts imposed on the biblical writings in an arbitrary manner, they are therefore rejecting what the fathers would have described as the faith delivered to the church by the apostles and thus the true meaning of the Bible itself. Anyone has the right to reject the message of the Bible, but no one has the right to hijack the Bible and claim that it says something foreign to its true meaning so as to domesticate it and turn it into the property of a neopagan religion of a decadent culture. The Reformation slogan of "the Word and the Spirit" must be reclaimed; there can be no Word without the Spirit, and the Spirit is never known apart from the Word.

62. Augustine, *Expositions of the Psalms, 51–72*, 470–71.

6

Letting the Literal Sense
Control All Meaning

> In the usual prophetic manner, however, figurative and literal expres-
> sions are mingled here, so that sober attentiveness may, by useful
> and salutary labor, arrive at the spiritual meaning. In contrast,
> carnal indolence or the slowness of the uninstructed and untrained
> mind is content with the literal meaning that lies on the surface
> and presumes that there is no more inward meaning to be sought.
>
> Augustine of Hippo[1]

This chapter continues the task of recovering the classical interpretation of Scripture begun in the previous one. Whereas chapter 5 dealt
with the hermeneutical implications of the unity and clarity of the Bible,
the present chapter continues to explore how unity and clarity are present in
the biblical text by specifically addressing the issue of meaning. To this end,
we will consider some of the most fundamental questions in hermeneutics.
What does the text mean? Does it have a spiritual sense in addition to its literal sense? How does the literal sense relate to the historical sense? Can the
literal sense be the historical sense, as history is understood within Christian
Platonism, or should it be restricted to the sense of history as advocated by
the Enlightenment? How does the literal sense relate to the canonical context?
Finally, in light of the discussion of such questions, we must come to some

---

1. Augustine, *City of God* 20.21, p. 426.

conclusions about what it means for the literal sense to control the meaning. The purpose of this chapter is to suggest that the Great Tradition of Christian biblical interpretation has been wrestling with these confusing and complex questions for centuries and has developed some hard-won answers, which modern hermeneutics has been, until recently, largely guilty of ignoring.

The word "literally" is one of the most misused and abused words in the contemporary English language. In popular usage today, it often means "with no exaggeration," as in "When I was a boy, we literally walked three miles to school every day." What is the point of using the word "literally" in this context? Is someone likely to think that "walking to school" is a euphemism for flying or getting there via a Star Trek transporter? Even worse is the slang expression "I literally died laughing." Well, if so, how is it that you have come back from the grave to tell us about it? It seems to be used for emphasis and to convey the idea that one is not exaggerating, which are characteristics of *how* the meaning is conveyed. In chapter 1, we saw Stephen Fowl imply that the "plain sense" (which historically is closely related to the "literal sense") is whatever the reading community says it is.[2] Can the word "literally" be saved, or is its meaning so vague and diverse that it has become useless?

If we want to use the word "literally" in a useful manner to get at some of the central issues in the Christian exegetical tradition, the first step is to see the roots of the meaning of the word as descriptive of *the meaning conveyed*, rather than in *how meaning is conveyed*. Let us consider what this would mean. When we use the word "literal," we can refer either to the proposition being asserted or to the figure of speech used to assert the proposition. This double meaning is the source of much confusion. For example, if we say "Josh Donaldson stole second base last night," is that a literal statement or not? Did he "literally" steal second base? The statement means that the baseball player advanced from first to second base without being thrown out by running quickly while the pitcher was delivering his pitch to home plate. Did he literally get from first base to second base? Most certainly he did—literally. But if we were to picture him sneaking out of the clubhouse and walking down Front Street in Toronto with a big, white base under his coat, we would misunderstand what was being asserted, and we would do so by taking the statement literally in the wrong way. We need to see that a *literal* fact is being asserted here by means of a *metaphor*. Understanding the metaphor rightly is essential to grasping exactly what fact is being asserted. It is possible either to believe or to disbelieve a proposition while acknowledging that the proposition is conveyed in either a literal or nonliteral way.

2. See chap. 1 above and also Fowl, *Engaging Scripture*, 119–26.

The legendary Southern Baptist preacher W. A. Criswell once wrote a book titled *Why I Preach That the Bible Is Literally True*. This way of putting it is familiar to many conservative Christians who object to the rejection of the fundamentals of the faith by theological liberals. But does anyone really suppose that Criswell's point was that there are no metaphors in the Bible? Of course not. So the proper way to express the orthodox criticism of liberal theology is not that liberals do not take biblical statements literally in all cases—who does? But rather, the essence of the concern is that what the text asserts—whether literally or through a figure of speech—is to be believed and not denied. We are to believe the literal truth of the proposition even when it is conveyed by means of a metaphor. When someone says that a biblical statement is "just a metaphor," one should immediately ask "A metaphor for what?" That will expose the motive behind the statement. Theological liberals often equate the "meaning" of biblical metaphors with their own common sense or progressive thoughts or higher religious sentiments in such a way that no one can specify the exact nature of the connection between the biblical text and what the metaphor in the text supposedly signifies. That lack of connection allows the worldview of the interpreter to become the real source of theological convictions, thus silencing the Bible, which then is reduced to functioning as a symbol of contemporary culture's highest values. Anything that erases the vital connections between what the text says and the content of the doctrine taught in the church undermines the authority of Scripture. This is the legitimate source of the suspicion of any sort of spiritual sense of Scripture, and we must ensure that in talk about any deeper or fuller or christological meaning attributed to the text, especially that of the Old Testament, we articulate the way in which this meaning is related to the literal sense. If it is not related to the literal sense—that is, to the meaning conveyed—it undermines the authority of Scripture.

All discussions that focus on the contrast between "allegory" and "typology" or that contend that "figural" is a legitimate way to read Scripture but that "allegory" is not are missing the main point. The main point at stake in the orthodox tradition of Christian exegesis is not method, but meaning. It is not the way meaning is conveyed, but what meaning is conveyed. In much of the history of hermeneutics, the meaning of "literal" is contrasted with "allegorical" in such a way that to take a text allegorically is to obscure or reject its real meaning. And that is surely a bad thing. But representatives of the Great Tradition, who are opposed to obscuring or rejecting what the text asserts, are not at all opposed to accepting truth conveyed through a metaphor, figure, symbol, or even allegory. The concern they typically have is the use of nonliteral interpretation to silence or reject the real meaning in the text.

In talking to laypeople and pastors, I find that most who insist on a "literal" interpretation of Genesis 1, for example, do so because, in their experience, it is the only way to protect the meaning of creation *ex nihilo*, and I, for one, share that concern. After all, many of those who have claimed that we ought to take Genesis 1 as a metaphor (or parable, poetry, or allegory) actually have been interested in substituting a very different creation story for the orthodox one. They typically affirm an understanding of creation that features eternal matter being shaped and molded by a demigod who is neither infinite nor transcendent, or else they tell a story of random chance with matter and energy interacting eternally in a universe that is in constant flux with no purpose, no design, and no transcendent Creator providentially guiding it to its eschatological destiny through Christ. The amusing thing is that they seem to want us to believe their story as the "literal truth"! If refusing to take Genesis 1 "literally" ends up meaning that we accept a pagan myth as literally true, then it seems like a shell game designed to deceive the faithful into accepting what the apostle Peter referred to as "cleverly devised myths" (2 Pet. 1:16). The instinct many people have—that taking Genesis 1 seriously means taking it literally—is perfectly sound when we are talking about the meaning conveyed rather than the way in which the meaning is conveyed. But if someone were to propose that we read Genesis 1 as a "parable that teaches creation *ex nihilo*," I would have to consider that reading to be a serious possibility.

The thesis of this chapter is that we need to let the literal meaning of Scripture control the interpretation of the text, but that doing so does not necessitate ruling out a spiritual meaning that can be described as a *sensus plenior* or the spiritual or christological sense of the text. Just as we can distinguish between *what* the text means and *how* that meaning is conveyed, so we can also distinguish between the meaning conveyed by the text and the human authorial intent. One of the goals of this chapter is to show how the Great Tradition of Christian exegesis was right to advocate seeing a spiritual sense of Scripture in addition to the literal sense. As Henri de Lubac says, "To summarize the whole thing briefly: the Christian tradition understands that Scripture has two meanings. The most general name for these two meanings is the literal meaning and the spiritual ('pneumatic') meaning, and these two meanings have the same kind of relationship to each other as do the Old and New Testaments to each other. More exactly, and in all strictness, they constitute, they *are* the Old and New Testaments."[3]

In chapter 1 I described my dilemma as a young pastor in knowing that Isaiah 53 speaks of the crucifixion and resurrection of Jesus Christ but not

---

3. De Lubac, *Medieval Exegesis*, 1:225.

knowing *how* this could be so, given what I had been taught about herme-neutical theory. How I wish I had read these words of de Lubac's while in seminary and before I had to preach my first Good Friday service! Eventually, by God's grace, I discovered that the Great Tradition of Christian exegesis had always seen a christological sense in Isaiah 53, but I still could not see how that christological sense could rightly be called the *literal* sense as long as I understood the literal sense within the narrow constraints of the Enlight-enment view of history. I could not see how a nonliteral sense could be true. Many people I know seem to have this same dilemma.

From a methodological naturalist perspective, Isaiah 53 could not be about an event seven centuries in the future (or even five or three centuries in the future on the assumption of a later date). But if the christological sense is not the literal sense, how is that other sense (whatever we call it) connected to the literal sense? How could it be something other than free-floating subjectivism? (I did not want to preach my own feelings about the text; I wanted to preach the Word of God.) This is a perennial question in the history of Great Tradi-tion hermeneutics. What this chapter seeks to show is that the spiritual sense is not in contradiction to, nor does it float free from, the literal sense. This will be done by showing that the Great Tradition, at its best, moved gradually in the direction of viewing the spiritual sense as contained within, or as an expansion of, the literal sense. The spiritual sense is not read into the text, nor is it a matter of individual subjective opinion. Instead, it is what Calvin, who brings the Great Tradition of Christian exegesis to its peak, calls "the plain sense of the text." I contend that this plain sense of the text is what scientific exegesis needs to engage.

It is ironic that modern historical-critical exegesis, for all its purported concern for the "scientific" meaning of the Bible, actually fails to be scientific enough.[4] Modern historical criticism understands the scientific meaning to be identical with the historical meaning and insists on restricting the definition of "historical" to the constricted and narrow sense allowed by philosophical naturalism. The modern period therefore actually has brought a major swerve *away* from the literal meaning of the text, which is considered too dangerous,

---

4. This point is made forcefully by Karl Barth in his preface to the second edition of his *Epistle to the Romans*:

> The critical historian needs to be more critical. The interpretation of what is written requires more than a disjointed series of notes on words and phrases. . . . True apprehen-sion can be achieved only by a strict determination to face, as far as possible without rigidity of mind, the tension displayed more or less clearly in the ideas written in the text. Criticism . . . applied to historical documents means for me the measuring of words and phrases by the standard of that about which the documents are speaking. . . . The Word ought to be exposed in the words. (8)

too foreign, too intrusive, too demanding, and too subversive and therefore in need of domestication and restriction to what interpreters can handle safely within their worldview. The literal meaning of the text thus has been subverted, circumvented, ignored, demoted, and replaced by various forms of modern exegesis, and to cap it all off, the modern interpreters have had the audacity to invent a narrative in which, supposedly, it was the exegesis of the *fathers* that allowed allegory to subvert the literal sense. Moderns claim that, unlike the fathers, they honor the literal sense, because they make the historical sense primary. There is a subtle but very deceptive sleight of hand at work here.

We readily acknowledge that the Great Tradition has stressed that the re-vealed message of Scripture centers on history. God acts in history and then speaks through his prophets to give the authoritative interpretation of those acts of judgment and salvation. To detach the gospel from history, therefore, would be to destroy it. Thus it seems right to most people that to honor the "historical" meaning of the text would be to honor the literal sense and, in one way, that is perfectly true. That is what Christians have tried to do ever since Peter wrote "For we did not follow cleverly devised myths when we made known to you the power and coming of our Lord Jesus Christ, but we were eyewitnesses of his majesty" (2 Pet. 1:16). Did not Paul also warn against turn-ing away from the truth and wandering off into myths? Indeed he did (2 Tim. 4:4). The biblical text makes statements about what God has done *in history*; not to recognize this fact is to risk drifting off into gnosticism and mythology.

The problem, however, is that ever since the Enlightenment, modern in-terpreters have been smuggling philosophical naturalism into the definition of history, so that history no longer means what the Scriptures and Great Tradition mean by history. (The idea that Peter and Paul meant history under-stood naturalistically is preposterous.) This is why the continuing ecclesiastical tradition of preaching and teaching that has resisted the pagan, philosophical naturalism of the Enlightenment by continuing to operate on the basis of the traditional definition of "history" is in ongoing tension with hermeneutics as practiced in the modern academy. W. A. Criswell and his ilk must be dismissed as "fundamentalists" by the modern academy, which is a good example of name-calling replacing reasoned argument. Are John Calvin, Thomas Aquinas, Augustine, Athanasius, and Irenaeus also to be dismissed as "fundamental-ists"? Should everyone prior to Baruch Spinoza be summarily labeled and dismissed? Perhaps we should think this over before deciding.

For the Great Tradition of Christian orthodoxy, the "literal sense" refers to the *meaning* of the biblical text, whether that meaning is conveyed through literal statements or through some sort of figural language and whether that meaning is what the human author consciously intended or is an extension of the human author's intention implanted in the text by the Holy Spirit through inspiration. The meaning of the biblical text, for the Great Tradition, cannot be reduced to what fits within the narrow confines of naturalistic metaphysics any more than the content of the text, the *res* to which the text points—that is, the living God who created the cosmos—can be fit into a naturalistic metaphysics. We find ourselves in the curious position of having to oppose something named "the historical-critical method" in order to do justice to what the Bible means by history. To top it off, we find that only by such opposition can we hope to preserve the *literal* sense of Scripture.

Many interpretive methods have been used in the history of Great Tradition exegesis to understand the literal meaning of the biblical text. The use of a method is far from being a panacea; as a matter of fact, every single reading method ever used has created problems as well as solved them. All reading methods—including allegory, typology, rhetorical analysis, form criticism, and all the rest—are in need of adaptation in view of the fact that the Bible is a book *unlike* any other, contra Spinoza. All methods—ancient and modern—are secondary to the pursuit of the meaning of the Holy Scriptures; yet all these methods must be revised in light of the meaning of the sacred texts to cope with the reality that commandeers those texts and speaks through them—namely, the living God. Method is subject to revision in the process of encountering the reality that we use the method to encounter. This basic point is often missed by those who write about hermeneutical theory in the contemporary academy, but it is a point that impresses itself on preachers of the Word with such force that it demands to be taken into consideration constantly.

What David Steinmetz once scathingly referred to as the "endless deferral of meaning"[5] is only possible in the academy and other artificial environments. It is impossible in real life; the opposite of the endless deferral of meaning is the constant engagement with the meaning of the text. When God speaks through the text to me, my sins and shortcomings are exposed—including my hermeneutical sins and shortcomings. The graduate seminar may end in uncertainty about the meaning of the text week after week, but when one has to preach next Sunday morning, one is forced to grapple with the text for as long as it takes to come to grips with its meaning. Very often the preacher cannot get ready to preach without repenting, which is part of what the fathers were talking about when they spoke of exegesis as a process of sanctification. Can a biblical scholar repent?

5. Steinmetz, "Superiority of Pre-critical Exegesis," 14.

In serious biblical interpretation, we need to understand the literal sense in terms of what the text actually means, and we must understand what the text actually means in terms of both human and divine authorship. It is an axiom of biblical interpretation that the true meaning of the Bible cannot be discerned unless one interprets it in a way that the meaning could be there only on the assumption of divine authorship. The Bible is a library of books written by over forty different human authors in three languages over a period of 1,500 years. Its unity—if it actually has a real unity—cannot have a merely human cause.[6] Methodological naturalism can never find unity in the Bible; it is helpless to do so in the face of the diversity of historical backgrounds that constitutes the context of the various biblical writings. It is the divine authorship of the Bible that makes it not just a library of books, but also one book. It is the divine authorship of the Bible that makes it not just the words of Moses, Isaiah, John, and Paul but also the Word of God. It is the divine authorship of the Bible that gives it one message and one theme: God. It is the divine authorship of the Bible that is the basis for one of the most basic of all hermeneutical rules—namely, that the Bible does not contradict itself—and therefore any interpretation of a text that contradicts the plain meaning of other texts in the Bible cannot be right. The Bible does not contradict itself because God inspired the Holy Scriptures, and God does not contradict himself.

The doctrine of inspiration, as we saw in chapter 2, also means that there can be no final conflict between the *divine* authorial intent and the *human* authorial intent, even if the divine authorial intent goes beyond what the human author consciously intended, which it often does (1 Pet. 1:10–12). The meaning of the text is what God is saying to us *through* the human prophets and apostles, who were his appointed messengers to all generations. Getting to this meaning has never been easy, because it involves prayer, piety, obedience to our Lord Jesus Christ, careful reading, contemplation, and the illumination

6. Frances Young writes, "The unity of the Scriptures is recognized to have been a dogma among the Fathers. The effect of this on exegesis, however, has not previously been discussed" (*Biblical Exegesis and the Formation of Christian Culture*, 7). Young attempts to show, especially in chap. 2, how the assumption of unity affected the exegesis of Scripture by the fathers. She shows that the Arian controversy was essentially a dispute over exegesis, and she shows further that Athanasius appealed to the unity of Scripture to support his interpretation of key texts in such a way that belief in the unity of Scripture was decisive for deciding the issue. She demonstrates that the debate with the Arians focused attention on the meaning of the text: "It also made Athanasius aware that one needed to probe behind the words to the 'mind' of scripture" (34). This is a very valuable discussion. I regret not having time to treat the exegesis of Athanasius more adequately in this book, but I have decided to discuss him more extensively in my upcoming book on the doctrine of God.

of the Holy Spirit. But *that* meaning, and nothing less than that meaning, is what biblical interpretation is after.

In the rest of this chapter we will examine two lines of argument in support of what has been asserted so far. In the first section, we will examine the development of the hermeneutical thought of the single most influential figure in the history of the Christian exegetical tradition, Augustine of Hippo. By looking at his actual practice of exegesis, it is possible to discern a movement in which the literal and spiritual senses are first pulled apart in order to uncover the richness of meaning contained in the text and later reunited in order to guard against Scripture being divided against itself. To see this, it is necessary to consider his actual exegesis in *Expositions of the Psalms* rather than only his theoretical reflections in *On Christian Doctrine*. It was primarily his actual practice of exegesis (especially of the Psalms and John) that shaped the Christian Great Tradition.[7]

Then, in the second section, we turn to the broader tradition of Christian exegesis to show that a pattern similar to the one observed in Augustine can be discerned in the tradition as a whole. To elucidate this pattern, we will consider briefly figures such as Origen, Theodoret of Cyrus, Thomas Aquinas, and John Calvin to argue that the tradition culminates in an expanded literal sense of the meaning of the text in Calvin's exegesis—an understanding of the literal sense that contains within itself most of the christological meaning that previous theologians had seen as part of the spiritual sense. Calvin usually refers to this as the plain sense. My proposal is that this process, as seen both in Augustine as an individual and in the tradition as a whole, is best understood as a process of gradually Christianizing the pagan tradition of allegorical reading in the service of developing a specifically Christian hermeneutics appropriate to Holy Scripture understood as a canon of writings inspired by a transcendent-personal God who graciously stoops to communicate in a saving way with his sinful creatures.[8] This Christianization of allegory necessarily involves drawing the spiritual or allegorical sense back into close proximity to the literal sense, precisely because the Christian faith is about God's mighty acts in history and the inspired interpretation of the meaning of those acts by his appointed and inspired prophets and apostles.

7. Michael Cameron makes this point in *Christ Meets Me Everywhere*, his extremely important study of Augustine's early hermeneutics: "The Tractates on John's Gospel and especially the Expositions of the Psalms, both endlessly copied in medieval times, made Augustine the most widely read patristic commentator on Scripture in the west for more than a thousand years" (18).

8. In the terminology made popular by Arthur Holmes, this is an exercise in the integration of faith and learning. See A. Holmes, *Idea of a Christian College*, esp. chap. 4.

In continuity with the exegetical practice of Irenaeus and Augustine and in harmony with the Christian Platonism of Thomas Aquinas, at the culminating moment of the Christian hermeneutical tradition, Calvin was able to describe the christological meaning of the Old Testament as the "plain sense" of Scripture. Calvin's ability to do so should be seen as the triumph of the specifically Christian theological reading of Scripture that undergirds Nicene and Chalcedonian orthodoxy. As such, it constitutes a rival and superior tradition to the crude rationalism and shallow naturalism of the Enlightenment and also to the human-centered reaction of the romantic tradition, not to mention the relativistic mess of postmodern theories of meaning designed to eliminate the intention of the author (especially the divine Author) from the meaning of the text, which are used today to turn Scripture into a wax nose by those unwilling to submit to its plain sense.

The Spiritual Meaning Grows out of the Literal Sense: Augustine

This section will address the question of the relationship between the literal and spiritual senses of Scripture in Augustine, the greatest of the church fathers and the spiritual founder of Christendom. We will proceed by unfolding a thesis.

Thesis: The spiritual meaning of the text often goes beyond the limits of what the literal sense says, but all spiritual meaning must be consistent with, and grow out of, the literal sense of the text (1 Pet. 1:10–12).

To unfold this thesis, we will describe the development of Augustine's hermeneutics from his conversion to about 400, when he had finished writing his *Confessions*, become a bishop, and found his feet as a biblical interpreter. Augustine was a man who changed and grew; he once wrote in a letter, "I count myself among those who write by making progress and make progress by writing."[9] There are three steps in this development. First, Augustine sees the need for and the value of the spiritual sense of Scripture in addition to the literal sense. Second, he realizes the need to anchor the spiritual sense in God's historical revelation culminating in the incarnation of the Son, Jesus Christ. Third, he begins to treat the spiritual sense as included in the literal sense.

In what follows in this section, I acknowledge my indebtedness to the work of Michael Cameron in his excellent monograph, *Christ Meets Me Everywhere: Augustine's Early Figurative Exegesis*, in which he gives the best account that I have read of Augustine's actual practice of exegesis. Incidentally,

---

9. Cameron, *Christ Meets Me Everywhere*, 13; see 294n13.

I see significant support for the thesis of my book in the fact that Cameron achieves such clarity in describing Augustine's hermeneutics by means of intensive study of Augustine's actual exegetical practice, rather than by deducing what Augustine's hermeneutics must have been like by examining his more theoretical statements and the philosophical influences on his thought. It is also significant that Augustine's theory changes and deepens as he works away at the practical task of exegesis and preaching. Cameron comes to understand Augustine's hermeneutics in much the same way as Augustine came to understand how to interpret Scripture well. Noting that Augustine learned his hermeneutics "on the run," Cameron says that he wants to "go beyond abstract statements about Scripture to try to catch his hermeneutic in the act of rising out of his practice."[10] I suggest that Cameron's approach to Augustine can be broadened into a way of approaching the history of biblical interpretation in general. Coming to understand the theological exegesis of the Great Tradition is more a matter of apprenticeship in the school of biblical interpretation and preaching than a matter of theoretical construction. It is the actual practice of preaching the Word that makes us into good exegetes, if we approach the task with humility, faith, obedience, a strong work ethic, prayer, and openness to the Holy Spirit.

First, we must look at Augustine's situation in the important year 384. It was in that year that Augustine moved to Milan, came under the influence of Ambrose's preaching, and began to study Platonic philosophy. As an adolescent, Augustine had fallen under the influence of a gnostic cult known as Manichaeism. As a student in Carthage, he had chanced to read Cicero's now-lost work, *Hortensius*, and had been inflamed with a desire to know truth through philosophy. So at the age of nineteen he decided to read the Bible but was put off by what he perceived as its failure to live up to the Ciceronian principle that truth and good form appeared together. The Bible seemed to him to be simplistic and incoherent. Augustine writes, "When I studied the Bible and compared it with Cicero's dignified prose, it seemed to me unworthy. My swollen pride recoiled from its style and my intelligence failed to penetrate to its inner meaning."[11] Notice the connection drawn by Augustine between his pride and the failure of his intelligence to penetrate to the "inner meaning" of the Scriptures. He failed to understand the Bible because he approached it without faith, humility, and openness to the Holy Spirit. It was not that he understood it and rejected it; rather, it was that he was unable to understand it and therefore rejected it. The understanding of the

10. Cameron, *Christ Meets Me Everywhere*, 11.
11. Augustine, *Confessions*, 3.5.9, p. 80.

Word of God is primarily a spiritual issue, as we saw in the previous chapter. To grasp the meaning of any scriptural text, one must be spiritually open to the saving and transforming message of the Bible as a whole.

All this leads us to understand what happened in Milan and what kind of influence Ambrose had on Augustine in a different light than it is sometimes depicted. Instead of the older, two-stage conversion theory (first a conversion to Neoplatonism and then a conversion to Christianity), we need to see that what Augustine learned in Milan was how to understand the Bible's spiritual message. Some Platonic ideas, especially that of spiritual substance, helped him grasp the true meaning of the Holy Scriptures.[12] But his conversion was primarily to the message of the Bible as a two-Testament witness to Jesus Christ as the revelation of the one, true, and living God.

In Ambrose's preaching, Augustine repeatedly heard 2 Corinthians 3:6 quoted: "For the letter kills, but the Spirit gives life." As Augustine explains, Ambrose did this in the context of showing the true, spiritual meaning of the Scriptures: "This he would tell them as he drew aside the veil of mystery and opened to them the spiritual meaning of passages which, taken literally, would seem to mislead."[13] It is worth noting that the context of 2 Corinthians 3:6 is Paul's discussion of the relation between the old and new covenants and specifically the difference the Spirit makes in enabling the believer to keep the new covenant, as opposed to trying to keep the old covenant by our own powers, which always leads to failure and death. Just as the Spirit empowers the believer to keep the new covenant, so the Spirit enables the believer to understand the truth of Scripture. The old covenant by itself leads to death because we cannot obey God's law perfectly; the new covenant leads to life because the Spirit enables believers to keep it. As Paul puts it, "Our sufficiency is from God" (2 Cor. 3:5). Augustine is absorbing a crucial lesson: the Old Testament is true but not complete without the New, and the New is true but not comprehensible without the Old. It is the unity and clarity of Scripture that demonstrate its authority. It was at this point that Augustine decided that orthodox Christianity was not absurd and that the Old Testament was not a liability when properly understood (that is, when understood christologically).

Next, we need to look at a key period in Augustine's development as an interpreter of Scripture, during the years 391–396, when the young priest of the Catholic Church immersed himself in the study of the writings of the apostle Paul to deepen his understanding of Christian truth in preparation for

12. See the section "Why Christian Platonism?" in chap. 3 above for a discussion of how Platonism helped him grasp the biblical nature of God.
13. Augustine, *Confessions*, 6.6, p. 140.

a teaching and preaching ministry as bishop. Augustine came to understand that the crucified man Jesus Christ is the core of God's plan of redemption.[14] What Augustine learned from Paul was "how to read salvation historically."[15] He came to see that salvation unfold through time and that the key to understanding the meaning of Old Testament texts was their fulfillment in the life, death, resurrection, ascension, and future return of Christ.

Augustine began to conceive of salvation history in four stages: (1) before the law when sin was in the world and death reigned even though transgression had not yet been exposed; (2) after the revelation of the law when sin began to be reckoned under the law, and fear of God's punishment became clear; (3) the age of Christ when through his grace, sin began to be overcome, though remnants remain in the heart; and (4) the future age when sin will be eradicated, and humanity will dwell in peace. The most critical transition in this scheme was the shift from being "under law" to being "under grace."

Augustine's attention was captured by the Pauline teaching that we as believers have been crucified with Christ; he found Deuteronomy 21:23, "Cursed is everyone who hangs on a tree," to be deeply significant for reading the Old Testament. As Cameron observes, Augustine grasped that spiritually astute people see that "words and ideas of one age of salvation history point to spiritual realities of the next."[16] Christ carried our sins (1 Pet. 2:24) and was made sin for us "so that in him we might become the righteousness of God" (2 Cor. 5:21). Up until this point, Augustine had understood the Christian life as the soul's striving to imitate the example of Christ in scorning worldly life and fear. But now he had a framework for understanding the human person as purified in Christ and as mortifying the sinful passions that push the soul away from God in a journey of ascent to God through and in Christ. During this time for Augustine, the cross became less a mere symbol of this journey and more a nonfigurative description of "the very mechanism of salvation." As Cameron puts it, "Christ took up this curse not only to teach, but also to redeem."[17] The cross became for Augustine not only a picture of God's love but a power in and of itself. Salvation, Augustine realized, was not merely something that happened in history; rather, salvation is itself essentially historical.[18] Thus, in his commentary on Galatians 3, Augustine saw that the gospel was preached to Abraham, who was justified by faith, not just prior to the coming of Christ but also prior to the giving of the law at Sinai. The

14. Cameron, *Christ Meets Me Everywhere*, 9.
15. Cameron, *Christ Meets Me Everywhere*, 139.
16. Cameron, *Christ Meets Me Everywhere*, 142.
17. Cameron, *Christ Meets Me Everywhere*, 149.
18. Cameron, *Christ Meets Me Everywhere*, 151.

cross brings together figure and reality in one event. As mediator, Christ in his humanity dies on the cross to put salvation into effect. Cameron summarizes:

> The cross therefore recast Augustine's way of understanding the relation between the divine and the human, not by juxtaposing them, but by interrelating them. . . . The realism inherent in the effective act of redemption, Christ's double-edged death on the cross, required an expanded concept of "likeness." He adapted the figure of associative metonymy in the direction of synecdoche, wherein a part stands for a greater whole. . . . So Christ died as one part of humanity representing the whole race . . . he "became a curse for us" (Gal. 3:13) so that we might be crucified with him and "the body of sin might be emptied out" (Rom. 6:6–7).[19]

Cameron points out that this combination of "associative metonymy and part-whole synecdoche" led to "a figuratively real concept of 'sacrament.'"[20]

This new appreciation of Christ's death gave Augustine a new conception of the unity of Scripture "from which his practice of figurative reading flowed."[21] Israel's story has now been reconceptualized within the scope of Christology, but not in such a way that the Old Testament was merely predictive of the New. Rather, for Augustine, Christ was "virtually incarnate"[22] in the Old Testament; his body already existed there in the form of Israel. The faith of the Old Testament saints was faith in Christ, who was really already present among them as the mediator of the covenant in the form of angels. Often we find statements that an angel spoke and that the Lord spoke appearing interchangeably in the Old Testament as though one statement is equivalent to the other. For example, in Exodus 3:2 we read "And the angel of the Lord appeared to him in a flame of fire out of the midst of a bush"; then in verse 4 we read "When the Lord saw that he turned aside to see, God called to him out of the bush." Christ was active in the creation and in the divine redemption of Israel; the relation of his activity in the Old Testament to his work in the incarnation is one of promise and fulfillment, yes, but also one of figure and reality.

In the first decade of the fifth century, Augustine enters on his preaching ministry as a bishop of the church, and his exegesis begins to mature. When he was a young believer just making his way out of Manichaeism and learning to appreciate the Bible, Ambrose's preaching helped him see that the Old

19. Cameron, *Christ Meets Me Everywhere*, 159.
20. Cameron, *Christ Meets Me Everywhere*, 159.
21. Cameron, *Christ Meets Me Everywhere*, 160.
22. Cameron, *Christ Meets Me Everywhere*, 161.

Testament had a spiritual meaning that went beyond the letter of the text by pointing to greater realities than the earthly themes with which the letter is concerned. Then Augustine learned that these realities were not merely future and not mere symbols but were activities of the Triune God who is at work in history to redeem his people through the death of Christ. It is Christ, the one sent by the Father, who enters history, takes our sin upon himself, and offers the sacrifice by which sin is forgiven and by which Christ's righteousness is made to be ours. This Christ is not merely the man Jesus; as the eternal Son of the Father, he is the Word by whom and through whom the cosmos came into being. This Christ interrelates the two Testaments in himself; therefore, figurative readings always point to him. This is why Paul can say that Christ was the rock from which the Israelites drank spiritually in the wilderness (1 Cor. 10:4). For Augustine, what we need to grasp is that the manna, for example, was not just a picture or symbol of a future reality that would some-day come into existence, that is, Christ as the bread of life. For Augustine, Christ was already sacramentally present in the manna, just as he was in the rock. Here we see his Christian Platonism put to good use in the service of a christological reading of the Old Testament that recognizes that Christ was ontologically real and sacramentally present before his incarnation, just as he is in the current age after his incarnation.

The upshot of all this is that Christ is *literally* present in the Old Testament, so the texts that speak of him do so in a literal sense. The distinction between the literal and the spiritual senses that once seemed so significant to the young Augustine eventually recedes into the background as the gap between the two senses is closed by what Jason Byassee terms his "christological literalism."[23] What I hope is clear by this stage of the argument is that the metaphysics, the dogma, and the exegesis are interdependent. Without a Nicene dogma of the Trinity with its high Christology, and without a theological metaphysics in which God is not limited to one point on the timeline of history but encloses time within himself and transcends time in the incomprehensible mystery of his unique being, it is not possible to think of Christ's relationship to the Old Testament as Augustine does. Christ is never absent from salvation history; he is with his people, saving and sanctifying them at every point of time simultaneously. We time-bound creatures can perceive this truth only by faith as we hear God proclaim it in his Word. But we can ourselves par-ticipate in Christ and in so doing experience the illumination, redemption, and sanctification made possible by Christ to those who are in him by faith. When Paul says "and the Rock was Christ" (1 Cor. 10:4), he is using a figure

23. Byassee, *Praise Seeking Understanding*, 205–10.

but is nonetheless speaking *literally*. The rock in the wilderness was figural language that witnesses to something real, not just for us or for Paul's first-century audience, but also for the children of Israel in the wilderness on the way to the promised land. Christ was with them and is with us—literally—and this has been made possible by his incarnation, death, resurrection, and ascension. When we penetrate beyond what Augustine calls "the letter" of Scripture to its spiritual meaning, we perceive the literal truth of the presence of Christ in the salvation of his people. The spiritual sense thus becomes an aspect of the literal sense, and the literal sense is not detached from history but is grounded in the history of Jesus Christ.

All Meaning Is Contained in the Plain Sense: The Tradition from Origen to John Calvin

In this section we will examine the Great Tradition of Christian exegesis more broadly and suggest that the pattern we see in Augustine's thought can be discerned in major elements of the tradition as a whole. First of all, we will see how the early fathers distinguished sharply between the literal and spiritual senses of especially the Old Testament and then, second, observe the reaction this provoked among those concerned not to let the spiritual sense float free of its moorings in the literal sense. Then, third, we will see how, in the thought of Thomas Aquinas and Nicholas of Lyra, the literal sense is expanded to include within itself much of what had previously been understood to be the spiritual sense. In both Augustine and in the tradition as a whole, we see a tendency to distinguish between the literal and spiritual senses to bring out the continuity between the Old and New Testaments, but we also see a concern to keep the two senses together, rather than allowing them to contradict each other. This process culminates in John Calvin's emphasis on the plain sense of Scripture as inclusive of all its meaning, including the christological meaning of the Old Testament. Once again, we will organize our thoughts around a thesis statement.

Thesis: All meaning is found in the plain sense, which can be understood as a combination of the literal and spiritual senses, which are unified by Jesus Christ as the great theme and center of the Old and New Testaments understood as one book (Luke 24:27).

It is well known that the Alexandrian tradition in the second and third centuries emphasized allegorical interpretation of Scripture. What is not as well known is the motivation behind the adoption of allegory and other Hellenistic reading methods for the interpretation of the Bible. Frances Young's seminal work, *Biblical Exegesis and the Formation of Christian Culture*, shows that the third-century fathers were involved in a grand project of fashioning a Christian culture based on the Bible as an alternative to Jewish and Hellenistic cultures, both of which were based on sacred writings as well. She notes that culture and religion were not separate entities in antiquity; the concept of the secular did not exist. As Robert Markus explains, Augustine invented the concept of the "secular,"[24] which is thus a Christian concept. "Secularism," however, is the absolutizing of the concept of the secular; it is the attempt of modernity to eliminate all vestiges of Christian culture from the West, which inevitably leads to neopaganism in an ill-fated attempt to return to a pre-Christian past.

Clement of Alexandria (ca. 150–215) was a major figure in early Christian attempts to show that Christian faith is not irrational, but consistent with sound reason and science. Brevard Childs emphasizes that Clement of Alexandria's goal was "the scientific knowledge of reality."[25] Childs is critical of Clement, however, for allowing a symbolic meaning of certain biblical texts to negate their historical meaning. Clement's conviction that the Old Testament can be interpreted christologically motivated him to adopt allegorical interpretations that detach the meaning from history. The use of allegorical methods was motivated by the desire to adapt the methods used to reconcile Homer and Greek philosophy in the service of reconciling the Bible and philosophy.

Origen (185–254), the greatest biblical scholar of his century, continued the attempt to relate biblical revelation to Greek philosophy. As was noted in chapter 3, this type of scholarly effort is not unlike the attempt by most contemporary theologians to explore the relationship between Genesis and modern natural science; in principle, it is unobjectionable.[26] All truth is God's truth, after all. However, Origen's work opened up a great deal of controversy in patristic theology, which ultimately led to criticism of Origen by the

---

24. For the mature Augustine, Rome is secular. R. A. Markus writes that "in the final analysis, there are only the two 'cities'; there is no hierarchy of related societies. Augustine sharply rejected the notion that any society might be modeled on the heavenly city, or reflect it as an image reflects its archetype" (*Saeculum*, 125). Again Markus: "Notwithstanding Constantine or even Theodosius, then, the Empire has remained 'secular' in Augustine's estimation" (126). It is not that no standards of value apply to political structures. Rather, it is that human political structures are not the kingdom of God. The state can be virtually demonic or relatively just, but it cannot merge with the church, because it is part of the secular, that is, the current age that is passing away.

25. Childs, *Struggle to Understand Isaiah*, 57.

26. Childs, *Struggle to Understand Isaiah*, 63.

Antiochenes such as Diodore of Tarsus (d. ca. 390), Theodore of Mopsuestia (ca. 350–428), and Theodoret of Cyrus (ca. 393–460).

Origen distinguished between the literal and spiritual senses of the text. Henri de Lubac suggests that this may be the remote origin of the later medieval scheme of the fourfold sense of Scripture.[27] Quoting de Lubac, Childs notes that the literal sense is not necessarily to be identified with the original sense of the human author and that recognition of the spiritual sense of a text does not necessarily imply rejection of the passage's historicity. Much confusion has been caused by a failure to understand these points, especially in modern times when Origen's allegorizing tendencies have been misunderstood and often rejected out of hand. Childs is quite aware that moderns do not define the literal sense in the same way the fathers do, but he does not mention the different definitions of history in play here.

Childs makes a vitally important point, however, when he says "Often when Origen speaks negatively of the literal sense, it is in the context of a debate with Jewish interpretations that would limit a passage's meaning to its alleged plain sense, thus explicitly rejecting its spiritual rendering."[28] This is of crucial importance, because what is often at issue here is the christological meaning of Old Testament passages such as Isaiah 53 or Psalm 110. This issue is a far cry from Origen's supposed "gnostic tendencies." The question is not whether the literal sense should be abandoned in favor of mythology but whether Christ is contained in the literal sense of the text as the New Testament writers claimed. Childs points to the issue of reference when he writes, "Because language and reality have become dissociated in modern thought, it has become difficult to understand that meaning lies in that to which it refers. Thus, in Origen the difference between the literal and the allegorical was not absolute, but lay within a spectrum. Allegory was a figure of speech among others and was symbolic in nature. The crucial question turned on the nature of the reference."[29]

This supports my argument at the beginning of this chapter that the word "literal" should be understood as referring to the meaning that is conveyed rather than the way in which that meaning is conveyed. I would add that language and reality have become dissociated in modern thought (as Childs says) because of the reductionist, narrow metaphysics of naturalism that limits history to nonsupernatural events. Since history is no longer able to speak of all that has happened in the past, it becomes detached from reality.

27. De Lubac, *Histoire et Esprit*, 178ff. as quoted by Childs, *Struggle to Understand Isaiah*, 67.
28. Childs, *Struggle to Understand Isaiah*, 67. Childs is following de Lubac here.
29. Childs, *Struggle to Understand Isaiah*, 68.

We must let reality shape our understanding of history, and reality is determined by the fact of God, who is real but beyond the reach of naturalistic explanation or description. Since naturalism cannot describe all of reality, it is unscientific and false. A false metaphysics inevitably distorts reality and leads to confusion. Modern failure to understand what Origen is up to is one example of such confusion.

Childs describes Origen's exegesis as usually beginning with the pursuit of the literal sense, then moving to a careful intertextual appeal, and finally ascending to the spiritual meaning from the literal sense. Origen struggled to do justice both to the particularity of "the literal, plain sense of the text" and to its "fuller theological function" as witness to Jesus Christ.[30] Origen refused to limit the meaning of the text to the single historical context of the original writer and was alert to the vertical, as well as the horizontal, dimension of the text. In all these ways, Origen was much closer to the center of the Great Tradition than he is often perceived to be.

Much of the confusion about the supposed heterodoxy of the Alexandrian approach to exegesis has arisen as a result of a tendency to overplay the contrast between the Alexandrian and Antiochene traditions. The caricature was that the Alexandrians demonstrated a lack of concern for history by offering wildly speculative allegorical interpretations that imported meanings into the text that were unrelated to its literal sense or historical context and that the Antiochenes were concerned about history in something like a modern sense. Even when the qualification is offered that not all Alexandrian exegesis was illegitimate, it was still thought that some of it was. Even when it was acknowledged that the Antiochenes did not have a view of history based on philosophical naturalism, it was still held that they were more loyal to the historical context of the text than the Alexandrians. These caricatures proved to be impossible to qualify and nuance and have had to be dropped altogether as patristic scholarship in the second half of the twentieth century reassessed the situation from the ground up.[31] As the hegemony of the Enlightenment dissipates in the future, we can expect the perceived gulf between the Alexandrians and Antiochenes to narrow considerably, and we can further expect that both schools will be seen as contributing to the Great Tradition consensus on exegesis.

Theodore of Mopsuestia (ca. 350–428) was the Antiochene who reacted most strongly against Origen. Childs summarizes Theodore's exegetical

30. Childs, *Struggle to Understand Isaiah*, 71.

31. For a summary of recent scholarship on the Antiochenes, see Nassif, "Spiritual Exegesis of Scripture," 437–70. For a recent monograph on Origen that focuses on his approach to exegesis as a form of participation in the quest for salvation, see Martens, *Origen and Scripture*.

method as follows.[32] Central is his view of history as composed of two successive epochs. The Old Testament, Theodore argued, is not to be interpreted allegorically as teaching the same message as the New Testament. He found only four psalms (2, 8, 45, and 110) to be predictions of Christ, and he argued for a single meaning for each psalm. He employed a highly restricted form of typology, rather than allegory, to relate the Old Testament to the New. What really brought him into conflict with the Alexandrians (and most of the church fathers) was his reluctance to recognize a Platonic contrast between earthly and heavenly realities. His strong eschatological emphasis led him to view the relation between the Testaments in horizontal terms only and not in vertical ones. As a result, he fell into an overly literal reading that ultimately rendered him unable adequately to account for prediction and fulfillment, which imperiled the relation between the Testaments. Theodore thus anticipated some of the worst features of modern historical criticism, but in so doing he stood outside the orthodox consensus.

Theodoret of Cyrus (ca. 393–460) is presented by Childs as playing a crucial role in mediating between the extremes of Alexandrian allegory and the overly literal, historicist interpretation of Theodore of Mopsuestia. Like all the fathers, Theodoret assumes the inspiration and unity of Scripture and the centrality of Jesus Christ as the key to understanding the Bible. He also stressed the necessity of having the right spiritual disposition to be able to interpret rightly. Theodoret's major contribution to the tradition was his emphasis on the need to see the figurative sense as an extension of the literal sense rather than as an arbitrary addition to it. He sees the literal sense as basically a paraphrase of the text, and the figurative sense as "extending rather than denying the significance of the literal."[33] Theodoret also employs a form of interpretation that is best described as neither literal nor figurative but typological. He argued for internal fulfillment within the history of Israel as well as for external fulfillment in the New Testament. Thus he preserved Theodore's concern for the integrity of the Old Testament while going beyond him in providing a theory for how the two Testaments are bound together. Childs recognizes Theodoret's sincere interest in history, while also recognizing the difference between his understanding of history and the understanding of the Enlightenment.

Childs stresses that Theodoret's exegesis shows that the line between the literal and the figurative senses of a text is often fluid, noting, for instance, that Theodoret saw the parable of the vineyard in Isaiah 5:1–7 and 28:23–28 as an

32. Childs, *Struggle to Understand Isaiah*, 132–33.
33. Childs, *Struggle to Understand Isaiah*, 137.

example in which the metaphorical reading is the literal meaning. Rather than being eccentric, this concern to hold together the literal and figurative senses is central to the Great Tradition. The center of the Great Tradition continued the trajectory of Theodoret in seeking various methods of maintaining the crucial links between the literal and spiritual senses of the text.

In the Middle Ages, we see this tendency in the work of Thomas Aquinas and Nicholas of Lyra. To appreciate Thomas's contribution to the exegetical tradition, it is necessary to examine his actual biblical interpretation in, for example, his Isaiah commentary and his three-volume commentary on the Gospel of John. Childs discusses Thomas's treatment of Isaiah and observes that even though he pays lip service to the fourfold sense in the *Summa Theologica* and never criticizes the figurative tradition, he nonetheless focuses on the literal sense. But the literal sense, for Thomas, includes much of what was previously thought to be part of the spiritual sense. Thomas emphasizes the divine authorship of Scripture, which is the most significant feature of his theological hermeneutics. He follows Augustine when he says that words signify things but that things can signify other things as well. The first signification is the literal sense, but the things signified by the things signified by the words are the basis of the spiritual sense. After discussing the traditional threefold division of the spiritual sense (allegorical, moral, and anagogical), he writes, "Since the literal sense is that which the author intends, and since the author of Holy Writ is God, Who by one act comprehends all things by his intellect, it is not unfitting, as Augustine says (Conf. XII) if, even according to the literal sense, one word in Holy Writ should have several senses."[34]

Childs notes in his Isaiah commentary that Thomas usually gives a literal reading of each text, but many of his literal interpretations are christological, including his view that Isaiah 7, 9, and 11 prophesy Christ. The sign of Isaiah 7:14 is the future Messiah; what is striking is that Thomas considers this a literal reading.[35] Cyrus is interpreted as both a historical figure and a type of Christ. When he comes to chapter 53, Thomas stands with the entire Christian tradition in understanding it christologically. Childs makes an important observation when he writes, "In a real sense, Thomas's interpretation of Isaiah 40–66, but especially of chapter 53, is not directed primarily to the text itself—that is, not just to the words, but to their substance. He does not distinguish between literal and figurative senses according to the Alexandrian tradition, but passes through the words of the text to their theological

---

34. Thomas Aquinas, *Summa Theologica* pt. I, q. 1, art. 10, p. 7.
35. Childs, *Struggle to Understand Isaiah*, 157.

substance, which inevitably transcends the verbal sense of the passage."[36] What is happening here is something familiar to many preachers who read the text, study the text, meditate on the text, pray over the text, and then find that the veil parts and the ontological reality of which the text speaks suddenly appears in glory and majesty. When this happens, the preacher is ready to preach the Good News! The goal of exegesis in the Great Tradition is not racking up publications in scholarly journals or getting tenure; the goal is to know God and to be transformed in the process. The goal is salvation. The goal of reading Isaiah 53 is to believe in Jesus Christ, who is the incarnate revelation of God, and to know him whom to know aright is life eternal. Thomas Aquinas understood this perfectly, and so have all the great preachers of evangelicalism from John Wesley and George Whitefield to Billy Graham and John Stott. It is past time for theological hermeneutics to catch up with what saints, fathers, and evangelists have practiced for centuries.

The Great Tradition of Christian exegesis exhibits a clear trajectory toward drawing the spiritual or christological sense of the text back into close proximity with the literal sense. The initial appreciation of the Old Testament involved stressing the existence of a spiritual meaning that pointed beyond the Old Testament realities themselves toward their fulfillment in Christ, but the use of Jewish and Hellenistic reading methods such as allegory threatened to pull the senses so far apart that a danger arose of meaning being imported from outside Scripture; the disastrous consequences of this threat became all too obvious in the rise of various forms of gnosticism that threatened the faith. As the medieval period developed, the tendency to pull the christological sense into closer and closer proximity is evident in Thomas Aquinas and also in Nicholas of Lyra.[37]

As the Reformation dawned, the Reformers engaged in rhetoric that sounded like opposition to allegory and seemed to foreshadow later historical-critical developments. They exhibited a strong emphasis on history and a preference for the literal sense along with a fondness for utilizing the linguistic tools of the new, rising humanism of the Renaissance. But appearances can be deceiving. Just as the Antiochenes are better understood as a corrective to Alexandrian excesses and mistakes than as a totally opposite tradition, so the Reformers are better understood as refiners of the Great Tradition of Christian exegesis than as founders of an alternative tradition. In an essay titled "Biblical Interpretation in the Era of the Reformation: The View from

36. Childs, *Struggle to Understand Isaiah*, 159.
37. See Childs's discussion of Nicholas of Lyra in chap. 12 of *Struggle to Understand Isaiah*, 167–79.

the Middle Ages," Richard A. Muller laments the paucity of studies of the thought of the Reformers on biblical interpretation in the light of the medieval tradition, but he observes that this situation is beginning to change, in part because of the work of David Steinmetz and those inspired by him. Muller argues in this essay that there is not total continuity but nevertheless "a fundamental continuity of exegetical interest that remained the property of precritical exegesis as it passed over from the medieval fourfold model into other models that, in one way or another, emphasized the concentration of meaning in the literal sense of the text."[38]

Muller says that Luther and Calvin did not simply trade in allegory for literal interpretation. Rather, they "strengthened the shift to letter with increased emphasis on textual and philological study, and then proceeded to find various figures and levels of meaning . . . in the letter itself."[39] Muller highlights the continuity between Calvin and the concentration of the literal sense that characterized Thomas Aquinas's exegesis. In both cases, the literal sense was an expanded literal sense that included, in the case of Old Testament texts, a christological *sensus plenior*. In support of these claims, we will examine Calvin's exegesis in the rest of this chapter.

Calvin lived at a crucial moment between the medieval era, when the Great Tradition flourished, and the Enlightenment era, when historical criticism departed from the Great Tradition. We need to examine Calvin's relationship to allegory to see the degree of continuity between Calvin and Thomas Aquinas, insofar as Thomas represents the central thrust of the Great Tradition. Calvin was not averse to finding a deeper spiritual meaning in addition to the literal or plain sense. Although he had sharp criticisms of certain allegorical interpretations, his mind was subordinated to the text of Scripture, and he fearlessly described what he found there, whether it fit with his theory or not. For example, consider his comments on the command to Moses to put off his shoes because he stood on holy ground during his encounter with the LORD at the burning bush (Exod. 3:5). Calvin writes, "If any prefer the deeper meaning (*anagoge*) that God cannot be heard until we have put off our earthly thoughts, I object not to it; only let the natural sense stand first, that Moses was commanded to put off his shoes, as a preparation to listen with greater reverence to God."[40] Notice that his terminology is "natural sense" versus the "anagogical sense." Calvin was aware of the truth contained in the medieval fourfold sense of Scripture. For him the fourfold sense truthfully holds that

38. Muller, "Biblical Interpretation in the Era of the Reformation," 12. The article is a contribution to a Festschrift for David Steinmetz.
39. Muller, "Biblical Interpretation in the Era of the Reformation," 12.
40. Calvin, *Commentaries on the Four Last Books of Moses*, 64.

the first or surface or plain meaning of the biblical text does not necessarily exhaust the full meaning of the text. A *sensus plenior* is possible providing that it grows organically out of the literal or plain sense.

In his commentary on Galatians, Calvin considers Galatians 4:24, where Paul asserts, "Now this may be interpreted allegorically." First, he engages in ritual castigation of "Origen and many others along with him" who are guilty of "torturing Scripture, in every possible manner, away from the true sense."[41] Notice that Origen's sin is in deviating from the true sense of Scripture, not allegory per se. Calvin then acknowledges, "Scripture is a most rich and inexhaustible fountain of all wisdom; but I deny that its fertility consists in the various meanings which any man, at his pleasure, may assign. Let us know, then, that the true meaning of Scripture is the natural and obvious meaning; and let us embrace and abide by it resolutely."[42] So Calvin is engaged in controversy over the "true" meaning of Scripture and the "natural" meaning, as opposed to "speculations" and subjective interpretations. In the next paragraph, he asks, "But what reply are we to make to Paul's assertion, that these things are *allegorical*?" Calvin's words are worth quoting:

> Paul certainly does not mean that Moses wrote the history for the purpose of being turned into an allegory, but points out in what way the history may be made to answer the present subject. This is done by observing a figurative representation of the Church there delineated. And a mystical interpretation of this sort (*anagoge*) was not inconsistent with the true and literal meaning, when a comparison was drawn between the Church and the family of Abraham. As the house of Abraham was then a true Church, so it is beyond all doubt that the principal and most memorable events which happened in it are so many types to us. As in circumcision, in sacrifices, in the whole Levitical priesthood, there was an allegory, as there is an allegory in the house of Abraham; but this does not involve a departure from the literal meaning.[43]

For Calvin, the issue is whether an allegorical interpretation is or is not the natural meaning, and he seems to equate the "natural" or "true" meaning with the "literal" meaning. The literal meaning can be an *anagoge*—a mystical interpretation.

This is an example of Calvin standing squarely in the trajectory of Great Tradition exegesis insofar as he views any legitimate spiritual sense as an extension of the literal sense. Note that he says that circumcision, the sacrifices, and

41. Calvin, *Galatians*, 135.
42. Calvin, *Galatians*, 135–36.
43. Calvin, *Galatians*, 136.

the Levitical priesthood are all "allegories," as also is the house of Abraham. But the reason the house of Abraham can be an allegory is that the church was ontologically present in it. One could say that an extended literal or spiritual sense is legitimate for Calvin *when it is really there*, and it is really there when it is there ontologically. The meaning of a given text is not determined by method or terminology but is inherent in the text or not; our business as interpreters is to sit humbly before the text and let it open up to us its true, natural, literal meaning. Sometimes that meaning will include a *sensus plenior*—a surplus of meaning that inheres in the text because of inspiration and points us to Christ.

In his *Institutes of the Christian Religion*, Calvin discusses allegory and/or the allegorical method in six different passages. All six are refutations of doctrinal error. Three are arguments against Roman Catholic doctrines: one opposes medieval semi-Pelagianism,[44] another argues against transubstantiation,[45] and one opposes required oral confession to priests.[46] Two of the other passages defend infant baptism, one with regard to Anabaptists in general[47] and one with regard to Michael Servetus in particular.[48] The sixth passage is one in which Calvin condemns Servetus for denying the ontological reality of the three persons of the Trinity.[49] What is striking about these passages is that he does not say that his opponents are wrong because of their use of the allegorical method of biblical interpretation. Instead, he himself shows a willingness to interpret Scripture allegorically when the text warrants. His point is that his opponents have interpreted Scripture *poorly* and used allegory in the *wrong way*, which is why they got the wrong result.

For example, with regard to the man whom the robbers left "half alive" (Calvin's words) in the good Samaritan parable (Luke 10:30), Calvin opposes the allegorical interpretation that we are "half alive" and thus able to cooperate with divine grace, as put forward by his Roman Catholic opponents. He writes, "First, suppose I do not want to accept their allegory. What, pray, will they do? For no doubt the fathers devised this interpretation without regard to the true meaning of the Lord's words. Allegories ought not to go beyond the limits set by the rule of Scripture, let alone suffice as the foundation for any doctrines."[50] Here Calvin does not rule out using allegory; he refuses to

44. Calvin, *Institutes* 2.5.19, p. 339.
45. Calvin, *Institutes* 4.17.15, pp. 1376–79.
46. Calvin, *Institutes* 3.4.4–5, pp. 626–29.
47. Calvin, *Institutes* 4.16.15–16, pp. 1337–39.
48. Calvin, *Institutes* 4.16.31, pp. 1353–58.
49. Calvin, *Institutes* 1.13.22, pp. 147–48.
50. Calvin, *Institutes* 2.5.19, p. 339.

accept their allegory. Why? Is it because it is allegory? No, it is because it is an allegory that is devised "without regard to the true meaning of the Lord's words." Calvin's criticism is that this allegorical interpretation is not rooted in the plain sense of the text and is therefore to be rejected. One can easily imagine Thomas Aquinas or Theodoret of Cyrus agreeing with Calvin on this point.

Calvin agrees with Augustine that this sort of allegory cannot be the foundation of doctrine. It can be used to illustrate doctrine that is based on the literal sense of another passage, but it cannot replace a textual foundation in the literal sense.[51] When Calvin accuses his opponents of taking refuge in allegories, he is referring to allegories that embody interpretations that do not grow organically out of the literal sense and are thus "mere allegory." He does this, for example, in book 3 of the *Institutes*, where he refutes the Roman Catholic interpretation of Jesus's sending the lepers to the priests after he had cured them.[52] Calvin's opponents ("canon lawyers and the Scholastic theologians," he calls them) claimed this act as a precedent for the need of sinners to go to confession. Denying that this idea is in the text at all, Calvin says that their allegory confuses the civil law with the ceremonies and is therefore "unsuitable." He says further that the reason Christ sent them to the priests was in obedience to the law and so that his miracle would be validated. The question for him is, as always, "What does the text mean?"

Calvin is not so much opposed to any interpretation that contains a spiritual meaning—or even an allegorical one—as he is to the sloppy misuse of Scripture by reading ideas into it that are not there. However, he shows no interest whatsoever in arguing for a single-meaning theory as the Enlightenment does; he merely wants to find whatever meanings may be in the text and ensure that there is an organic connection between the literal and the spiritual senses. In this he is continuing a trajectory that Childs and others have documented in the late medieval period, especially in Thomas Aquinas and Nicholas of Lyra, a trajectory that is already found within the writings of Augustine, who gradually moved away from the term "allegory" but never lost his enthusiasm for finding the spiritual sense of Old Testament passages.

51. Jason Byassee says that Augustine takes the same position: "Figurative reading cannot add anything new to Christian teaching that was not already present in literal form elsewhere in Scripture. Otherwise we would have a gnostic approach to scripture, in which a creative genius could find whatever she or he wished lurking wherever she wished in Scripture. No Christian exegesis can rest merely on allegorical exegesis for its foundation" (*Praise Seeking Understanding*, 111).

52. Calvin, *Institutes* 3.4.4, pp. 626–27.

Summary and Conclusions

In this chapter we have examined the centrality of the literal sense in the Great Tradition of Christian exegesis of Scripture. We have seen that the literal sense has suffered a drastic reduction in modern Enlightenment thinking because of the narrowing of the definition of history in deference to philosophical naturalism. The literal sense of Scripture has a broader and more robust character in the Great Tradition. It cannot be detached from either history or the intention of the human author; neither can it be fully grasped apart from consideration of the intention of the primary author, the God who inspires, preserves, and illumines the text.

God exists and has created the cosmos. Scripture is a series of signs set in place by the Lord for the illumination of his people within the economy of time and space. Scripture participates in the sacramental reality of the spiritual realm as well as the material realm and is a suitable revelation to us creatures, who, made up of both bodies and souls, inhabit both the material and spiritual realms. So biblical interpretation involves both a vertical and a horizontal dimension. The meaning of biblical texts is discerned by historical trajectories of promise and fulfillment, but meaning is also discerned by words signifying things that themselves stand for other things—some material and some spiritual in nature. The Bible is a book about heaven as well as earth, because Jesus Christ sits at the right hand of the Father in heaven yet rules on the earth, and we pray "Your will be done on earth as it is in heaven" (Matt. 6:10). The two central facts of biblical interpretation are (1) *God* speaks and (2) God speaks to *us*.

What God says in Scripture can be termed the literal sense or the plain sense. The trajectory within the thought of a central figure in the Great Tradition, Augustine, and that of the tradition as a whole, is to recognize first that the Old Testament has a spiritual sense that points beyond itself to the Christ-event, but then to draw the spiritual sense back into the literal sense when it threatens to become detached from history and from the primary meaning of the text as written. The extended literal sense or double-literal sense comes to be seen as containing the christological sense that the church, following the lead of Jesus and the apostles, saw in the Scriptures. Terminology varies from writer to writer and from century to century, and many reading strategies are employed in Great Tradition hermeneutics. Perhaps the best term to use today is "christological literalism."

Various techniques are used, some borrowed from the wider culture, such as allegory, and others, such as typology, developed specifically for biblical interpretation. But in the end, the tradition has never concluded that biblical interpretation can be reduced to a question of method or technique. Many methods can be used; none are adequate by themselves. Much more important in biblical interpretation are the following characteristics of the interpreter and the process of interpretation. Here are ten theses on biblical interpretation that summarize the findings of chapter 5 and 6:

1. The interpreter must be a believer who is open to God revealing himself and who is willing to obey what God commands.

2. The interpreter must proceed in prayer and humility in conscious dependence on the illumination of the Holy Spirit.

3. The interpreter must strive with all effort possible to study the Bible as a whole and to read, reread, meditate on, memorize, and pray over the text.

4. The interpreter must believe that the Bible is a unity with Jesus Christ as the central theme.

5. The interpreter must recognize that Scripture is inspired and that no legitimate interpretation can ever contradict the plain sense of another passage of Scripture.

6. The interpreter must seek the literal sense as the first priority. Sometimes the literal sense will also be the spiritual sense, but other times there may be a *sensus plenior*.

7. If the spiritual sense is not simply identical with the literal sense, then the interpreter must seek to determine what the spiritual sense is and show that it grows organically out of the literal sense without contradicting the literal sense.

8. A text will have several contexts including the immediate literary context, the broader literary context, the canonical context, and the historical context. The interpretation should not contradict any of these contexts, but the canonical context is the most important one.

9. Most of the historical information needed for accurate interpretation of biblical texts will be found within the canon of Scripture itself. Therefore, the one essential area of knowledge for biblical interpretation is a deep and broad knowledge of the canon of Scripture itself.

10. The Bible was given by God to the church to be read and understood by the people, and therefore it can be read and understood by ordinary laypeople who are willing to study diligently and to humbly seek the Spirit's leading.

These points are meant to summarize the essential features of the science of biblical hermeneutics to make clear that the Bible belongs to the church and must be interpreted within the church if it is to be understood properly. Insofar as the university is founded by the church as part of a Christian culture, it can be a fruitful site for biblical interpretation, but insofar as the university adopts a non-Christian identity and insists on all academic disciplines operating on the basis of methodological naturalism, it becomes a hostile environment for biblical hermeneutics. The modern, secularized university, however, cannot carry out its mission of seeking truth effectively in general; the case of biblical hermeneutics is just a single instance of a general deficiency. Without recognition of natural theology, the natural moral law, and the natural laws of science, a university is handcuffed with regard to the pursuit of truth in its faculties of theology, law, and the liberal arts and sciences, respectively.

The only way biblical hermeneutics can be a science is for it to recognize that the nature of the Bible is revelation. Therefore, the Bible is not an end in itself; it is a means to a greater end, the knowledge of God. Insofar as biblical study leads one to God, it is dealing with the true and proper end of theology. But insofar as God is bracketed out of the equation in advance by means of methodological naturalism, the whole enterprise takes on an air of unreality. In that case, all one can expect to hear from the text is an echo of one's own thoughts, the thoughts of other human beings, or the highest values of the culture reflected back to one's consciousness. This makes it possible for the Bible to be turned into a tool that can be wielded like a weapon in the service of various and sundry ideologies. In the postmodern, relativistic, academic climate of today's university, the Bible thus becomes a pawn in the clash of wills that characterizes the humanities and social sciences and, increasingly, even the natural sciences as well.

The one absolutely crucial thing that the church cannot ever agree to do is to give up the priority of the literal sense of Scripture as the controlling sense for all valid meanings. Calvin tended to use the phrase "plain sense" to speak of all the true meaning contained in any given text, and a given meaning can be the plain sense only if it is rooted in the literal sense. The Enlightenment insists that the literal sense be restricted in a crippling manner to what fits within its truncated metaphysics, but the church can never agree to do that. To do so would be to make exegesis unscientific, because the object of study—God—would not be permitted to dictate the method used to study that object. In a day of rising barbarism and general cultural decline, it is necessary to utter a firm no to the request to bow before the demands of metaphysical naturalism. This no is not merely a negative; it has the positive function of protecting the scientific character of biblical hermeneutics and the integrity of the literal sense. The Bible is about what it says it is about; nothing the culture says or does can change that. We approach the Bible as God's Word in a posture of humility, saying, "Speak, LORD, for your servant hears" (1 Sam. 3:9). The Great Tradition is made up of people who cannot get over the wonder that God actually does just that—God speaks.

7

Seeing and Hearing Christ in the Old Testament

Let us listen now to something our Lord said on the cross: "Into your hands I commit my spirit" (Luke 23:46). When we hear those words of his in the gospel, and recognize them as part of this psalm, we should not doubt that here in this psalm it is Christ himself who is speaking. The gospel makes it clear. . . . He had good reasons for making the words of the psalm his own, for he wanted to teach you that in the psalm he is speaking. Look for him in it.

Augustine of Hippo, commenting on Psalm 31[1]

*T*his final chapter of part 2 is the climax of the book. Here we build on the theological and metaphysical foundations laid in part 1 as we continue our soundings in the exegetical heritage of the early church fathers in order to bring to light long-forgotten ways of reading the Scriptures that the influence of rationalism, materialism, and various forms of antirealism have rendered so incredible to the "modern mind" that most contemporary theologians do not even know they exist, let alone put much stock in them. The recovery of a pro-Nicene culture of biblical interpretation requires us to grasp the interaction of exegesis, dogma, and metaphysics as part of a spiritual discipline by which the believing reader is united to Christ by being transformed and purified by the sanctifying work of the Holy Spirit. In this

---

1. Augustine, *Expositions of the Psalms, 1–32,* 330–31.

chapter, we will discover a way of interpreting the Old Testament that brings the spiritually receptive reader into a direct relationship with the living Lord Jesus Christ, who is not only seen in the text but also speaks in and through it.

The first section of this chapter will consider a kind of exegesis that was used extensively by the New Testament writers, the second- and third-century church fathers, and the major pro-Nicene theologians of the fourth and fifth centuries—namely, "prosopological exegesis." This is likely to be a new term to many, even to those who have taken a hermeneutics course, so I will carefully define and illustrate it in the first section of this chapter. In the second section, I will examine how Augustine applied this reading technique to his exegesis of the Psalter and how he Christianized it by rooting it in New Testament Christology and ecclesiology. In the final section, I will argue that the christological literalism of the Great Tradition is truly scientific exegesis.

Prosopological Exegesis: A Primer

In two recent books,[2] Matthew Bates has rendered great service to the church by recovering and explaining the importance of a method of interpreting the Scriptures that was used widely by the New Testament apostles, the postapostolic fathers, and other early Christian interpreters up to Augustine, whose magisterial expositions of the Psalms caused the method to become central to Christian interpretation of the Psalms for the following millennium. In this section, we will define prosopological exegesis and then discuss some examples from both the New Testament authors and some of the second- and third-century fathers. In the next section, we will look at Augustine's christological interpretation of the Psalms, in which he employs this reading method extensively.

According to Bates, prosopological exegesis can be defined as follows:

> Prosopological exegesis is a reading technique whereby an interpreter seeks to overcome a real or perceived ambiguity regarding the identity of the speakers or addressees (or both) in the divinely inspired source text by assigning nontrivial *prosopa* (i.e., nontrivial vis-à-vis the "plain sense" of the text) to the speakers or addressees (or both) in order to make sense of the text.[3]

The earliest Christians were convinced that "a few special humans in the past had in fact obtained an otherworldly glimpse into divine affairs—the

---

2. Bates, *Hermeneutics of the Apostolic Proclamation*; and Bates, *Birth of the Trinity*.
3. Bates, *Hermeneutics of the Apostolic Proclamation*, 218.

ancient Hebrew prophets."⁴ These prophets, such as David and Isaiah, were enabled to overhear conversations between God the Father and God the Son. The prophets took on the *prosopa* of the members of the Trinity and spoke in character in their writings.

Bates begins his book on the importance of prosopological exegesis for development of the doctrine of the Trinity by pointing to the way the author of Hebrews identifies the speaker in Psalm 40:6–8 as Christ himself:⁵

Consequently, when Christ came into the world, he said,

"Sacrifices and offerings you have not desired,
　but a body you have prepared for me;
in burnt offerings and sin offerings
　you have taken no pleasure.
Then I said, 'Behold, I have come to do your will, O God,
　as it is written of me in the scroll of the book.'" (Heb. 10:5–7)⁶

Then the author of Hebrews explains the meaning of the text quoted from Psalm 40:

When he said above, "You have neither desired nor taken pleasure in sacrifices and offerings and burnt offerings and sin offerings" (these are offered according to the law), then he added, "Behold, I have come to do your will." He does away with the first in order to establish the second. And by that will we have been sanctified through the offering of the body of Jesus Christ once for all. (Heb. 10:8–10)

Who is the speaker in Hebrews 10:5? It is, clearly, the author of Hebrews. Who is the speaker in 10:6–7, which is a quotation from Psalm 40? It is, according to Bates, the Messiah.

The English Standard Version Study Bible note here follows the majority of modern interpreters in identifying this as a Davidic psalm and treating the quoted words as the words of David. The note speaks of David's awareness that God desires faithful hearts rather than mere sacrificial rituals. Bates, however, observes that the author of Hebrews seems to attribute the words of Psalm 40 to the Messiah, that is, to Christ. The context of Hebrews 10 seems to support Bates as one can see from the words in verse 8. Notice that

---

4. Bates, *Birth of the Trinity*, 5.
5. Bates, *Birth of the Trinity*, 1.
6. The words in Heb. 10:7, "Behold, I have come to do your will, O God, as it is written of me in the scroll of the book," are the quotation from Ps. 40:6–8.

the author of Hebrews resumes speaking in verse 8 and refers to "he" as in "When *he* said above." The question is: "Can the 'he' in verse 8 plausibly be taken to be David?" That does not seem to be possible. After all, this speaker speaks to God ("I have come to do your will, O God"), and the author of Hebrews says that this speaker—"he"—does away with the sacrificial system in order to do God's will and goes on to explain further that this involves our sanctification through the offering of the body of Jesus Christ once for all (v. 10). David neither abolished the sacrificial system nor sanctified us through the offering of his body. The Messiah did these things. The words of Psalm 40 make perfect sense when read as the words of the Messiah, Jesus Christ, which is exactly what the author of Hebrews does. But how can Jesus Christ be speaking in Psalm 40, a millennium prior to the incarnation of God in the birth of Jesus? This is the question answered by prosopological exegesis.

Bates explores the background of prosopological exegesis in ancient literary criticism, classical Greek drama, and classical rhetoric.[7] As a reading technique, it was well known in ancient Greco-Roman culture. The essence of it was distinguishing carefully and accurately between various characters (*prosopa*) in texts, dramatic productions, and speeches so as to facilitate correct understanding. When the apostles and fathers took over this technique, they adapted it to their own purposes by understanding the texts they were interpreting within the divine economy of the God who inspired Scripture. But how did they adapt it?

Most modern interpretations of Hebrews 10:5–10 (at least those that do not simply dismiss this kind of interpretation as inept and ridiculous) rely on some sort of typological move. Bates discusses the views of Richard Hays, who is an outstanding representative of the typological approach. Hays sees that there are instances in Paul's writings, as well as in other strands of the New Testament, in which Christ's voice is heard in the Psalms.[8] To the question "How can it be possible that the Messiah speaks in the Psalms?" Hays provides a complex typological explanation in which he argues that early Judaism saw the royal lament psalms "as paradigmatic for Israel's corporate national sufferings in the present time, and their characteristic triumphant conclusions would be read as pointers to God's eschatological restoration of Israel."[9] He then claims that the early church regarded the sufferings of the

---

7. Bates, *Hermeneutics of the Apostolic Proclamation*, 187–99. For other brief discussions of prosopological exegesis in the ancient world in general and in Augustine in particular, see Cameron, *Christ Meets Me Everywhere*, 162–64, 172–74; and Fiedrowicz, "Introduction," in Augustine, *Expositions of the Psalms*, 1–32, 50–60.

8. Hays, *Conversion of the Imagination*, 107.

9. Hays, *Conversion of the Imagination*, 110–11.

king who represents Israel in these psalms as having been accomplished in "an eschatologically definitive way by Jesus on the cross, and to see the vindication of Israel accomplished proleptically in his resurrection."[10] Bates, however, is not convinced that a typological explanation is sufficient to explain what is going on in Hebrews 10.

According to Bates, the typological approach has serious weaknesses. Chief among them is that typology is a modern invention, intricately bound up with modern preoccupations about certain notions of history and referentiality that were not on Paul's radar. Frances Young says that "typology is a modern construct" and that it is "born of modern historical consciousness."[11] As Hans Frei demonstrated a generation ago in his groundbreaking work, *The Eclipse of Biblical Narrative*, biblical interpretation prior to the Enlightenment assumed that the literal reading of biblical narrative involved reading it as referring to actual historical occurrences.[12] But during the Enlightenment, as I discussed in chapter 4 above, the repudiation of Christian Platonism and the accompanying rise of Epicurean naturalism caused the truncated modern notion of history to come to prominence. Once history was viewed through the restrictive prism of naturalism, biblical narrative became detached from "reality" (according to the narrow Enlightenment construal of "reality"). Before this time, as Frei argued, the Bible was regarded as telling the story of reality into which we needed to fit ourselves somehow. But after this point, the problem was how to fit as much of the biblical narrative as possible into the new construal of reality derived from an extrabiblical worldview (Epicurean philosophical naturalism). A gap now existed between the biblical narratives and the present "naturalistic" reality; typology became a way to bridge that gap. Young quotes A. C. Charity, who states that *typologia* appears for the first time in Latin in 1840 and the English form "typology" for the first time in 1844. Young summarizes Charity's view: "He argues that allegory and typology are only distinguished in the aftermath of the post-Reformation rejection of allegory."[13]

The gap between the past (the text) and the present in modernity can be bridged from our side only by an "imaginative construal" (Brueggemann)[14]

10. Hays, *Conversion of the Imagination*, 111.
11. Young, *Biblical Exegesis and the Formation of Christian Culture*, 152, 153.
12. Frei, *Eclipse of Biblical Narrative*, 2.
13. Young, *Biblical Exegesis and the Formation of Christian Culture*, 194n20.
14. See Childs, *Struggle to Understand Isaiah*: "His attack is built upon a widespread assumption of postmodern literary studies that meaning is never a fixed property of a text, but a process of interpretation involving an interaction between text, reader and context. The acquiring of meaning is therefore not a search for a stable given, but a fluid exchange within an ongoing activity" (315–16). It should be clear by now that I reject Brueggemann, postmodern hermeneutics,

or by a typological reading (Hays). But what this move amounts to in both cases is that it is "from our side"; that is, it is basically a "reading into" the text by modern interpreters.[15] It should be obvious at this point in history that we cannot overcome the problem of the contemporary loss of confidence in Enlightenment ideals of neutrality and objectivity by means of postmodern theories in which the reader brings the meaning to the text. This would be like fighting fire by pouring gasoline on it; it is to use heightened subjectivity to overcome the problem of subjectivism. This only intensifies the problem.

Bates notes that, after the collapse of the twentieth-century biblical theology movement over "problematic notions of history," later studies seemed to show that "typology could seemingly get along just fine operating in the narrative space opened up between two pieces of literature apart from any question of historical referentiality."[16] This is precisely what makes typology less objectionable to the modern mind and explains its popularity among biblical scholars trying to operate within a guild dominated by philosophical naturalism while struggling to take the plain sense of Scripture seriously. But it seems to me that, in the end, typology is a modern solution to a modern problem and that we would be wise to heed Bates's warning not to "foist our peculiar modern notions of history and referentiality onto Paul."[17] Modern concepts of typology serve more to mask the problem than to solve it.

the Epicurean philosophical naturalism on which it rests, and the whole idea that meaning cannot and does not reside in the text in a stable manner. While certainly alert to the weaknesses of Brueggemann's position, Childs, however, fails to offer an adequate alternative to Brueggemann's subjectivism and relativism, because he does not directly challenge Brueggemann's position on the level of metaphysics. In place of modern Epicureanism and the subjectivism into which late modern hermeneutics has fallen, I recommend Christian Platonism, the Nicene doctrine of God, and a robust doctrine of inspiration as the basis for seeing a stable and true meaning in the text of Scripture itself under the illuminating guidance of the Holy Spirit. The key point as it relates to prosopological exegesis is that the New Testament writers did not "imagine" or "read into" the Old Testament text the conversations between the Father and Son; rather, those conversations are actually in the Old Testament text because of inspiration waiting to be discerned in the light of the Christ-event by those who believe in Christ and are led by his Spirit.

15. Perhaps I am not being fair to Hays at this point. Perhaps he sees typology as depending on meaning that inheres in the Old Testament text because of inspiration. That may well be; it certainly is the case that most biblical interpreters who are sympathetic to the Great Tradition do speak of typology in that way, as I would myself. The word "type" (τυπικῶς) is, after all, used by Paul (1 Cor. 10:11; for examples of Paul's typological interpretation, see Rom. 4:23–24; 1 Cor. 9:10). My point is not to indict Hays, but to stress that if one uses typology as referring to meaning inhering in the Old Testament text because of inspiration, one runs afoul of modern philosophical naturalism just as much as if one had used allegory or any other form of *sensus plenior* or the spiritual sense. If typology escapes modern censure, it does so only by sacrificing objective meaning and becoming a "reading into" the Old Testament text.

16. Bates, *Hermeneutics of the Apostolic Proclamation*, 135.

17. Bates, *Hermeneutics of the Apostolic Proclamation*, 135.

Bates, however, does see Paul as using typology language to refer to "deliberately anticipatory types" in the Old Testament. In 1 Corinthians 10:6, Paul says that the wilderness wanderings of Israel in Numbers have become types (τύποι) of us. No one is denying the existence of some sort of mimetic correspondence between Old Testament persons, events, and things and New Testament ones. But as Bates points out, it is crucial to notice that Paul does not reason forward from scriptural past events to prove the imitative instantiations in his present.[18] Rather, he sees them through the lens of the apostolic *kerygma* in mimetic terms. Because of the congruence of the work of God in Israel and Christ, there are patterns that can be identified as consistent, which makes the Old Testament narratives instructive for us.

I would add to Bates's account that these patterns are just the sort of thing one would expect in a Christian Platonist metaphysics in which things in the world of flux participate in universals in the realm of unchanging realities. And if these universals are understood, as often they are in the Great Tradition, to be ideas in the mind of the God who is the author of Scripture, then it is easy to see why such mimetic correspondences would exist. These patterns can be discerned on the basis of the ontological reality of the God who acts in both Testaments in what John Webster calls "the domain of the Word."[19] This is what makes the world sacramental. It explains how scriptural patterns reflect heavenly patterns as, for example, in Hebrews 9–10 where the sanctuary, priesthood, and sacrifices of the old covenant, and the old covenant itself, are described as "shadows" (σκιάν, Heb. 10:1) and "copies" (ὑποδείγματα, Heb. 9:23) of heavenly realities. Christ has offered a once-for-all sacrifice that fulfilled the sacrificial system; then he entered into heaven and sat down at the right hand of God (Heb. 10:12). The interplay between the earthly and the heavenly, the material and the spiritual, realities is not static, however, but historical in that it involves the actions of the incarnate Son in history, accomplished through his incarnation, death, resurrection, and ascension, which are decisive for redemption. Christ comes from heaven to earth to redeem the earth and then ascends to heaven to await his second coming, at which point the heavens and earth will be joined together in the final act of the

18. Bates, *Hermeneutics of the Apostolic Proclamation*, 147.

19. Webster, *Domain of the Word*, 3–31. Webster writes: "Holy Scripture and its interpretation are elements in the domain of the Word of God. That domain is constituted by the communicative presence of the risen and ascended Son of God who governs all things. His governance includes his rule over creaturely intelligence: he is Lord and therefore teacher. In fulfillment of the eternal purpose of God the Father (Eph. 1:9, 11), and by sending the Spirit of wisdom and revelation (Eph. 1:17), the Son sheds abroad the knowledge of himself and of all things in himself" (3). Although Webster does not use the term "Christian Platonism," this description of the "domain of the Word" lucidly expresses the concept I have in mind when I use that term.

drama of redemption (Rev. 21). So Christian Platonism provides a hospitable metaphysical context for prosopological exegesis.

Bates lays the foundation for understanding how prosopological exegesis works in Paul's writings in the first two chapters of *The Hermeneutics of the Apostolic Proclamation* by carefully analyzing 1 Corinthians 15:3–11 and Romans 1:1–6, which he sees as containing two very early protocreeds.[20] He understands these protocreeds as playing a crucial hermeneutical function in Paul's writings. When analyzed carefully, they set out the summary of a metanarrative centered on Jesus Christ, which undergirds the Bible as a whole and is the context for Paul's biblical interpretation. The metanarrative consists of the following elements:

1. Preexistence
2. Human life in the line of David
3. Death for sins
4. Burial
5. Existence among the dead
6. Resurrection
7. Initial appearances
8. Installation as Son of God in power
9. Subsequent appearances to others
10. Appearance to Paul
11. Apostolic commissioning
12. Mission to the nations[21]

I do not have time or space here to develop Bates's discussion in all of its nuance and depth. The reader is referred to his excellent book, especially chapter 2. What Bates shows convincingly is "that certain pre-Pauline protocreedal materials are foundational for his hermeneutic, in the sense that they define what being 'according to the Scriptures,' and 'promised in advance,'" actually mean for Paul.[22] Bates shows that when Paul quotes Old Testament passages, he is doing so with an overall master narrative in mind by which Christ fulfills the Old Testament. This master narrative is, in Paul's judgment,

20. How early? In order to appear as they do in Paul's letters to Corinth and Rome, they would likely need to have been common in the very early Christianity of the first two decades or so after Christ's resurrection.

21. Bates, *Hermeneutics of the Apostolic Proclamation*, 100.

22. Bates, *Hermeneutics of the Apostolic Proclamation*, 107.

derived from the Old Testament Scriptures and functions as a guide to interpreting those Scriptures. So when Bates comes to his analysis of Paul's prosopological exegesis, he argues that Paul is guided by this master narrative in his discernment of who is being addressed by whom in Old Testament passages where the speakers are difficult to identify, which allows us to understand Christ as preexistent and the Old Testament as inspired witness to the preexistent Christ. The parallel to this approach in Irenaeus of the function of the rule of truth is impossible to miss; I will say more about this parallel below. Bates also notes that, obviously, "the assumption of ultimate divine authorship" is critical to this overall hermeneutical strategy.[23]

Bates also shows that second- and third-century church fathers—including Justin Martyr, Tertullian, and others—employed prosopological exegesis. He quotes Justin as follows:

> But whenever you hear the sayings of the prophets spoken as from a person . . . you must not suppose [the sayings] to be spoken from the inspired persons themselves, but from the divine *Logos* . . . who moves them. For sometimes he speaks as one announcing in advance things which are about to happen; sometimes he speaks as from the person of Christ; sometimes as from the person of the people giving answer to the Lord and his Father—such as is seen in your own writers, when the one person is the writer of the whole, but many people are put forward as participating in dialogue.[24]

Bates then points out four things about this passage.[25] First, Justin affirms that the divine Logos is the ultimate author of the prophetic words; therefore, the prophets were able to predict future events under inspiration. Second, Justin says that the Spirit may inspire the prophet to adopt a past tense in speaking of a future event, especially when the prophet has stepped into a different role. For example, Justin notes that in Psalm 22:18 Christ is the speaker and says (in the past tense), "They cast lots for my clothing," even though this event is future for David. Third, the divine Logos sometimes speaks as the person of God the Father, sometimes as the person of Christ the Son, and sometimes as the people giving answer to the Lord and his Father. Finally, Justin compares the role of the Logos, as the true author of Scripture, to the role of pagan authors of dramatic works.

23. Bates, *Hermeneutics of the Apostolic Proclamation,* 217. It is very encouraging to see that in Bates's work the doctrine of inspiration is actually allowed to do some work, which is in stark contrast to much contemporary biblical interpretation.

24. Justin Martyr, *1 Apology* 36.1–2, as quoted in Bates, *Hermeneutics of the Apostolic Proclamation,* 200.

25. For the four points, see Bates, *Hermeneutics of the Apostolic Proclamation,* 200–203.

How should this method of prosopological exegesis be evaluated? Bates has mounted a very strong case in his two books for three crucially important points that hermeneutics needs to take into consideration going forward.

First, biblical authors use prosopological exegesis, and their example is followed by the early church fathers. Much New Testament study today assumes that Second Temple Judaism is the source we should mine for understanding New Testament hermeneutical methods. Bates himself is a trained scholar of Second Temple Judaism, yet his work shows that placing Paul in his Greco-Roman milieu and comparing his hermeneutics to early patristic exegesis yields valuable insights into how the apostles interpreted the Old Testament christologically.

Second, viewed from the perspective of patristic exegesis, one grasps the value of New Testament prosopological exegesis as setting an example for how the church should go about seeing and hearing Christ in the Old Testament. In other words, prosopological exegesis is not just a technique used by apostles, but also one that can and should be used by Christian followers of the apostles, including both the early church fathers and contemporary interpreters.[26]

Third, Bates has offered impressive evidence for prosopological exegesis having had a major influence on the development of trinitarian thought in the patristic era, especially in his second book, *The Birth of the Trinity*. In so doing, he has made a major contribution to the issue of how to evaluate the quality of the patristic exegesis that led to the formulation of pro-Nicene theology in the fourth century. Prosopological exegesis is, by no means, the *only* reading strategy employed by the patristic exegetes in their trinitarian interpretation of Scripture. But it is an outstanding example of the kind of patristic exegesis that is both (1) generally held in low regard in modernity, and (2) crucial to the emergence of patristic trinitarian theology. As Andrew Louth points out, it is necessary to ask how we can accept the results of the Nicene fathers' exegesis in the form of the doctrine of the Trinity but at the same time reject the exegetical methods they employed to obtain those results.[27] If we find it possible to recover prosopological exegesis as an act of *ressourcement*, we will find ourselves in the happy situation of being able to receive with gladness *both* patristic exegesis and the dogmatic conclusions of Nicaea and Chalcedon based on that exegesis.

26. This point can be taken as support for the thesis put forward in the second part of chap. 5 above, where I argue that the apostles are our models in interpretation.

27. Louth writes, "The Fathers, and creeds, and Councils claim to be interpreting Scripture. How can one accept their results if one does not accept their methods?" (*Discerning the Mystery*, 100).

If we compare the hermeneutical function of Bates's apostolic *kerygma* with the hermeneutical function of the rule of truth (or rule of faith) in Irenaeus, which was discussed in chapter 5, we see important similarities. Irenaeus was locked in a life-and-death struggle against the gnostics; the key battleground was the interpretation of Scripture. The gnostics operated with a metaphysical cosmology and interpreted individual passages of Scripture from within that worldview. Since their worldview was coherent in the sense of being a consistent set of beliefs joined together as a whole, their biblical interpretation was not altogether self-contradictory but rather somewhat unified. This unity gave it a superficial illusion of plausibility, which made it dangerous for deceiving the faithful. By interpreting Scripture out of the *skopos* of Scripture, as summarized in the rule of truth, Irenaeus opposed the gnostic worldview with a different metaphysical worldview. The crucial difference between the interpretive matrix Irenaeus used to interpret Scripture and the one used by the gnostics was that Irenaeus's hermeneutical worldview was the apostolic proclamation, *which arose out of Scripture itself*, while that of the gnostics was a worldview derived from a foreign source unrelated to Scripture. Irenaeus could interpret Scripture rightly because he worked within the rule of truth, which was itself derived from Scripture.

Irenaeus's interpretation of Scripture resulted in a beautiful picture of a great king (the Lord Jesus Christ), while that of the gnostics resulted in an ugly representation of a dog or fox (a debased and degenerate image of the king). It is crucial that we both see Christ depicted and hear Christ speaking in the Old Testament. Bates's explanation of how Paul did prosopological exegesis enables us to understand how Paul set the example for Irenaeus in these matters, and it enables us to see patristic exegesis (and therefore also patristic dogma) as arising out of Scripture itself in continuity with apostolic biblical interpretation.

Augustine's Christological Interpretation of the Psalms

A number of years ago, I learned an interesting fact about Benedictine spirituality in reading *The Rule of St. Benedict*. I discovered that the monks have traditionally chanted the entire Psalter in worship every week.[28] My initial reaction to learning this was probably a typically evangelical Protestant one. I asked, "Why the Psalms?" I did not grasp why the Psalms would be so central to monastic worship on a daily basis. Why not the Gospels? Why not Romans?

---

28. "No matter what, all 150 psalms must be chanted during the week" (Benedict of Nursia, *Rule of St. Benedict*, chap. 18, p. 68).

Why not the Bible as a whole? The Psalms to me were an ancient Israelite hymnbook that expressed the religious piety of God's people prior to Christ.

From having taken a course on the Psalms in seminary and being shaped by historical-critical methods, especially form criticism, I regarded the Psalms as mainly of historical value. I could see the Psalter as containing examples of piety for the people of God of all ages. Thus I could preach that it is acceptable for us as Christians to lament evil as the psalmists do and that the psalms of thanksgiving offer us rich examples of how to worship our Creator and Redeemer properly. The imprecatory psalms proved to be a bit more complicated; the historical reflex was to assign them to a more primitive stage of progressive revelation. The psalms of David also occasionally provided typological anticipations of Christ in which David functioned, from a New Testament perspective, as a type of the Messiah. In the cave of Adullam, David's enemies beset him; in the scourging and torture prior to the crucifixion, Christ was beset by his enemies. Thus we can see David as a type of Christ. Nevertheless, the Psalter still seemed somewhat more distant to me than the warm piety of the apostle Paul or the intimate portrayal of Christ's love for us in the Gospels. In Augustine's interpretation of the Psalms, however, we discover a way to understand the Psalms that makes perfect sense of the Benedictine devotion to chanting them so frequently that they were actually memorized by many monks. Why? It is because, for Augustine, both Christ and the church speak frequently in the Psalms. Augustine sees the Psalter as a thoroughly Christian book.

In 390 Augustine made the "mistake" of visiting the city of Hippo in search of recruits for his planned monastic community, only to be called by surprise to the priesthood by the aged bishop Valerius, who was in search of a competent teacher for his church. All of a sudden Augustine's plans for a quiet life of meditation and scholarship were interrupted by a call to pastoral ministry, and he begged for time to study in preparation for this task. He imagined Valerius wondering why a learned man like himself might need to study at this point and wrote the following in "Letter 21":

> But perhaps your Holiness says, "I should like to know exactly how your instruction falls short." Let me count the ways! I can more easily list what I have than what I wish to have. I dare to say that I know and hold with complete faith what belongs to salvation. But the question is: How (*quomodo*) do I minister this thing for the salvation of others, "not seeking what is advantageous (*utile*) to me, but what is advantageous to the many (*multa*), that they may be saved" (1 Cor. 10:33)?[29]

---

29. Augustine, "Letter 21," as quoted in Cameron, *Christ Meets Me Everywhere*, 135–36.

As Michael Cameron points out, the issue for Augustine at this moment was *how to minister*.[30] It is at this exact moment in Augustine's pilgrimage that he has a deeper and more profound encounter with the writings of the apostle Paul than he'd ever had before. The existential question looming before him was how to preach and teach for the salvation of the people—the same question I faced before my first Good Friday service as a young pastor (see my anecdote that opens chap. 1). In its most concise form, this dilemma is how to preach salvation through Christ from the whole Bible. My specific form of the question was how to preach Christ from Isaiah 53 on Good Friday. What Augustine learned in his years of study of the apostle Paul was how to preach Christ from the Psalms.

As a Platonist who was a Christian, Augustine needed at this point in his career to become a more thoroughly *Christianized* Platonist, and Paul was exactly the right author to help him do it. As a Platonist, Augustine had no trouble seeing how Scripture could be interpreted figurally or allegorically. Any Platonist believes that there are such things as universals; a Christian who is a Platonist also believes in the Word of God and the Wisdom of God. Therefore, believing that there are ideas in the mind of God that could be mirrored in the created works of God comes naturally to such a person. But what was missing in Augustine's thinking was how this happens in *history*. He needed to come to a deeper appreciation of the historical nature of salvation without losing his basically Platonist metaphysics; that is, he needed to see that we can read the Bible figurally only because at a certain point in time salvation was accomplished on the cross. The cross is a sign of salvation, but not merely a sign. It is "a nonnegotiable, *nonfigurative* description of the very mechanism of salvation."[31] Christ redeems us on the cross; this is what Augustine learned from Paul's Epistle to the Galatians. Salvation is not something abstract and eternal that is figurally pictured in the cross but something that actually *occurred* on the cross. As Cameron puts it, Augustine came to understand that "salvation took place not despite the temporal process but through it, by means of a man 'born of a woman, born under the Law' (Gal. 4:4)."[32] Augustine became a distinctively Christian kind of Platonist by coming to understand more clearly that the incarnation means not only that God created a cosmos in which there is a spiritual dimension in addition to the material dimension but also that God entered the material cosmos in the form of a man in order to give history a *telos* or end point—a goal and source

30. Cameron, *Christ Meets Me Everywhere*, 136.
31. Cameron, *Christ Meets Me Everywhere*, 149, italics in original.
32. Cameron, *Christ Meets Me Everywhere*, 151.

of meaning. Platonism is all about vertical relations; Christian Platonism is
about vertical *and* horizontal relations. It is *crucially* the intersection of the
vertical and the horizontal—of time and eternity—in Christ. Henri de Lubac
speaks for the Great Tradition when he characterizes Christ as "a scriptural
exegete par excellence in the act by which he fulfills his mission."[33] Christ
"unlocks" the meaning of Scripture by his action: "His cross is the sole and
universal key."[34] De Lubac here reflects the mind of Augustine.

Michael Cameron points out that Augustine read and reread both Paul and
the Psalms throughout his ministry. He observes that when Augustine read
the Psalms in light of Paul's insights about Christ's crucified human humility,
Scripture opened up to him. One way this happened was that he now saw
Christ using the Psalms to explain himself. Cameron explains:

> The canonical Gospels portrayed Jesus using psalms to explain his identity, his
> message, and above all his passion. The Synoptics cast the story of the crucifix-
> ion in terms of lament psalms, especially Psalm 21 (Matt. 27:46; Mark 15:34),
> Psalm 30 (Luke 23:46), and Psalm 68 (Matt. 27:34). Luke's post-resurrection
> Jesus is said to have explicitly taught the apostles "everything about himself in
> the Law, the Prophets *and the Psalms*" (Luke 24:44). The apostles are portrayed
> as preaching and teaching the Psalms as prophecies of the messianic age in
> general and of Messiah in particular (Acts 2:25–28; 4:25–26; 13:33–37; Rom.
> 15:8–11; Heb. 1:5–13). But Christians also read the Psalter as the Book of Christ
> in another way: not only as an "objective" account of fulfilled prophecy but
> also as a spiritual revelation of his human soul, in fact as a virtual transcript
> of his inner life while accomplishing the work of redemption. Paul particularly
> taught Christians to read the Psalms as echoes of the voice of Christ.[35]

The Psalms do not merely speak of Christ; rather, in the Psalms Christ actually speaks.[36] Augustine discovered prosopological exegesis as a result of his
encounter with Paul, although many other church fathers had discovered it
before him. Like Bates, Cameron also notes that the fathers continued to read
the Psalms in this way in the second and third centuries: "Second-century
writers like Ignatius of Antioch, Justin Martyr, and Irenaeus continued this
Christological reading; so did Tertullian, Cyprian, Clement of Alexandria, and

33. De Lubac, *Medieval Exegesis*, 1:239.
34. De Lubac, *Medieval Exegesis*, 1:239.
35. Cameron, *Christ Meets Me Everywhere*, 167–68. Cameron is using the traditional Septuagint numbering of the psalms here, so he is actually referring to Psalms 22, 31, and 69 in
our English Bibles.
36. For another good discussion of Augustine's christological reading of the Psalms, see
Byassee, *Praise Seeking Understanding*, esp. chap. 2.

Origen, in the third century. In the fourth century, the Christ of the Psalms was important to Athanasius, Basil of Caesarea, Gregory of Nazianzus, Gregory of Nyssa, and John Chrysostom in the east and Hilary of Poitiers, Jerome and Ambrose of Milan in the west."[37] Augustine thus represents the mainstream of the early church in finding Christ speaking and being spoken of in the Psalms. A century later, Benedict would draw on the common patrimony of the church in making the Psalms central to monastic worship. Augustine was thus no innovator, but he was a highly influential figure for a millennium of church history, which begs the obvious question of why his reading of the Psalms is so little known today. My answer to this question was developed in chapter 4; we live after the great disruption of the Great Tradition's consensus on biblical interpretation, and we need to push aside the veil of the misnamed "Enlightenment," which casts such a dark shadow over the Holy Scriptures and their christological meaning.

Cameron analyzes Augustine's Christology after 390 as developing along the lines of seeing Christ's kingship and priesthood coming together in the cross. He writes, "To emphasize the King-Priest's union with his people before God, Augustine adverts to a striking figure of speech that extends but also transcends prosopological exegesis: impersonation. . . . The device of impersonation goes beyond prosopological analysis by hearing a second voice speaking within the first voice."[38] I am not sure that viewing impersonation as something other than prosopological exegesis is the best way to understand what Augustine is doing, but it does get at a real and highly complex phenomenon in Augustine's exegesis of the Psalms that needs to be described in some way. Let us look at an example of what Cameron is talking about.

Michael Fiedrowicz points out that Augustine's understanding of the Psalms as a prophecy of the mystery of Christ in his totality—head and body (the *totus Christus*)—gave him a hermeneutical key to plumb the depths of the Old Testament.[39] He also points out that, in this regard, Augustine was following the practice of the New Testament writers. Psalms that were interpreted christologically became "as clear as the gospel."[40] Augustine made use of prosopological exegesis to understand how it is possible for human beings "to share in the immortal life of God."[41] Christ identifies with his church and speaks at some points as the body and at other points as the head. For Augustine, the church has a kind of preexistence in the prayer of Christ even

37. Cameron, *Christ Meets Me Everywhere*, 168.
38. Cameron, *Christ Meets Me Everywhere*, 179.
39. Fiedrowicz, "Introduction," in Augustine, *Expositions of the Psalms, 1–32*, 43.
40. Augustine, *Expositions of the Psalms, 1–32*, 144.
41. Fiedrowicz, "Introduction," in Augustine, *Expositions of the Psalms, 1–32*, 51.

as spoken prophetically through David and other prophets in the Old Testament.[42] We can see how these ideas are worked out by a brief examination of Augustine's treatment of Psalm 3.

Augustine's Interpretation of Psalm 3

In his exegesis of Psalm 3, Augustine considers a short psalm of David that many modern commentators read historically, guided by the title, which points clearly to the historical background of the psalm. The title is "A Psalm of David, When He Fled from Absalom His Son." Many modern interpreters also extend the historical interpretation typologically, so that David is regarded as a type of Christ. For Augustine, however, the question of who is speaking is not settled by appeal to the incident in the life of David mentioned in the title, because David speaks prophetically and thus not simply about himself. Those who see David as a type of Christ here implicitly acknowledge that fact, but Augustine thinks that it is worth investigating who is actually speaking. His exposition of the psalm is fascinating, because he offers no fewer than three separate answers to the question of who is speaking in the space of just over eight pages—all three of which he views as valid. How does he work this out?

Augustine is not concerned to deny or diminish the importance of the historical meaning of the psalm; he discusses the situation in the life of David as basic to the literal sense. As we saw in chapter 6, the literal sense cannot be contradicted by any *sensus plenior*. But Augustine also relates the situation in David's life to the life of Christ. The betrayal of David and the rising up of a host of enemies against him seem to Augustine to be paralleled clearly in the betrayal of Jesus by Judas and the rising up of Jesus's enemies against him. To the historical interpretation suggested by the psalm's title, Augustine adds, "But it also has a spiritual interpretation as follows: the Son of God, that is, the power and wisdom of God, deserted the mind of Judas, when the devil took possession of him deep within."[43]

In verses 2–3 Augustine hears an echo of Matthew 27:42, "Let him come down from the cross, if he is the Son of God," and "Others he saved, himself he cannot save." In verse 4 he sees Christ's trusting of his heavenly Father even to the uttermost. The reference to "sleep" in verse 5 is taken to mean "death" on the basis of several scriptural usages of the word "sleep" as a euphemism for death (such as 1 Thess. 4:13). Thus "I woke again" is naturally a reference to the resurrection. In verse 7 Christ appeals to God for salvation; verse 8

42. Fiedrowicz, "Introduction," in Augustine, *Expositions of the Psalms, 1–32*, 55. See also Cameron, *Christ Meets Me Everywhere*, 201–2.
43. Augustine, *Expositions of the Psalms, 1–32*, 77.

declares that salvation comes from God and is a blessing for the people of God. So Augustine's first interpretation of the psalm is to see it as spoken by Christ. David speaks as a prophet, and his words are the words of Christ by the inspired action of the Holy Spirit.

Then Augustine does something quite unexpected. He offers a second interpretation in which we see his famous concept of the *totus Christus* in operation: "This psalm can also be understood with reference to the person of Christ in another way—namely, that the whole Christ is speaking."[44] By "the whole Christ" (*totus Christus*), he means the body of Christ of which he is the head. Here we see the fruit of Augustine's engagement with the Christology and ecclesiology of Paul: Christ not only became incarnate as the man Jesus, but he also created a body for himself in the form of the church of which he is the head. This body of Christ lives in the material world in an ongoing form between the first and second comings of Christ, that is, in our age.

Augustine quotes Ephesians 4:15–16 as the basis for his extended interpretation, noting the way the church experiences persecution just like her Lord and head. He exhorts God's people to say in the words of the psalm, "I have slept and taken rest, and I arose because the Lord will uphold me; let them pray so, that they may be joined and connected to their Head. For to this people it is said, 'Arise, sleeper, and rise from the dead, and Christ will take hold of you' (Eph. 5:14)." Note that he is encouraging Christians to identify with Christ and to regard themselves as sharing his sufferings and, in so doing, to share in his resurrection. He is exhorting them to imitate Paul, who wrote,

> But whatever gain I had, I counted as loss for the sake of Christ. Indeed, I count everything as loss because of the surpassing worth of knowing Christ Jesus my Lord. For his sake I have suffered the loss of all things and count them as rubbish, in order that I may gain Christ and be found in him, not having a righteousness of my own that comes from the law, but that which comes through faith in Christ, the righteousness from God that depends on faith—that I may know him and the power of his resurrection, and may share his sufferings, becoming like him in his death, that by any means possible I may attain the resurrection from the dead. (Phil. 3:7–11)

Augustine sees the identification of the church with Christ in Pauline terms as the union of believers with Christ as members of his body.

But Augustine is not done yet; he offers a third interpretation of the psalm. This time he applies it to each of us in our personal struggles against the vices and sinful desires that rise up against us. He writes, "Lord how numerous are

---

44. Augustine, *Expositions of the Psalms, 1–32*, 81.

those who afflict me! Look how many rise up against me!"[45] He locates the basis of our hope in that "God has deigned to take on human nature in Christ."[46]

Let us stop and take stock for a moment. What is going on here? Augustine is reading Psalm 3 as a psalm of David, just as anybody who pays attention to the title would do. The psalm is literally about David. But the psalm is also *literally* about more than merely an incident in the life of David; it is prophetic speech, which can be understood to have been spoken by Christ, who inspired the prophet David and speaks through him. What Christ says is made clear by the fact that Christ is the one spoken of in the New Testament, that is, the one who died and rose again to redeem his church and to unite believers to him in his body. But this is not a matter of reading New Testament content into an Old Testament text, because the preincarnate Word, the Son and Wisdom, was really inspiring David so that David's psalm became Christ's own speech. Jesus Christ speaks through his prophet to his people, and this is an extension of the literal meaning of the text. Jason Byassee helpfully comments that Augustine's exegesis of this psalm is a "thoroughly *historical* vision of exegesis, rooted in the history of the incarnation."[47]

Since we can regard Augustine's three interpretations as extensions of the literal meaning understood historically as David speaking of his situation during the rebellion of Absalom, they could be regarded as the legitimate spiritual sense of the text. Alternatively, since these three spiritual senses do not contradict the literal sense, they can actually be regarded as extensions of the literal sense *if* we can grant the ontological reality of the preexistent Son speaking in the text.[48] These are literally the words of the preexistent Son. And all three can be seen as growing out of the literal sense *if* we grant the reality of inspiration. If the preexistent Son can really and did really inspire David, and if David could and did really speak as a prophet of both himself and of more and better than he knew, then it is not inappropriate to see Christ in the text and to hear Christ speaking through the text.[49] And if Christ really has in history become the head of his body the church, it cannot be impossible that the speaking head speaks for the entire body, which after all is exactly what heads normally do. And if what is said is true of the body as a whole, then it is also true for each individual who makes up a part of that body. The

45. Augustine, *Expositions of the Psalms, 1–32*, 83.
46. Augustine, *Expositions of the Psalms, 1–32*, 83.
47. Byassee, *Praise Seeking Understanding*, 63.
48. This is an example of the relationship between the literal and the extended literal sense that we developed in chap. 6 above.
49. Here we see the crucial importance of the matters discussed in chaps. 2 and 3 above for seeing and hearing Christ in the Old Testament.

difference between prosopological exegesis and typological exegesis is that in typological exegesis (at its best) we may *see Christ opaquely* in the Old Testament text, but in prosopological exegesis we actually *hear Christ speak clearly* in the text.

Augustine's Interpretation of the "Psalms of the Crucified"

We now turn to Augustine's exegesis of the "psalms of the crucified" in order to clarify further how patristic prosopological exegesis differs from modern typological exegesis. In the block of psalms from 15 through 31, Augustine identified seven as the "psalms of the crucified": Psalms 16, 17, 18, 22, 28, 30, and 31.[50] In these seven psalms, Christ speaks from the cross. For Augustine, Psalm 22 is the central psalm in this group and could be regarded as the center (or holy of holies) of the Psalter as a whole because it reveals the central mystery of the faith, which is the saving death of our Lord. Three of these psalms (16, 22, and 31) are explicitly quoted in the New Testament passion narratives. The other four (17, 18, 28, and 30) can be read as exploring the meaning of the cross. We will survey each of these seven psalms, noting how Augustine interprets it, and then conclude with some observations about the significance of his exegesis for our interpretation of the Old Testament today.

PSALM 16

This psalm is a cry to God for preservation (v. 1) coupled with a confession of faith in Yahweh as "my Lord" (v. 2). The speaker says that the LORD is "my chosen portion and my cup" (v. 5); he blesses the LORD who "gives me counsel" (v. 7). He says, "I have set the LORD always before me" and on this basis is confident, "because he is at my right hand, I shall not be shaken" (v. 8). This confidence is further expressed in the words "For you will not abandon my soul to *Sheol*, or let your holy one see corruption" (v. 10). Instead, the speaker expresses confidence:

50. I am using the numbering in our English translations of the Psalter in the text of this book. Augustine's numbering is different from ours between Psalms 9 and 146, because he is using the Septuagint numbering system. Thus his Psalm 9 is a combination of our Psalms 9 and 10; his Psalm 147 is a combination of our Psalms 146 and 147. So between our Psalms 9 and 147, Augustine's number is one behind the English number. In Psalms 1–8 and 148–50, the numbering is the same. The reader who consults the sources quoted in this book (such as Bates or Cameron) or who reads Augustine's *Expositions* in either the Latin originals or the English translation will need to bear in mind that Augustine's numbers are one behind the numbers in both this book and our English translations of the Bible. When he talks about Psalm 15, he means our Psalm 16. When he talks about Psalm 21, he means our Psalm 22. When he talks about Psalm 30, he means our Psalm 31.

> You make known to me the path of life;
>   in your presence there is fullness of joy;
>   at your right hand are pleasures forevermore. (16:11)

Psalm 16:8–11 is quoted by Peter on the day of Pentecost (Acts 2:25–28) to argue that Jesus is the Messiah. Peter points out that the text cannot be referring to David, who died and was buried and whose tomb is "with us to this day" (Acts 2:29). He says that David was a prophet and knew that God had sworn an oath to place one of his descendants on the throne (v. 30). Peter also asserts that David "foresaw and spoke about the resurrection of the Christ, that he was not abandoned to Hades, nor did his flesh see corruption" (Acts 2:31). In Acts 13:35, Paul's sermon in the synagogue at Antioch in Pisidia also cites Psalm 16:10, "You will not let your Holy One see corruption," as a prophecy of Christ's resurrection.

Augustine's initial observation with regard to this psalm is that in it "our king speaks from the standpoint of the human nature he assumed. At the time of his crucifixion the royal title written above him stood out clearly."[51] The entire psalm is then interpreted as Christ speaking through his prophet David, just as Peter says is the case. While the New Testament writers do not explicitly state that the entire psalm is Christ speaking, they do attribute the key section in verse 10 to the Messiah, and it seems plain that verse 10 is a continuation of the same speaker who has been speaking throughout. Cameron calls attention to the significance for Augustine of the future tense that is used throughout the psalm: "Augustine carefully observes the future tense of these verbs because they were spoken by the Prophet as anticipations of God's saving acts; however, also carefully setting them in the scene of the crucified Christ, they continue to anticipate God's deliverance in resurrection."[52]

As in many passages of Scripture, the tenses almost get in the way of the thought, because what is past, present, and future is all known simultaneously to God. The church already exists in the Savior dying on the cross, but it actually exists already in a sense in the speaking Messiah in the psalm of David in the Old Testament. Cameron comments on the church: "In Christ it has a kind of 'preexistence' and is already the subject of his intercession before he died. The Church is a reality not merely from the moment of his redemptive death but from the eternity of his ever-living love, and so must be seen as existing even 'before the foundation of the world.' . . . Because he has forever been alive Christ has also forever loved the Church, for 'where the

---

51. Augustine, *Expositions of the Psalms, 1–32*, 182.
52. Cameron, *Christ Meets Me Everywhere*, 201.

head is, there too is the body.'"[53] Here is an idea that is not easy to process except within the context of Christian Platonist metaphysics. Because the Son is eternally begotten of the Father, the Son is eternal. And since the reality of the individual members of the church—their essence—is derived from the Son, there is a sense in which the essence of the church exists eternally in an ideal sense prior to taking flesh in history. Yet this time sequence is valid only from our point of view as creatures encased within time. From the point of view of the divine Messiah, what is future (to us) is just as certain and just as real as the past and present. This line of thought seems to fit securely within Paul's concept of the lordship of Christ over both creation and the church in Colossians 1:15–20. There Christ is said to be the one through whom "all things were created in heaven and on earth, visible and invisible" (v. 16); he is also said to be the "head of the body, the church" (v. 18). In sum, it says, "He is the beginning, the firstborn from the dead, that in everything he might be preeminent. For in him all the fullness of God was pleased to dwell, and through him to reconcile to himself all things, whether on earth or in heaven, making peace by the blood of his cross" (Col. 1:18–20). Christ's identity is the same yesterday, today, and forever (Heb. 13:8), but his identity is progressively revealed to creatures as the mission of the Messiah unfolds in history.

Psalm 17

This psalm is not quoted in the New Testament, but it is an individual lament understood by Augustine to have been spoken in the voice of Christ during the crucifixion. Augustine notes that it is a prayer of David himself, but is "to be assigned to the Lord in person, together with the Church, which is his body."[54] He relates the words "my deadly enemies who surround me" (v. 9) to the words of Christ's mockers: "Hail, King of the Jews!" (Matt. 27:29).[55]

Psalm 18

This is an individual lament, which is understood by Augustine to be spoken in the voice of Christ. It has the same title as the previous psalm, "A prayer of David himself." As Cameron notes, this is the first use of Augustine's famous concept of the *totus Christus*, "whole Christ."[56] In his comments on verse 2, Augustine writes: "Accordingly Christ and the Church, the whole Christ (*totus Christus*), Head and body, are speaking here when the psalm

53. Cameron, *Christ Meets Me Everywhere*, 202.
54. Augustine, *Expositions of the Psalms*, 1–32, 185.
55. Augustine, *Expositions of the Psalms*, 1–32, 186.
56. Cameron, *Christ Meets Me Everywhere*, 204.

begins, I will love you, Lord, my strength. I will love you, Lord, through whom I am strong."[57] As he goes through this psalm, Augustine hears the voice as alternating between the head and the body. David's voice becomes that of Christ and then it becomes that of Christ's body; this is possible because of the close identification of the body with its own head.

PSALM 22

In the opening paragraph of his first exposition of Psalm 22, Augustine writes:

> "To the end," because the Lord Jesus Christ himself speaks, that is, prays for his own resurrection. Now, his resurrection happened on the morning of the first day of the week. He was "taken up" into eternal life, and death will no longer be his master [Rom. 6:9]. But these words are spoken in the person of the Crucified One (*ex persona crucifixa*). The beginning of this psalm has the words that he cried out as he hung upon the cross while also holding fast (*servans*) the person of the "old man" whose mortality he carried (*portavit*). Now this "old man" was nailed to the cross with him [Rom. 6:6].[58]

This statement sets the agenda for the exposition of this psalm and of the other six in this group. As Cameron points out, for Augustine these words carry "bedrock spiritual authority"[59] because they come from the lips of the dying Savior himself as he hung on the cross (Matt. 27:46; Mark 15:34). The significance of Christ speaking this psalm on the cross can hardly be overstated from the perspective of biblical theology. Cameron points out that for Augustine, "Christ takes as his own the voice of the sinner Adam. . . . In order to submerge himself in humanity's sinful ego the crucified Christ spoke in the voice of Adam. . . . Christ drinks to the dregs Adam's terrible cup of torment while confessing to the ignominy of 'my' sins."[60]

For Cameron, the significance of Augustine's reading here is that it marks his emergence from "a religious-philosophical to a distinctly Christian mode of spiritual reasoning."[61] Cameron writes that, for Augustine, Christ's use of the word "me" in this psalm is "a figurative act of *prosopopeia* raised to the power of redemption."[62] What Cameron is saying is that here we see

57. Augustine, *Expositions of the Psalms, 1–32*, 189.
58. Augustine, *Expositions of the Psalms, 1–32*, 221.
59. Cameron, *Christ Meets Me Everywhere*, 197.
60. Cameron, *Christ Meets Me Everywhere*, 198.
61. Cameron, *Christ Meets Me Everywhere*, 198.
62. Cameron, *Christ Meets Me Everywhere*, 197–98.

prosopological exegesis being used in a distinctively Christian manner in order to express the idea that the historical action of Christ on the cross is the means by which the redemption of sinners is accomplished. Christ takes humanity's sin and in exchange gives us his righteousness. Augustine sees this as a sacramental action; here the words of Scripture mediate the power of salvation that has arisen from the self-sacrifice of Christ on the cross on behalf of Adam's fallen race. God is interacting with the world—that is the vertical dimension—and God is shaping history and moving it toward its appointed end—that is the horizontal dimension. The cross is where the vertical and horizontal intersect, so it is divine action in a human act—in other words, it is a sacrament.

Psalm 28

In his exposition of this individual lament, Augustine says that the speaker here is "the Mediator himself, strong of hand in the conflict of his passion."[63] He identifies with Christ and interprets the psalm as expressing the truth that the "eternity of your Word never ceases to unite itself to me."[64]

Psalm 30

This is a psalm of praise at the dedication of the temple; Augustine interprets it as a psalm of the resurrection. He sees it as the whole Christ vowing to praise the Lord because "you have taken me up and have not let my enemies gloat over me."[65] Verses 9–10 are Christ's prayer for resurrection.

Psalm 31

This psalm contains the cry of Christ on the cross: "Into your hand I commit my spirit" (v. 5), which is quoted in Luke 23:46. In his first exposition of this psalm, Augustine paraphrases: "To your power I entrust my spirit, knowing that I will swiftly receive it back."[66] In his second exposition, Augustine notes that Luke 23:46 quotes this verse and stresses that this proves that Christ really is speaking in this psalm. As far as Augustine is concerned, Christ quotes it because these are his own words, spoken beforehand prophetically and now spoken appropriately in the fulfillment of the prophecy. Augustine writes:

63. Augustine, *Expositions of the Psalms, 1–32*, 291.
64. Augustine, *Expositions of the Psalms, 1–32*, 291.
65. Augustine, *Expositions of the Psalms, 1–32*, 297.
66. Augustine, *Expositions of the Psalms, 1–32*, 317.

He had good reason for making the words of the psalm his own, for he wanted to teach you that in the psalm he is speaking. Look for him in it. Bear in mind how he wanted you to look for him in another psalm, the one . . . where he said, "They dug holes in my hands and my feet, they numbered all my bones. These same people looked on and watched me. They shared out my garments among them, and cast lots for my tunic" [Ps. 22:16–18]. He wanted you to understand that this whole prophecy was fulfilled in himself, so he made the opening verse of that same psalm his own cry: "O God, my God, why have you forsaken me?" Yet all the same he transfigured the body's cry as he made it his own, for the Father never did forsake his only Son. "You have redeemed me, Lord God of truth carrying through what you promised, unfailing in your pledge, O God of truth."[67]

Christ exegetes Scripture by fulfilling it; he also gives us verbal clues to its meaning to help us understand it clearly.

What can we learn from Augustine's expositions of the "psalms of the crucified" about prosopological exegesis and the way in which the early church interpreted the Old Testament? I suggest three points, which are of the greatest significance.

First, Augustine views the validity of prosopological exegesis as being grounded in the reality of biblical inspiration and in the unity of the Bible as centered on Jesus Christ. So everything we said in chapter 5 is in the background here as presupposed by Augustine and necessary for his exegesis.

Second, the literal sense is the controlling sense, as we saw in chapter 6, in that the fundamental and crucial meaning of these psalms, in Augustine's view, is the historical action of God in Christ on the cross of Calvary. The cross is not merely a figure of something else, such as an idea, principle, or ideal. The cross is where redemption actually is accomplished in history; everything else that is done in terms of interpretation here depends on that fact.

Third, the self-interpreting character of the Bible is on display here; since Christ indwells the text, it is Christ himself who, by his Spirit, speaks in the text. The sacramental-historical nature of redemption means that what the Bible says, God says. God is not detached or remote from us; God is active and alive in our midst, speaking in the midst of his church just as John saw in the opening chapters of Revelation (Rev. 1–3).

In Revelation 5 we read of John's vision of the Lamb, who looks as though it had been slain (v. 6), and we are told that the four living creatures and the twenty-four elders sing a new song when they find that this Lamb is worthy to open the scroll (v. 9). What is the scroll? It is said to be "a scroll written

67. Augustine, *Expositions of the Psalms, 1–32,* 331.

within and on the back, sealed with seven seals" (v. 1), which could be symbolic of God's covenant with humanity, which is the meaning of history. Only the slain Lamb who is now alive is able to open the scroll. Jesus Christ is both the *content* of Scripture and the *interpreter* of Scripture; in his exposition of the "psalms of the crucified," Augustine allows Jesus Christ to exercise his lordly prerogative to determine the meaning of his own Word. This is the highest and most profound implication of the early church's use of prosopological exegesis, and it comes to its climax in Augustine's sermons.

The Christological Literalism of the Great Tradition as Scientific Exegesis

In this chapter I have so far suggested that the reason the fathers borrowed the technique of prosopological exegesis from the broader culture and applied it in a unique way to the Scriptures is that they perceived that the Scriptures speak of the being of the one true God and that this One speaks through the text as a living presence in the text. Therefore, in order to engage with such writings, one has to take into account the pressure exerted on interpretation by the presence and reality of this One who speaks in the text as both author *and* main character. The understanding of God and God's relationship to the world that they perceived in the text generated the theological metaphysics that I refer to in this book as Christian Platonism. The fathers' doctrine of God also funded a doctrine of inspiration that allowed them to understand the sovereign Lord speaking through the words of the Old Testament prophets in such a way as to reveal himself to readers who acknowledge, and submit to, the reality of his being in the text. As the transcendent and immanent One, God can be both *in* the text and *above* the text, making use of the text in order to reveal himself to the reader in a saving and sanctifying way. Thus reading Scripture was a sacramental-historical exercise with both vertical and horizontal dimensions. Seeing and hearing Christ in the Old Testament was, for them, the happy outcome of reading as humble recipients of revelation and as sinners being progressively united by faith to the very being of the Triune God through the grace of our Lord Jesus Christ in the power of the Holy Spirit.

In chapter 1 I argued that the term "theological interpretation" has been overused and defined too vaguely in contemporary discussion; chapters 5, 6, and 7 have attempted to provide a thick description of the kind of theological interpretation we need to recover and place in the center of future theological work. My main reservation about the term "theological interpretation of Scripture" is that using it risks misunderstanding what we are talking about, as if it is just another technique or method in the toolbox of biblical scholars to be pulled out as needed. This understanding would permit some biblical scholars to do historical-critical studies and others to do theological interpretation, as if the latter were just another possible method to be applied by those so inclined when they deem appropriate. But that understanding of theological interpretation of Scripture fails to capture the significance of the argument of this book. What this book is arguing is that without being theological in the way I have described, the interpretation of Scripture will fail to do justice to the reality of the biblical text. Any kind of interpretation that neglects theology is bad interpretation. Now, of course, this is not to say that we should not have archaeological, philological, and other kinds of historical studies of places mentioned in the text, words used in the text, and events that form the background to the text. I am simply saying that these good things by themselves do not constitute "interpretation" and that we have not finished interpreting the text when we have exhaustively covered the ground in terms of the language, background, and historical situation. I am pleading for recognition that while sound exegesis of Scripture *uses* historical tools, it *is* theological in nature. Theological interpretation is not an option or an extra; it is the heart of good biblical interpretation and always has been. All good exegesis *must* be theological.

In modernity, biblical interpreters like to think of themselves as practicing "scientific exegesis" in contrast to premodern exegesis, which they regard as "simplistic" or "subjective" or as having a tendency to read meaning into the text with no controls on what the text can be made to mean. Origen is the favorite whipping boy, and allegory is the besetting sin. But the problem with such oversimplifications is that premodern exegesis is a complex and variegated phenomenon that includes competent practitioners, incompetent ones, and occasional spiritual geniuses. It also attracts fakes and charlatans, as well as deceptive heretics bent on destroying the faith once delivered. So if one wants to refute premodern exegesis, one needs to take its strongest proponents, such as the apostle Paul, Augustine, Thomas Aquinas, and Calvin; one also needs to distinguish between practices that gradually drop away in the tradition and ones that rise to the top as "best practices" among recognized doctors of the church.

The marks of a healthy and effective science are that it is an organized body of knowledge with a defined subject matter and employs a method appropriate to the study of that subject matter. The genius of premodern exegesis is that it produced classical orthodoxy (as symbolized in the creeds), has a clear focus on God as the subject matter being studied, and employs the method of contemplating the self-revelation of God in Holy Scripture.

Therefore, classical Christian exegesis can be regarded as scientific. It is also the case that the modern historical-critical method (or methods) tends to display (rather ostentatiously at times) the trappings of science—having a form of science but denying the power thereof, one might say. But modern historical criticism's method is not really fit for the purpose because it is a method that presumes the nonexistence or irrelevance of the subject matter it is supposed to be studying. Its method permits it to see only what exists as part of the material world. It screens out spiritual reality. In modernity, theology largely has ceased to have as its real objective the study of God. It has pulled back from that lofty goal to focus on the study of human ideas and opinions about God. If this is a science, it is not theological science.

Consider the following thought experiment. If astronomy ceased to use telescopes and never looked at the stars, focused all its attention on mentions of the stars in literary sources and the history of human thoughts about the stars, all the while entertaining an ongoing discussion of the sense in which stars could legitimately be said to exist, with the most radical astronomers expressing doubts about the very existence of the stars in the traditional sense, and if astronomers debated endlessly about what earthly realities the idea of "star" might be said to refer to and whether and to what extent traditional ideas about stars reflected class, gender, and racial bias—would we be justified in viewing this endeavor as "astronomy"? There might still be university departments of astronomy, learned societies at which papers were presented, journals of astronomy, conferences on topics of interest to astronomers, and doctoral programs in astronomy, but would it be astronomy? Or would it be something else operating under the name "astronomy"? And if we were persuaded to call it a science, would it really be the science we know today as astronomy?

"Biblical studies" may be the name of a department in many seminaries, but it is not really a science in the Aristotelian sense of an inquiry of study with an organized body of knowledge, a particular subject matter to study, and a method appropriate to the study of that object. The giveaway is the word "studies" attached to the subject matter. All modern academic disciplines that use this nomenclature are *derivative* in the sense that they base themselves on other disciplines, which have more of a claim to be sciences and actually have a disciplinary methodology of their own.[68] The science from which mainstream, academy-approved biblical studies most often derives its

68. E.g., religious studies draws on methods used in archaeology, anthropology, history, philology, literary theory, philosophy, and so on. Women's studies draws on methods used in psychology, sociology, political theory, economics, literary theory, history, and so on. The term "studies" usually indicates a multidisciplinary focus on something that is not precisely defined;

method is history. History is a science in that its focus of study is the human
past, and its method is the interpretation of empirical artifacts in the form of
oral or written testimonies and records. Historians have never quite come to
universal agreement as to whether history is one of the "humanities" or one
of the "social sciences." But no matter how that question is settled, there is
little question that there is a desire among many historians to be regarded
as more than "opinion mongers" and to be seen as somehow practicing a
scientific method that yields objective truth rather than mere prejudices or
opinions.

Since the awe-inspiring rise of modern technological science based on the
so-called hard sciences, including physics, chemistry, and biology, many other
academic disciplines have aspired to be regarded as objective sciences. One
way they have sought to do so is by imitating the methods of the empirical
sciences in what Andrew Louth (following George Steiner) referred to as "the
fallacy of imitative form."[69] So historians have tried to model their methods
as far as possible on those of physics, which has led to historians adopting a
modern, neopagan set of metaphysical beliefs (Epicurean naturalism), whose
prestige depends on its association with modern technological science, even
though that association is merely accidental. Modern science did not grow
out of Epicureanism. It grew out of a medieval Christian worldview in which
the doctrine of creation made it plausible to think two things about the world:
(1) that events in nature are not random, purposeless, or temporary but rather
reliable, purposeful, and permanent; and (2) that the human mind is capable
of grasping the laws of nature that govern events in the world because the
same Logos by which the universe was created is part of our minds insofar as
we have been created in the image of God. Epicurean metaphysics undercuts
both of these assumptions. The identification of philosophical naturalism
with the success of technological science is therefore unwarranted and the
result of Enlightenment propaganda rather than clear thinking.

The development of modern science took place on the basis of Christian
Platonism, which supported the belief that natural law and rational order are
imprinted on the universe. Formulating hypotheses in the form of lawlike for-
mulae as mathematical descriptions of how events in nature are connected and
refining those hypotheses through repeatable, empirical experiments should
be possible on the basis of the Christian doctrine of creation. The incredible
success of technology or applied science in the modern era has proved that

---

the result is a lack of scientific rigor and, in particular, a failure to specify what constitutes
falsifiability in the theories advanced by scholars in the field.
    69. Louth, *Discerning the Mystery*, 10.

natural science is an approach that comes to grips with the truth about the way things are in this world.

Unfortunately, in the early stages of modern science, the goal of technological control of nature was seen as being hindered by the existence of teleology in nature. Teleology is a bedrock assumption of Christian Platonism. But if things have inbuilt natures, and if they flourish only when those natures are fulfilled, then there are definite limits to how far we should go in manipulating nature (including human nature). The problem was that such limits were seen by early modern science and philosophy as undesirable constraints to be shaken off by the triumphant and sovereign will of the autonomous individual. So teleology was out, and so was the Christian Platonism of the Great Tradition of Christian orthodoxy. Scientists sawed off the branch on which science was perched, although the full implications of this move did not become visible right away. We discussed the process of the point-by-point rejection of Christian Platonism in chapter 4, and we saw that the end point of that process was late modern skepticism and relativism, through which the foundations of modern science itself are eroded and undermined. The Enlightenment's replacement of Christian Platonism with Epicurean philosophical naturalism has led, over time, to the erroneous identification of "science" with "naturalism." As a result, the academic discipline called "history" has sought to be a science in the wrong way, that is, by adopting the modern metaphysics of philosophical naturalism. This has led to a definition of "history" in which what is understood as "historical" is arbitrarily reduced to what can be conceived within the narrow confines of strict philosophical naturalism. Historians tried to do history in the same way that physicists did physics.

Biblical studies developed as a discipline separate from theology by seeking the patronage and prestige of history at the precise moment in history when the scientific character of history was being deformed and diminished by its adoption of philosophical naturalism as its understanding of what it means to be "scientific." This resulted in biblical studies becoming a secularizing force within the church, which will never be able to digest the antibiblical metaphysical assumptions built into the modern concept of history. As David Steinmetz noted in his famous article "The Superiority of Pre-critical Exegesis," it is astonishing but true that the modern historical-critical method still struggles for a foothold in the church after *two centuries* of dominating the academy.[70] It seems to me that if it has not gained universal acceptance in the church by now, it never will. Historical-critical approaches dominate only declining, liberal Protestant denominations and those who wish to imitate

---

70. Steinmetz, "Superiority of Pre-critical Exegesis," 14.

them among Roman Catholics and evangelicals. The vibrant and growing evangelical churches of the Global South, along with a strong minority within the West, continue to resist the hegemony of historical criticism. Another approach must therefore be found. My view is that biblical studies is the prodigal that needs to come home. But where is "home"?

Biblical studies needs to be brought back into the academic discipline of what Augustine called Christian philosophy and Thomas Aquinas called sacred doctrine, which we today call theology. Theology is exegesis plus dogmatics; in other words, it is contemplation of the philosophical implications of the revelation derived from Scripture. As Hans Boersma puts it, "Exegesis is in the first place a theological discipline: it aims to place before us the God we know in Jesus Christ."[71] Hermeneutics is merely biblical interpretation reflecting on its method, and so hermeneutics needs to be integrated into theological methodology, of which it is a key part. This is the sound instinct that has led to such a strong interest in our day in the various iterations and kinds of what is called theological interpretation of Scripture. It is surely right that the interpretation of Scripture should be "theological," but the question is what does this mean?

Theology is a science. The object of study is God and all things in relation to God. The method is meditation on revelation derived from biblical exegesis and reflection on philosophical questions that arise from meditation on revelation.[72] Historic Christian orthodoxy is the body of knowledge produced so far by this science. So biblical interpretation is integral to doing theology, and exegesis is incomplete without theological reflection. My intention in the last section of this chapter is to describe as clearly as I can what I mean by theological interpretation of Scripture—what I described earlier in this book as the recovery of a pro-Nicene culture in which exegesis can be done in continuity with the Great Tradition of Christian orthodoxy. In so doing, my understanding is that I am simply describing all good biblical interpretation, not an esoteric offshoot or minor subset of biblical interpretation.

According to Jason Byassee, christological literalism means that "the text refers literally to Christ, the *res* of all scripture's *signa*."[73] The Bible is literally about Christ (the *res* of Scripture), because the Bible is Christ's Word

71. Boersma, *Scripture as Real Presence*, 41.

72. See Levering, *Scripture and Metaphysics*: "The thesis of this book is that 'renewal of the theology of the triune God' requires that theologians reject the alleged opposition between scriptural and metaphysical modes of reflection, without conflating the two modes. Scriptural and metaphysical modes of reflection came unglued, I argue, when theologians no longer recognized contemplation as the rightful 'end' of Trinitarian theology" (2). Levering's book is a good example of *ressourcement* theology and of the kind of theology that helps us become "God-centered" (3).

73. Byassee, *Praise Seeking Understanding*, 224.

spoken by Christ himself through his appointed prophets and apostles. These prophetic and apostolic words are signs (*signa*). Michael Fiedrowicz says of Augustine that he was persuaded that a sign could be understood only by someone with knowledge of the reality (*res*) to which the sign pointed.[74] Another way to express this is to say with Byassee that allegory is incarnationally shaped.[75] Byassee helpfully distinguishes between christological literalism and allegory as follows. The former refers to the words of Scripture when they *directly* refer to Christ. An example would be Psalm 16:10, which was discussed above. Christ was literally raised from the dead rather than being left to suffer corruption; Psalm 16:10 is a prophecy of that event. For Byassee, the latter term, allegory, refers to the *indirect* application of the words of Scripture to Christ even when their literal meaning does not directly speak of Christ. An example would be to see Isaac prefiguring Christ as a sacrificial victim (Gen. 22). Here we identify a connection between the Son of God and the son of Abraham because we are reading the story of Abraham and Isaac in the context of the Bible as a whole; since God is working everywhere in the Bible, we can expect to see recurring patterns that reflect the universals in which individual things in this world participate. Sacrifice would be an example of a recurring pattern that participates, to a greater or lesser extent in individual cases, in a universal reality that partially constitutes creation.

For Augustine, language is sacramental. Cameron describes how this works:

> Christ impersonates Adam in order to reveal the structure of redemption that he later calls "the marvelous exchange, the divine transaction." Augustine had a shorthand term for this: "sacrament." Christ's will-to-death gives what it portrays, and so makes all other events, words, and signs *sacramental* insofar as they partake of it. Because that includes the Old Testament's words and deeds, it too is sacramental. And that sacrament legitimates Augustine's figurative reading of Scripture.[76]

As noted above, Byassee says that allegory is, for Augustine, "incarnationally-shaped."[77] Fiedrowicz points out that Augustine's exegesis is made possible by his doctrine of biblical inspiration.[78] So how do we sum this up?

74. Fiedrowicz, "Introduction," in Augustine, *Expositions of the Psalms, 1–32,* 25. This is why the fathers saw biblical interpretation as a spiritual discipline requiring faith, as we saw in chap. 5 above.

75. Byassee, *Praise Seeking Understanding,* 227–28.

76. Cameron, *Christ Meets Me Everywhere,* 199. See Boersma, *Scripture as Real Presence,* 43–55, for an excellent discussion of Augustine's understanding of the literal sense as sacramental.

77. Byassee, *Praise Seeking Understanding,* 227–28.

78. Fiedrowicz, "Introduction," in Augustine, *Expositions of the Psalms, 1–32,* 26.

I argued in chapter 6 that we can see a gradual move, both in Augustine and in the tradition as a whole, toward the christological sense being understood as the extended or expanded literal sense and toward the view that the literal sense must control the meaning of the text. But need we go so far as to say that the allegorical or spiritual sense is totally illegitimate? Is it possible to see christological literalism as the controlling sense of the text, but also to make room for seeing the spiritual sense of texts as having a secondary and dependent form of validity as well? Cameron, Byassee, and Fiedrowicz all agree that Augustine would do so, even though he recognized the dangers of uncontrolled speculation and eisegesis and employed the term "allegory" less and less as time went on, probably because of a concern to avoid misunderstanding by those fearing the danger of subjectivism.[79] As we have seen throughout this book, terminology is extremely varied and difficult to pin down. Yet we have seen an enormous amount of shared conviction and similar approaches embedded in the spiritual practices of the Great Tradition, especially in sermons and theology written in support of preaching.

Childs rightly sees the Great Tradition of biblical interpretation including much allegorical interpretation even as it "struggles" to let the literal christological sense have the central and controlling position. Calvin ends up focusing almost solely on christological literalism and makes little use of the spiritual sense (or allegory) except where the plain sense indicates Christ in a literal fashion. Perhaps we should simply disavow the use of allegory and focus exclusively on christological literalism. Perhaps we are tempted to make such a move because we think it would be a retreat to an apparently more defensible position against the onslaughts of philosophical naturalism, but maybe the time is right to go on the offense. After all, it is only realistic to admit that philosophical naturalism will never rest content until it totally eliminates Christ from the Old Testament. There can be no predictive prophecy, no typology, and no christological content in the Old Testament (except for our imaginative construals) if philosophical naturalism is not challenged. Perhaps we should bite the bullet, refuse philosophical naturalism, and see where things go from there. Our theology should be exegetical, and our exegesis should be theological. Both should be in the service of preaching, and we should be attentive to the best preachers of the church in assessing how to evaluate allegory.

79. See Byassee's discussion of this point in *Praise Seeking Understanding*, 219–20. Also, see Cameron's insightful comments in *Christ Meets Me Everywhere*, 17. Both agree that Augustine increasingly used the term "figural" instead of "allegory," and both suggest that his reason for doing so was not a loss of conviction about the christological surplus of meaning in Old Testament texts but rather to minimize misunderstanding among his audience and readers relating to subjectivism and arbitrariness. Apparently, some things have not changed much in 1,600 years.

In the end, the issue comes down to whether we see Scripture as sacramental, and that depends on whether we have a Christian Platonist metaphysics that can support a sacramental understanding of language, Scripture, and interpretation. And that, in turn, seems to depend on whether we have a doctrine of God that is sufficiently biblical to fund an understanding of inspiration, providence, and miracle that allows for the kind of interpretation that expects and finds the unity and clarity of the Bible's message centered on Jesus Christ. In the end, all of these things hang together: christological literalism (Scripture as sacramental), Christian Platonism (sacramental ontology), inspiration of Scripture (the domain of the Word), and the Nicene doctrine of God (trinitarian classical theism). Can we see through the diversity of terminology to a common faith? My purpose in writing this book has been to commend the Great Tradition to evangelicals and other orthodox Christians today and to encourage us all to interpret Scripture with the Great Tradition by recovering the genius of premodern exegesis. Nothing is more important to the growing and flourishing of healthy churches and the powerful, biblical preaching of the gospel.

Conclusion

8

The Identity of the
Suffering Servant Revisited

Now the passage of Scripture that he was reading was this:

> "Like a sheep he was led to the slaughter
>   and like a lamb before its shearer is silent,
>   so he opens not his mouth.
> In his humiliation justice was denied him.
>   Who can describe his generation?
> For his life is taken away from the earth [Isa. 53:7–8]."

And the eunuch said to Philip, "About whom, I ask you, does the prophet say this, about himself or about someone else?" Then Philip opened his mouth, and beginning with this Scripture he told him the good news about Jesus.

Acts 8:32–35

*T*he purpose of this final chapter is to circle back to the dilemma that I described at the beginning of chapter 1: how to preach Jesus from Isaiah 53 without violating valid hermeneutical theory. According to one of the greatest Old Testament scholars of the twentieth century, Brevard S. Childs, this is "the most contested chapter in the Old Testament."[1] What stands out to me in reflecting on this statement is, first, how utterly and obviously true

---

1. Childs, *Isaiah*, 410.

it seems in the context of modern historical-critical study of the Bible, and, second, how utterly and obviously false it is in the context of the Great Tradition of Christian exegesis. Tremper Longman III writes of the gap between the church and the academy: "While most Christians today wonder why anyone could miss seeing how Jesus so precisely fulfilled Old Testament prophecy, scholars are apt to wonder how the New Testament authors could presume to use these texts in application to him."[2]

Christian scholars today find themselves under considerable pressure to qualify, dial back, or even give up the claim that Isaiah 53 speaks prophetically of the death and resurrection of Jesus Christ. Ironically, many of these scholars, who think of themselves as practical biblical interpreters with no particular metaphysical presuppositions, actually are unwitting slaves of some Enlightenment *philosophe* who despised everything Christians hold dear.[3] It is easy to be in the academy, and it is easy to be a Christian; what is difficult is to be a Christian in the academy. If Philip had been a member of today's Society of Biblical Literature, would he have been able to answer the Ethiopian eunuch's question in such a way that a baptism would have taken place in Acts 8?

In the introductory chapter to this book, we noted the existence of these two solitudes (academy and church), and we wondered if there was any way to bring them together. In part 1 of this book, we established that the gap is not between two chronological ages (premodern and modern) but rather between two rival traditions: the Great Tradition of Christian exegesis, which characterizes the preaching ministry of the church from the apostles to the present, and the tradition of historical criticism stemming from the Enlightenment's rejection of Christian Platonism in favor of ancient Epicurean naturalism, which dominates the modern research university. In part 2 of this book, we examined the exegesis of the premodern tradition and found that it is more scientific than that of the historical-critical tradition because it employs a method that allows the interpreter to engage with the true *res* of the text, the living God to whom the text points. The recovery of the genius of premodern exegesis involves the recovery and rebalancing of three pillars of scientific exegesis: the Nicene doctrine of God, the theological metaphysics that flows

---

2. Longman, "Messiah: Explorations in the Law and Writings," 13.

3. I am adapting the oft-quoted words of John Maynard Keynes written in another context: The ideas of economists and political philosophers, both when they are right and when they are wrong, are more powerful than is commonly understood. Indeed the world is ruled by little else. Practical men, who believe themselves to be quite exempt from any intellectual influence, are usually the slaves of some defunct economist. Madmen in authority, who hear voices in the air, are distilling their frenzy from some academic scribbler of a few years back. (*General Theory of Employment*, chap. 24, 386)

from that doctrine, and the christological literalism of patristic exegesis. Only this kind of exegesis is capable of engaging with the reality of God, who is both in the text and above the text speaking through it. Theological exegesis both sees and hears Jesus Christ in both Testaments.

Given all this, it is unsurprising that the Great Tradition has been virtually unanimous in affirming that Isaiah 53 depicts the crucifixion and resurrection of Jesus Christ. But the self-involving nature of theological exegesis as a spiritual discipline requiring faith in the God who speaks through the text means that unbelievers cannot see and hear Christ in the text merely by applying the tools of historical research on the basis of methodological naturalism. It is not merely a matter of the spiritual resistance of sinners to the acknowledgment of the holy presence of the living God, although that is part of the equation; it is also a matter of philosophical presuppositions screening out anything supernatural or transcendent. In discussing the dual-focus purification of the church fathers, we noted that it is not easy to disentangle the twin problems of knowing and desiring God, that is, the moral and epistemological issues. Does the non-Christian scholar not *know* that Isaiah 53 is about Christ? Or does that person not *want to know* that Isaiah 53 is about Christ? The noetic effects of sin are real and difficult to parse precisely, and it must be noted, human beings are individuals, so exact details may vary from person to person. Some people are much less hostile to God than others; it is perfectly possible to believe that, in certain cases, the person is honestly searching but just not yet at the point of faith. All that we can be certain of is that "without faith it is impossible to please him, for whoever would draw near to God must believe that he exists and that he rewards those who seek him" (Heb. 11:6).

Within the ranks of biblical scholars, things are far from monolithic. At one end of the spectrum are those who reject Great Tradition exegesis almost totally (think, for example, of the Jesus Seminar). At the other extreme are those who are burdened by the thought that they must go back and forth between two incompatible worlds, the world of the secular academy, where the Bible is often treated merely as a jumble of incoherent human thoughts about divine matters, and the world of the church, where people expect you to preach sermons that presuppose the unity, clarity, necessity, sufficiency, and authority of Holy Scripture. There are, of course, also many points in between. Compromises are rampant. For example, we noted in chapter 4 Strauss's accurate observation that biblical scholars of his day were much more inhibited in applying to the New Testament the same theories about myth that they so readily applied to the Old Testament. It is not unusual for scholars to come right out and admit that they believe the historical events of the Old Testament from creation to exodus need not have actually happened, but then quail at the prospect of applying the same logic to the miracles and resurrection of Jesus. Faced with the pressure of living in these two worlds, many scholars reflexively compartmentalize; that is, they do the opposite of integrating faith and learning. They bend over backward to keep their employment of methodological naturalism in Gospel criticism or biblical prophecy completely separate from their confession of faith in church and their preaching.

To bring this book to a conclusion, I wish to do three things. First, I want to compare three commentaries on Isaiah 52:13–53:12 and make some observations about how they deal with the passage. I will discuss the International Critical Commentary on Isaiah 40–55 by John Goldingay and David Payne, the commentary by J. Alec Motyer, and the Old Testament Library commentary by Brevard Childs. Thus we can examine a historical-critical commentary, an evangelical commentary, and one that tries to hold together both historical criticism and theological interpretation on a canonical basis. Second, I want to offer a sermon that I preached in my home church last year on Isaiah 53, followed by a few comments on it. It is fair that the reader expect the author of a book like this one to make clear what I think good theological interpretation of Scripture applied to preaching looks like. Third, I want to bring the book to a close with some comments in dialogue with two interlocutors representing evangelicals who have a great deal of credibility in biblical interpretation and are concerned with the "theological interpretation of Scripture movement" that is currently under way. The two persons I have selected are D. A. Carson, who has expressed a mixture of cautious optimism and certain concerns in an article titled "Theological Interpretation of Scripture, Yes, But . . . ," and Kevin Vanhoozer, who has tried to chart a course between skepticism and enthusiasm in an article titled "Ascending the Mountain, Singing the Rock: Biblical Interpretation Earthed, Typed, and Transfigured." My goal is to highlight points of common agreement with these authors in hopes of identifying a future direction for evangelicals to move in the days ahead.

Three Treatments of Isaiah 53: Goldingay and Payne, Motyer, and Childs

In approaching this passage, all three of these commentaries display some important similarities. I will summarize these first, before turning to differences. All three work from the Hebrew text and take the Septuagint into account at various points. All three quote other commentaries and various scholarly works extensively, although they focus primarily on giving their own interpretation.

Similarities in the Analysis of Structure and Literary Character

All three see the passage as a distinct literary unit, although Goldingay and Payne spend some time considering the possibility that 52:13–15 might be a separate unit. All three see basically the same structure of five stanzas (52:13–15; 53:1–3, 4–6, 7–9, 10–12). Childs notes that the confession of the "We" in 53:1–11a is bracketed by two divine speeches in 52:13–15 and 53:11b–12. Goldingay and Payne and also Motyer see the passage as a chiasm with some small variations as seen below:

Goldingay and Payne (ABCDC′B′A′)

My Servant will triumph despite his suffering (52:13–15)
  Who could have recognized Yhwh's arm? (53:1)
    He was treated with contempt (53:2–3)
      The reason for his suffering was us (53:4–6)
    He did not deserve his treatment (53:7–9)
  By his hand Yhwh's purpose will succeed (53:10–11a)
My servant will triumph because of his suffering (53:11a–12)[4]

Motyer (ABA′)

A^1 Enigma: exaltation and humiliation (52:13–15)
  B Revelation: human testimony, based on divine revelation, witnessing to the fact and meaning of the Servant's suffering and death (53:1–9)
    B^1 Suffering observed and misunderstood (1–3)
    B^2 Suffering explained (4–6)
    B^3 Suffering, voluntary and undeserved (7–9)
A^2 Solution: exaltation through sin-bearing (10–12)[5]

As is obvious, these two outlines are compatible with Childs's approach in that both see the LORD as the speaker in the first and fifth stanzas.

When identifying the genre of literature, all three see the passage as poetry, even though there is a lack of clear meter. Goldingay and Payne mention that synthetic parallelism and repetition are key features. All agree that there are significant textual difficulties, although Motyer tends to focus the most on what the text does say as opposed to what it might be conjectured to have originally said. There is some discussion in Goldingay and Payne about whether the unit should be considered a psalm of lament or a psalm of thanksgiving, but

---

4. Goldingay and Payne, *Isaiah 40–55*, 277.
5. Motyer, *Prophecy of Isaiah*, 423.

they conclude that the passage seems to be unique. Form criticism does not really help us to pin down the kind of thing we are dealing with here, which seems more like a record of a visionary experience than anything else. The lack of literary polish and awkward phrases may signal that the material is somewhat opaque even to its writer. I was reminded of 1 Peter 1:10–12 when reading this observation, although none of the commentaries references it.

The Contrast between Great Tradition Exegesis and Historical-Critical Exegesis

Now we must examine how the commentaries differ. I want to focus my comments around four issues: focus, goal, context, and meaning. We will consider these one at a time.

FOCUS: ON THE TEXT VERSUS ON THE HISTORICAL SITUATION BEHIND THE TEXT

First, we ask whether the commentaries focus on the text itself or on the historical situation behind the text. All three commentaries focus primarily on interpreting the text itself, but there are differences. Motyer emphasizes the context of Isaiah as a whole; the links he notes are theological and serve to highlight the meaning of the passage. Goldingay and Payne do draw attention to some links, such as the "Behold, my servant" of 52:13 echoing 42:1, but most of the time they make little of the theological significance of such links.[6] For the most part, they are content simply to note parallels or echoes. For example, they note that the same Hebrew word is used in 52:13 to describe the Servant (exalt) and also in 6:1 to describe the LORD. But they make nothing of it; does this hint at the divine nature of the Servant? Does it indicate a link conceptually or theologically between chapters 6 and 53? They do not say. No one commentator can be expected to say everything relevant, but my point is that there is a pattern in Goldingay and Payne of not interpreting this passage as part of a unified theology as expressed in the book of Isaiah as a whole. Earlier passages are primarily historical sources that are helpful in establishing which part of the semantic range of a word might be in view here. This is helpful, but insufficient as interpretation.

Childs spends some time arguing against taking the word "sprinkle" (or "splatter," *yazzeh*) in 52:15 in a cultic context. However, he resists the more radical critics' tendency to eliminate the word from the text and instead proposes a noncultic solution. Some commentators make things much too easy

6. Goldingay and Payne, *Isaiah 40–55*, 288.

for themselves by emending the text whenever they cannot understand it. This is not really an overstatement, as perusal of various critical commentaries will quickly confirm. Sometimes it seems that the essence of historical criticism is the permission scholars give themselves to chop up the text when they cannot makes sense of it as it stands. Both Childs and Goldingay and Payne resist this temptation for the most part. However, Motyer goes further, in that for him apparent tensions in the text are spurs to theological contemplation. The excellence of his interpretation is displayed in his ability to integrate all the statements in the passage into his overall understanding of what it says. It is neither forced harmonization nor passive acceptance of contradiction, but thoughtful exposition. Motyer's analysis of "sprinkle" emphasizes the cultic background in Leviticus, but he stresses that the use of the term here points to the universal salvation of the LORD and the inclusion of the gentiles that is a constant emphasis throughout the book of Isaiah. This interpretation takes account of both the more immediate context (the book of Isaiah) and the canonical context (the law).

GOAL: SYNTHESIS VERSUS ANALYSIS

Second, we consider what the goal of the commentaries is: synthesis or analysis. Here we see real differences. For Goldingay and Payne, the stress is on analysis to the point that it sometimes feels like reading a lexicon. One reads page after page of notes on endings, roots, interesting cognates, textual variants, proposed emendations, and so on. Please do not misunderstand; my complaint is not "too much detail" or "too much scholarship." Rather, my complaint is that the elephant has labored and brought forth a mouse! The scholarly detail is not matched by textual illumination. Even after all the effort of reading and considering the philological details, one still wonders what the text means, and one does not feel that the analysis has led to better synthesis.

Motyer's commentary is filled with comments on linguistic matters as well. Practically every line addresses the Hebrew text in some way but always with an eye to theological exposition. One outstanding example is his treatment of verses 4–5 of Isaiah 53. He begins his analysis of verse 4 by saying, "With neither co-operation nor understanding from us, the Servant took on himself all that blights our lives." He shows that "'took up' means 'to lift up' (off someone in this case)." He stresses the distinction between the "we," which contrasts with the "he." He says that "smitten by God" and "afflicted" express the objective and subjective sides of his suffering. Then, turning to verse 5, he stresses that the Servant deals with our sinful state, our "alienation from God," and our "broken personhood." He asks: "When they recalled how 'the Arm of the Lord' pierced the dragon after they had called for him to act (51:9–10), could they have foreseen they were calling him, himself, to be pierced to death?" Quoting Franz Delitzsch, he then points out that the Servant is pierced on account of our sins, which he had taken on himself. Then he concludes: "Thus verse 4 demands the noun 'substitution,' and verse 5 adds the adjective 'penal.'"[7] Here he is saying that the thought expressed in "penal substitution" is found in verses 4–5, which synthesizes several things said in these verses. Motyer is able to synthesize the thought of verses 5–7 by noting the link to chapter 6:

> The towering theological genius of Isaiah is nowhere more apparent than here. Substitutionary sacrifice lay at the heart of his own experience of God (6:5–7). Of all people he knew the efficacy of the altar and the sacrifices God had appointed, yet (though he does not tell us how) somewhere between the profoundly real experience of 6:7 and the vision of the substitutionary role of the Servant in 52:13–53:12 the awareness dawned that (as Heb. 10:4 puts it) the blood of bulls and goats cannot take away sins. Within the horizons of the Old Testament this was daring in the extreme. Our brothers and sisters in the Old Testament church, as we meet them in the Psalms, were people in actual enjoyment of the benefits of forgiveness, peace with God and spiritual security. There is no suggestion that, under the old covenant, they knew that they enjoyed these benefits only on the ground of a perfect sacrifice yet to come. In every essential their position was the same as ours; the Lord attached promises (of forgiveness, peace, acceptance etc.) to the sacrifices and they offered the sacrifices, resting in faith on the promises. It took a man of remarkable insight to see that something greater and better was needed. But this is what Isaiah did. . . . In Isaiah 53, and particularly in verses 7–9, Old Testament and biblical soteriology reaches its climax.[8]

I have quoted this lengthy passage because it epitomizes what theological interpretation can be and should be. It is not merely reading and defining words but coming to grips with the totality of the thought being expressed and relating it to us as sinners who need a Savior.

CONTEXT: CANON VERSUS RECONSTRUCTED HISTORICAL SITUATION

What is the decisive context for proper interpretation of this passage? There are always multiple contexts for every biblical passage: the historical-cultural

---

7. Motyer, *Prophecy of Isaiah*, 430.
8. Motyer, *Prophecy of Isaiah*, 432–33.

context, the literary unit, the book (or in the case of larger books, the section of the book), the Testament, the Bible as a whole, and the reception history of the text in the exegesis of the church. There are three main possibilities in approaching this problem. One is to make the canon of Scripture, that is, the Bible as a whole, the authoritative context. A second is the Enlightenment higher-critical approach that sees a historical situation reconstructed on the basis of methodological naturalism as the decisive context. The third is to see the reception history of the text, that is, the history of exegesis and dogma in the church as decisive. I contend that patristic exegesis and the Great Tradition culminating in Calvin would be variations on the first approach. Vosian biblical theology and the best of evangelical preaching (as, e.g., J. R. W. Stott) would come the closest to this approach of the available options today. Most higher criticism would be examples of the second approach. The Roman Catholic Church would perhaps be the example of the third approach, though many Catholic theologians would dispute that characterization of their position. In terms of the commentaries we are discussing, Motyer would exemplify the first position and Goldingay and Payne the second. Childs is a unique case in that he wants to move dialectically between the first and second positions. I offer the following comments on each commentary.

Goldingay and Payne insist on interpreting Isaiah 53 in the context of the exilic situation. They write, "The passage constitutes the prophet's final attempt to picture how the problem of Jacob-Israel's rebellion may be resolved. How does forgiveness and renewal come about?"[9] They say that the prophet brings together four fields of metaphors: (1) Israel as an afflicted people, (2) the prophet in his experiences of affliction, (3) the kingship, and (4) cultic images linked to the "splattering" in verse 15.[10] They never say exactly how these metaphors explain the meaning of the passage. After canvassing the various suggestions for who the Servant might be, they dismiss a number of them without giving their own view clearly. The only clue we have is that there is nothing in this commentary to suggest that its authors believe that the Servant could have been anyone other than a contemporary figure of the exile, whether that be Deutero-Isaiah, Jeremiah, an unknown (to us) contemporary, or perhaps someone known to the people of that time such as Moses. There is no suggestion that the Servant might actually be Yahweh himself come to suffer on behalf of his people.

Motyer, however, situates the passage in its canonical context and stresses the importance of the Bible as a whole as the decisive context for interpreting

---

9. Goldingay and Payne, *Isaiah 40–55*, 283.
10. Goldingay and Payne, *Isaiah 40–55*, 283–84.

chapter 53. Motyer sees the Servant as the LORD come to Zion to suffer for the sins of the people. He notes that in 52:6 the LORD "promised action on behalf of his people in which he would be personally present."[11] The Servant is the coming of the LORD, even at the same time as the Servant is separate from the LORD. This tension is not resolved in the text; the interpreter must resist the temptation to flatten it out in either direction, and Motyer does so successfully. He emphasizes that the Servant's purpose is to deal with the sin-problem of the people. He writes, "So much of the enigma and dramatic intensity of the poem focuses in the 'many'; they start back from the sufferer only to find, once the truth has been revealed, that in his suffering lies their highest benefit."[12] Throughout the Bible, the main obstacle to divine-human fellowship and peace is the problem of sin; it is this problem that Isaiah 53 deals with.

Childs wants to view the context in a double way: as the exile (Isa. 40–55) and as the two-Testament Bible. This means that he needs a double reference in the form of a figure from the exilic period and Jesus Christ in the New Testament. Before proceeding, it should be pointed out that there is nothing wrong with a double reference in principle. It happens in typology all the time. Moses can be a type of Christ without actually being Christ. This typological relationship works because Moses is not given divine attributes in the Old Testament; he does not die for the sins of the world, rise again, ascend to the right hand of majesty, and so forth. Typology is a rather strict form of analogy; the analogy works only on one particular point of comparison. Childs is vague as to the identity of the Servant. Rightly locating the question in the context of Isaiah 40–55, Childs points out the echo of 42:1 in 52:13, "Behold, my Servant," and notes that although the Servant initially is Israel, the office is transferred from the nation Israel to the individual prophetic figure of 49:3.[13] The individual prophetic figure *represents* Israel and *is* Israel. He is "divinely commissioned to the selfsame task of the deliverance of the chosen people and the nations at large."[14] So the Servant is a prophetic figure called and commissioned by the LORD to act in a saving manner on behalf of Israel and the nations. So far so good.

The question I have for Childs is whether the kind of things Isaiah 53 says about this figure could originally have been applied to the kind of human prophet he envisions and then, only later, have been applied to Christ. Did someone during the exile suffer an atoning death for the world? Or did someone during the exile undergo horrific suffering and die and then Christ did the

11. Motyer, *Prophecy of Isaiah*, 424.
12. Motyer, *Prophecy of Isaiah*, 423.
13. Childs, *Isaiah*, 412.
14. Childs, *Isaiah*, 387.

same but added the vicarious and substitutionary layer to it? But surely those questions are answered for us by the text of Isaiah 53. The description there is of substitutionary suffering; the Servant deals with the sin-problem decisively. Also, the idea that the servant was a human prophet is in tension with the idea that it was the LORD come in person.[15] Childs says, "In the suffering and death of the servant of Second Isaiah, the selfsame divine reality of Jesus Christ was made manifest"; he argues that the servant of Isaiah 53 was linked ontologically to Jesus Christ and is "not just a future promise of the Old Testament awaiting its New Testament fulfillment."[16] It remains unclear to me why Childs is so adamant that Isaiah 53 is not to be understood as prophecy and the New Testament as fulfillment when that has been the overwhelming consensus of the Great Tradition. No doubt he is right that there is an ontological link between Isaiah 53 and the New Testament proclamation of Christ, but the question is the nature of this link. The most natural explanation of the nature of the ontological link, from my perspective, is that of prophecy and fulfillment.

MEANING: WHAT IT MEANS TO US VERSUS WHAT IT MEANT TO THEM

Finally, we come to that last point of contrast. What does it mean? We have already anticipated some of this discussion in the last two sections. Synthesis, context, and meaning are inextricably intertwined. For Goldingay and Payne, Isaiah 53 must be understood primarily in the context of the exile and Isaiah 40–55. For Motyer, it must be understood in the context of the Bible as a whole. Childs wants to have it both ways. One basic principle of the historical-critical approach is that the meaning of the text must be understood within the historical context in which it was written. This is a fine rule, but it can be pushed too far. One way it can be pushed too far is to insist that without parallels in the culture, a meaning cannot possibly be seen in the biblical text under consideration. So, for example, if there is no creation *ex nihilo* in ancient Mesopotamian and Egyptian texts, then it cannot be found in Genesis 1:1. Such an approach eliminates the possibility of God revealing anything truly new in the Bible, which emasculates revelation and empties it of its power, not to mention that it limits God. Another way the principle of historical context can be pushed too far is to say that God never tells us ahead of time what he is going to do in the future. The idea of Isaiah 53 not being completely comprehensible to the people of the Old Testament

---

15. The sacrifices of the temple—birds, animals, etc.—constitute the anticipatory type of Christ in the Old Testament context of Isaiah 53. The Servant is the Antitype, not the type.

16. Childs, *Isaiah*, 423.

and that the promise remained unfulfilled for centuries do not necessarily make it irrelevant to the people of Isaiah's day. The second coming of Christ is a prophecy that has remained unfulfilled for nearly two thousand years, yet it would be false to say that it is not meaningful to Christians today.

Hope is a basic category of biblical theology and closely related to faith: "Now faith is the assurance of things hoped for, the conviction of things not seen" (Heb. 11:1). How could the meaning of Isaiah 53 not be that the people are called to live in hope and by faith? The hope is that the divine sin-bearer will one day come and suffer and die for the sins of the nation and the world. Faith is in the LORD who promises this through his prophet. When Isaiah speaks of the "new heavens and a new earth" in Isaiah 65:17, we do not usually hear the objection: "But that cannot be relevant to Isaiah's hearers since it did not occur in their lifetime." We live in hope and by faith when it comes to eschatology. And strictly speaking, from a New Testament perspective, the coming of the Suffering Servant with his death and resurrection is the beginning of the end of history; it is eschatological. We now live in "the last days." The problem with the historical approach to biblical interpretation is not that it is concerned to ensure that we do not detach the meaning from history; that is a good thing. The problem with historical interpretation is its limited, reductionist view of history that excludes the action of God in the midst of history, even as he guides history to its appointed destiny in Christ. Both the present and the future are under his sovereignty, and the future hope is therefore a source of hope and comfort for the believing community.

For Motyer, Isaiah 53 is primarily a prophetic vision of a divine sin-bearer who will come and finally solve the problem of how a sinful people can be transformed into the new covenant people and united with the saved of the nations in the new heavens and new earth. For Goldingay and Payne, Isaiah 53 is a confusing prophetic oracle about a human prophet in exile who dies a shameful death and is viewed by Deutero-Isaiah as heroic and admirable in spite of his humiliation. For Childs, the view of Goldingay and Payne is basically right, yet there is an ontological link that justifies the church seeing a similarity between this figure and Christ. They are all theological interpretations, but in my view Motyer's is clearly the better one.

A Sermon on Isaiah 53 and Some Reflections on It

What follows is a sermon preached at Westney Heights Baptist Church in Ajax, Ontario, in August 2016. It was the second of a two-part series. The week before I had preached on "The Impossible Dilemma and the Divine Hope" (Isa. 6).

The Divine Messiah as the Only Hope of Salvation

(Isa. 52:13–53:12)

Today we come to the holy of holies of Holy Scripture. We come into the presence of the source and basis of our salvation. We catch a glimpse into that awful moment when the beloved Son of God experienced the wrath of God that was aimed at sinners and by taking that wrath upon himself, Jesus Christ saved us from having to experience it for ourselves. This is the marvelous exchange: he gets our sins and we get his righteousness in return. Is it fair? No. It is mysterious? Definitely. Is it our only hope of escaping the wrath justly directed toward rebellious, fallen, sinful, disobedient, ungrateful sinners like us? You bet your life it is.

Last week we peeked into the temple where Isaiah had his vision of Almighty God in chapter 6. These two chapters are the two most important chapters for understanding the book of Isaiah as a whole and quite possibly the two most important chapters in the entire Bible. If we understand them both, we grasp the essence of the gospel.

Let us review quickly. In chapter 6 the heavens open for Isaiah, and he sees directly into the throne room of God. What does he see? Isaiah 6 tells us that he sees the LORD high and lifted up. And he sees seraphim—majestic, angelic creatures with six wings each, and one called to another and said:

> Holy, holy, holy is the LORD of hosts;
> the whole earth is full of his glory! (6:3)

The foundations of the thresholds shake at this voice, and the house was filled with smoke. And that, take note, was just the voice of the angel, not the voice of God!

Isaiah's reaction is understandable. He is overcome with fear: "Woe is me! For I am lost; for I am a man of unclean lips, and I dwell in the midst of a people of unclean lips; for my eyes have seen the King, the LORD of hosts!" (v. 5). Isaiah knows he is a sinner, and he knows Israel has sinned and broken God's covenant. And the overpowering idea of God that fills his mind in this encounter is that of God's holiness.

This is the basic problem of the book of Isaiah. Isaiah knows that Judah's problem is not really political, and it is not really a military one. It is not really one of class division or war or immorality. All these are symptoms of the deeper issue, which is that Judah is a sinful people, and Judah serves a holy God.

Then, in verses 6–7, we see the angel take a coal from the altar and apply it to Isaiah's lips, and he hears these astonishing words: "Your guilt is taken away, and your sin atoned for." Then he hears a voice saying "Whom shall I send, and who will go for us?" and he shouts "Here am I! Send me" (v. 8).

Isaiah receives a strange commission. He is told to go and preach judgment and exile and devastation (vv. 9–10). He asks: "How long, O Lord?" and the answer is astonishing: "Until cities lie waste . . . and the LORD removes people far away" (vv. 11–12). What a call to ministry! Preach with no hope of any great response. Isaiah had a few followers, a remnant, but he never saw repentance on a national scale. Isaiah's mission was to prepare the nation for exile.

At the very end of this answer from the LORD, however, we see a tiny, little ray of hope. In verse 13 we read of a stump and a holy seed. What does this mean? In 7:14 we hear of a mysterious birth of a child who will be called "Immanuel" (God with us). In 9:6–7 he speaks of a child who will have incredible names like "Wonderful Counsellor, Mighty God, Everlasting Father, Prince of Peace." In 11:1 we are told that there shall come forth from the stump of Jesse a shoot, and a branch from his roots will bear fruit. This one will be a mighty one on whom the Spirit of the LORD rests, and the description of his kingdom is one of righteousness, peace, renewal, and joy. And yet, although all this is true, Isaiah never wavers from his prediction of the judgment of the coming exile, the destruction of the city of Jerusalem and its temple, and the end of the Davidic monarchy. All this must occur, yet the promise of salvation stands.

In chapter 40 the focus of the book changes. Suddenly, Isaiah is speaking to the exiles in Babylon, and his message is one of hope. In chapters 44–45 we find an amazing prediction of a king named Cyrus who will come to power and allow the captive exiles to return home to Jerusalem. In chapters 40–55 Isaiah begins to speak of a mysterious figure known as the Servant of the LORD, who will deliver Israel and save the nations.

Who is this Servant? Is it Israel? Yes, at least at first, but not just Israel. It seems to be an individual who arises out of Israel and stands for Israel. In 49:4, after the LORD speaks to the Servant, the Servant speaks to the LORD. Down through the ages biblical commentators have debated who the Servant is. Is it Israel? A remnant within Israel? One of the prophets? Or is it the LORD God himself come down to Zion to save and redeem?

We get a clue from 42:5–9, where the LORD says that he himself will save his people. In 43:3 we read:

> For I am the LORD your God,
>   the Holy One of Israel, your Savior.

In this passage the LORD states clearly that the people have failed: "But you have burdened me with your sins; you have wearied me with your iniquities" (v. 24). And yet, he says, "I am he who blots out your transgressions for my own sake" (v. 25). The Servant will do what Israel failed to do.

Who is the Suffering Servant of Isaiah 53? It is the divine LORD who comes to Jerusalem in salvation. This brings us to Isaiah 52:13–53:12. What we see here is a description of this Suffering Servant of the LORD. He both is the LORD and is a being separate from the LORD. There is no explanation for how this can be in the text. Isaiah is presented with a fact: this is the Servant. His prophetic vision is described as best he can, but not everything is comprehensible to Isaiah, to his original hearers, or even to us. This figure of the Suffering Servant is shrouded in mystery, and he evokes awe and worship. What does Isaiah 53 tell us about this Suffering Servant? What we have here is a five-stanza poem with three verses in each stanza. We will look at each stanza.

I. A Shocking Servant (52:13–15)[17]

Note that God is speaking: "Behold, my servant" (v. 13). Also note the words "high and lifted up" (v. 13). These are the same words in Hebrew as we saw in Isaiah 6:1 applied to the LORD. Is it possible this Servant is the LORD himself?

In Isaiah 2:6–22 we have a harsh condemnation of the pride of man and the statement that only the LORD will be lifted up and exalted (esp. v. 17). This is a clue. It cannot be Israel or a merely human prophet who is exalted to the level of God.

But then—a wrenching shift—we read that the appearance of the servant is "marred, beyond human semblance" (v. 14). What kind of suffering is this? It says: "As many were astonished at you" (v. 14). Note the past tense here. It is describing a past event.

It also says: "kings shall shut their mouths" (v. 15). The nations will be shocked speechless by what they see.

II. A Scorned Servant (53:1–3)

Here the speaker changes. Who is speaking in vv. 1–12 ("us," "we," "our")? It is the prophet speaking to and for Israel. When the Servant was finally revealed to Israel, Israel did not believe it was her Messiah-Savior. The question "Who

---

17. I honestly do not remember where the alliteration in this sermon originally came from; I am not usually creative enough to make up my own homiletical alliteration, so I probably read it somewhere years ago. I just cannot remember where! If a reader knows the source of these five adjectives starting with *S* as applied to the Servant, please let me know so that I can give proper credit to the author in the future.

has believed . . . ?" (v. 1) may reflect the rejection of Isaiah's message in his own day. Note that the phrase "the arm of the LORD" (v. 1) is a metaphor for the power and strength of God, yet here it is revealed through weakness and death!

In these verses we have a narrative of the life of the Servant and his rejection by his people. He is "a young plant—a root out of dry ground" (v. 2)—not a mighty oak or fruit tree in bloom. The ground is Israel, and the plant is the Messiah-Servant. This points to the birth of a baby in the Roman Empire who is born in a stable, not a palace, and sprouts from the most unlikely soil. "He was despised and rejected" (v. 3)—he was considered an embarrassment; no one wanted even to look at him.

III. A Suffering Servant (53:4–6)

This third stanza is the heart of the poem and the center of Isaiah's vision. The same speaker continues; the prophet is speaking for Israel—and all of us. This is the culmination of the shocking revelation of the Servant-Messiah.

We are now in the holy of holies. He suffers for us in our place:

> "borne our griefs and carried our sorrows"
> "smitten by God and afflicted"
> "pierced for our transgressions"
> "crushed for our iniquities"

In verse 5 we see the result of his suffering:

> "The chastisement that brought us peace"
> "with his wounds we are healed"

In verse 6 we are compared to sheep; this is not really a compliment!

> "All we like sheep have gone astray"
> "and the LORD has laid on him the iniquity of us all"

The stress in all three verses is that he suffered for a purpose—for us.

IV. A Slaughtered Servant (53:7–9)

Here we see the extent of his suffering—it is a suffering all the way to death. But wait: now the *Servant* is compared to a sheep—actually a lamb "led to the slaughter" (v. 7). What is going on here? We are compared to sheep in verse 6, and he is compared to a sheep in verse 7. The Servant has become one of us! But the points of the two comparisons are opposite to each other: *his sinlessness* versus *our sinfulness*. We cannot help thinking here of his silence before Pilate like a sheep before its shearers is dumb.

In verse 8 we read "By oppression and judgment he was taken away," which is a prediction of his trials, then "he was cut off out of the land of the living," a clear reference to his death. We read that he "made his grave with the wicked and with a rich man in his death" (v. 9). Commentators struggle to understand what Isaiah may have meant here, but to the reader of the Gospels it could not be plainer. His innocence is reiterated: "he had done no violence and there was no deceit in his mouth."

V. A Successful Servant (53:10–12)

If the poem ended here, it would make no sense: How could the Servant die if he was *Yahweh*? And how could the death of the Servant by itself save anyone? But the fifth stanza speaks of resurrection, or at least it implies it strongly: "he shall see his offspring; he shall prolong his days" (v. 10).

And what is the "spoil" (v. 12)? It is those who are saved through his atoning sacrifice. Note that the Servant makes "an offering for guilt" (v. 10). This links back to 6:7, where it says that Isaiah's guilt is taken away and his sin atoned for. How was Isaiah saved? It was by looking forward in faith to God's gracious provision of a way of salvation through the atoning sacrifice of the Servant-Messiah. Note that the Servant is alive and "makes intercession for the transgressors" (Heb. 7:25).

Isaiah 53 is actually an outline of the life of Christ:

   I. A *Shocking* Servant (52:13–15): His birth—low and unrecognized

  II. A *Scorned* Servant (53:1–3): His life—rejected by his own people

 III. A *Suffering* Servant (53:4–6): His death—unjust suffering for others

 IV. A *Slaughtered* Servant (53:7–9): His burial—he was buried just like the wicked

  V. A *Successful* Servant (53:10–12): His resurrection—he is our eternal high priest

When the Ethiopian eunuch asked Philip "About whom, I ask you, does the prophet say this, about himself or about someone else?" (Acts 8:34), is it any wonder that Scripture next says "Philip opened his mouth, and beginning with this Scripture he told him the good news about Jesus"?

Conclusion: Behold Your God!—The Suffering Servant!

This chapter is a prophetic vision of the incarnate Savior seven centuries prior to Christ's birth in Bethlehem. The response of the Ethiopian eunuch was to believe, repent, and be baptized. If you have not done this, will you do it today? If you have done this, then the natural response is to worship our God.

Hymn of Response: "And Can It Be!" (Charles Wesley, 1738)

Comments

This sermon was preached in the context of regular Sunday morning worship to a congregation of about 450 people. It is a typical sermon for our church in that it is heavily expositional and not loaded with illustrations or stories. Not every congregation would be ready for this type of preaching, but Westney has a long tradition of this sort of sermon. At the time, I had been teaching through Isaiah for over a year in the adult Sunday school class of over 125 people. The majority of adults in our church own ESV Study Bibles and attend a weekly Bible study of one kind or another.

The sermon treats the passage as a prophetic vision of the future. The only attempts to develop any historical context are the references to the exile. The main thrust is to present the chapter as the solution to the problem of a holy God dwelling in the midst of a sinful people, which inevitably leads to divine judgment. This is the main problem of the book of Isaiah: divine judgment by a holy God leads to the exile. Yet Isaiah insists that exile is not the end and that God is not finished with his wayward people. One sermon cannot say everything important. I did not have time to talk about 2 Samuel 7 here, but in Sunday school we looked at the Davidic covenant in depth, and I showed that the central problem that Isaiah was wrestling with was how God can keep his promise that a descendant of David would reign on the throne of Jerusalem forever without denying his own holiness. This is why Isaiah 53 is so significant; it holds out hope that God would himself come among his people and do for them what they could not do for themselves. Only God can take the wrath of God upon himself and survive the ordeal. This is why there must be a divine sin-bearer. This is why chapter 53 is the heart of the book of Isaiah.

For me, theological interpretation of Scripture means interpreting the meaning of each passage in the context of the overall theology of the Bible as a unified whole centered on Jesus Christ. This commitment, coupled with a high doctrine of inspiration, is what leads me to interpret Isaiah as the solution to the great problem of the book of Isaiah, which is the great problem of the

Bible as a whole. Adam and Eve were expelled from the garden because sin had to be separated from the holy God. How do we get back? That is finally what Isaiah 53 is all about.

The "Evangelicals and Evangelicals Together" Project: The Perils and Promise of Theological Interpretation of Scripture

This whimsical section heading is an allusion to "Evangelicals and Catholics Together" and is meant to convey the wry awareness that among evangelical theologians there is no paucity of disagreement: "You worry about getting evangelicals together with Catholics; I find it enough of a challenge to get evangelicals together with other evangelicals!" But in all seriousness, it does seem to me that there is a great deal of common ground for us to share. My goal here is to clear away the obstacles that obscure the view of that common ground.

As we come to the end of modernity, when universals like the good, the true, and the beautiful have been dissolved in the acids of Enlightenment rationalism, thus opening the door to the triumph of relativism and skepticism in the late, decadent, "postmodern" phase of Western modernity, it is now time to consider where we can find a new basis for rebuilding the foundations. This is as true in biblical interpretation as in any other cultural endeavor. Natural theology, natural law, and scientific law have all been undermined and weakened by late modern relativism; in a cultural situation such as this, it would be strange if hermeneutics were to be untouched by rampant subjectivism.

In fact, one observes that evangelical biblical interpreters have been boxed into a corner regarding subjectivism. On the one hand, we are understandably wary of postmodern hermeneutics in which the autonomous individual of modernity simply dominates the text and turns it into a battleground for a clash of wills over issues of race, gender, and class. The Bible becomes a club in the hands of battling barbarians who seek to use it to assert their own "will to power" over and against the "enemy." The study of English literature in the late modern academy has been reduced to a series of attacks on enemies in the name of ideologies of race, gender, and class—in short, a power struggle. If present trends continue, this is the unappealing future in store for biblical studies in most Western universities. On the other hand, the only source of objectivity that anyone still recognizes as an alternative to the will to power of the autonomous individual seems to reside in the "historical" meaning of the text, that is, what it is supposed to have meant to the original readers in the original situation as determined by the human author's intention. It is not surprising that evangelicals, therefore, gravitate toward theories of interpretation in literary theory and law that stress the single meaning of the original author.

Vanhoozer on Biblical Interpretation

We see this trend in the early work of Kevin J. Vanhoozer, who appeals to the defense of the single meaning of a text as determined by the author's intention. Perhaps no book has been more influential on evangelical hermeneutics in the past twenty years than Vanhoozer's *Is There a Meaning in This Text?* This book draws heavily on the literary theory of E. D. Hirsch, who famously defended the intention of the author as decisive for the meaning and stability of texts.[18] Vanhoozer describes Hirsch's view approvingly: "For Hirsch, the author's intention is the only practical norm, the sole criterion for genuine consensus, the sole guarantor of the objectivity of meaning. . . . It is the author who determines verbal meaning."[19] Vanhoozer claims that commentators in the tradition of Calvin have agreed. He quotes from Calvin's preface to his commentary on Romans: "It is the first business of an interpreter to let his author say what he does say, instead of attributing to him what we think he ought to say."[20] It is difficult to imagine any theologian of the Great Tradition, including Origen and Augustine, disagreeing with that sentiment. But who is the author, in the particular case of Holy Scripture? Vanhoozer notes that Calvin was a product of his training as a Renaissance humanist and shared a passion for recovering the original intention grounded in the mind of the author. None of this is objectionable, but what is missing is attentiveness to the Christian theological understanding of the dual authorship of Scripture: Are we speaking of the human author only or of the divine Author only or of the divine Author speaking through the conscious intention of the human author only? Hirsch's literary theory was developed for reading texts written by humans, not for reading inspired Scripture. That does not mean his concern for respecting authorial intention cannot be shared by Calvin or by us, but it does mean that theological hermeneutics must give careful consideration to the question of who the author is whose intention must be respected.

There is nothing in principle wrong with Vanhoozer using Hirsch's literary theory or, for that matter, speech-act theory, as he also does extensively in his work; the fathers utilized reading techniques originally developed for interpreting the Greek and Roman classics. But the fathers also modified those

18. See Hirsch, *Validity in Interpretation*.
19. Vanhoozer, *Is There a Meaning in This Text?*, 47.
20. Calvin as quoted by Vanhoozer, *Is There a Meaning in This Text?*, 29.

techniques by focusing on the question of what God means to say through the text. How does Vanhoozer make Hirsch's literary theory specifically *theological*? The first thing to note is that Vanhoozer clearly sees the necessity of doing so; he explicitly titles his approach "Augustinian Hermeneutics."[21] In a section titled "The Theological Dimension of Interpretation,"[22] Vanhoozer observes the effect of the postmodern death of God on texts in general. In essence, the death of God logically entails the death of the author: "The death of God is linked to the disappearance of the authority of the human author too."[23] He quotes Roland Barthes, who points to how the modern, revolutionary refusal to assign a fixed meaning either to the world or to texts "liberates an activity we may call counter-theological, properly revolutionary, for to refuse to halt meaning is finally to refuse God."[24] If I am understanding him correctly, Vanhoozer is saying that belief in God is the prerequisite for believing in the stability of the meaning of the text, because it is the existence of God that guarantees the authority of the human author of any text; this applies as much to the Bible as to the US Constitution or a Shakespearean play. The stability of meaning depends on the intention of the author, which depends on the interpreter bowing before the Creator and accepting reality, including the existence and authority of the author, rather than rebelling against it.

What do we make of all of this? Well, in general it is fine as far as it goes; the problem is that it does not go far enough. However, in an insightful and highly suggestive article published in 2013, Vanhoozer takes several large steps in the direction I am recommending in this book.[25] In this article, he is in conversation with Hans Boersma, among others. He agrees with Boersma's identification of a crucial deficit in evangelicalism: "an anemic ontology."[26] While applauding the evangelical focus on grammatical-historical interpretation, he raises the pressing question of "whether divine authorship is simply human discourse writ holy."[27] He identifies the key question: "Does the divine address coincide with that of the human author without remainder or is there a surplus of meaning?"[28] To answer this question, he discusses the Song of Songs and comes to the conclusion that reading the Song as Middle Eastern love poetry only, as has been done in modernity, is unnecessarily reductionist

---

21. Vanhoozer, *Is There a Meaning in This Text?*, 29.
22. Vanhoozer, *Is There a Meaning in This Text?*, 30.
23. Vanhoozer, *Is There a Meaning in This Text?*, 30.
24. Roland Barthes as quoted by Vanhoozer, *Is There a Meaning in This Text?*, 30.
25. Vanhoozer, "Ascending the Mountain, Singing the Rock," 207–25.
26. Vanhoozer, "Ascending the Mountain, Singing the Rock," 208. We have discussed Boersma's "sacramental ontology" at various points in this book.
27. Vanhoozer, "Ascending the Mountain, Singing the Rock," 209.
28. Vanhoozer, "Ascending the Mountain, Singing the Rock," 210.

and that it is crucial to read it on several levels: the Song is about the goodness of created sexuality, God's love for Israel, and Christ's love for the church.[29]

Along the way, Vanhoozer shows how Edmund Clowney, an evangelical interpreter, reads Paul's statements about the rock in the wilderness wanderings in 1 Corinthians 10:4 in a way that sees the Old Testament as being full of signs that point to Christ.[30] Vanhoozer proposes a particularly Protestant contribution to theological interpretation by suggesting that there must be a connection between the literal and spiritual senses; meaning does not change but is extended: "It is not that a new meaning has been added, but rather that the original meaning has finally achieved its Christological *telos*. . . . The typological meaning *is* the literal meaning of the discourse when viewed in canonical, which is to say redemptive-historical context."[31] Vanhoozer prefers to speak of a "covenantal ontology" rather than a "sacramental ontology"[32] and of "transfigural interpretation"[33] rather than "allegorical interpretation," but the uniquely Protestant character of his contribution to catholic biblical interpretation seems to be very comfortably companionable to the Great Tradition and very ill at ease with modernity. He writes, "It should be clear that the transfigural readings I have set forth here, while affirming the literal sense, are a far cry from methodological naturalism."[34] Indeed they are, and I commend Vanhoozer for taking the position he has at this point.

Carson on Biblical Interpretation

In an essay published in 2011, D. A. Carson offers some praise tempered with friendly criticism and probing questions for the theological interpretation of Scripture movement. I would like to mention and respond to eight points Carson makes in this article. Overall, I share almost all of Carson's concerns.

First, Carson says that TIS[35] attempts to "transcend the barren exegeses generated by historical-critical methods," especially ones that are "frankly anti-supernatural interpretations determined by post-Enlightenment assumptions about the nature of history."[36] But his concern is that "this emphasis in TIS is

29. Vanhoozer, "Ascending the Mountain, Singing the Rock," 234.
30. Vanhoozer, "Ascending the Mountain, Singing the Rock," 216–17. See Clowney, *Unfolding Mystery*, chap. 6.
31. Vanhoozer, "Ascending the Mountain, Singing the Rock," 218.
32. Vanhoozer, "Ascending the Mountain, Singing the Rock," 224–25.
33. Vanhoozer, "Ascending the Mountain, Singing the Rock," 220–23.
34. Vanhoozer, "Ascending the Mountain, Singing the Rock," 224.
35. Carson uses this abbreviation (TIS) for "Theological Interpretation of Scripture"; I follow his usage when quoting him.
36. Carson, "Theological Interpretation of Scripture," 188.

often cast in terms of the conflict between history and theology, with history made out to be the villain."[37] This is a valid concern that I share, and I hope I have made it clear in this book that one of my major goals is to separate the classical understanding of history as the interpretation of past events from the Enlightenment redefinition of history as the interpretation of past events on the basis of philosophical naturalism. The antisupernatural definition of history is gnostic and not really history. Rather than simply defending "history" in general, we need to make these distinctions and turn the charge back against those who try to tar orthodoxy with the brush of gnosticism.

Second, Carson says, "a historical reading is determinative for a great deal of theological interpretation."[38] Again he is right, and I agree. I would argue that my interpretation of Isaiah depends on history in that the entire history of Israel up to Isaiah's day is in the background of the whole "holy God–sinful people" scheme. As noted above, I interpret one of the central problems of Isaiah to be how God can keep the promise (made to David in 2 Samuel 7) that one of his descendants will sit on the throne forever with the word that comes through Isaiah that Jerusalem, the temple, and the Davidic monarchy will be destroyed. This tension is fundamental to understanding Isaiah 7–8, which is not comprehensible apart from the historical background.

However, all the examples Carson gives involve what I call "intrabiblical history" as opposed to the reconstructed history depicting what supposedly happened behind the text. These are two different matters. God has given us in the canon of Scripture the historical knowledge that we need in order to interpret the Bible in a theologically responsible way. This is why Isaiah 36–39—four chapters of prose historical narrative—are in the middle of a book composed mostly of prophetic oracles and poetry. The history contained in those four chapters is crucial for proper theological interpretation of the book.

Third, Carson affirms that TIS strives to bring biblical studies and theology closer together, and that this is a good thing. But he has some worries about which theology, and surely he is right to raise such concerns.[39] I have tried to say much the same in this book. Stephen Fowl's interpretation of the implications of the Jerusalem Council for the contemporary church's handling of homosexuality is wrong, despite being a theological interpretation, because he is using bad theology that exalts experience over revealed propositions. Arianism has a theological interpretation of the Bible; it just happens to be untrue. It misinterprets Scripture. Just because someone does exegesis does

---

37. Carson, "Theological Interpretation of Scripture," 189.
38. Carson, "Theological Interpretation of Scripture," 190.
39. Carson, "Theological Interpretation of Scripture," 193–96.

not automatically make the conclusions true, and it is the same with theological interpretation.

Fourth, Carson is open to learning from precritical exegesis, but he wonders why the emphasis is on the fathers and not the Reformers.[40] I would agree, and that is why I have made Calvin the hero of my narrative of the development of the Great Tradition. I also seek to promote Thomas Aquinas, which should be a clue to how I feel about post-Reformation Protestant scholasticism. It is time to reclaim the riches in John Owen, for example, as John Webster was engaged in doing during the final period of his life. There is much more of value in the Great Tradition than just the fathers, but I am probably more enthusiastic about the fathers than Carson is, although I might be slightly less enthusiastic about them than Boersma is. Can we make Augustine an honorary Reformer?

Fifth, Carson is worried about allegory.[41] There is nothing surprising here. Allegory is a slippery word, and all the terminology in this area is complex. I have tried my best to tidy things up, but I am under no illusions in this regard. All I can do is ask Carson and others with his concerns to consider what I have written about "christological literalism" and see if they can agree with it.

Sixth, Carson wonders if anybody has a kind word for the poor maligned Enlightenment.[42] I am afraid I do not. Here I acknowledge that I am oversimplifying and painting with a broad brush; I have left myself open to challenge from scholars who claim that the Enlightenment was not the same in every country. It is true that I have focused primarily on Germany and France, but I have tried to make clear exactly what it is about the Enlightenment that I have a problem with, which is the rejection of Christian Platonism, as explained in chapters 3 and 4. If by Enlightenment you do not mean *that*, well, then we can talk. I think both Carson and TIS people need to think more precisely about what is wrong about the Enlightenment.

Seventh, Carson writes that it would be good if TIS people noticed that confessional evangelicalism has written some good stuff that is in the Great Tradition.[43] I agree totally and have tried to show this throughout this book. John Calvin, Charles Spurgeon, John R. W. Stott, James Hamilton Jr., Geerhardus Vos, Scott Swain, Michael Allen, and many more make cameo appearances in white hats as the "good guys." John Webster, of course, is a major inspiration. Thomas Oden was an inspiration too, and J. Alec Motyer, of course. The list could go on and on. The whole-Bible Vosian biblical theology that has been

40. Carson, "Theological Interpretation of Scripture," 196–98.
41. Carson, "Theological Interpretation of Scripture," 198.
42. Carson, "Theological Interpretation of Scripture," 200–201.
43. Carson, "Theological Interpretation of Scripture," 202.

written lately and, I could add, the New Studies in Biblical Theology series edited by Carson are the kind of things we need more of and are very much in the Great Tradition. Any TIS person who cannot recognize this would be suspect in my eyes.

Eighth, Carson is tired of the "endless swipes at propositions."[44] So am I and would just point out that all such "swipes" come in the form of propositions! Carson also mentions that it is good to see that the Bible has a story line that can enrich our understanding of Scripture, but he also says that just noting that the Bible has a narrative structure "does not mean that one is reading that story line richly and well." Exactly right. Liberation theology, for example, has an understanding of the story line of the Bible, but it puts peripheral things in the center and central things on the periphery. Just doing theological interpretation is not necessarily doing it well.

I believe that Carson and Vanhoozer inhabit the Great Tradition and do so with intellectual integrity and substance. Like John Webster, Hans Boersma, and many others, they stand in opposition to modernity in the sense in which I have defined it. All of them would want to affirm that to be an evangelical Protestant is, ideally, to be catholic in the best sense of the word and that nowhere is this more true than in the interpretation of Scripture. The fact that we have a few disagreements left over means we are part of a living tradition rather than a dead orthodoxy. On the one hand, as long as we all read our Bibles in anticipation of an encounter with the living God, we will continue to inhabit a living tradition and will have eternity to hash out the details. On the other hand, maybe we will all be too busy for the first few millennia just adoring the Suffering Servant of the LORD, Jesus Christ, the Lamb slain from before the foundation of the world, now raised from the dead and adored by the prophets, apostles, saints, and angels in heaven.

---

44. Carson, "Theological Interpretation of Scripture," 206.

Appendix

Criteria for Limiting the Spiritual Sense

*C*an you make the Bible say anything you want it to say?

I. Prerequisites for Faithful Interpretation

1. *Reverence for God and his Word.* A high view of Scripture and submission to the authority of God are needed; without docile, teachable hearts we cannot hope to be taught by the Spirit.
2. *Repentance of all disobedience and sin.* We cannot expect God to reveal more truth until we are obedient to the truth already revealed.
3. *Willingness to work hard.* Scripture study requires much labor and time.

II. Criteria for Limiting the Range of Meaning

1. *Canon.* The sixty-six canonical books constitute the presupposition of exegesis.
2. *Skopos.* The overall message or theme of the Bible.
3. *Creed.* The Apostles' Creed is a baptismal creed that summarizes the *skopos*.
4. *Jesus Christ.* The entire Bible is ultimately focused on him.

III. Four Positions on Limiting Theological Interpretation

1. *Protestant*. The canon of Scripture is the limit of the possible range of meanings; the *skopos* and creed are subordinate but important guides to determining the meaning. Ultimately, it is God the Holy Spirit who interprets Scripture using Scripture to do so.

2. *Roman Catholic*. The teaching office of the church (centered on the bishop of Rome) has the responsibility to determine which possible meanings can be valid and which cannot.

3. *Liberal*. The communal sense of the community of faith (the church) based on its experience (or the experience of groups within it) is the final authority on what meanings can be read out of *and* into the text. Contemporary, communal consensus trumps canon, *skopos*, creed, and even Christ.

4. *Enthusiast*. Individual experience (i.e., "God told me!") is the final arbiter of what the text means, and this can trump canon, *skopos*, creed, and even Christ.

Note: All Christians agree that Christ is in some sense the ultimate authority, but some groups fail to allow Christ to be the final authority in practice.

Note: The first position is one that evangelicals strongly affirm. The second one is not technically heretical: the Roman Catholic Church does not say that the bishop of Rome can overturn canon, creed, or Christ. Rather, he is subordinate to them. There is room for discussion about what the proper role of the bishop of Rome might actually be. The last two are heretical, however, and those who hold them have separated themselves from the body of Christ.

Bibliography

To make this book more accessible for a general audience, only English-language works appear in the notes and bibliography. Thankfully, many patristic writings are now available in English translation, allowing those without special training in the original languages to have firsthand acquaintance with the rich heritage of the Christian tradition. The Works of St. Augustine series from the New City Press and the Ancient Christian Commentary series from InterVarsity Press, to cite two prominent examples, are of the very highest value to biblical and systematic theologians.

This bibliography includes all works cited in the notes as well as a few others that are important for theological interpretation of Scripture. The literature is vast and far beyond the scope of any one scholar. Solomon had no idea how right history would prove him to be when he said, "Of making many books there is no end" (Eccles. 12:12). Important new books will no doubt become available while the present work is being prepared for publication. With such an abundance of relevant and important literature, the would-be theologian faces a spiritual struggle to remain focused on the Bible itself, which must be the main preoccupation of anyone who aspires to be a true theologian.

Patristic, Medieval, and Reformation Sources

Ambrose of Milan. "On the Holy Spirit." In *Ambrose: Select Works and Letters*, vol. 10 of *The Nicene and Post-Nicene Fathers*, 2nd series, edited by Philip Schaff and Henry Wace. Reprinted, Peabody, MA: Hendrickson, 1994.

Augustine of Hippo. *The City of God*. Translated by William Babcock. 2 vols. Works of St. Augustine I/6–7. Hyde Park, NY: New City, 2012–13.

———. *The Confessions*. Translated by Maria Boulding. Edited by John E.

Rotelle. Works of St. Augustine I/1. Hyde Park, NY: New City, 1997.

———. *Expositions of the Psalms, 1–32.* Introduction by Michael Fiedrowicz. Translated by Maria Boulding. Edited by John E. Rotelle. Works of St. Augustine III/15. Hyde Park, NY: New City, 2001.

———. *Expositions of the Psalms, 51–72.* Translation and notes by Maria Boulding. Edited by John E. Rotelle. Works of St. Augustine III/17. Hyde Park, NY: New City, 2001.

———. *Teaching Christianity; De Doctrina Christiana.* Translation and notes by Edmund Hill. Edited by John E. Rotelle. Works of St. Augustine I/11. Hyde Park, NY: New City, 1996.

Benedict of Nursia. *The Rule of St. Benedict.* Translated with introduction and notes by Anthony C. Meisel and L. M. del Mastro. New York: Image Books, Doubleday, 1975.

Calvin, John. *Commentaries on the Four Last Books of Moses Arranged in the Form of A Harmony.* Vol. 1. Translated by Charles William Bingham. Calvin's Commentaries, vol. 2. Grand Rapids: Baker Books, 2005.

———. *Commentary on the Prophet Isaiah.* Translated by William Pringle. Calvin's Commentaries. Reprint of the Calvin Translation Society edition. Grand Rapids: Baker Books, 2005.

———. *Galatians.* Translated by William Pringle. Calvin's Commentaries. Reprint of the Calvin Translation Society edition. Grand Rapids: Baker Books, 2005.

———. *Institutes of the Christian Religion.* Edited by John T. McNeill. Translated by Ford Lewis Battles. 2 vols. Library of Christian Classics. Philadelphia: Westminster, 1960.

Elliott, Mark W., ed. *Isaiah 40–66.* Ancient Christian Commentary on Scripture. Downers Grove, IL: InterVarsity, 2007.

Irenaeus of Lyons. *Against Heresies.* In *The Ante-Nicene Fathers.* Edited by A. Cleveland Coxe. Vol. 1. 1885. Reprinted, Peabody, MA: Hendrickson, 1999.

———. *On the Apostolic Preaching.* Translated and introduced by John Behr. Popular Patristics Series. Crestwood, NY: St. Vladimir's Seminary Press, 1997.

Justin Martyr. *Dialogue of Justin, Philosopher and Martyr with Trypho, A Jew.* In *The Ante-Nicene Fathers.* Edited by A. Cleveland Coxe. Vol. 1. 1885. Reprinted, Peabody, MA: Hendrickson, 1999.

———. *The First Apology of Justin.* In *The Ante-Nicene Fathers.* Edited by A. Cleveland Coxe. Vol. 1. 1885. Reprinted, Peabody, MA: Hendrickson, 1999.

Thomas Aquinas. *Commentary on the Gospel of John.* Translated by Fabian Larcher and James A. Weisheipl. 3 vols. Washington, DC: Catholic University of America Press, 2010.

———. *Summa Theologica.* Translated by the Fathers of the English Dominican Province. 5 vols. Notre Dame, IN: Ava Maria, 1920.

Modern Sources

Adams, Samuel V. *The Reality of God and Historical Method: Apocalyptic Theology in Conversation with N. T. Wright.* New Explorations in Theology. Downers Grove, IL: InterVarsity, 2015.

Allen, R. Michael, ed. *Theological Commentary: Evangelical Perspectives.* London: T&T Clark International, 2011.

Allen, R. Michael, and Scott R. Swain. *Reformed Catholicity: The Promise of Retrieval for Theology and Biblical Interpretation.* Grand Rapids: Baker Academic, 2015.

Allis, Oswald T. *The Unity of Isaiah: A Study in Prophecy.* Eugene, OR: Wipf & Stock, 2000.

Ayres, Lewis. *Nicaea and Its Legacy: An Approach to Fourth-Century Trinitarian Theology.* Oxford: Oxford University Press, 2004.

Barth, Karl. *The Doctrine of Creation,* vol. 1. Translated by J. W. Edwards,

O. Bussey, and H. Knight. Vol. III/1 of *Church Dogmatics*, edited by G. W. Bromiley and T. F. Torrance. Edinburgh: T&T Clark, 1958.

———. *The Doctrine of Creation*, vol. 3. Translated by G. W. Bromiley and R. J. Erlich. Vol. III/3 of *Church Dogmatics*, edited by G. W. Bromiley and T. F. Torrance. Edinburgh: T&T Clark, 1960.

———. *The Epistle to the Romans*. Translated from the 6th edition by Edward C. Hoskyns. Oxford: Oxford University Press, 1968.

Bartholomew, Craig G. *Introducing Biblical Hermeneutics: A Comprehensive Framework for Hearing God in Scripture*. Grand Rapids: Baker Academic, 2015.

Bartholomew, Craig G., and Heath A. Thomas, eds. *A Manifesto for Theological Interpretation*. Grand Rapids: Baker Academic, 2016.

Bates, Matthew W. *The Birth of the Trinity: Jesus, God, and Spirit in the New Testament and Early Christian Interpretations of the Old Testament*. Oxford: Oxford University Press, 2015.

———. *The Hermeneutics of the Apostolic Proclamation: The Center of Paul's Method of Scriptural Interpretation*. Waco: Baylor University Press, 2012.

Beale, G. K. *A New Testament Biblical Theology: The Unfolding of the Old Testament in the New*. Grand Rapids: Baker Academic, 2011.

———. *The Temple and the Church's Mission*. New Studies in Biblical Theology. Downers Grove, IL: InterVarsity, 2004.

Betz, Otto. "Biblical Theology, History of." In *The Interpreter's Dictionary of the Bible*. Edited by George A. Buttrick, 1:432–37. Nashville: Abingdon, 1962.

Beyer, Bryan E. *Encountering the Book of Isaiah: A Historical and Theological Survey*. Grand Rapids: Baker Academic, 2007.

Billings, Todd. *The Word of God for the People of God: An Entryway to the Theological Interpretation of Scripture*. Grand Rapids: Eerdmans, 2010.

Blenkinsopp, Joseph. *Isaiah 40–55: A New Translation with Introduction and Commentary*. Anchor Yale Bible 19A. New Haven: Yale University Press, 2008.

Boersma, Hans. *Embodiment and Virtue in Gregory of Nyssa: An Anagogical Approach*. Oxford Early Christian Studies. Oxford: Oxford University Press, 2013.

———. *Heavenly Participation: The Weaving of a Sacramental Tapestry*. Grand Rapids: Eerdmans, 2011.

———. *Nouvelle Théologie and Sacramental Ontology: A Return to Mystery*. Oxford: Oxford University Press, 2009.

———. *Sacramental Preaching: Sermons on the Hidden Presence of Christ*. Grand Rapids: Baker Academic, 2016.

———. *Scripture as Real Presence: Sacramental Exegesis in the Early Church*. Grand Rapids: Baker Academic, 2017.

Boersma, Hans, and Matthew Levering, eds. *Heaven on Earth? Theological Interpretation in Ecumenical Dialogue*. Malden, MA: Blackwell, 2013.

Brown, Michael L. "Jewish Interpretations of Isaiah 53." In *The Gospel according to Isaiah 53: Encountering the Suffering Servant in Jewish and Christian Theology*, edited by Darrell L. Bock and Mitch Glaser, 61–83. Grand Rapids: Kregel, 2012.

Burrell, David B. *Knowing the Unknowable God: Ibn-Sina, Mamonides, Aquinas*. Notre Dame, IN: University of Notre Dame Press, 1986.

Byassee, Jason. *Praise Seeking Understanding: Reading the Psalms with Augustine*. Grand Rapids: Eerdmans, 2007.

Cameron, Michael. *Christ Meets Me Everywhere: Augustine's Early Figurative Exegesis*. New York: Oxford University Press, 2012.

Carson, D. A. "Theological Interpretation of Scripture: Yes, But . . ." In *Theological Commentary: Evangelical Perspectives*, edited by R. Michael Allen, 187–207. London: T&T Clark International, 2011.

Carter, Craig A. "The Recovery of a Sacramental Ontology as the Basis for

Developing a Sacramental Theology of Baptism." In *Ecclesia Semper Reformanda Est = The Church Is Always Reforming: A Festschrift on Ecclesiology in Honour of Stanley K. Fowler*, edited by David G. Barker, Michael A. G. Haykin, and Barry H. Howson. Kitchener, ON: Joshua, 2016.

Childs, Brevard S. *Biblical Theology in Crisis*. Philadelphia: Westminster, 1970.

———. *Biblical Theology of the Old and New Testaments: Theological Reflection on the Christian Bible*. Minneapolis: Fortress, 1992.

———. *Introduction to the Old Testament as Scripture*. Philadelphia: Fortress, 1979.

———. *Isaiah: A Commentary*. Old Testament Library. Louisville: Westminster/John Knox, 2001.

———. *The New Testament as Canon: An Introduction*. Philadelphia: Fortress, 1984.

———. *The Struggle to Understand Isaiah as Christian Scripture*. Grand Rapids: Eerdmans, 2004.

Clowney, Edmund P. *The Unfolding Mystery: Discovering Christ in the Old Testament*. 2nd ed. Phillipsburg, NJ: P&R, 2013.

Cooper, John W. *Panentheism—the Other God of the Philosophers: From Plato to the Present*. Grand Rapids: Baker Academic, 2006.

Coyle, J. Kevin. "Mani, Manichaeism." In *Augustine through the Ages: An Encyclopedia*, edited by Allan D. Fitzgerald, 520–25. Grand Rapids: Eerdmans, 1999.

Crawford, Matthew R. *Cyril of Alexandria's Trinitarian Theology of Scripture*. Oxford Early Christian Studies. Oxford: Oxford University Press, 2014.

Daley, Brian E. "'In Many and Various Ways': Towards a Theology of Theological Exegesis." In *Heaven on Earth? Theological Interpretation in Ecumenical Dialogue*, edited by Hans Boersma and Matthew Levering, 13–32. Malden, MA: Blackwell, 2013.

———. "Is Patristic Exegesis Still Usable? Some Reflections on Early Christian Interpretation of the Psalms." In *The Art of Reading Scripture*, edited by Ellen F. Davis and Richard B. Hays, 69–88. Grand Rapids: Eerdmans, 2003.

Daniélou, Jean. *From Shadows to Reality: Studies in the Biblical Typology of the Fathers*. London: Burns & Oates, 1960.

Davies, Brian. *An Introduction to the Philosophy of Religion*. 3rd ed. Oxford: Oxford University Press, 2004.

Davis, Ellen F., and Richard B. Hays. *The Art of Reading Scripture*. Grand Rapids: Eerdmans, 2003.

de Lubac, Henri. *See* Lubac, Henri de

Dodaro, Robert. *Christ and the Just Society in the Thought of Augustine*. Cambridge: Cambridge University Press, 2004.

Doolan, Gregory T. *Aquinas on the Divine Ideas as Exemplar Causes*. Washington, DC: Catholic University of America Press, 2008.

Driver, Daniel R. *Brevard Childs, Biblical Theologian: For the Church's One Bible*. Grand Rapids: Baker Academic, 2010.

Duvall, J. Scott, and J. Daniel Hays. *Grasping God's Word: A Hands-On Approach to Reading, Interpreting and Applying the Bible*. 3rd ed. Grand Rapids: Zondervan, 2012.

Feser, Edward. *The Last Superstition: A Refutation of the New Atheism*. South Bend, IN: St. Augustine's Press, 2008.

Festugière, André-Jean. *Epicurus and His Gods*. Translated by C. W. Chilton. Cambridge, MA: Harvard University Press, 1956.

Fitzgerald, Allan D., ed. *Augustine through the Ages: An Encyclopedia*. Grand Rapids: Eerdmans, 1999.

Fowl, Stephen E. *Engaging Scripture: A Model for Theological Interpretation*. Eugene, OR: Wipf & Stock, 1988.

———. *Theological Interpretation of Scripture*. Cascade Companions. Eugene, OR: Wipf & Stock, 2009.

Frei, Hans. *The Eclipse of Biblical Narrative*. New Haven: Yale University Press, 1974.

Gaffin, Richard B. Introduction to *Redemptive History and Biblical Interpretation:*

The Shorter Writings of Geerhardus Vos. Edited by Richard B. Gaffin. Phillipsburg, NJ: P&R, 1980.

Gay, Peter. *The Enlightenment: An Interpretation.* Vol. 1, *The Rise of Modern Paganism.* New York: Norton, 1966.

———. *The Enlightenment: An Interpretation.* Vol. 2, *The Science of Freedom.* New York: Norton, 1969.

Gentry, Peter J., and Stephen J. Wellum. *Kingdom through Covenant: A Biblical-Theological Understanding of the Covenants.* Wheaton: Crossway, 2012.

George, Timothy. *Reading Scripture with the Reformers.* Downers Grove, IL: IVP Academic, 2011.

———. "Reformational Preaching." *First Things*—Web Exclusives—January 2017. https://www.firstthings.com/web-exclusives/2017/01/reformational-preaching.

Gerson, Lloyd P. *Aristotle and Other Platonists.* Ithaca, NY: Cornell University Press, 2005.

———. *From Plato to Platonism.* Ithaca, NY: Cornell University Press, 2013.

Gignilliat, Mark. *Karl Barth and the Fifth Gospel: Barth's Theological Exegesis of Isaiah.* London: Routledge, 2016.

———. *Old Testament Criticism: From Benedict Spinoza to Brevard Childs.* Grand Rapids: Zondervan, 2012.

Gillespie, Michael Allen. *The Theological Origins of Modernity.* Chicago: University of Chicago Press, 2008.

Goldingay, John, and David Payne. *Isaiah 40–55: A Critical and Exegetical Commentary.* 2 vols. International Critical Commentary. London: Bloomsbury T&T Clark, 2006.

Goppelt, Leonhard. *Typos: The Typological Interpretation of the Old Testament in the New.* Translated by Donald H. Madvig. Eugene, OR: Wipf & Stock, 2002.

Greely, Henry T. *The End of Sex and the Future of Human Reproduction.* Cambridge, MA: Harvard University Press, 2016.

Gregory, Brad S. *The Unintended Reformation: How a Religious Revolution*

Secularized Society. Cambridge, MA: Belknap Press of Harvard University Press, 2012.

Hamilton, James M., Jr. *God's Glory in Salvation through Judgment: A Biblical Theology.* Wheaton: Crossway, 2010.

Harrisville, Roy A., and Walter Sundberg. *The Bible in Modern Culture.* 2nd ed. Grand Rapids: Eerdmans, 2002.

Hays, Richard B. *The Conversion of the Imagination: Paul as Interpreter of Israel's Scripture.* Grand Rapids: Eerdmans, 2005.

———. *Echoes of Scripture in the Gospels.* Waco: Baylor University Press, 2016.

———. *Echoes of Scripture in the Letters of Paul.* New Haven: Yale University Press, 1989.

———. *Reading Backwards: Figural Christology and the Fourfold Gospel Witness.* Waco: Baylor University Press, 2014.

Heiser, Michael. *The Unseen Realm: Recovering the Supernatural Worldview of the Bible.* Bellingham, WA: Lexham, 2015.

Hill, Andrew E., and John H. Walton. *A Survey of the Old Testament.* 3rd ed. Grand Rapids: Zondervan, 2009.

Hirsch, E. D. *Validity in Interpretation.* New Haven: Yale University Press, 1967.

Holmes, Arthur F. *The Idea of a Christian College.* Grand Rapids: Eerdmans, 1975.

Holmes, Stephen R. *The Quest for the Trinity: The Doctrine of God in Scripture, History and Modernity.* Downers Grove, IL: InterVarsity, 2012.

Howard, Thomas. *Chance or the Dance: A Critique of Modern Secularism.* Wheaton: Harold Shaw, 1969. Reprinted, San Francisco: Ignatius, 1989.

Huxley, Aldous. *Brave New World.* Toronto: Vintage Canada, 2007.

Jaki, Stanley J. *Genesis 1 through the Ages.* London: Thomas More, 1992.

John Paul II. *Man and Woman He Created Them: A Theology of the Body.* Translated and introduced by Michael Waldstein. Boston: Pauline Books and Media, 2006.

Kant, Immanuel. "What Is Enlightenment?" In *What Is Enlightenment? Eighteenth Century Answers and Twentieth Century Questions*, edited by James Schmidt, 58–64. Philosophical Traditions 7. Berkeley: University of California Press, 1996.

Keynes, John Maynard. *The General Theory of Employment, Interest and Money*. Amherst, NY: Prometheus Books, 1997.

Kreeft, Peter. *C. S. Lewis for the Third Millennium: Six Essays on the Abolition of Man*. San Francisco: Ignatius, 1994.

———. *The Philosophy of Tolkien: The Worldview behind the Lord of the Rings*. San Francisco: Ignatius, 2005.

Legaspi, Michael C. *The Death of Scripture and the Rise of Biblical Studies*. Oxford Studies in Historical Theology. Oxford: Oxford University Press, 2010.

Letham, Robert. *The Message of the Person of Christ*. The Bible Speaks Today. Downers Grove, IL: InterVarsity, 2013.

Levering, Matthew. *Participatory Biblical Exegesis: A Theology of Biblical Interpretation*. Notre Dame, IN: University of Notre Dame Press, 2008.

———. *Scripture and Metaphysics: Aquinas and the Renewal of Trinitarian Theology*. Malden, MA: Blackwell, 2004.

Lewis, C. S. *The Abolition of Man*. New York: HarperCollins, 2001.

———. *The Screwtape Letters and Screwtape Proposes a Toast*. New York: HarperCollins, 2009.

Longenecker, Richard N. *Biblical Exegesis in the Apostolic Period*. 2nd ed. Grand Rapids: Eerdmans, 1999.

Longman, Tremper, III. "The Messiah: Explorations in the Law and Writings." In *The Messiah in the Old and New Testaments*, edited by Stanley E. Porter, 13–34. Grand Rapids: Eerdmans, 2007.

Louth, Andrew. *Discerning the Mystery: An Essay on the Nature of Theology*. Oxford: Oxford University Press, 1983.

———. *The Origins of the Christian Mystical Tradition: From Plato to Denys*. 2nd ed. Oxford: Oxford University Press, 2007.

Lubac, Henri de. *History and Spirit: The Understanding of Scripture according to Origen*. Translated by Anne Englund Nash. San Francisco: Ignatius, 2007.

———. *Medieval Exegesis: The Four Senses of Scripture*. Vol. 1. Translated by Mark Sebanc. Grand Rapids: Eerdmans, 1998.

———. *Medieval Exegesis: The Four Senses of Scripture*. Vol. 2. Translated by E. M. Macierowski. Grand Rapids: Eerdmans, 2000.

———. *Medieval Exegesis: The Four Senses of Scripture*. Vol. 3. Translated by E. M. Macierowski. Grand Rapids: Eerdmans, 2009.

Lyotard, Jean-François. *The Postmodern Condition: A Report on Knowledge*. Minneapolis: University of Minnesota Press; Manchester, UK: Manchester University Press, 1984.

Machen, J. Gresham. *Christianity and Liberalism*. Grand Rapids: Eerdmans, 1923.

MacIntyre, Alasdair. *After Virtue*. 3rd ed. Notre Dame, IN: University of Notre Dame Press, 2007.

Markus, R. A. *Saeculum: History and Society in the Theology of St. Augustine*. Cambridge: Cambridge University Press, 1970.

Martens, Peter. *Origen and Scripture: The Contours of the Exegetical Life*. Oxford: Oxford University Press, 2012.

McCarthy, Michael. *The Revelatory Psalm*. Ann Arbor, MI: University Microfilm, 2003.

Milbank, John. *Theology and Social Theory: Beyond Secular Reason*. Oxford: Blackwell, 1990.

Moberly, R. W. L. *Old Testament Theology: Reading the Hebrew Bible as Christian Scripture*. Grand Rapids: Baker Academic, 2013.

Molnar, Paul D. *Divine Freedom and the Immanent Trinity*. 2nd ed. London: Bloomsbury T&T Clark, 2017.

Motyer, J. Alec. *Look to the Rock: An Old Testament Background to Our Understanding of Christ*. Leicester, UK: InterVarsity, 1996.

———. *The Prophecy of Isaiah: An Introduction and Commentary*. Downers Grove, IL: IVP Academic, 1993.

Muller, Richard A. *After Calvin: Studies in the Development of a Theological Tradition*. Oxford Studies in Historical Theology. Oxford: Oxford University Press, 2003.

———. "Biblical Interpretation in the Era of the Reformation: The View from the Middle Ages." In *Biblical Interpretation in the Era of the Reformation: Essays Presented to David C. Steinmetz in Honor of His Sixtieth Birthday*, edited by Richard A. Muller and John L. Thompson, 3–22. Grand Rapids: Eerdmans, 1996.

———. *The Unaccommodated Calvin: Studies in the Foundation of a Theological Tradition*. Oxford Studies in Historical Theology. Oxford: Oxford University Press, 2000.

Muller, Richard A., and John L. Thompson, eds. *Biblical Interpretation in the Era of the Reformation: Essays Presented to David C. Steinmetz in Honor of His Sixtieth Birthday*. Grand Rapids: Eerdmans, 1996.

Nassif, Bradley. "The Spiritual Exegesis of Scripture: The School of Antioch Revisited." *Anglican Theological Review* 75 (1993): 437–70.

Nelson, R. David, Darren Sarisky, and Justin Stratis, eds. *Theological Theology: Essays in Honour of John Webster*. London: Bloomsbury T&T Clark, 2015.

North, Christopher R. *The Suffering Servant in Deutero-Isaiah: An Historical and Critical Study*. 2nd ed. Oxford: Oxford University Press, 1956.

Oden, Thomas C. *Agenda for Theology: After Modernity, What?* Grand Rapids: Zondervan, 1990.

———. *Classic Christianity: A Systematic Theology*. San Francisco: HarperOne, 1992.

———. *The Rebirth of Orthodoxy: Signs of New Life in Christianity*. San Francisco: HarperSan Francisco, 2003.

———. *Requiem: A Lament in Three Movements*. Nashville: Abingdon, 1995.

Osborn, Eric. *Irenaeus of Lyons*. Cambridge: Cambridge University Press, 2001.

Oswalt, John N. *The Bible among the Myths: Unique Revelation or Just Ancient Literature?* Grand Rapids: Zondervan, 2009.

———. *The Book of Isaiah 1–39*. New International Commentary on the Old Testament. Grand Rapids: Eerdmans, 1986.

———. *The Book of Isaiah 40–66*. New International Commentary on the Old Testament. Grand Rapids: Eerdmans, 1998.

Pinnock, Clark. *Most Moved Mover: A Theology of God's Openness*. Grand Rapids: Baker Academic, 2001.

Provan, Iain. "Canons to the Left of Him: Brevard Childs, His Critics and the Future of Old Testament Theology." *Scottish Journal of Theology* 50, no. 1 (February 1997): 1–38.

Provan, Iain, V. Philips Long, and Tremper Longman III. *A Biblical History of Israel*. 2nd ed. Louisville: Westminster John Knox, 2015.

Quinn, Patrick. *Aquinas, Platonism and the Knowledge of God*. Hants, UK: Ashgate, 1996.

Ramm, Bernard. *Protestant Biblical Interpretation: A Textbook of Hermeneutics*. 3rd rev. ed. Grand Rapids: Baker, 1970.

Schall, James V. *The Regensburg Lecture*. South Bend, IN: St. Augustine's Press, 2007.

Schreiner, Thomas R. *The King in His Beauty: A Biblical Theology of the Old and New Testaments*. Grand Rapids: Baker Academic, 2013.

Scobie, Charles H. H. *The Ways of Our God: An Approach to Biblical Theology*. Grand Rapids: Eerdmans, 2003.

Shepherd, Charles E. *Theological Interpretation and Isaiah 53: A Critical Comparison of Bernhard Duhm, Brevard Childs, and Alec Motyer*. London: Bloomsbury T&T Clark, 2014.

Smith, Wesley J. *Consumer's Guide to a Brave New World*. San Francisco: Encounter Books, 2004.

Solzhenitsyn, Alexander. "The Relentless Cult of Novelty and How It Wrecked the Century." Paper presented to the National Arts Club, New York, 1993. Available online at *Catholic Education Resource Center*. http://www.catholicedu cation.org/en/culture/art/the-relentless -cult-of-novelty.html.

Sonderegger, Katherine. *Systematic Theology*. Vol. 1. Minneapolis: Fortress, 2015.

Spurgeon, Charles. "Spurgeon's Verse Expositions of the Bible: Isaiah 53." *Study-Light.org*. https://www.studylight.org /commentaries/spe/isaiah-53.html.

Steinmetz, David C. "The Superiority of Pre-critical Exegesis." In *Taking the Long View: Christian Theology in Historical Perspective*, 3–14. Oxford: Oxford University Press, 2011.

Stendahl, Krister. "Biblical Theology, Contemporary." In *The Interpreter's Dictionary of the Bible*, edited by George A. Buttrick, 1:418–32. Nashville: Abingdon, 1962.

Stott, John R. W. *The Cross of Christ*. Downers Grove, IL: InterVarsity, 1986.

Strauss, David Friedrich. *Life of Jesus Critically Examined*. Translated by George Eliot. New York: Macmillan, 1898.

———. *The Old Faith and the New*. Introduction and notes by G. A. Wells. Translated by Mathilde Blind. Amherst, NY: Prometheus Books, 1997.

Strauss, Leo. *Spinoza's Critique of Religion*. Chicago: University of Chicago Press, 1965.

Swain, Scott R. *The God of the Gospel: Robert Jenson's Trinitarian Theology*. Downers Grove, IL: InterVarsity, 2013.

———. *Trinity, Revelation, and Reading: A Theological Introduction to the Bible and Its Interpretation*. Edinburgh: T&T Clark, 2011.

Swinburne, Richard. *The Christian God*. Oxford: Oxford University Press, 1994.

———. *The Coherence of Theism*. Rev. ed. Oxford: Oxford University Press, 1993.

Treier, Daniel J. *Introducing Theological Interpretation of Scripture: Recovering a Christian Practice*. Grand Rapids: Baker Academic, 2008.

Tyson, Paul. *Returning to Reality: Christian Platonism for Our Times*. Eugene, OR: Wipf & Stock, 2014.

Vanhoozer, Kevin J. "Ascending the Mountain, Singing the Rock: Biblical Interpretation Earthed, Typed, and Transfigured." In *Heaven on Earth? Theological Interpretation in Ecumenical Dialogue*, edited by Hans Boersma and Matthew Levering, 207–25. West Sussex, UK: Blackwell, 2013.

———, ed. *Dictionary for Theological Interpretation of the Bible*. Grand Rapids: Baker Academic, 2005.

———. *Is There a Meaning in This Text? The Bible, the Reader, and the Morality of Literary Knowledge*. Grand Rapids: Zondervan, 1998.

Voegelin, Eric. *The New Science of Politics*. Chicago: University of Chicago Press, 1987.

Vos, Geerhardus. *Biblical Theology: Old and New Testaments*. Grand Rapids: Eerdmans, 1948.

———. *Redemptive History and Biblical Interpretation: The Shorter Writings of Geerhardus Vos*. Edited by Richard B. Gaffin Jr. Phillipsburg, NJ: P&R, 1980.

Walton, John H. "New Observations on the Date of Isaiah." *Journal of the Evangelical Theological Society* 28, no. 2 (June 1985): 129–32.

Ward, Timothy. *Words of Life: Scripture as the Living and Active Word of God*. Nottingham, UK: Inter-Varsity, 2009.

Watson, Francis. "Does Historical Criticism Exist? A Contribution to Debate on the Theological Interpretation of Scripture." In *Theological Theology: Essays in Honour of John Webster*, edited by R. David Nelson, Darren Sarisky, and Justin Stratis, 307–18. London: Bloomsbury T&T Clark, 2015.

———. *The Fourfold Gospel: A Theological Reading of the New Testament Portraits of Jesus.* Grand Rapids: Baker Academic, 2016.

———. *Paul and the Hermeneutics of Faith.* 2nd ed. London: Bloomsbury T&T Clark, 2016.

———. *Text and Truth: Redefining Biblical Theology.* Grand Rapids: Eerdmans, 1997.

———. *Text, Church, and World: Biblical Interpretation in Theological Perspective.* Grand Rapids: Eerdmans, 1994.

Weaver, Richard M. *Ideas Have Consequences.* Chicago: University of Chicago Press, 1948.

Webster, John B. *Confessing God: Essays in Christian Dogmatics II.* Edinburgh: T&T Clark, 2005.

———. *The Domain of the Word: Scripture and Theological Reason.* Edinburgh: T&T Clark, 2012.

———. *God and the Works of God.* Vol. 1 of *God without Measure: Working Papers in Christian Theology.* Edinburgh: T&T Clark, 2016.

———. *Holiness.* Grand Rapids: Eerdmans, 2003.

———. *Holy Scripture: A Dogmatic Sketch.* Cambridge: Cambridge University Press, 2003.

———. *Virtue and Intellect.* Vol. 2 of *God without Measure: Working Papers in*

Christian Theology. Edinburgh: T&T Clark, 2016.

———. *Word and Church: Essays in Christian Dogmatics.* Edinburgh: T&T Clark, 2001.

White, Andrew Dickson. *A History of the Warfare of Science with Theology in Christendom.* New York: Appleton, 1901.

Whybray, R. N. *Isaiah 40–66.* New Century Bible Commentary. London: Marshall, Morgan and Scott, 1975.

Wilken, Robert Louis. "In Defense of Allegory." *Modern Theology* 14, no. 2 (April 1998): 197–212.

———. *The Spirit of Early Christian Thought.* New Haven: Yale University Press, 2003.

Wilson, Catherine. *Epicureanism at the Origins of Modernity.* Oxford: Oxford University Press, 2008.

Work, Telford. *Loving and Active: Scripture in the Economy of Salvation.* Grand Rapids: Eerdmans, 2002.

Wright, N. T. *The New Testament and the People of God.* Minneapolis: Fortress, 1992.

Young, Frances M. *Biblical Exegesis and the Formation of Christian Culture.* Cambridge: Cambridge University Press, 1997. Reprinted, Peabody, MA: Hendrickson, 2002.

Index of Scripture

Index of Persons

Whitefield, George, 182
Whitehead, Alfred North, xiv
Whybray, R. N., 6
Wilken, Robert Louis, 18, 96
William of Ockham, 11, 86–87
Williams, D. H., 19
Wilson, Catherine, 115

Wolff, Hans Walter, 7
Work, Telford, 35
Wright, N. T., 106

Young, Frances, 95, 168, 177, 194

Zeno, 63

Index of Subjects